D1121548

WITHDRAWN

This Is All a Dream We Dreamed

Also by Blair Jackson

Garcia: An American Life

Grateful Dead Gear: The Band's Instruments, Sound Systems, and Recording Sessions, From 1965 to 1995

Grateful Dead: The Music Never Stopped

Also by David Gans

Conversations with the Dead: The Grateful Dead Interview Book

Not Fade Away: The Online World Remembers Jerry Garcia

Playing in the Band: An Oral and Visual Portrait of the Grateful Dead

Talking Heads: The Band and Their Music

This Is All a Dream We Dreamed

An Oral History of the Grateful Dead

Blair Jackson and David Gans

FLATIRON
BOOKS

NEW YORK

THIS IS ALL A DREAM WE DREAMED. Copyright © 2015 by Blair Jackson and David Gans. All rights reserved. Printed in the United States of America. For information, address Flatiron Books, 175 Fifth Avenue, New York, N.Y. 10010.

www.flatironbooks.com

The Library of Congress Cataloging-in-Publication Data is available upon request.

ISBN 978-1-250-05856-0 (hardcover)
ISBN 978-1-250-05858-4 (e-book)

Book production by March Tenth, Inc.

Flatiron books may be purchased for educational, business, or promotional use. For information on bulk purchases, please contact the Macmillan Corporate and Premium Sales Department at 1-800-221-7945, extension 5442 or write to specialmarkets@macmillan.com.

First Edition: November 2015

10 9 8 7 6 5 4 3 2 1

This book is dedicated to my brother, Roger, who lit the flame; my wife, Regan—my partner in ecstasy and adventure; and my kids, Kyle and Hayley, who will carry the torch.

—Blair Jackson

I dedicate this book to the memory of Alan Feldstein (1952-2009), one of the most knowledgeable, opinionated, and passionate music lovers—and Deadheads—I ever knew.

We met in 1973, introduced as fellow musicians and fellow 'heads. The first "bootleg" Grateful Dead recording I ever heard was from March 23, 1974, at the Cow Palace; Al had it just a couple of weeks after the event. Hearing that tape in his apartment opened up a whole world to me.

"Fiddle" and I went to many shows together back in the day, and we played music together (our own, the Dead's, and more) off and on for more than thirty years. We carried on a deep conversation about this stuff, onstage and online and in person, for decades. Al's spirit suffuses this text, because my consciousness as a musician and a Deadhead evolved in concert with his.

—David Gans

Contents

Acknowledgments   ix

Introduction   xi

Who's Who   xix

1 More Than Human   3

2 San Francisco   47

3 All Graceful Instruments Are Known   95

4 Psychedelic Americana   127

5 Let it Grow   177

6 Independence   209

7 On the Road Again   245

8 Hungry for Color   291

9 I'll Get a New Start   325

10 Vince and the Early Nineties   373

11 Summer Flies and August Dies   405

Contents

Coda No. 1: Courtenay Pollock, Tie-Dye Man   415

Coda No. 2: The Deaducation of Gary Lambert   423

Coda No. 3: Ned Lagin: Electronic Whiz Kid   427

Coda No. 4: Editing *The Grateful Dead Movie*   431

Coda No. 5: Terrapin Trailways   435

Coda No. 6: Confessions of a Teenage Deadhead,
            Early Eighties   441

Coda No. 7: Jim and Doug Oade: A Tale of
            Two Tapers   445

Coda No. 8: Hanging Loose with Al and Tipper   451

Sources   453
Bibliography   463
Photo Credits   471
Index of Speakers   473
Index of Names   477

Acknowledgments

This book grew out of the wreckage of another book that didn't happen. Stephen Power had a very cool idea, but we weren't able to get it all the way into print. The demise of that deal led to a conversation with Bob Miller, the editor of David's first book and now the head of Flatiron Books. The authors are grateful to Bob for embracing this project with great energy and creativity; thanks also to his colleagues Jasmine Faustino, Karen Horton, David Lott, Marlena Bittner, Steven Boriack, Lisa Goris, Liz Keenan, and Molly Fonseca.

The authors are profoundly thankful to our agent, Sandy Choron, for applying her inspired brand of creativity to every step of this book's life, from inception to editing to marketing. Sandy and her husband/partner, Harry Choron, designed and produced the book, too, and we appreciate their openness to our input in that process.

For assistance with exclusive material, we thank Rosie McGee, Howard Rheingold, Stephen Talbot, and Steve Silberman.

We share a deep admiration and respect for the many writers who came before us or were contemporary fellow travelers in chronicling the Grateful Dead world over the past half-century. From *Mojo Navigator* to *Crawdaddy*, *Rolling Stone* to *Creem*, *Circus* to *Musician*, *BAM* to *Guitar Player*, *Zig-Zag* to *Dupree's Diamond News*, the rich tapestry of Grateful Dead history and the surrounding culture has been documented by literally hundreds of journalists, critics, radio and TV folks, and, of course, fans, all sharing glimpses of the Dead's inexplicable magic. We have referred to the work of many of them, as we acknowledge in the endnotes and bibliography of this book.

We also want to especially thank these fine (and kind) interviewers for their contributions to our project: Bud Scoppa, Miles Hurwitz, Michael Goodwin, Charlie Haas, Andy Childs, Ann Heppermann and Kara Oehler, Michael Wanger, Charles Reich, and Jann S. Wenner.

Thanks to Molly Brown Strachan, Beth Card, Damien Palermo, Roger Sideman, and Bob Trudeau for help with transcribing. For all-around assistance, we're grateful to Barbara Bernstein, Bob Merlis, and Mark Simoncic.

David thanks his wife, Rita Hurault, for endless support, encouragement, and inspiration.

Finally, we acknowledge these vital resources: Corry Arnold, *Lost Live Dead* (lostlivedead.blogspot.com); Joe Jupille; Nicholas Meriwether, Grateful Dead Archive; David Lemieux, Grateful Dead Productions; the Deadlists Project (deadlists.com); DeadBase (deadbase.com); Grateful Dead Family Discography (deaddisc.com); jerrygarcia.com; Bonnie Simmons; Marty Martinez; and Paul Grushkin.

Introduction

You got turned on to the Grateful Dead by your older brother, or by a classmate. You were given a concert tape or a vinyl copy of *Workingman's Dead* or a cassette of *Skeletons from the Closet*. You were a pothead, probably, and you were or became an acid head (or at least tried it).

You were a member of one or more Deadhead tribes. You went to a Dead show, and then another, and another, and over time you developed connections. You had a group of people you always sat with at the show, and a larger group who would meet somewhere before and after the show. There are people you got tapes from, and people you gave tapes to. You knew people who wore tie-dyed clothing from head to toe, and people who sported high-end Jerry Garcia ties with their four-hundred-dollar suits and recognized other guys doing the same on the subway or at business meetings. Maybe they still do. You had friends and maybe even relatives whose holiday gifts to you tended to be Grateful Dead–branded pint glasses or golf club covers or calendars, dancing bear beanbag dolls, baseball hats, and Grateful Dead–related books.

Or perhaps none of that applies. You are too young to ever have seen the Grateful Dead, even two decades ago, during the last years. Or you were old enough to have caught the Dead live, but for whatever reason your path just never crossed theirs. You were into other stuff; maybe you even actively disliked them for any number of reasons, but time and exposure have changed your opinion and now you can't get enough. Maybe your exposure to contemporary jam bands led you back in time to the group that started it all.

There are as many routes to the Grateful Dead as there are people who enjoy(ed) them. No membership card was required. There was no acid test to pass, exactly. "Getting it" on whatever level, wavelength, or intensity you defined made you a Deadhead. You might even have hated that term and all the sociological baggage that came with it: "I'm a fan, but I'm not a Deadhead." That was fine, too. In a way, a line from "Dancing in the Street"—one of the first cover tunes the Grateful Dead adapted in their early days—perfectly captured the ebullient spirit at the group's core: "It doesn't matter what you wear / Just as long as you are there."

The Grateful Dead was about collaboration, spiritual and social democracy, trust, generosity, and fun. It meant a hell of a lot to a hell of a lot of people, and whatever its punk/outlaw/pirate/libertine/bourgeois origins, it became a legitimate American success story by the only standard America understands: money. More important, the Grateful Dead created a unique and eloquent musical language and established a society that sustained—and continues to sustain—the interest and loyalty of millions.

It takes a whole lot of blind men to fully describe an elephant of this size, so we are telling this tale by weaving together stories told by members of the band, their collaborators, their peers, and their fans. The authors are members of this community: each of us was a fan first and then a journalist covering the Grateful Dead world. As such, we helped to shape the culture to some small degree.

David engaged with the Grateful Dead as a musician and strove in his writing to elucidate what was going on musically. Both of us have had the privilege of producing archival recordings and writing liner notes for both Grateful Dead and Jerry Garcia releases. David wandered into the radio business by way of *The KFOG Deadhead Hour* and (without ever intending to) wound up producing and hosting the nationally syndicated *Grateful Dead Hour* for thirty-plus years. He has also presented Grateful Dead (and other) music on KPFA, Berkeley's pioneering nonprofit radio station, since the 1980s, and for many years has produced an annual sixteen-hour fund-raising marathon for the station, presenting Grateful Dead and related music to a global audience.

Blair gave David his first Dead-related writing assignment, at *BAM* magazine in 1976, and the two of us interviewed Jerry Garcia together twice in 1981. Blair and his wife, Regan McMahon, published a Dead fan magazine, *The Golden Road,* from 1984 to 1993. His book *The Music Never Stopped* (1983) was the first linear history of the band, and later books, such as his biography, *Garcia: An American Life* (1999), and *Grateful Dead Gear* (2006), illuminated other aspects of the band's rich and enthralling multi-layered universe.

We are both members of various (and variously overlapping) Deadhead tribes.

The music is central to the Grateful Dead culture, but the culture created itself around that music in a number of ways, which in turn affected the music. In the early days, in smaller venues, the band and audience were in very close contact. In larger halls, the distance from the stage to the back of the room required a grander presentation, gestures big enough to communicate across a distance. It is not possible for the atmosphere and flavor and dynamics of a gig at the Fillmore to be scaled up for 70,000 people in a stadium.

The Grateful Dead changed and grew and outgrew and re-grew greatly over the years; the Dead you heard when you became a 'Head was probably your favorite Grateful Dead. Mileage varied on these questions, and varied loudly at times. David favors the Americana-jam era of the early seventies; that's when he got on the bus. Blair jumped on with *Live Dead* in late '69, first saw the band at the Capitol Theatre in Port Chester, New York, in the spring of 1970, and remained a Grateful Dead optimist for the next quarter-century, through good times and bad. He saw many life-changing Dead shows in the seventies, but he actually had more fun at shows in the eighties, when his show-going circle had expanded, and the Dead regularly played such wondrous outdoor venues in California as the Greek Theater in Berkeley, Frost Amphitheater at Stanford, Cal Expo in Sacramento, and the Ventura County Fairgrounds on the beach north of Los Angeles.

The drama appealed to lots of different types, which David likened to baseball fandom in an essay for *The Official Book of the Dead Heads* in the early eighties. Many people came for the ecstatic real-time experience, dancing or tripping or listening carefully (or all three together!) with a critical ear. Many kept set lists and/or wrote notes as the show progressed. And many people brought recording equipment so they could take the experience home and share it with others. That practice was great evangelizing for the Dead and surely played a tremendous role in expanding their audience.

The Dead made their living from live performance much more than from records and airplay. Defying the conventional wisdom that "home taping is killing music," the Grateful Dead tolerated and eventually legalized taping and non-commercial trading of their recordings. And the taping network the Dead scene fostered found its way to thousands of shows by other acts, from the Rolling Stones to Dylan to Springsteen to the up-and-coming bar band at your local club.

The reason people are still talking about the Grateful Dead fifty years after the band's founding is that they made an absolutely unique and deeply compelling—to a small number of people—kind of music. They created something musical and something more than musical. If you understood it, if you vibrated with it, it was just incredibly attractive. They played differently every time; they really did. And the charisma of the individuals! They were like the Beatles in the sense that every one of those guys had a persona that people in the audience related to. Plus they looked like just a bunch of schmucks like us: they dressed in T-shirts and comfortable clothes; no rock-star accoutrements at all. It started out as a neighborhood scene in San Francisco, with them playing for their peers and their friends, and it got bigger because people wanted to get in on it. It grew organically because of its power, its beauty, and also its imperfectness. There was a sort of mystique around it.

The San Francisco music scene came up in the sixties when the doors were blown wide open in the culture. Recorded music only became available in the twentieth century, and a group of smart, alienated, young, middle-class kids in Palo Alto, California, had access to music from all over the world. A bunch of musicians with different interests and different styles came together to play, first in a jug band—an interesting phenomenon in its own right—and then found the limitations of that acoustic style of music and went electric, inspired by a couple of different things, including the Beatles' movie *A Hard Day's Night*. That seemed to get everybody who was alive interested in being in a band. So these guys were playing in a jug band and they all got electric instruments and started playing music a little more seriously and a little louder. And then they hooked up with Ken Kesey and his Merry Pranksters and started taking LSD to play music, and that sort of liquefied everybody's individual psyche and allowed them to merge their musical sensibilities to create something entirely new.

An important part of this—and the thing that made the Grateful Dead unique within their cohort and pretty much in the history of rock music—was collective improvisation: their uncanny ability to invent music out of thin air and create a sort of spontaneous midair architecture. They were creating brand-new structures on the fly, everybody playing and listening to one another with equal intensity. It depended on everybody having an open mind and a generous spirit, and not (as Dead lyricist Robert Hunter later put it in another context) "dominating the rap." They could go from one song off into uncharted space and literally go anywhere that the music could take them, including utter silence, cacophonies free of key signature and/or time signature, everybody playing as furiously as they could all at once with no particular cohesion, and every possibility between those extremes. At its best it was incredibly beautiful music, and it made people want to hear how the experiment would come out the next time. That's how they built a culture. The people around them who were drawn to this music wanted to participate: we wanted to listen in on this conversation among really smart people who were creating an eclectic blend of musics, taking familiar ideas and recasting them by juxtaposition, inversion, recontextualization, repetition, non-repetition—endless possibilities, all based on a vocabulary of mostly accessible themes.

Along the way, they wrote more than a hundred amazingly satisfying songs. And that is another key component of it, because it doesn't matter how good your jams are if your songs are lame. The Grateful Dead had so many great songs, and they stitched them together with improvisation in a conversational manner.

As Mikal Gilmore, the great *Rolling Stone* writer, reflected in his book *Night Beat: A Shadow History of Rock and Roll,* "To see the Grateful Dead onstage was to see a band that clearly understood the meaning of playing together from the perspective of the long haul. . . .

"At their best, they were a band capable of surprising both themselves and their audience, while at the same time playing as if they had spent their whole lives learning to make music as a way of talking to one another, and as if music were the language of their sodality, and therefore their history."

The Grateful Dead believed that you can make something real and spontaneous and compelling happen with other musicians in the moment if you trust each other, love each other, encourage each other, and play your brains out. When it worked, there was nothing like it, and the Grateful Dead were really good at it for a really long time.

Some people got into the Dead when they were a feral psychedelic dance band in 1967–68; others heard a blues band fronted by Pigpen; by the early seventies folks heard a country-rock band with appealing sing-along tunes. Everybody loved a different Grateful Dead. But the gestalt is what made it click.

The Grateful Dead became an attractive destination; the culture itself became a destination. And there came a time when a lot of the people who were coming weren't necessarily there for the music— they were there for the party, which annoyed the folks who wanted to pay attention to the music. The band's paychecks got bigger, but the Dead did their very best to maintain their integrity and keep one another honest through all of that. It got really big and out of hand after a while, but that happened because what they were doing was so incredibly charming and thought-provoking and honest, and it didn't pander to anybody. They were acting out their drama and their art in front of people in a way that, if you got it, was irresistible.

Oral history, by definition, has limitations. This book is not the place for a detailed chronology. Dennis McNally's *A Long, Strange Trip* (2001) and Blair's *Garcia: An American Life* (1999) would be good places to start for that.

The Dead's social and business structures were sui generis. The road crew and office staff had more power and greater voices in running things than in most conventional bands or other businesses. Accordingly, we gathered stories from many non-performing members of the tribe.

What you'll find here is a combination of archival interviews—the authors have nearly eighty years of Grateful Dead journalism between them, and have spoken at one time or another to nearly every significant person to float through the Dead scene—and material gathered specifically for this book in 2014, plus bits borrowed from other published and unpublished sources. Inspired by the musicians' concerted sense of quest, we have made this a collaborative effort, presenting key events from a number of perspectives.

Like the Dead's music, our approach is conversational. In the pursuit of assembling a coherent narrative, some quotes have been edited and/or rearranged, and, in a few cases, combined from more than one interview for storytelling purposes. All of the sources are meticulously accounted for. You'll find some stories you haven't heard before, possibly from voices that may be unfamiliar to you. We hope the way these tales unfold will shed new light on history you might already know.

— Blair Jackson and David Gans
Oakland, California, December 2014

Who's Who

ALLAN ARKUSH: Fillmore East usher, Fillmore East production staff, Joe's Lights, filmmaker

BROOKS ARTHUR: Recording engineer (*Anthem of the Sun*, 1968)

KEN BABBS: Merry Prankster

STEPHEN BARNCARD: Recording engineer (*American Beauty*, 1970)

BOB BARSOTTI: Producer of concerts for Bill Graham Presents

PETER BARSOTTI: Producer of concerts for Bill Graham Presents

BILL BELMONT: Grateful Dead road manager and record-biz consultant

BERNIE BILDMAN: Grateful Dead fan; founding board member, Rex Foundation

DICK BOGERT: Recording engineer (*The Grateful Dead*, 1967)

BOB BRALOVE: Musician, MIDI/electronic music consultant, producer of *Infrared Roses*, 1991

JERILYN BRANDELIUS: Family Dog member, longtime life partner of Mickey Hart

STEVE BROWN: Grateful Dead Records employee

BETTY CANTOR-JACKSON: Grateful Dead recording engineer/ producer

JOHN CIPOLLINA: Quicksilver Messenger Service guitarist

TOM CONSTANTEN: Grateful Dead keyboardist

JOHN BYRNE COOKE: Janis Joplin's road manager

DAVID CROSBY: Musician (the Byrds; Crosby, Stills, and Nash)

SUSAN CRUTCHER: Film editor (*The Grateful Dead Movie*, 1977)

JOHN CUTLER: Grateful Dead technical staffer, co-producer of
   In the Dark (1987), *Without a Net* (1989), *Built to Last*, (1990), etc.

SAM CUTLER: Grateful Dead road manager

MILES DAVIS: Musician

TOM DAVIS: Comedian (*Saturday Night Live*)

JOHN "MARMADUKE" DAWSON: New Riders of the Purple Sage
   guitarist and songwriter

LEN DELL'AMICO: Grateful Dead video director

SPENCER DRYDEN: Jefferson Airplane and New Riders of the Purple
   Sage drummer

ROB EATON: Dark Star Orchestra guitarist, Grateful Dead fan

JON EZRINE: Guitarist, Grateful Dead fan

DAVID FREIBERG: Quicksilver Messenger Service, Jefferson Starship
   keyboardist/bassist

DAVID GANS: Musician, Grateful Dead fan, writer

CAROLYN "MOUNTAIN GIRL" GARCIA: Merry Prankster, second
   wife of Jerry Garcia

CLIFFORD "TIFF" GARCIA: Jerry Garcia's older brother

ANNABELLE GARCIA: Daughter of Jerry and Mountain Girl

JERRY GARCIA: Grateful Dead band member

BILL GILES: British Grateful Dead fan

DONNA JEAN GODCHAUX: Grateful Dead band member

BILL GRAHAM: Concert promoter

LAIRD GRANT: Early Grateful Dead road crew member

WAVY GRAVY: Merry Prankster, Hog Farm commune member,
   Grateful Dead fan

DAVID HARRIS: *MoJo Navigator* magazine

MICKEY HART: Grateful Dead drummer

DAVE HASSINGER: Record producer (*The Grateful Dead*, 1967; *Anthem of the Sun*, 1968)

DAN HEALY: Grateful Dead sound engineer

GAIL HELLUND: Grateful Dead secretary

FREDDIE HERRERA: Owner of Keystone Berkeley, the Stone (clubs)

BRUCE HORNSBY: Grateful Dead keyboardist

ROBERT HUNTER: Early musical partner of Jerry Garcia et al., lyricist for the Grateful Dead

JESSE JARNOW: Writer, Grateful Dead fan

PAUL KANTNER: Jefferson Airplane guitarist

ALTON KELLEY: Poster artist

KEN KESEY: Merry Prankster

JIM KOPLIK: Concert promoter (Watkins Glen, etc.)

ROB KORITZ: Dark Star Orchestra drummer, Grateful Dead fan

BILL KREUTZMANN: Grateful Dead drummer

NED LAGIN: Musician, composer of *Seastones*, 1975

GARY LAMBERT: Musician, Grateful Dead fan, editor of the *Grateful Dead Almanac*

EILEEN LAW: Grateful Dead fan liaison

DENNIS "WIZARD" LEONARD: Grateful Dead/Alembic engineer

DAVID LEOPOLD: Grateful Dead fan

PHIL LESH: Grateful Dead bassist

RICHARD LOREN: Grateful Dead booking agent and manager

STEVEN MARCUS: Grateful Dead Ticket Sales manager

BOB MATTHEWS: Grateful Dead recording engineer/producer

JEFF MATTSON: Dark Star Orchestra guitarist, Grateful Dead fan

COUNTRY JOE McDONALD: Country Joe and the Fish guitarist

ROSIE McGEE: Grateful Dead family member, photographer, author

(*Dancing with the Dead: A Photographic Memoir,* 2013)

JON McINTIRE: Grateful Dead manager

RON "PIGPEN" McKERNAN: Grateful Dead band member

DENNIS McNALLY: Grateful Dead publicist (1984–95), author of *A Long Strange Trip,* 2003

PETER McQUAID: Grateful Dead Merchandising

BOB MERLIS: Columbia University student, later publicist for Warner Bros. Records

CONNIE BONNER MOSLEY: Early Grateful Dead family member

STANLEY MOUSE: Poster artist

BRENT MYDLAND: Grateful Dead keyboardist

MICHAEL NASH: Grateful Dead fan, writer

DAVID NELSON: New Riders of the Purple Sage, Jerry Garcia Acoustic Band, etc., guitarist

DOUG and JIM OADE: Grateful Dead tapers

KEITH OLSEN: Record producer (*Terrapin Station,* 1977)

STEVE PARISH: Grateful Dead road crew member, Jerry Garcia Band manager

DAVE PARKER: Grateful Dead accountant

COURTENAY POLLOCK: Tie-dye artist

RON RAKOW: Grateful Dead manager

JONATHAN RIESTER: Grateful Dead manager

DANNY RIFKIN: Grateful Dead manager

BRIAN ROHAN: Music lawyer, co-founder of Haight-Ashbury Legal Organzation

SARA RUPPENTHAL: Jerry Garcia's first wife

NORM, SANDY, JASMINE, JUSTIN, AND TASHA RUTH: Grateful Dead fans, Terrapin Trailways bus

MERL SAUNDERS: Musician, longtime partner of Jerry Garcia outside the Dead

JOHN SCHER: Concert promoter

ROCK SCULLY: Grateful Dead manager

TIM SCULLY: Grateful Dead technical crew

CAMERON SEARS: Grateful Dead manager

ROY SEGAL: Recording engineer (*Grateful Dead from the Mars Hotel*, 1974)

ALAN SENAUKE: Columbia University student

STEVE SILBERMAN: Writer, Grateful Dead fan

JAN SIMMONS: Assistant to Bill Graham, later assistant to Cameron Sears

OWSLEY STANLEY: Co-founder of Alembic, Grateful Dead patron, LSD chemist, sound system designer

RHONEY STANLEY: Grateful Dead secretary

SUE SWANSON: High-school classmate of Bob Weir, later Grateful Dead employee

PETER TORK: Musician, emcee at Monterey Pop Festival

ALAN TRIST: Ice Nine Publishing

RICK TURNER: Co-founder of Alembic, Grateful Dead technical crew

RON TUTT: Drummer (Jerry Garcia Band)

GEORGE WALKER: Merry Prankster

BOB WEIR: Grateful Dead band member

VINCE WELNICK: Grateful Dead keyboardist

RON WICKERSHAM: Co-founder, Alembic

SUSAN WICKERSHAM: Co-founder, Alembic

JOHN ZIAS: Musician, Grateful Dead fan

This Is All a Dream We Dreamed

CHAPTER 1

More Than Human

For our purposes, this story starts on New Year's Eve, 1963, in Palo Alto, California, south of San Francisco, part of a web of small cities known as the Peninsula.

Twenty-one-year-old Jerry Garcia had lived in the area since his release from the Army near the end of 1960, and also had some roots there—he had spent a few years of his adolescence living in Menlo Park. A native San Franciscan, he took up the electric guitar in his mid-teens, learning Chuck Berry songs and other early rock 'n' roll tunes, but during his brief Army stint (Pvt Garcia had some problems with authority) he learned the rudiments of finger-picking guitar from another soldier, and when he returned to civilian life, it was acoustic music, exclusively, that he wanted to pursue. Living in poverty on the Peninsula, he devoted most of his waking hours to mastering the guitar so he could dabble in old-time country music with friends (including future Grateful Dead lyricist Robert Hunter), then threw himself wholeheartedly into the banjo in order to play bluegrass. Through the early sixties he played in a succession of old-time and bluegrass groups that are known today only because they were part of the musical apprenticeship of future rock star Jerry Garcia. Talk to serious Deadheads and they'll reel off names such as the Thunder Mountain Tub Thumpers, the Wildwood Boys, the Hart Valley Drifters, the Black Mountain Boys—bands that lasted a few weeks to a few months and rarely played outside the Peninsula. To earn a little money to help support his wife, Sara (a fine singer herself) and baby daughter, Heather, Garcia got a job teaching guitar and banjo at a Palo Alto music store called Dana Morgan Music.

One of Garcia's musical mates on the Peninsula, Ron McKernan—nicknamed Pigpen, after the unkempt Peanuts character created by cartoonist Charles Schulz—was a blues and R&B kid through and through. His father was an R&B DJ, and he grew up listening to black music. School was never his thing; he was more interested in becoming the next T-Bone Walker or Lightnin' Hopkins. He played serviceable blues guitar, strong harmonica, and some piano. Pigpen and Garcia played a few gigs together in a rock/R&B cover band called the Zodiacs, headed by a local guitarist named Troy Weidenheimer, but mostly stuck to acoustic performances at coffeehouses and clubs.

Boyish Bob Weir had bounced around various schools in Northern California and Colorado but never quite found his niche. He took up the acoustic guitar in his early teens and learned the basics, copying records by Joan Baez and other popular artists and aping the technique of local pickers such as Garcia and the hot blues player on the Peninsula in this era, Jorma Kaukonen (later lead guitarist of Jefferson Airplane). Though Weir was briefly in a group called the Uncalled Four, he was still very green when he wandered into Dana Morgan Music one fateful night . . .

BOB WEIR: I was with a couple of friends walking the back streets of Palo Alto on New Year's Eve at about seven-thirty, headed to a coffeehouse to get some music and celebrate. We heard banjo music coming out of the back of a local music store and just knocked on the door and got invited in. We knew who it was; we knew it was Jerry. He was waiting for his banjo students, and I said, "Jerry, listen, it's seven-thirty on New Year's Eve, and I don't think you're going to be seeing your students tonight." He agreed and asked if we played instruments. We all eagerly nodded yes and broke into the front of the store to grab some instruments. We played all night and had a wonderful time. We decided at that point we had enough amateur talent to start a jug band; they were popular at the time. We started practicing that week and got a gig shortly thereafter. Off it went from there.

BOB MATTHEWS: It goes back to [TV's] *The Beverly Hillbillies*. In 1960, people were just transitioning out of being beatniks into what they didn't know until a few years later was being hippies. Folk music was a key issue. Everybody was buying guitars and getting guitar lessons. I heard Flatt and Scruggs playing the theme song to *The Beverly Hillbillies* and fell in love with that hard-as-nails banjo sound.

There were lots of guitar teachers around. I was trying to find a banjo teacher. My mother, who was teaching first-graders to read at a local progressive private school called Peninsula School, had a Stanford film undergraduate doing a documentary on her unique teaching, and when my mother articulated her difficulty [in finding me a banjo teacher], Sara Garcia turned around and said, "My husband teaches banjo." That's how I met Jerry.

Bob Weir and I were really into the jug bands. We liked Gus Cannon [of Cannon's Jug Stompers, a black, Memphis-based jug band in the late twenties] and Jim Kweskin. The Jim Kweskin Jug Band was playing at the Cabale [in Berkeley]. You had to be at least eighteen, if not twenty-one, to get in. We snuck in, and we were up in the front row. Geoff Muldaur had an incredible voice, and we were really digging on the band. And then this cute, Daisy Mae–looking creature, whose name was Maria D'Amato, came out and sang "I'm a Woman." Most of the males in the building were drooling. She was a gorgeous girl. She became Maria Muldaur, of course. The next day, Bob and I cut class and hitchhiked into Palo Alto to Dana Morgan Music, where

Jerry was teaching banjo. As we walked into his little cement cubicle, he was playing banjo—noodling, as he always did. I think I said, "We went to see the Kweskin Jug Band last night, and we're starting a jug band." Jerry looked up, didn't drop a beat, and said, "Good. I'm in it. I know a great harp player, this guy named Pigpen."

ROBERT HUNTER: I was offered the position of jug player, but I didn't have the embouchure. So I dropped out and didn't pick up performing again for about ten years.

CONNIE BONNER MOSLEY: I remember in high school, the hallways would clear when Pigpen walked down the hallways—with a woman on each arm, maybe. I remember his last days at Palo Alto High School, before he was expelled, and then running into him a few months later at the guitar store.

BOB MATTHEWS: I got to be in Mother McCree's Uptown Jug Champions. First I was washboard player, and then I was kazoo player, then I was the second kazoo player. Bobby loved to hyperventilate himself blowing on the jug. He also played one-string washtub bass—went out and got a zinc washtub, a broomstick, and a piece of twine. That was what he did—and sang and looked pretty. Jerry was

BOB MATTHEWS: He was so mean-lookin'. He was the same age we were, barely eighteen, but we could run over to East Palo Alto, to Maroney's liquor store, send him in with money, and he'd come out with whatever you asked for. Weir and I used to drink Green Death—Rainier Ale. We'd pay for Pig's Thunderbird, and he'd buy us two or three big bottles of Green Death.

CLIFFORD "TIFF" GARCIA: Weir and Jerry were both working at the music store. Weir was giving lessons, Jerry was giving lessons and trying to repair instruments but he wasn't very mechanically inclined. But anything to make ends meet—[Jerry and Sara] had a baby on the way. I remember seeing Bob there and hearing him play and listening to him give lessons. He was just a kid but he was pretty good. He was still going to school at the time; Jerry was older and out of school. Anyway, when I first heard Jerry had gotten together with Weir and Pigpen, I knew it would be a good nucleus for a group.

JERRY GARCIA (1964): I think there are about four major categories of music that we actually play, and we boil it down under the name of jug band music. Actual jug band music is a sort of early blues-band music that was recorded during the 20s and 30s, not sophisticated music; it might feature guitar and harmonica played blues-style, kazoo, possibly a five-string banjo, possibly a jug, which acts as a tuba does in an old-time Dixieland band. That is one of our major areas of material, one of our sources. Another is early Dixieland; New Orleans jazz. We get some 20s, 30s popular music, and a certain amount of more recent blues, from within the last ten or fifteen years, that includes some very recent—within the last three or four years—rhythm & blues songs. So we have quite a large area, and it makes it more fun for us, and certainly more satisfying, because it doesn't restrict us to one particular idea or one particular style, and the result I think is pretty interesting, and it's great—just a gas.

I think we'll play the music probably as long as we're together; we all live in the same area. Like I say, it's fun, it's rewarding, it's great to get together. We don't expect to make a fortune at it, or ever be popular or famous or worshipped, or hit *The Ed Sullivan Show,* or anything like that, or the circuses or the big top, or whatever. Anyway, we play at a few places in the area; I think that we may be restricted to that, just because it's impractical to travel too long a distance. But as long as we can play, we'll play, regard-

playing the banjo [and guitar] and leading the band. He was playing the five-string banjo. It's a different genre of music, but he was playing Jerry Garcia banjo. We were playing a tune— "Washington at Valley Forge," or something—and Jerry leaned over and said, "Hey, why don't you take a break?" What he meant was, "Take a solo." I thought he meant "take a break," so I left the stage.

7

less of what it's for, who it's for, or anything. It's fun for us, that's the important thing.

CAROLYN "MOUNTAIN GIRL" GARCIA: The jug band was fantastic; God, they were good! They rotated people in and out of there so you never knew who was going to do what. It seemed like every song they did would have a different set of musicians. But it was great, great fun. Their gigs were packed and fun and really upbeat. The energy was there and it was good, good energy. They had the Top of the Tangent [a coffee house in Palo Alto] rockin'. Plus, with the jug band there was the opportunity to display all kinds of crazy schtick—vaudevillian jokes and insults and banter, which also happens in some bluegrass bands. I think I saw [Mother McCree's] twice and then they formed the Warlocks and that was a different thing altogether. I was not interested in amplified music at the time. I liked folk music and classical music. I loved the banjo, too.

BILL KREUTZMANN: I saw Jerry play with Mother McCree's Uptown Jug Champions at the Tangent in Palo Alto. I sat right in front of him and watched him playing, and man, he had the whole place in the palm of his hand. Everybody was watching him and he was giving off this incredibly beautiful energy. I said, "Man, I'm gonna follow that guy forever!" I never said that to anyone; I just said it to myself.

About three weeks later, I got a phone call. It was Jerry, saying, "Do you want to be in a band?"

While Mother McCree's Uptown Jug Champions were playing the local clubs on the Peninsula, writer Ken Kesey, who had been at the center of a libertine, Bohemian scene at his house on Perry Lane in Palo Alto, near Stanford University (where he had studied writing with Wallace Stegner), was increasingly dabbling in psychedelics and hanging out with a bunch of like-minded inner-space adventurers who became known as the

Merry Pranksters. Kesey—and Garcia's friend Robert Hunter— had been involved in secret government-sponsored tests on the effects of psychedelics, but by 1964, the genie was out of the bottle and LSD was finding its way to receptive groups of people in the Bay Area, Los Angeles, New York, and a few other places.

Kesey moved from Palo Alto to La Honda, deep in the forest southwest of Palo Alto, and many of the Pranksters followed him. In the summer of 1964, he took some of the money he'd earned from the publication of his best-selling first novel, *One Flew Over the Cuckoo's Nest,* and bought a 1939 International Harvester school bus. He gutted it, replacing the seats with mattresses and sound and film equipment, had an acid-fueled DayGlo painting party to create the wildest and most colorful bus anyone had ever seen on Planet Earth, and christened it Further. Kesey and the Pranksters—including Ken Babbs and Neal Cassady—anti-hero of some of Jack Kerouac's best known books, including *On the Road* and *The Dharma Bums*—embarked on a legendary LSD-soaked trip across America in the bus, an epic voyage immortalized (among other episodes) in the Tom Wolfe book *The Electric Kool-Aid Acid Test.*

The Peninsula buzzed with tales of Further's travels for months afterwards, but the bus trip turned out to be just a warmup for the psychedelic evangelism Kesey and the Pranksters would unleash during 1965 and 1966. Sometime in early 1965, acid found its way to Garcia's circle of friends.

DAVID NELSON: I think it was Rick Shubb [Nelson's bandmate in the Pine Valley Boys bluegrass band] who found this house on Gilman Street [in Palo Alto]. It was the most wonderful place. It had a porch with brick steps. You could come out and just sit in the afternoon. There's nothing like the afternoon in Palo Alto. It's really amazing.

That's the first place that we took acid. And it was 'cause of Rick Shubb. He had a contact in Berkeley and he said, "I can get some hits of acid." Everybody was like, "Okay, I want to do it, I want to do it!" And Hunter's back there shaking his head, because he had been through this two years before that. He said, "You guys are nuts. You don't realize what you're in for."

So Shubb comes over on that day. I think it was thirteen people that all took acid at the same time for their first time. It was Jerry and Sara, me, Eric Thompson, David and Bonnie [Parker], Rick Shubb, and some more. We said, "What if there are dangerous pitfalls and things to watch out for? We gotta go ask Hunter! He's done it before." And so we all run down over to Ramona Street and knock on his door and he looks at us and he goes, "Do you always jump out of planes without a parachute?" We said, "Please, please, Mr. Man, will you please help us here?" So he says, "Okay, just a minute," and he set these chairs up facing him. I remember him talking and it sounding really profound, but I remember he made a gesture [with his hand] and I saw *brrd, brrd, brrd, brrrrrrrrrrrd*—the fingers fan. The visual stuff was just fantastic!

Then we went back to the house and we discovered looking at yourself in the mirror is a total thing. It's like, "Who is that? I didn't know I looked like that!" You don't look the same; you really don't. And you look at your hand, it doesn't look like the same hand. There's all kinds of stuff; really fun.

DAVE PARKER: In those days you could be wandering around and feeling the weirdest way imaginable and feeling obvious, but nobody would notice. It wouldn't even occur to somebody to think that you're on drugs. We were wandering around the house and in and out of the house and walking up and down the streets and around the block, looking up at the streetlights. Police cars would go by and they paid no attention. I remember feeling as demented and bizarre as I could imagine and then some, and yet it was all very soft and innocent walking around Palo Alto. There was no sense of threat or paranoia; it was all happy and wonderful, though very strange at the same time. I thought later what a weird scene that must have been for the other people in the neighborhood. But I'm sure it didn't look as weird as it felt.

DAVID NELSON: Anyway, so that started the thing of, "I think we're going to go electric" [with the band]. I remember right after [the first trip] that there was a lot of buzz about it. There was a lot of talk on what we called the "trips couch" about going electric.

PHIL LESH: I couldn't believe that was Bob Dylan on AM radio, with an electric band [on "Subterranean Homesick Blues" in mid-1965]. It changed my whole consciousness: if something like that could happen, the sky was the limit. Dylan and the blues, and some folk music, were the foundation of our repertoire in the year or so before we started touring and going out—before the Trips Festival, say. That was a paradigm for us. That was how we, in a way, learned to interpret songs. You can add or extend or elaborate on very simple tunes, very simple stuff, like blues songs or folk songs, which have two chords or three chords.

> Mother McCree's heyday, such as it was, coincided with the rise of the Beatles and, shortly after, the Rolling Stones in America. Bob Weir once commented that the Beatles made being in a rock band look "impossibly attractive," and in their early days, the Stones were driving crowds wild playing rock 'n' roll, blues, and R&B—all of which Mother McCree's dabbled in. So in early 1965, Garcia, Weir, and Pigpen decided to start an electric band, the Warlocks. Dana Morgan, Jr., son of the music store owner, was the original bassist, and eighteen-year-old Bill Kreutzmann, already a well-established rock/R&B drummer in the area, was enlisted to be the skinsman.

JERRY GARCIA: Our earliest incarnation was kind of a blues band in a way. We were kind of patterned after the Rolling Stones. This was during the British Invasion. Everybody went and saw [the Beatles'] *A Hard Day's Night*—"Yeah, that looks like fun! Let's go play rock 'n' roll!" Me and Pigpen both had that background in the old Chess Records stuff—Chicago blues like Howlin' Wolf and Muddy Waters, and people like Jimmy Reed, Chuck Berry. It was real natural for us, and we even did those kinds of tunes in the jug band. So it was an easy step to make it into sort of a proto-blues band. The

Stones were already doing all the old Muddy Waters stuff.

Remember that old Junior Walker and the All-Stars instrumental, "Cleo's Back"? That was also real influential on the Grateful Dead—our whole style of playing. There was something about the way the instruments entered into it in a kind of free-for-all way, and there were little holes and neat details in it—we studied that mother-fucker! We might have even played it for a while, but that's not the point—it was the conversational approach, the way the band worked, that really influenced us.

When we first started the Warlocks, I thought, "Wow, Pigpen is this guy who can play some keyboards, some harmonica, and he's a powerhouse singer." He was the perfect frontman, except that he hated it; getting him to do it was really a bitch. I think he was just a shy person.

SUE SWANSON (One of the band's first fans): It was always Jerry's band. But Pigpen was the only one who was really a showman. He'd get out there and work the audience and the band would be behind him. They would let him take the reins and back him up. But by no means were they a backup band for him nor did he ever really lead them. I guess he had a lot of influence on the type of music they played, but they all had that bent, too.

The first fans were Connie [Bonner] and me and Bob Matthews, Barney [Laird Grant], and Bobby Petersen. Connie and I were pretty wild. We used to do all kinds of crazy things, and we were up for it all. We were not exactly the kind of girls who stayed home and behaved. We were gone, we were history. One of the things we used to do was practice getting into hotels—any band that came around we would [sneak into their hotels] for practice so when the Beatles came to town we'd be ready! We always got in, too—Eric Burdon and the Animals, the Dave Clark Five, Chad and Jeremy, Sonny and Cher, the Rolling Stones. I asked Keith Richards, "I know these guys who have a band—what can you tell them? What's your advice?" He said, "Write your own songs." So I passed along that information to Jerry .

We told [the Warlocks], "We'll make you famous, but we want to meet the Beatles!"

BILL KREUTZMANN: We used to rehearse at Dana Morgan's Music store in Palo Alto, and we practiced there mostly because we got the instruments for free, because the bass player's father owned the music store. So after hours Pigpen used to [take] instruments off the wall when the shop was closed and we'd start a jam session. Those were our first rehearsals, in this little music store. I had a little drum set out there and they'd take guitars off the wall to play. And Dana, God bless him, wasn't the best bass player, but really generous—he gave us all the instruments and never asked for them back; it was very kind.

BOB MATTHEWS: Their first gig was at Magoo's Pizza, on the main drag of Menlo Park, California. It was in May of 1965, about a month before I graduated high school—Bob Weir, by that time, had determined that high school wasn't for him—and a whole bunch of people from my high school would come down on Friday nights to hear this band, because they were a good dance band.

JERRY GARCIA: We did . . . we stole a lot of . . . well, at the time, the Kinks and the Rolling Stones' "King Bee," "Red Rooster," "Walkin' the Dog," and all that shit. We were just doing hard, simple rock 'n' roll stuff, old Chuck Berry stuff—"Promised Land," "Johnny B. Goode"—[and] a couple of songs I sort of adapted from jug band material. "Stealin'" was one of those, and that tune "Don't Ease Me In"—it was our first single, an old ragtime pop Texas song.

The first night at the pizza place, nobody was there. The next week, when we played there again, it was on a Wednesday night, there were a lot of kids there, and then the third night there was three, four hundred people, all up from the high schools. . . . We were playing, people were freaking out.

SUE SWANSON: Jerry used to have this little Corvair, and we'd be going down to Magoo's or whatever, and I can remember he and Pig would be behind us in their car and Matthews and I would be laughing, laughing, laughing, because they had what was for the time real long hair and Pig had the big, droopy mustache. We called them the Ugly Sisters.

Pigpen was like a professional dirty old man. He was always there with the sexual innuendo. But at the same time, he was a total gentleman, so you knew he was kidding. I mean, he would never force his attentions on a woman who wasn't interested in him. But he always talked *dirrrrty,* so dirty. I didn't even know what he was talking about most of the time; didn't have a clue—that's how naïve I was. All he did was embarrass me. That's who he was—he wore those clothes and talked that talk, but he was a very soft, sweet, gentle guy. He just had this persona.

> Once the band got rolling, it became clear that Dana Morgan, Jr., was too busy working at the music store to give his all to the Warlocks, and he was only a serviceable bass player to begin with. Something had to give.
>
> Then along came Phil Lesh. He was a couple of years older than Garcia and had traveled a very different path from the other guys in the Warlocks. As a kid growing up in the East Bay cities of El Cerrito and Berkeley, he initially studied classical violin but later switched to trumpet; he played in the school marching band but soon gravitated toward jazz. After graduating from Berkeley High, he was part of the jazz band at the College of San Mateo, but found himself increasingly drawn to composing and electronic music. He briefly enrolled in UC Berkeley's music program (meeting future Grateful Dead keyboardist Tom Constanten along the way), but, intimidated by the academic requirements, quickly dropped out. Instead, he audited a course at Oakland's Mills College taught by the brilliant avant-garde composer Luciano Berio, and for a while immersed himself in the world of modern music. That wasn't paying the bills, though, so he took a series of dead-end odd jobs (in a Las Vegas casino, the San Francisco post office, etc.), and spent his spare time writing esoteric music. He also grew his hair, tried LSD and speed, and got into listening to rock 'n' roll for the first time.

PHIL LESH: I met Jerry when I worked briefly for KPFA. I was an engineer for *The Midnight Special*. I went to a party in Palo Alto and Jerry was there singing and playing his guitar. I just had this flash— "This guy sounds really good; he makes the music live." I had always been impressed by somebody who could sing and play, and Joan Baez was big-time. That quickened my interest in that kind of music, and so I listened to it closer and found that there were things to enjoy in it, things to listen to that were not so much alien to classical music but just part of music as a whole—just like classical is part of music as a whole.

I was at the party and Jerry was playing and singing and I asked if I could make a tape of him to play for Gert Chiarito, who was the host of *The Midnight Special*. He said okay, so we got in a car and went to Berkeley to get the tape recorder—this is when we had all the time in the universe—and he sang and played five or six songs. I played the tape for Gert and asked her if she thought he was good enough to play on *The Midnight Special*. She said this guy could have a show all to himself. They did an hour show of Garcia on KPFA, and after that he was almost a regular.

> Phil later took acid with some friends and went to see Garcia's new electric band, the Warlocks.

PHIL LESH: Good God, it sure was a great scene! We'd just been to see the Rolling Stones, and the Byrds had been in town—this was '65, their first gigs ever—and I just happened to mention it to Garcia —he was at the party, too; we were both stoned out of our minds. Weir came along with some grass and we went to the car and got high, and I happened to mention sometime during that evening to Garcia, "I think I'll take up the electric bass and join a band." The next month, or the next whatever it was, we go down to hear the band and Garcia takes me aside and puts a beer in my hand and says, "Listen, man, you're gonna play bass in my band." "But I . . . er . . . who, me? Well, Jesus, that might be possible." Actually, it excited the shit out of me because it was something to do. And the flash was, "Oh, shit, you mean I can get paid for having fun?"

Of course it was so ironic because before, I'd gotten to the point where I just wanted to quit music entirely. I hated rock 'n' roll music; I didn't think it was anything. I thought it was so lame. I said, "What can you do with three chords?"

JERRY GARCIA: [Phil] decided he wanted to do something that was happening right now; he didn't want to wait to hear his music performed, so in two weeks he learned how to play the bass. The guy is really gifted. I showed him a few things—the sense of the bass—for each tune, and the rest he figured out for himself.

PHIL LESH: [I learned in] two weeks before the first gig, yeah. I didn't play too good, man; it was a real wooden sound, real stiff. But we actually did play a gig two weeks afterwards. And for three or four years after that when I would tell people how long I had been playing bass, they would say, "Amazing!"

JERRY GARCIA: We played in clubs, mostly, and bars—the Fireside, the In Room, [places] like that—for about three or four months, six nights a week, and that's where we really learned how to play. Five sets a night, you really get hot by the third or fourth set, and you can start playing some really insane stuff.

STEVE BROWN: In '65 I left KSFO and went to work in record distribution, doing promotion: going to radio stations from south of San Francisco to Monterey and also going to all the major record stores on the Peninsula and down to Santa Cruz and Monterey. So I would have this word coming to me from these stores about the bands they'd been seeing. And it inevitably came up "Warlocks, Warlocks." People would give you a heads-up on what's cool.

I spent time going to see them at the In Room in Belmont to check 'em out. The In Room was interesting, because it was right there on El Camino Real, in suburbia, and the people who were going there were stewardesses and insurance salesmen, sort of a *Mad Men* kind of deal with lots of cigarette smoking back in the day, and drinks. So you go in the door and it's the bar and there are stools and tables and all these people, and then it made an L, and at the rear was the stage and there was an area to dance, I think, and the sound would sort of go out around the corner into the bar. You could still see the band a little from the bar. So the people who came to see the Warlocks would be in that dance area.

[One night] we went out in somebody's old Plymouth and smoked a joint and laughed it up and gabbed it up. There was a lot of smoking going on behind the club during the breaks. Everybody in the club would be smoking cigarettes and everyone out back was smoking pot. The people in the bar pretty much ignored the band; they probably thought they were just there to entertain the people in the back, and we were pretty well entertained!

BOB MATTHEWS: I remember watching them in that first year, after Magoo's, doing the In Room for six weeks; doing the [San Francisco] Mime Troupe benefit. They were a dance band: people loved to dance to them, and they didn't like it when the song ended. And the band didn't like it either, because they'd come up with a groove, and once you've got a groove, you go with it.

They started extending "Gloria" out to fifteen minutes. I saw the evolution of improv: playing a tune longer than its formatted arrangement was. They would start to explore rhythmic variations. And as they'd start to do that, they'd start tripping themselves out. That was one of the things I loved so much about Bill Kreutzmann as a drummer. He was so intuitive and interactive; he had an incredible capacity in his mind to see mathematical solutions musically. I remember watching Billy play, and the way he would pose himself, interact. I still say he's the greatest rock 'n' roll drummer who ever existed. I'm very biased, but I'll stand by that. He's really a great drummer. A musical drummer.

BILL KREUTZMANN: We played extended pieces from the very beginning. We just never thought of stopping; it never crossed any of our minds to play three-minute songs. We played this bar called the In Room that was a terribly weird gig on some levels, but a great learning gig for us—six nights a week, five sets a night. The weekends were all these heavy straight juicer types, and they'd be looking up at us as we played all these long, long songs and they didn't know what to make of us. They wanted us to quit, but the men didn't want to admit they were tired of dancing and look shitty to their girls. We played every new Rolling Stones song that'd come out, and Pigpen would sing some blues. We just kept playin'.

JERRY GARCIA: We'd do songs and suddenly they'd be ten or fifteen minutes long. Really, the phonograph record is the thing that says, "Hey, a song is three minutes long." Not music itself, certainly not for dancing.

Stuff like Ravi Shankar, Ornette Coleman, [John] Coltrane. I was listening to Ornette's *Free Jazz* record and it was like, "Hey, new idea! That sounds like fun!"

A lot I got from Phil. I've heard him listen to stuff I thought sounded like shit, and he says, "Oh, it's great," then later I realize it is cool.

BILL KREUTZMANN: Phil was my big influence in jazz. During that rough first year after Phil and I joined the band and we were playing at Magoo's pizza parlor and joints like that, Phil lived near me in Palo Alto and he turned me on to all sorts of stuff—not just jazz, but Charles Ives and people like that. It really turned my head around. Then, when we lived together in San Francisco, he turned me on to Coltrane and I just bit on that. I thought, "Jeez, I gotta learn to play this stuff." I really listened to [Elvin Jones] a lot. He was a major influence, no question about it.

JERRY GARCIA: I first had the experience of having a player just exceed what you would normally expect [with] this bluegrass fiddle player named Scotty Stoneman, who was a real tragic case; he's dead now. He was a hopeless alcoholic when I heard him play, and was just about totally burned out, in fact, but he just played amazing. He'd take these medium-tempo fiddle tunes and stretch them out to about fifteen minutes of completely free improvisation that wasn't bound in any way by the normal structure of the songs. It was just completely flowing over the top like John Coltrane or anybody who plays in a stream of consciousness style of playing. It had amazing emotional content, but also with tremendous technical control at the same time; a beautiful combination of those two things, and for me that's always been a model for how powerful music can be. And it didn't have anything to do with loudness.

During the summer of 1965, a San Francisco band called the Charlatans traveled up to Virginia City, Nevada, a true old West town, and transformed the Red Dog Saloon into a psychedelic rock 'n' roll venue. The band and their friends, who loved to dress in Edwardian/Western garb, were heavily into LSD, and played ear-splitting rock and country-flavored music at the Red Dog in front of a primitive light show for several weeks before the "authorities" essentially drove them out of town. By the time they returned to San Francisco, psychedelics had taken hold in several bands there, too, including Jefferson Airplane, who debuted at the Matrix club in August, and the Great Society (featuring Grace Slick), who turned up a short time later. That fall, some of the folks who had been involved with the Red Dog and who were now living in a commune in San Francisco started putting on dances in the city as the Family Dog.

Meanwhile, the Warlocks, who were getting more and more into acid themselves, and increasingly enjoying the colorful psychedelic scene that was fast evolving in San Francisco, were looking for a new name. Apparently, "Warlocks" was already taken by some other band somewhere. When the group went to record their first demo tape at Golden State Studios on November 3, 1965, they called themselves the Emergency Crew, but that didn't cut it.

JERRY GARCIA: We were trying to think of a name for the band. Our name was originally the Warlocks. We discovered that there was a band back East or something like that recording under that name, and we decided, "Oh, no, we can't have that. We can't be confused with somebody else." So we were trying to think up names, and for about two or three weeks we went on the usual thing of coming up with thousands and thousands of very funny names, none of which we could use, like Skinny Minnie and the Vivisectionists. We were standing around in utter desperation at Phil's house in Palo Alto. There was a huge *Webster's New World Dictionary*, I believe—big monolithic thing—and I just opened it up, and there in huge back letters was "Grateful Dead."

It canceled my mind out, kind of, and I thought, "Well . . ." So we decided to have it, but it was funny, 'cause we really didn't like it too much at first, and it kinda made us shudder. We were worried that nobody was gonna go for it, it's too weird, and whatever. But finally, enough people called us that, and we called ourselves that enough times, that that's who we are now.

BOB MATTHEWS: It was time to change the name. Bazillions of names, all on pieces of paper, and everybody kept throwing them back and forth, and nothing was making it. There was so much dissension, and nothing coming out of it, that Phil stood up and said, "Enough is enough."

Phil is a very intellectual person and always had sources of knowledge around him. One of the things he had was an *Oxford Unabridged,* on a dictionary stand. [Jerry] said, "It's gonna come to us." He put his hands over his eyes, went over to the dictionary, opened the dictionary, and still with his hands over his eyes, moved his finger down, and stopped in an arbitrary place. We were there, and watching, and it was totally arbitrary. He opened his eyes and said, "grateful dead?!" And he read the definition. The first definition was, "ethnomusicological term dealing with ballads of unrequited love." It's a very old term.

JERRY GARCIA (1967): It's a genre ballad, like there are "murdered girl" ballads. Well, there are "grateful dead" ballads. So it tied in nicely in a way. Plus the fact that a lot of people have mentioned *The Tibetan Book of the Dead* in connection with it, although I don't know whether that particular phrase ever appears in it. I don't think it does. It's also like a very brief phrase you could describe as being the psychedelic condition. If you wanted to talk about it like that. It's any number of things. It's just a loaded phrase. It looks good in print, it sounds good—it's got a sort of euphonic thing going for it.

DAVID NELSON: Jerry takes me and Sara into my room and says, "You've got to hear this. I'm really wondering what the general reaction is going to be, and I just want to have an idea." I remember his big eyes lookin' at me. I said, "What's the idea?" and he said, "Grateful Dead."

I said, "Let me think about it." I was lookin' at the straight world—the lamebrains and the dodos, you know. Those people just react instantly, and they think they're right and all that.

But I said, "It's a fantastic name," and that's what Sara said, too. They went with it and it turned out to be the best band name ever. Didn't it? Did it not?

Rock 'n' roll was supposed to say, "Hey, I don't care about your fuckin' straight music and all your namby-pamby rules. We're just playin' this for fun, period, and that's all it is."

SUE SWANSON: Everybody's mom hated it, so we knew we loved it!

It was inevitable that the Peninsula's leading psychedelic band would eventually cross paths with Ken Kesey and the Merry Pranksters, who had been throwing acid parties up in the La Honda redwoods for some time and were looking to expand beyond Kesey's sylvan wonderland. It helped, too, that the Bay Area now had access to a mother lode of high-quality LSD, thanks to one Owsley "Bear" Stanley, who, with his girlfriend, Melissa Cargill, began making thousands of hits of the still-legal psychedelic in various locations and distributing much of his product for free. He, too, was destined to hook up with Kesey's crowd.

CAROLYN "MOUNTAIN GIRL" GARCIA: The Pranksters usually had

parties on Saturday, and that was when people could come out from Berkeley or come over the hill from Palo Alto. We would set up the sound system and show movies out in the woods.

GEORGE WALKER: It was kind of like a psychedelic show-and-tell. People would get high and do little skits and stuff. Some of it was musical, some of it was just silliness. We realized there was something about the way we were relating to ourselves and the rest of the world that was a little different.

As the scene at Kesey's got bigger and bigger, he realized, "This is too easy to spot. We need to get this out of my house or we're all going to end up seriously in trouble." And so he said, "Let's go rent places and do it somewhere else," and he came up with the term *the acid test*. We put up posters that said, "Can You Pass the Acid Test?" Before LSD became illegal, we would give people a dose of acid when they came in. It was kind of a "test" to see how well people could function in this situation.

CAROLYN "MOUNTAIN GIRL" GARCIA: They were really meant to be a safe place to get high.

[The Warlocks] were the natural addition to the scene. First of all, they were hungry and scuffling, and we could give them something for their time. They were very talented, for amateurs, at the time—they weren't playing the kind of music that you could go out and sell, even in a bar. Typically, in one of their early shows, by the second set there would be like thirty or forty die-hards in the place. They basically drove everybody out. They were noisy, they were really brash, they played excruciatingly long songs incredibly loud, and most folks just weren't ready for it.

But taking what they were doing with the blues, Lightnin' Hopkins tunes, and so on, putting that into the Acid Test format, and with them being stoned, you'd get these long, drawn-out, peculiar [passages] where they would be sort of fooling around with their instruments. It was just wonderful.

And it had a lot to do with the way they are today, I think. We played enough of those shows for that to become part of their show, and for the people who go to Grateful Dead shows to expect that sort of thing. They've perfected it, at this point.

DAVID NELSON: I remember going to San Jose [the Acid Test, at "Big Nig's" house, December 4, 1965]. I think it was with Eric [Thompson] or somebody, and walking up—we made the mistake of dropping first—and I go, "Oh, I guess we're more than a little fashionably late," because there were people already out on the lawn, going *"blahty-blah-blah-blah."* It looked kind of like a well-lit uptight party, and then somebody said, "Oh, the band's actually not ready yet. It's questionable whether they're going to play or not." The problem with that Acid Test was, it was at a house, and the person who owned it—or rented it—started looking at what was going on and said, "Please! No, no! I didn't say you could do that!" In that day and age, you'd say, "Aw, somebody was just too uptight!" So I went back and had a wonderful time just walking around Palo Alto.

The first Acid Test where the Grateful Dead really played was the Big Beat Acid Test [in Palo Alto, December 11, 1965]. I remember they played a tune, and they were so stoned that they orbited completely out of the tune, and they're looking around and saying, "What are we playing?" Now it's up to somebody to make the call, and of course Jerry was playing lead at the time, so he goes, "What? What are we doing?"— Jerry not knowing himself; I could see that look on his face. But he was saying, "I don't know, but let's keep it going. Don't stop!" and he would suggest a real simple idea, and of course Phil is a quick study and got it, and it just started to develop—Billy hears it, Weir hears it, and all of a sudden they're into this new thing and Garcia is still looking at them. In those early days,

CAROLYN "MOUNTAIN GIRL" GARCIA: We were colorful, we were fun, we were athletic. To . . . us this was an American tradition. If you believe in the pursuit of life and liberty and happiness . . . we felt like we'd discovered a certain kind of magic, and this was magic that needed to be shared.

23

all the jams would be him looking at the band and they're looking at him. It was like an adventure. That's the secret of jams. If a band doesn't have eye contact and they call themselves a jam band, what the hell has the world come to? But that was the first time I saw it; it really was. That was the actual evolutionary moment.

CAROLYN "MOUNTAIN GIRL" GARCIA: There was no barrier between the audience and the participants. The audience and the performance was one. We would set up a strobe light. We had boxes of instruments people could play, and there would be live microphones spotted around the room. We also realized this was revolutionary work, because we were introducing people to a set and setting that really hadn't been done before. We wanted to sell this concept that your brain can do a lot of things you didn't know it could do.

KEN KESEY: [It was] like a new tribe on a new seashore, and they're pounding on new drums. . . . For all those people doing the psychedelic dancing, there was absolutely nothing for them to base their dancing on. They're making it up right there in front of you. All those people there, high and dancing, had never seen anything like this before. Up until then, if you were going to a dance, you did what had been done before—you danced the jitterbug or the boogaloo or the mashed potato, or whatever was happening in the culture at the time. But when the Dead's sound started to spark that acid consciousness, the way people moved to music absolutely changed. It was absolutely new and spontaneously creative. I don't think that kind of movement had ever happened before. It's not like Krishna. It's not like aborigines. It's not like Africans, really. It's its own thing.

There's this funny scene [in the Merry Pranksters' film footage of one Acid Test] with these guys who look like they just stepped in from the fraternity house. They're wearing cardigan sweaters and dress shirts, and they're trying to do the jerk to this incredibly weird music. They keep looking around as if they don't quite know where they are—whether they're making a spectacle of themselves or whether they're doing the right thing, or what. And you can see on their faces the dawning consciousness of "Hey, there might be more to life than what we're learning in college!"

OWSLEY STANLEY: For most people, the proper dose is 150 to 200 micrograms. When you get to 400, you just totally lose it. I don't care who you are. Kesey liked 400. He wanted to lose it.

Kesey was playing around with something he did not understand. I said to him, "You guys are fucking around with something people have known about forever. It's sometimes called witchcraft, and it's extremely dangerous. You're dealing with part of the unconscious mind that they used to define as angels and devils. You have to be very careful because there are all these warnings. All the occult literature about ceremonial magic warns about being very careful about these areas in the mind." And they laughed at me.

JERRY GARCIA: A lot of people freaked out [at the Acid Tests]. A lot of people came completely unglued, absolutely. I can't unqualifiedly say that this was really totally great. My personal experiences were absolutely great.

People used to say it all the time about the Acid Tests: "Too high energy, it's dangerous." The kind of stodgy, Tim Leary school of the East Coast—"This is a sacrament."

We said, "Well, who said that we are all doing the same thing? I mean, we aren't researching, we're partying. We're having fun."

That was the difference between us and them. For me, it was very profound on a lot of levels. Going off into the woods and being meditative didn't cough up anything for me except for how pretty everything is. I got my flashes from seeing other people and interacting with other people, because I was looking for something in this world, not out of it. I was looking for a way to get through this life, not transcend it.

[What was great about the Acid Tests was] the freedom . . . and the synergy—lots of things happening at once. No specific focus, which meant that kind of pattern beyond randomness. The whole study of chaos has been an interesting affirmation of this sense that when you take away the order, something is left; another level of order comes to the surface.

BILL KREUTZMANN: [Playing on acid] changed the tempo a lot. Actually, a lot of the time there was no tempo. It also created more extendedness and amplified what was going on—it made things go on longer, or just seem like a blink, depending. It was totally musical or not musical at all. Who knows? When you're high on acid you can't be expected to be too analytical about things; you're going more with a free flow. Sometimes you would be synchronous with what the other guys were playing, and sometimes you'd be in your own world playing. But we weren't examining what we were doing. I remember once when I was high on acid it took me what seemed like fourteen years to take my drums apart. It seemed like lifetimes had gone by—I'd gone gray, grown old, died, been reborn—all in the time it took to put one cymbal in the case.

JERRY GARCIA: There's a thing about playing stoned without having pressure on you to play competently. If you can have the space in your life where you can be high and play and not be in a critical situation, you can learn a lot of interesting things about yourself and your relation to the instrument and music. We were lucky enough to have an uncritical situation, so it wasn't like a test of how stoned we could be and still be competent—we weren't concerned with being competent. We were concerned with being high at the time.

KEN KESEY: By putting the tape recorder on "tape" instead of "input," you'd get a little lag on each channel. Then we'd put one speaker at one end of the hall and one at the other, and a microphone in front of each speaker so the sound would be going out of a speaker, into a microphone, back into the tape recorder, and into the other speaker, and so on, until the sound just washed around in the hall.

CAROLYN "MOUNTAIN GIRL" GARCIA: This short lag on your voice was just long enough to be really uncomfortable, and it would really fuck you up. It was exactly the length of time it would take you to form a thought, so just as your next thought was formed, you heard your voice speaking the previous thought. It was really hard to make progress through that.

KEN KESEY: Even when the Dead were playing through their own equipment, that sound was washing around the hall. Nobody had ever heard anything like this—where they were part of the ambience of the sound.

WAVY GRAVY: I was amazed, absolutely amazed that for a dollar at the door, somebody could make the floor change color. [At the Muir Beach Acid Test] I started making a sculpture out of chairs, and got people into that. That was a lot of fun, and what a soundtrack to watch the floor change colors!

CAROLYN "MOUNTAIN GIRL" GARCIA: [After an Acid Test] you'd be so burned out. It was a lot of work—loading, unloading, unrolling [wires], plugging, going and getting stuff and making it happen. You had to have that shit together by showtime. And you'd work and play all night long, and then you had to load everything back up. You'd get out of there at about ten in the morning and you'd be a complete frazzle.

We kept moving them around so we'd get different people coming all the time and we wouldn't get into a rut. But how we ever managed to sell more than one ticket is beyond me. It was word of mouth. We'd get a poster out about three days before the thing, send out a postering crew, and that was it.

OWSLEY STANLEY: The Acid Test was like a circus, and the Grateful Dead was just one of the acts in that circus. All that weird shit that was going on with the sound was happening when they weren't performing.

We have tapes of some of them. Most of them are unlistenable. It's hard to really judge it on a regular musical level. Musically speaking, it might be one thing, but so far as magic or consciousness is concerned, it's something else. Some of the Acid Tests were up and going and fun, and some of them were real dark. It was the full gamut.

CAROLYN "MOUNTAIN GIRL" GARCIA: [When] we started to add

music, with what became the Grateful Dead, it turned into another kind of thing, which was more of a stage presentation. Early on, there were two parts to the show: music and events. The two didn't really mix. Musicians like to give a performance. They don't like too many events going on while they're giving their performance. As soon as they were done, or there was a break, then the events would begin again.

JERRY GARCIA: It wasn't one of those things where people paid to come see us specifically, so we had the option to be able to not play, and there were times when we would play maybe twenty bars and everybody would come unglued and we'd all split. So there were times we really didn't want to play, but there were times we really did want to play, and not only could we play, but since nobody had any expectations of what we were going to play, we could play anything that came into our minds.

PHIL LESH: All I can say is you had to be there. That was the *baptismo del fuego*. When you're up there and your face is falling off and you've still got to play, and you do this over and over again, spilling your guts in front of thousands of people . . . you develop a certain flip attitude, even toward performing. You begin to believe that you could go out there naked and nobody'd notice, as long as you played loud enough.

CAROLYN "MOUNTAIN GIRL" GARCIA: I think the Acid Tests were really a deliberate attempt to move consciousness expansion out into the public marketplace of ideas. We wanted to sell this concept that your brain can do a lot of things you didn't know it could do. America needs the antic spirit that the Merry Pranksters embodied. I think that the spirit of play and the fun is antiwar, it's anti-establishment, and we need to keep our creativity; we need to keep our personal freedoms—they're precious.

BOB WEIR: When I fell in with Ken Kesey and Neal Cassady, it seemed like home sweet home to me, to be tossed in with a bunch of crazies. There was some real serious crazy stuff going on. Jesus, where do you start? For one thing, I had to abandon all my previous conceptions of space and time. It was pretty conclusively proven to me that those old concepts were shams. I thought I was pretty well indoctrinated into the "anything goes" way of dealing with life. But I found much more than anything goes with the Pranksters. There was a world of limitless possibilities. It was . . . God, it's hard to say anything that doesn't sound clichéd. But it was really a whole new reality for this boy. We were dealing with stuff like telepathy on a daily basis.

It might have been partly because of the LSD or the personal chemistry of everyone involved, and the times. We picked up a lot from those guys. Particularly from Cassady. He was able to drive fifty or sixty miles an hour through downtown rush-hour traffic, he could see around corners—I don't know how to better describe it. That's useful if you're playing improvisational music; you can build those skills to see around corners, 'cause there are plenty of corners that come up. We gleaned that kind of approach from Cassady. He was one of our teachers, as well as a playmate.

JERRY GARCIA: We all saw different aspects in Neal. He'd show different aspects of himself to everybody. He was able to refer to lots and lots of different things in one conversation. He had lots of levels going. Some of them you knew about, some of them you didn't know about, but there was continuity there. Each time that you talked to him, he would pick up from where you left off last time you'd seen him, even if it had been months.

BOB WEIR: If there was something on your mind, if you had a problem or an observation or something, you know, you'd bring it to Dad—you'd bring it to Neal. If there was something on your mind, you'd bounce it off him. And it sure as hell would bounce.

JERRY GARCIA: Yeah. So he filled the role of the person you go to for advice. You know, ask Dad.

We were all malleable. He was the guy speaking to us from the pages of Kerouac. He was a breeze, some kind of incredible super-

American mythos personality blasting through the highways of 1947 America. America owes more to that period of time than it realizes, I think.

BOB WEIR: It's still working, and it's still working right well for us. Basically, Neal was the hood ornament on the chrome Zephyr that came floating through American culture.

SARA RUPPENTHAL: I came to love the man dearly, but at first I found him very intimidating. It wasn't until the Big Beat Acid Test that I really came to appreciate him. That was the night I saw him do that thing where he could tune into everybody's reality. He had an extraordinary gift. He really was a "Martian policeman," as he called himself. Doing his monologue with a hammer—juggling a hammer—and talking. And somehow managing to touch everybody in this circle of people watching him, to call each of them on their trip or let them know what they were thinking and could never say. He was a genius, maybe psychopathic. Probably really psychic and a brilliant psychologist. And a very gentle soul. A very compassionate person, although he would always head for the medicine cabinet and help himself to whatever you had.

> As 1965 turned into 1966, the Grateful Dead were still living on the Peninsula but were spending more time in San Francisco, where the psychedelic counterculture was growing exponentially by the week, it seemed, and more dances and other events were taking place all over the city. At the beginning of the new year, the Acid Test moved up to Portland for a weekend, then came right back to San Francisco for their most high-profile event yet—a happening at the Fillmore Auditorium, which would become ground zero for the San Francisco ballroom scene during the first months of 1966, under the aegis of Bill Graham and Chet Helms (who later branched off to run the Avalon Ballroom). Then, on January 22, the biggest Acid Test of all took place at Longshoreman's Hall in San Francisco, where the Pranksters and the Dead unleashed their mind-bending, anar-

chic reveries on a crowd numbering in the thousands, for the middle of the three-night Trips Festival, a multimedia "coming-out" party for the burgeoning psychedelic scene and alternative art/music culture. Organized primarily by Stewart Brand (later publisher of the *Whole Earth Catalog*), the Trips Festival might well have been the largest public gathering of stoned and tripping people ever in the United States up to that point.

RON "PIGPEN" McKERNAN: We were roaring up toward Portland. Neal was driving and rapping into the microphone like always. We burned out a back wheel bearing and had to stop. We rented a truck—one of these big Avis or Hertz trucks with a big box on the back. We rigged up lights on the inside of the box, rigged up an intercom system between the cab and the back, and took off for Portland.

I was sitting up in the front with Neal. We had this big speaker in the front so we could [talk] back and forth with the guys in the back, who were cramped up like sardines with all the equipment. Anne Murphy was sittin' between me and Neal. So there we were roaring up through this winding mountain road, with snow drifts eight or ten feet high on the sides—icy roads and a blizzard—and Neal has one hand on the bottle of wine, the other hand poppin' speed, and the other hand playin' with Anne, and the other hand talkin', and the other hand drivin' the truck . . . and on and on and on. There it was, man. "*Aaaugh!* Give me some of that wine, quick!"

We finally got to Portland and found the place and went in and it was still snowing. I spent quite a bit of time in the cloak room sleeping on the floor with about nine other people.

ROCK SCULLY: The Fillmore Acid Test [January 8, 1966] was one of those Acid Tests where you really had to pay attention to hear how the music was coming together. You weren't going to a "concert" at one of these things. The stage was all over the place—it was wherever Babbs would point the spotlight. There was interminable sound-checking going on. And Babbs is mumbling on and you couldn't tell whose microphone was on, and sounds are coming out and Babbs and Kesey would be talking to each other on different speakers across the hall.

I watched very carefully, and the Dead actually pulled off a really great blues set. It was indicative of what was to come once they got goin'. I think it had to do with the fact that the beat, the rhythm, was really in sync with the crowd, so as long as the crowd was up and bouncing, they could get away with just about anything. So they'd have these conversations, both literally and figuratively, with their instruments and with their voices talking about where they were going to go next. And Pigpen was sort of the straight man in the whole deal. It was kind of like the Marx Brothers, where there was one oddball who didn't speak their language.

| Some weirdness from the Fillmore Acid Test . . .

BOB WEIR: Hey, Ken! These microphones don't seem to be working.

PIGPEN: They fucked up!

WEIR: Nothing up here is working.

UNIDENTIFIED: Excuse upon it friends, the electronic wasteland . . .

PIGPEN: How 'bout a microphone? C'mon now!

UNIDENTIFIED: Just keep a-playin', boys. She'll come through one o' these days.

PIGPEN: They ain't no power on the stage!

UNIDENTIFIED: Just keep a . . .

PIGPEN: All the 'lectricity on the stage—just fix it!

KEN KESEY: This is the captain speaking. We have reached our first emergency, and we haven't even got by the boundaries of—

PIGPEN: Well, why don't you rectify it pretty damn quick?

KESEY: Let's everybody put their worries and frets to mind to produce some e-lectricity for the stage . . .

PIGPEN: It's about time to get it ready!
KESEY: There's wires all around here plugged into e-lectricity. Let's—

PIGPEN: Hey, man, stop your babbling and fix these microphones! We need some power!

> Owsley Stanley first heard the Grateful Dead at an Acid Test in December 1965.

OWSLEY STANLEY: I thought, "These guys are fantastic." But it was scary. The music was scary, pushing me to the edge. The sound of Garcia's guitar was like the claws of a tiger. It was dangerously scary. Very, very to the point. I thought to myself, "These guys are going to be greater than the Beatles some day." It was almost like a revelation, like looking into the future. I just instinctively knew that there was something like that. And in a way, they are, because the Beatles were a phenomenon of the universal attractiveness of their music, and the intense teenage involvement. We find that intense teenage involvement in dozens of different bands, we find excellent musical output in dozens of different bands, and they create a lot of fans, [but] they have not created the kind of thing that's associated with the Dead.

The next time I saw them was at the Fillmore Acid Test, and I met Phil. I walked over to him and I said, "I'd like to work for you guys." Because I had decided that this was the most amazing thing I'd ever run into. And he says, "Oh. We don't have a manager . . ."

I said, "I don't think I want to be the manager."

He said, "Well, we don't have a sound man." And I said, "Well, I don't know anything about that, either, but I guess I could probably learn. Sounds like more fun."

They were part of the scene that was doing something that was right out on the edge—the edge of consciousness, the edge of magic, the edge of music—that was very dynamic. A band composed of five guys that were among the smartest people I'd ever run across.

To find that many really smart people—people whose minds operated in the same function zone that mine did and could carry on the most tenuous and stratospheric of conversations with nobody gettin' lost—that blew my mind, number one. It's unusual to find that kind of bunch. I've worked for a lot of bands: I've been on the road; I've worked in halls where they come through, a different band every day; in festival situations. I've worked situations where I've had a lot of contact with a lot of musicians, and by and large I find that there's a great many really bright guys involved in the music, but to find that many all in one group is truly unique.

DAVID NELSON: The Trips Festival was the biggest one of all. And remember that the Trips Festival wasn't just an Acid Test. The Acid Test was the second night. [The event] was Friday night, Saturday night, and Sunday, and I went to every one of them because that was such an outlandish idea in 1966. "Are you kiddin' me? There's a thing called a Trips Festival?" I didn't know people knew what that word meant. Truly. *Trips* was a new word. There were all kinds of art things and a lot of literary things; literature was important back then. There were readings and there was what they call "art happenings." Like I saw some lady in a bikini come out and a guy climbs a ladder and pours buckets of paint on her and she goes, *"Ah, ah, ah,"* and the paint spills on her and creates different patterns.

The big one was, of course, that the Dead were going to play [on the Acid Test night] along with the Pranksters. [Jerry and I] were still living on Waverly Street [in Palo Alto] and Jerry was saying, "Don't miss this one!"

JERRY GARCIA: Everybody there was high. I mean every soul there—except for Bill [Graham]! And he was trying to organize the whole thing. It was a roomful of loaded people and he was trying to pull it together. I had heard the rumor that it was time for us to play; let's put it that way. So we went up onstage, and I'm looking around and the stage is total chaos, absolutely crowded with people milling around. So I go over to my guitar, and my guitar is broken; it's smashed. The bridge is pulled off of it, the strings are all over the place. I'm looking at it and it occurs to me that my guitar is wounded, it's hurting, it's broken.

Bill comes over and he says, "Why aren't you guys playing? You guys are supposed to play right now." Here he is, sweating and his eyes are buggin' out, and he's got his little sweater and clipboard. It was the way you could distinguish him from everyone else — he was the guy trying to make things happen. So I pointed at my guitar and said, "I think my guitar's broken." And he immediately drops what he was doing and falls down and he starts fumbling around trying to put the pieces of my guitar together. I looked at him and I thought, "What a hero! What a guy!"

DAVID NELSON: [After being in the balcony awhile] I went down into the hall and now I'm thinking, "Oh, I'm coming on this anxiety stage [of the acid trip]. Oh, man, that's right." The only thing I know to do is to walk with the people. So now it's getting packed and I'm going, "Hey give a fellow a little room here." Everybody is just smashed, plus the anxiety, and the thing of "Oh, they're starting to play," and the band was experiencing the same thing, too. All of a sudden everything had fallen apart on stage. I saw Garcia grab his guitar and tell Laird [Grant, a roadie], "Look, see?" And the bridge was dangling—*boing, boing, boing*, like that—and he's saying, "See, you gotta fix my fuckin' guitar. I'm too stoned."

It took forever for this to happen. So we're inching along, and then they started to play. I stepped out of the line, and as I stepped out I looked up, and the Pranksters were all over the place doing their little trip, which was like flashing lights or doing some strobe light thing, and I followed that and then turned around and—*blam!*—there's this clear space but nobody seems to see it. It was like a six-foot-diameter circle, right on the floor, right in the middle. I listened for a while and it just sounded like four-dimensional music. I was going, "Listen to this! They're goin' one way with one instrument and another way with another instrument. It's gyroscopic. The groove! It's goin' this way and it's also goin' that way. This is amazing." They were playing really slow, too, so you could see big spaces between the musical ideas. I was just goin', "Oh, my God, it's the best thing I've ever heard."

CAROLYN "MOUNTAIN GIRL" GARCIA: There was [Bill Graham], whacking people over the head with his clipboard. We're saying, "Who is this guy? Get him out of here. He's ruining our lovely trippy event with his clipboard and all that shouting." But Stewart had hired this schmo to come in and be in charge of the guest list, so there he was, and after that is when he started putting on his own dances regularly.

The Trips Festival was a shocking success. I think it was actually a sellout and we couldn't believe it. We'd never had a sellout before. Stewart Brand had done this incredible thing of getting everybody down from the techie world, and of course everyone from our crowd was there. It was amazing. There were reciprocating video loops and light machines and light sculptures; just incredible stuff that had never been done on this kind of scale before. Ken had set up this thing where he would write things on an overhead projector and we'd project that on the ceiling, so his writing was twelve feet tall. He had a hatful of phrases he'd culled from his desk drawer, so we'd project this on the ceiling and you couldn't believe the weight of these giant words—the energy of these words was immense.

DAVID NELSON: At the very end I'm wandering around because I can't even think about a ride home now. "I don't remember how I got here." So I wandered around, and Pigpen comes up, eyes sunken in, and I thought, "Oh, yeah, that's right—he didn't take acid so he doesn't connect with this. That must be rough." So I went, "What is it?" He said, "Can you carry my organ up the stairs? We gotta lock them up." They were sweepin' the floor. I'm still there, and me and [my friend] Paul Mittig said, "Sure, man." We grabbed his organ. We carried it upstairs, and they locked it up and now I'm thinkin', "How the hell am I gonna get home?" Sue Swanson comes up and goes, "Dave, you need a ride?" I said, "Yeah," and Weir comes up on my other side and says, "Yeah, yeah. We're takin' you home. Don't worry, man. But first we're gonna go to a little gathering in San Francisco. Is that okay?" I said, "Oh, yeah, sure." It was Kesey, Neal Cassady, and everybody flopped around on the floor. You had to step over people. And they carried on for as long as they wanted to, and then took me home to Palo Alto, to my home.

JERRY GARCIA (1966): That was the only Trips Festival. Probably the only really good one. Everybody in the place was stoned and all on the same trip, responding to everything that was going around, and doing stuff to change it; it was a responsive atmosphere. It was a great big party, is what it was. It wasn't a dance or anything else. It was a huge party—a very successful one. It was just the ultimate in entertainment. We've played a lot of things that were almost as wild, but I don't think there has been anywhere I felt as personally free.

CAROLYN "MOUNTAIN GIRL" GARCIA: We didn't invent light shows or most of the other things we did. There were other powerful heads out there doing all that and more. We didn't really originate any of this stuff. But Ken was better at publicizing things than most people, so as the years went by we got more of the blame or credit than we probably deserved.

But the Acid Test was a great idea. Some people did not have fun at the Acid Test. For some people it was a little too much. But gee, they paid to get in and there was no guarantee. It was strictly experimental. Ken felt strongly that LSD was something that was going to improve mankind. He felt it was an important tool. At the same time, though, I think there was an element of rebellion that we all shared against the sixties establishment. The Vietnam War was such a devastating thing in this country at that time, and we were the counterattack; the internal insurgents.

After the Trips Festival, the Dead and the Pranksters moved their scene to Los Angeles for about a month and a half. During that time, there were several Acid Tests, and the Dead also played a couple of more traditional gigs. The band lived together in a large house on the edge of Watts, along with Owsley (now their sound man and acid supplier), newly hired manager Rock

Scully, and a few friends, such as Phil's new companion, Florence Nathan (aka Rosie McGee).

RON "PIGPEN" McKERNAN: We moved into the place in L.A. and started trying to promote our band. Which worked okay, except the cops ordered us to take down the posters off the telephone poles we nailed them to.

DAVID NELSON: For me, [the Trips Festival] was an incredibly solid thing—one of the most solid hits in my life. The universe seemed like time stopped and molecules changed; it was so exciting. I realized that the world had changed and now it was going to go this way. There was nothing bad happening, there was no immoral stuff going on. There was no innuendo or hidden stuff. It was just plain, simple fun.

But everyone from the outside looking in was morally outraged, as if there was some betrayal there.

ROSIE McGEE: From the very beginning, they were completely dedicated to working, to rehearsing—just going for it, going for it, going for it. And those of us around them were peripheral to what they were doing. I don't mean this in a negative way! I came to understand that over time. My job was rolling joints and making sure there was food when they took a break. I understood that pretty early. We were all on the mission together; the women did this, that, and the other, and the guys did this, that, and the other. We all had our parts to play, and that was my part.

From day one, it was band-centered life. They all worked their asses off. Individually, at home, they all personally practiced their individual instruments; and they agonized over writing songs if they did write songs. It was completely obsessive, but it had to be. I mean, that's who they were. They're musicians. And then when they came together, they worked just as hard as a group. Not one of them was lazy. They got mad at each other. They certainly had ego in different ways, but I think at the heart of it, they got angry not because of their ego being invested in a point of view, but of the end result not being what they thought it could be.

When they started they were playing some pretty straightforward stuff. Some of it was pretty sloppy. It took a while before the mind-meld.

They moved to L.A. in January of '66. It was, "Let's

all go to L.A. and put on some Acid Tests down there. And let's see if we can break into the music business," which they had no idea how they were going to do. And they didn't. There was a vague idea of going from there to Europe which evaporated.

We didn't have very many gigs. I don't know if there was more than the one at Troupers Hall. Troupers Hall is a small room that's rented out; it's a retired actors' home and performance space. I don't know who got it. Maybe Rock obtained it for the night. We rented it probably for very little money, and put on a show there. It was totally homemade—we had a card table for the box office and a cigar box for the money. I was the one who went to the fabric store and bought the paisley cloths that we put behind the band to make stage decor.

JERRY GARCIA: We'd met Owsley at the Acid Test and he got fixated on us: "With this rock band I can rule the world!" So we ended up living with Owsley as he tabbed up the acid in the place that we lived. We had enough acid to blow the world apart. And we were just musicians in this house and we were guinea-pigging more or less continually. Tripping frequently, if not constantly. That got good and weird.

OWSLEY STANLEY: I never set out to turn on the world, as has been claimed by many. And I certainly never made a million dollars from drugs. I just wanted to know the dose and purity of what I took into my own body. Almost before I realized what was happening, the whole affair had gotten completely out of hand. I was riding a magic stallion. A Pegasus. I was not responsible for his wings, but they did carry me to all kinds of places.

WAVY GRAVY: Of course, the biggest and most famous [of the L.A. Acid Tests] was the Watts Acid Test, where I coined the phrase *electric Kool-Aid*. We had the two large galvanized garbage cans, brand-new. We had rented this enormous warehouse in Watts, which was still smoldering from "Black Power" and "the Revolution" and all of that stuff. As the people arrived, I kept saying, "Okay, pay attention here. The Kool-Aid on the right is the 'electric Kool-Aid,' and the Kool-Aid on the left is for the kids. Let's review . . ." But people would be dancing for three hours to the Grateful Dead, and just guzzle and start to melt until pretty much half the place was melting down.

We all took it, because that was part of the deal. And when we did take it, we became this whole interlocking unit; everybody was kind of like breathing at the same time, no matter where we were in the place. Everybody knew what everybody was up to. It was weird and wonderful, amazing, and it took us a while to get to that spot. Once we hit that spot, and we were in synch, I could have repaired a Swiss watch, and I don't know how to repair a Swiss watch.

But I did know how to go look for this girl who is screaming. And I got on the mic, and said, "A sister is unglued, and we're going to glue her back together, and I'll see you where she is." I started crawling around, and she was in this little side room, and when I got there, there were fifteen to twenty people that I recognized. We all joined hands and turned into jewels and light, and she stopped screaming. And she turned into jewels and light.

That's when, I maintain, I passed the Acid Test. When you get to the very bottom of the human soul—where the nit is hitting the grit, and you're sinking, but somebody is sinking worse than you are, and you reach down to help them—bingo! That's when everybody gets high. You don't even need LSD to do that, but that was a great one.

OWSLEY STANLEY: I think my knowledge of sound dates back to the period of the L.A. Acid Tests and, specifically, one of the rehearsals we had in the house in Watts when I actually saw sound coming out of the speakers. It was total synesthesia, and I'd never experienced that at any other time. It was just a unique experience. And it so completely blew my mind, and I realized, "Hey, no matter what, I've got to remember what this is doing." I spent a lot of time absorbing what it was doing and realizing how different it was from what I thought sound did. That became the foundation for all the sound work that I've done. I was able to convert information into a three-dimensional image that was all coming from my ears, of course, but transferring it into a visual form.

I always trusted what happened on acid. Everything that happens to you on acid is real. Everything you see is real, everything you experience is real, everything you think about is real. The thing about it is that a lot of the stuff you see is not stuff you see when you're straight, because when you're straight you're limited. The acid removes filters and lets the noise through. The noise is as real a part of the universe as what you allow through. It just hasn't been important for you, and when you open those flood-gates and let them through, you let through a lot of stuff that's as real as the stuff you do let through.

To me, psychedelics are a gift of nature that bring tribalism to people; they bring an understanding of the ecology of the planet and the interaction of all living things, because that's one of the first things you become aware of when you take psychedelics—how everything is alive and how everything depends on every-thing else. You go to every indigenous culture that has a respect for its environment—which is unlike the hierarchical approach of the feudalistic structures that the world is now run by—you find these people use psychedelics of some sort.

TIM SCULLY (Sound engineer): I remember one incident at the L.A. Acid Tests, probably at either the Sunset or Pico Acid Test. The band was traveling with Kesey's Pranksters because of the indescribable synergy that took place when the Dead played while the Pranksters were pioneering liquid projection, strobe lights, and such. Many of us thought there was something more hap-pening at Acid Tests, a kind of psychic linkage, which produced a gestalt group consciousness.

Theodore Sturgeon wrote a science fiction story, *More Than Human* [1953], which described a fictional gestalt entity formed by a group of physically handicapped but paranormally gifted youngsters. In the story, the gestalt was incomplete and the group searched for "missing" members of the final mature entity.

You could think of the early Acid Tests as a similar search, where the Dead and Pranksters traveled to throw parties where strangers were invited to take LSD and see if they could "link up" with the group. The result was an ever-growing "family" of people who had experienced this link-up.

ROCK SCULLY: We didn't have the wherewithal to crack the live market, by virtue of the fact that L.A. is so damn big. You have to have mass media of some kind. You've got to buy radio time, put posters on telephone poles and windows of stores. Except people don't get out of their cars.

KEN BABBS: We were going to have an Acid Test down there [at UCLA], on a Friday or Saturday night, and we went in to Pauley Pavilion during the afternoon to do a preview or soundcheck, to see if everything was the way it needed to be. Tiny Tim, who was a good friend of Wavy's, was there, playing his ukulele and singing. There was a grand piano on the stage and some of the guys from the Grateful Dead got in there and started picking the strings and making all these weird noises, and then Cassady got on the microphone and started rapping. This guy comes up to me and says that so-and-so—whoever the guy was that ran the place—wants to see you. And so I went up to his office and he said, "We can't have this here." I said, "Wait a minute—we signed the contract, it's all set up, we've got the fliers printed." He says, "Nope. Can't do it. Not here." And then, talking about Tiny Tim, he says, "Who was that girl up there playing the ukulele? She was the worst!" I was real discouraged. I was ready to leave right then and never go back to L.A. again in my life, but Wavy and all of them found another place and put out these fliers, and it turned out to be a pretty good evening.

CAROLYN "MOUNTAIN GIRL" GARCIA: The devolvement of the [L.A.] Acid Tests wasn't a great thing. Basically, there wasn't enough to go around. There wasn't enough sleeping space, there were too many people. And when the bus left for Mexico, I think there was a sigh of relief.

The way it happened is *Life* magazine sent over this asshole photographer to do a photo shoot of the Pranksters. And right in the middle of all this Babbs sent someone through the crowd saying, "You'd better come to the bus right now," but only to certain people. I guess he unloaded people's stuff by the side of the road and the people he had chosen got on the bus and everyone else was left behind. Cassady was among the uninvited. I was among the uninvited; the bus ducked me.

In order to get back on the bus, I had to hitchhike from San Francisco to San Juan Capistrano [north of San Diego], where there was a park on the beach where the bus was hiding. They were there provisioning for this trip to Mexico and resting up after the Acid Tests.

JERRY GARCIA: If the Acid Test had continued in its own natural progression without the laws coming out about acid, I think it would have been just incredible; in about five months it would have been the biggest thing on earth. Because it was increasing at an exponential rate; it was just gaining incredible momentum. Each time it was tremendously funny and good and entertaining—what life should be, really. There's been nothing that equals that for weirdness.

KEN BABBS: We were never in a position where we were trying to "make it" in the sense of being discovered and becoming famous. We were just doing what we liked to do and people came to [the acid tests] and we kept going like that. You go to a town, you find a place and you put on your show and then you leave. But there were no promoters or managers or anything like that around. It was all much more spontaneous than that.

JERRY GARCIA: I miss the looseness. You didn't have to worry about drugs or sex or much of anything else. Life had an adventurous quality to it, and when you're young you feel like you can take on the world, and the world was definitely ready to be taken on at the time. Somehow everything seemed possible at every level. But that only lasted a little while; pretty soon there were cops everywhere. And we knew we weren't going to be able to get away with all that for too long. The good times, playing the Acid Tests—these things were positive experiences that didn't have a downside.

OWSLEY STANLEY: When we left for L.A. the band was worth $100 a show, and three months later they were offered $375 for a show, so we'd moved up the ladder a bit, though I couldn't tell you why.

JERRY GARCIA: We came back from L.A. and moved into [Grateful Dead co-manager] Danny Rifkin's house on 710 Ashbury. We hung out there for about a week. We didn't actually move in, because we were looking for a place in the country.

We ended up with a ranch—Rancho Olompali, the site of the only Indian battle ever fought in California. It's up in Novato [Marin County]. It was a great place. It had a swimming pool and barns and that sort of thing.

ROSIE McGEE: [The main house] was a kind of Spanish-style pseudo-adobe structure with at least two stories and a whole bunch of rooms. This was the beginning of the end of Owsley's supreme reign, because he came to Olompali and decreed he was going to get this great big room upstairs. By then people were sick of his domination, and they said, "No, we're going to draw straws." So they did, and he ended up getting one of the worst rooms, which served him right. After a while he didn't hang out there so much.

JERRY GARCIA: Novato was completely comfortable, wide open, high as you wanted to get, run around naked if you wanted to, fall into the pool. Everything was just super-groovy. It was a model of how things could really be good, if they really wanted to be. All that was a firming up of the whole social world of rock 'n' roll around here, because the musicians in the Bay Area—most of them are from around here; they've known each other for really a long time in one scene or another—and that whole thing was like shored up, so to speak, at those parties [and jam sessions at Olompali]. The guys in Jefferson Airplane would get together with Quicksilver [Messenger Service] and different guys—eighty-one players would get together and get high and get loose and have some fun.

It was good times, unselfconscious and totally free.

DAVID FREIBERG: When the Dead were at Olompali, Quicksilver was living out in Olema [in rural western Marin] on a ranch. We had a barn to practice in, and what little money we had came from going into the city and playing at the Fillmore and the Avalon.

We had visited back and forth and hung out with the Dead a little here and there. They had a swimming pool, and I think one of their entourage was [Quicksilver guitarist John] Cipollina's girlfriend. One evening we were out at our ranch and we hear whoops and screams from outside, and it was the Grateful Dead, dressed up in Indian war paint, raiding the cowboys—us. We were sitting there with a big bowl of pot, after dinner or something, and they came in and we all smoked the dope. So we figured we were going to get them back for that raid.

We had a great plan. They were playing at the Fillmore with the Airplane, and since they put us in the role of cowboys and they were the Indians, we were going to raid them dressed up as cowboys, with bandanas over our faces, and with guns, and while they were onstage we were going to tie them to their amps, take their guitars away, and sing [Hank Williams's] "Kaw-Liga Was a Wooden Indian," then leave. And we had Bill Graham involved in this; he knew it was going to happen. We actually rehearsed "Kaw-Liga" for a while. We spent all day whooping it up around town, shooting cap guns out the window. Cipollina had a couple of antique rifles with leaded-up barrels. So we went over there to the Fillmore when the Dead were supposed to be on. We sent a spy in and everything was late, and the Airplane were still on. We didn't want to tip our hand by showing up; we wanted to appear out of nowhere. So we decided to wait. A couple of people went to get some coffee. [Quicksilver singer/guitarist] Jim Murray and my ex-wife, Julia—Girl—and I were sitting in our equipment truck, which was an old panel truck, smoking a joint, with all the cap guns in the back.

You've got to remember where this was—the Fillmore Auditorium; we were in the real Fillmore [district]. Well, unbeknownst to us, while we were sitting in this truck, a couple of blocks away, the police had shot a young black kid escaping from a robbery, and the famous riots of '66 had started. So here we were—some people had seen us throwing guns in the back of this truck, so they called the cops. So we're sitting in there and all of a sudden the front door opens and a gun comes in—Jimmy and I looked at each other and said, "Ha-ha, it must be Cipollina playing jokes on us." We looked again and it was a .357 magnum; there was no mistaking it. They ripped us out of there, put handcuffs on Murray, because he was six-foot-four. Girl and I they didn't worry about, and threw us in the back of a police car and proceeded to search the truck. Murray said, "I dumped a film [canister] of pot in there; they're going to find that." This is while I was taking about eight joints out of my pocket and giving four of them to Girl and keeping four of them and swallowing them.

We never got to do "Kaw-Liga."

ROSIE McGEE: [That summer] had *such* an impact, but the reality is we lived [in Marin] for six weeks and then we went back into the city [to 710 Ashbury]. Being out there was not the place to be. We had a wonderful summer there, but everything was happening in the city.

CHAPTER 2

San Francisco

In the winter of 1966, Chet Helms and the Family Dog and Bill Graham began producing regular shows at the Fillmore Auditorium in San Francisco, usually alternating each weekend. Their fractious relationship led to Helms leaving the Fillmore to begin putting on dances at the Avalon Ballroom in late April, and for the next year and a half, both ballrooms thrived and were central to the city's ever-growing counterculture scene, which was centered in the Haight-Ashbury neighborhood.

BILL GRAHAM: The Dead and the Airplane and Quicksilver Messenger Service—we were all born in '65–'66. I was thirty-five, so maybe I was reborn, but they came into adulthood in '65-'66. As far as I'm concerned, this life started then, and I was a baby and they were babies. I taught them, they taught me. If it wasn't for these groups—it was various members of the Grateful Dead and the Airplane, [Mike] Bloomfield, [Paul] Butterfield—I would never have known who Chuck Berry was, or Otis Redding or Luther Allison, Muddy Waters, Freddie King, Albert King, B. B. King. Right down the line. They were the ones who said to try this and that. That opened it all for me.

PAUL KANTNER (Jefferson Airplane): What was encouraged by the Fillmore shows was that kind of thinking. You want to present people with something staggering, unexpected, just to shift their brains into being open enough to go without even knowing what you were going to see. You could almost always go to the Fillmore knowing that something would be interesting. And if nothing was interesting onstage, the floor was almost always more interesting than any band. That's why we liked to be on the stage: 'cause it was the best view of the whole floor, relatively uncrowded—a nice place to be.

JERRY GARCIA: Graham used to be just a penniless hustler in San Francisco. He used to call up Kreutzmann and ask him for advice when he first started promoting rock 'n' roll dances.

ROCK SCULLY: Graham would call Danny and me for advice and he'd always ask us what Jerry's opinion was. He relied on us a lot in the beginning. We told him about Paul Butterfield. We told him about Otis Redding: "You gotta get Otis!"

JERRY GARCIA (1966): [Chet Helms and Bill Graham] are different but they're both good. I don't have a preference one over the other. I think they're doing a good thing.

STEVE BROWN: If you walked down Haight Street, there were like one or two hippie stores—places that appealed to the countercul-ture—in just about every block. Dress shops, the Psychedelic Shop, an incense shop, bookshops. There was a whole little mini-industry providing the accoutrements of the lifestyle—black lights, color wheels, incense, cigarette papers. You'd see the dance posters for the Fillmore and Avalon up in all these stores, taped to the windows and on the poles. And there was a lot more than just the Fillmore and Avalon, too. I imagine the band people pretty much hung out with each other at their various houses, but for the regular people, the meeting places were along Haight Street, in the Panhandle and Golden Gate Park, and of course the Fillmore and the Avalon, because the music was always the big thing that everybody was into.

[In those days, going to shows] was something to do and affordable. Talk about getting your money's worth: three bands doing two sets at each place! You could see the first sets at one place, drive down and catch the last three sets at the other place. It worked really great. When I was in the Navy [in San Diego] I used to fly up and do just that, so I could see everything that was going on.

The Avalon was a really great place. It supposedly had a spring suspension floor, so it was a wonderful place to dance. It had a bunch of old couches, it had its own food. It was very much a hippie, Diggers [anarchist/theater tribe who created a "free store" in the Haight and performed other works of practical social criticism], coming-from-within type of environment; really the epitome of what the San Francisco scene would be in a lot of ways. Bill Graham's shows at the Fillmore, even though they had some of the same bands and he incorporated some of the same niceties, didn't have the same feeling that the Family Dog, and the Avalon Ballroom particularly, had. It was a different kind of a vibe. The Fillmore was great for music—you could really get lost in that because it was so small and the sound was so great—but at the Avalon, you felt like meandering around more and being more social and letting loose even more. It was one of those places you could get really fucked up and not worry about it. Maybe because the Fillmore was in a district that was predominantly black, and it was during a time when there was a lot of shit going on in the inner cities everywhere, the Fillmore had an edge to it. You were sort of holed up in there when you were there and you hoped your car didn't get broken into while you were in there. The Avalon wasn't in a great neighborhood either, but it felt a lot safer.

The bands at the Avalon were definitely what you'd see as the first or second bands [on the bill] at the Fillmore, and then another local band or regional band would be added. Whereas the Fillmore would often have a touring act that was a national act, or a British band, and have that on the top and then be supported by a couple of local bands. Bill was out there grabbing every national act he could—"You gotta play for me!"—and Chet Helms was happy doing what he was doing, because he could sell it out on the weekends.

JERRY GARCIA: I think [psychedelics were] a very, very important part of it. Everyone at that time was looking hard for that special magic thing, and it was like there were clues everywhere. Everybody I knew had a copy of [Aldous Huxley's] *The Doors of Perception*, and wanted to find out what was behind the veil.

It was all those kids that read Kerouac in high school—the ones who were a little weird. The Haight-Ashbury was like that at first, and then it became a magnet for every kid who was dissatisfied—a kind of central dream, or someplace to run to. It was a place for seekers, and San Francisco always had that tradition anyway.

BOB WEIR: We were rebellious by nature, anti-authoritarian. And the resistance we got from society in general just fueled our fires. That was probably more important to us than LSD. And then on top of that, to encounter the resistance we got from society—that was all I really needed to know that we were on to something.

JERRY GARCIA: Back in the old days when we were taking acid and stuff, I learned some of my most important musical lessons. There were times I was so high and out there and felt so vulnerable that playing the guitar seemed like the only pathway to salvation. By taking it to that level of craziness and making it seem that important, which is obviously not the case, I learned there's no reason not to go all the way when you're playing. It's an emotional thing, and I've learned how to incorporate that somehow.

BOB WEIR: It taught me to keep my ears open, to listen and follow my whims. I'm not sure I wouldn't have naturally done that had I not taken acid, but I was taking acid at the time and that's what it did.

As far as the effect it had on the Grateful Dead, just the brotherhood that occurred behind us being a bunch of stoned crazies and having pretty much to depend on our collective wits to get us by probably had a lot to do with the Grateful Dead being as tight as they were.

JERRY GARCIA (1967): The thing that happens when you get high and play is new ideas present themselves, new possibilities. You're more open to the changes in the music, but more important, you're more open to the changes in the people. There's a very real kind of communication going on between the dancers and the musicians. If you're a little stoned, you're less into yourself, less into demonstrating your ability, you're less into your own thing and more into the total thing. Playing itself is a high. Playing is in fact the best high that I know. There's no comparable experience in drugs—nothing like it.

STEVE BROWN: A song like "Viola Lee Blues" could stretch out whatever drugs you were on even further. They played enough long songs to understand they enjoyed jamming and, as something I hadn't really grown up with—at least in rock 'n' roll—they were the first band that I remember thinking, "Oh, wow, let's go!" Snap on the seat belt, put the top down, and go.

> Besides playing relatively high-profile shows at the Fillmore and Avalon, the Dead also gigged all around the Bay Area, in clubs and armories and any place that would have them, honing their chops and slowly developing a following. They also spent some time recording in the Haight.

BOB MATTHEWS: We had been to a hippie recording studio on Buena Vista Hill, belonging to Gene Estribou. That was Scorpio Records. There was a single that came out of that—"Stealin'" and "Don't Ease Me In." It was late at night after we had played at California Hall. We'd loaded in—in those days it was Bear's Altec Voice of the Theater [loudspeakers], McIntosh power amps and pre-amps. Lug it up three flights of stairs to this attic recording studio. We were doing four-track in those days, and it was brand-new. We were still coming down from the show, Saturday night, and I remember watching the reels of tape going round and round. It enthralled me. I said, "I want to do that." I told Bob Weir, "I'm gonna be the guy who's going to record the Grateful Dead. I'm the guy in the family that's gonna do this."

BILL KREUTZMANN: I could carry most of the band's equipment in my gray '58 Dodge station wagon with a rebuilt engine. When we lived in Lagunitas [after leaving Olompali], we were recording at Gene Estribou's in San Francisco and I would drive the band in every day. To get the car to make it to San Francisco, I'd have to put half a container of oatmeal in the radiator to plug it.

JERRY GARCIA (1966): We did the first Grateful Dead single before we rushed off to L.A. The performances were bad and the recordings were bad and everything else was bad, so we didn't want it out.

DAVE HARRIS (*Mojo Navigator* magazine): It's better than a lot of the stuff on the radio.

BOB WEIR: Oh, the fuck it is!

JERRY GARCIA: Well, it might be, and then again, it might not be. The big thing about it is it doesn't sound like us.

> At the end of July 1966, the Dead went on their first major road trip since the Portland Acid Test, spending a week in Vancouver (July 29–August 6) playing what was billed as a Trips Festival, and a nightclub called the Afterthought. Owsley and Tim Scully (who also aided Bear in his chemical pursuits) handled the Dead's sound needs during this period, devising a revolutionary (for the time) sound reinforcement system out of high-end hi-fi components. Owsley also began the then-unheard-of practice of recording the band's gigs and rehearsals so they could evaluate his mixes and their performances.

ANNOUNCER (At the Vancouver Trips Festival): Good evening from Captain Consciousness. For your pleasure, we're going to start off with a group from San Francisco. They're called the Grateful Dead!

> Complete silence.

PHIL LESH: Our fame precedes us!

JERRY GARCIA (1966): The [Vancouver] Trips Festival wasn't really a Trips Festival; it was just a very complex light show, but in terms of what it did with the music it was pretty meaningless. There was one thing happening on the screen [and] another thing happening on the stage. It wasn't well run and it wasn't well conceived, and it was mostly done by people who weren't very experienced at it. They would do things like have every band [including Big Brother and the Holding Company, the Daily Flash, and others] every night, so a band would only get to play maybe one set a night and it would be a short one. You couldn't really get warmed up or get any kind of thing going. It wasn't really much fun to play. The next weekend [at the After-thought in Vancouver] was much better.

ROCK SCULLY: Back then, Pigpen was a real integral part of it musically, and held a certain beat or rhythm together, and then Kreutzmann's foot kept that thing anchored, because Phil, from the get-go, wasn't playing by rock 'n' roll rules—certainly not the blues bass. Phil was just learning the bass as an instrument, but he could hear symphonically where he wanted to be with his instrument. If he was going to play it, it was going to be "orchestra-ready"—first bass.

There were some musical battles worked out onstage, most of it friendly. But Jerry might yell at Weir to keep it simple—"Don't try to fill in every space. Pauses are as important in music as notes or chords." I know Phil and Jerry reached an understanding, but Phil would show his displeasure fairly often by turning his back and going over by himself and playing to his amplifier.

I think one of the neatest things the Dead had was they learned to weave this tapestry onstage. But it took some doing.

Tapes [of the night's show] would come back to the hotel with us and there would be a serious session. They developed some teamwork there, talking about variations and how come it fell apart there, or how to smoothly transition into whatever. For the first few years, there would be two or three nights of serious discussions about what they considered to be failures. Phil was often very uptight about how

53

an evening came out. But rather than argue about it, we decided to listen to it and see what happened. And that's part of how they became so smooth, doing it onstage. It was totally constructive. There was no finger-pointing. I think it made for a better performance the next night. Instead of keeping it locked in and being more and more uptight about something that's not working, these kinds of conversations they'd have at the hotel did a world of good.

STEVE BROWN: One of the things I spotted early on that kept drawing me to them was, when it was really cooking and they were really having fun, when it was making that magic—whether it was a full house of people supporting it, or just catching it alone, seemingly—there would be this thing where Jerry would turn to the band and get this smile, which was the smile that let you know that not only were you having fun, they were having fun, the whole place was having fun. It was like a perfect moment: "This is what we're here for!" And that was a thing I kept looking for every time I went to a Grateful Dead concert. Or maybe not so much looking for it, but being ready for it.

There was always something special about them. The qualities of musicianship having to do with other bands had more to do with me analyzing other players I seemed to like or I thought were really good, whereas the Grateful Dead were more of a whole that I felt more attached to as one engine of sound and song. I think the other bands—as much as I liked some of their songs and some of the musicians individually—didn't seem to have the full content of what the Grateful Dead offered to me. Technically, musicianshipwise, I would think the Airplane was over the Dead in that era, but there were these other elements that the Dead had: this chemistry of all of them together.

OWSLEY STANLEY: Everybody always liked the way Jerry played the guitar, and the guitar player in the standard rock 'n' roll band is always the hero. Either him or the lead singer, if there is one; it depends on who is the most up front. In the case of the Grateful Dead, Pigpen—he might have been cuddly to some people, but I don't think he affected people quite that strongly. I could never understand the cult of Garcia, because to me they were a band and the sum was so much greater than the parts. Plus, I knew from interacting with him, he didn't want to be looked on as the leader of the band. He didn't feel he organized the thing. They were already the Grateful Dead when I met them, so I have no idea how they actually got together. I do know that getting the Grateful Dead to do something required that you convince at least two people in the band to go in the same direction, and then the rest would tend to follow. But most of the time it was like taking five horses and hooking them to a ring with ropes and nothing went anywhere because they all pulled in different directions.

I could play you tapes that would make you cringe, they're so bad. They couldn't sing for shit. Any one of them could sing on his own okay, but they sounded terrible together, and I think part of that was that the technology of onstage monitoring was pitiful. It's absolutely essential that musicians clearly hear themselves in order to blend their voices together. If they were sitting around practicing their vocal harmonies without instruments, it was fine. But once they were onstage with the instruments going, each one would hear something else and they'd all be off-key. It was sometimes painful. In fact, at the beginning I remember saying to them, "Gee, guys, maybe you should stick to instrumentals, or songs where only one person sings." Fortunately, they didn't listen to me. The one thing I insisted on that they did listen to me about was I insisted on soundchecks, and I encouraged them to listen to tapes of their performances—not just so they could hear how they sounded, but also to correct me on what I was doing, because I tried to make the tapes as much like the way it sounded in the hall as possible. We did the best we could with the tools we had, but the tools were inadequate.

BOB MATTHEWS: Everything Owsley did soundwise was an experiment. In some ways it was a model of technical perfection. The problem was it took forever to do anything, to set it up and take it down and get it working. Bear had some great ideas, but it was difficult for him to remember that the show starts at eight, so you have to be

55

prepared and you have to be able to make decisions—"Yeah, it would be great to be able to do things that way, Bear, but we don't have the time nor can we take the risk." And that was the problem. You don't give Murphy enough credit: If you try to push the envelope every time, he's going to win. Ninety-nine percent of the time [Bear's] ideas were right on, but you could question the manner in which he tried to carry them out. And that's what eventually started to affect his direct involvement, which went through various cycles.

Owsley was a great thinker and a good teacher, but you had to be in the right place with him and accept things in a certain way. To get through the Owsley School was a challenge. Trying to stop him and communicate with him was only going to get you engrossed in what he was doing. You don't confront him, and you go around and do what you know needs to be done, the way you believe it should be done, in a way that can make it happen, because the musicians want to play for the audience.

That was the first punch in our Acid Test card. The Acid Test? Anyone could pass that. But could you pass the Bear Test?

BOB WEIR: We called it the "Owsleystein System."

RON "PIGPEN" McKERNAN: When it was working it was really good—the best in the world, literally. But it wasn't too often. You see, Owsley had this time lag—it took him so long to get things sorted out, and we couldn't put up with that if we were to function as a band.

JERRY GARCIA (1967): The thing was, there was so much paraphernalia we needed in order to make [the system work] that we spent five hours setting up and five hours breaking down every time we played. Our hands were breaking and we were getting miserable, and the stuff never worked. Sometimes it was so weird; we got some far-out stuff on that system. It had its ups and its downs, and we thought that if Tim [Scully] was able to work on it long enough and get enough parts made, we would be able to have a working system.

Then we went to Vancouver, and that was the downfall. Laird, who drives our truck, was stopped at the border and they wouldn't let him into Canada. The equipment finally got there somehow, and it was set up and we played through it without too much hassle, but it was lousy; it was just bad, and it brought us down. Then we had to work until dawn to pack it up. It was uncomfortable and it was very bad, very down, very unfortunate. [When we got back to the Bay Area] we decided to disassociate from his benevolence and [Bear's] experiment.

TIM SCULLY: I think Bear's idea of direct electrical recording of electric instruments was good. I also liked his idea of using theater speakers and good quality amplifiers. The use of low-impedance lines from instruments to pre-amps was also good.

I don't think any of us understood the abuse the equipment would have to withstand. We learned over time it needed to withstand immersion in Coca-Cola, getting dropped in stairways, etc. And some of the reliability issues may have been related to everyone being stoned on acid while setting up and operating the equipment.

The time when the band went back to conventional gear for a while coincided with the time Bear and I went off to make more LSD. He and I remember this differently. My memories are that the band was uncomfortable with having us too involved with them while actively making acid, while Bear remembers the parting being more over equipment.

BOB WEIR: With Tim and Bear with us, we were a bust waiting to happen, so it was a good idea we went our separate ways when we did.

TIM SCULLY: When the band asked me to stop living and traveling with them, I felt rejected. For a while it had felt like an extended family.

About July or August 1966, when I started working at Bear's Point Richmond [LSD] lab, was the end of the close relationship [with the band]. I had gotten involved with the band in the first place because that was what Bear asked me to do, more or less as a test so he could see if he could trust me to work in his lab making LSD, which was my main interest at the time. I never thought of a career in audio. I did get very fond of the band. Traveling with them was like running away to join the circus.

Psychedelic light shows were part of the ballroom environment from the outset, and so were posters: beginning in the spring of 1966, Helms and Graham commissioned posters for each weekend's dances at the Avalon and Fillmore. Wes Wilson pioneered the trippy, flowing style that came to be associated with the San Francisco poster movement, but he was quickly joined by a host of great artists, including Stanley Mouse and Alton Kelley, who created some of the most famous early images associated with the Grateful Dead, including the iconic skeleton and roses.

JERRY GARCIA (1967): There is a small, concentrated area of a lot of activity. There is a lot of creativity, but it's not always on levels you can observe because there are different trends happening in what we used to call "the arts." For example, six or seven years ago, if you were a painter in San Francisco, you never sold anything because nobody in San Francisco buys paintings and there's no place to sell them. But a guy with a light show can make money. The guys who run the light shows are the guys who were painters a few years ago, and they're finding out something about color and the eye, and about spontaneity. Those are all aspects the plastic arts have never had before.

Poster design and printing, all those things, are skills. [They] are a product of a lot of people working at something, and they're getting a return for it. The people who run the dance halls are doing a thing. The people who are being managers are doing something. There's a lot going on. People are opening stores. Not everybody is an artist or creative person, but not everyone has to be a bookkeeper or businessman to make it. They can get into something that turns them on a little. With our scene here, we've managed to employ just about everyone we know in some capacity, because everybody has something they can do.

ALTON KELLEY: [The first Grateful Dead dance poster Mouse and I did] was the one with Frankenstein on it [for a Family Dog dance at the Avalon, August 19–20, 1966]. I spelled the name wrong! It says "GREATFUL." What a fantastic name that was! It was the name of names.

[As for the skeleton and roses poster, for an Avalon dance August 16–17, 1966], we had been looking for some kind of image for the Grateful Dead because we had a poster coming up. I was just thumbing through some books [at the San Francisco Public Library] and I had the *The Rubaiyat of Omar Khayyam* with the illustrations by E. J. Sullivan, and I came to that picture.

STANLEY MOUSE: We said, "That's got 'Grateful Dead' written all over it!" I always tell people we Xeroxed it, but of course there weren't Xerox machines then. Then I came across the actual piece—Kelley had cut it out! It was a bad thing to do; really bad! So we took it and I colored it in and did the lettering around it, and it was spectacular.

JERRY GARCIA: [The skeleton] is a very potent image. It's been with us all along. Things that have to do with death—I mean, it's one of the biggies. As long as death remains mysterious, it's going to remain powerful. That was one of the luckiest things that ever happened to us in a way, because the name has always prevented us from being absolutely acceptable in a Michael Jackson sense. We've never been entirely acceptable. Death is always death.

ALTON KELLEY: [The San Francisco rock scene] was like the longest party I ever went to. It went on for a couple of years. It was literally every weekend—Friday, Saturday, and Sunday you would party down. Man, it was dance your ass off. The music was real fresh, everyone was young and fresh. Everything seemed brand-spanking-new. It was really the happening thing. Rock 'n' roll, the Beatles, the whole thing was just this wild time. What went on in the dance halls was outrageous. It was all very unselfconscious, completely on the natch, loose and out there.

EILEEN LAW: People really would help each other, and everyone seemed very open then. When the dances started happening, everyone danced. It was so easy to meet people. A band like Quicksilver or the Airplane might play a set, and then you'd see all the players out on the dance floor mingling with everyone else.

> By September 1966, most of the Dead and their growing "family" were ensconced in 710 Ashbury, or nearby. The roster of folks living at 710 was constantly shifting, as friends who needed a place to crash for days or more would turn up, or girlfriends would change, or other nuclear units would disperse to get more space and privacy. Neal Cassady lived in the attic for a while. The Dead also had influence over the property directly across Ashbury Street from 710, which became the headquarters for the Haight-Ashbury Legal Organization (HALO) and also had rooms to rent. Sue Swanson was among those who lived there, and at one point Mouse lived and worked there.

ROSIE McGEE: When [Phil and I] first moved into 710, everybody drew straws for who would get which bedroom, and we ended up sharing the front room with Jerry and his girlfriend at the time, with a little Chinese screen between us. That didn't last. Billy Kreutzmann at the time was still married and had a little girl, was looking for a new place. I found us a two-bedroom place in Diamond Heights.

CAROLYN "MOUNTAIN GIRL" GARCIA: You come in the front door [at 710] and on your left is the dining room/front parlor with big sliding doors that are open, so it's two rooms made into one. There are beautiful stained-glass borders on these bay windows that look out into the street. In that room is Weir's bed and a big green fold-out lounge chair that Bob Matthews lived in. There was another set of sliding doors at the end and that led into Pigpen's dark little room. He had another door going in there from the kitchen. The dining room had a big table and that's where a lot of the business got done, and a lot of the interviews were done there. The kitchen was straight back, and the staircase went up to the right. On the upper floor was

Rock [Scully]'s room, which had a few stairs going out onto a little gravel-roof deck over the kitchen, and there was Jerry's room, which was the one you see in the pictures with the American flag on the wall. So I moved into Jerry's room. And then there was the front room, with a beautiful old Victorian fireplace and old curtains that were falling apart, and really ancient rugs on the floor that were crumbling but you could still faintly see these gorgeous designs on them. Danny lived in the basement apartment with Laird, and sometimes Laird lived in the attic.

ROSIE McGEE: At the very beginning, [the Dead scene] was egalitarian, just because nobody was thinking about who was doing what; we were just doing it. There was no master plan and we were a group of friends. We lived communally at first, pretty much for financial reasons, and because it just evolved that way. We all liked each other. But you've got to remember that we came from all these different families and backgrounds and upbringings; then suddenly we were together. It's amazing it worked as well as it did. But when people talk about about the Grateful Dead in the same sentence with commune, that's not it at all. We were never truly a commune, as that word is generally used.

As far as the women's roles, at the time I never thought about it in terms of "women's lib" or "We're doing all the women's work and the guys are having all the fun." We were all having all the fun. We were this great group of friends where every person did what they did for the communal good. In that time, particularly, it was more natural for women to do the cooking and the cleaning. I'm sure there are some women who will beat me over the head for saying that, but in that era, coming out of the fifties and early sixties, that's the way it was. Even today, women tend to keep the home fires burning, because they're the ones who have the children, and generally they're the ones who raise the children in the home, if they're around. But we never felt put-upon. There was never a division over it.

STANLEY MOUSE: I had a firehouse on Henry Street [in San Francisco]. It had been an old horse-drawn buggy firehouse, so it had troughs and an upstairs. I had my studio upstairs. Big Brother used to practice downstairs. But then the Diggers moved in. They were shit-kickers and rabble-rousers, but supposedly doing a good function. It went with the whole morass that was happening in '67 with the runaway kids; they helped feed them and stuff. So that was good. One of them asked if they could fix their car at my place. So I said yes, and then pretty soon there were two cars and then three cars, and then the place was loaded with Diggers—like fifty Diggers. And they started sleeping there, so I just left. It drove me out.

When I got displaced by the Diggers, the Dead had two houses— their regular [710] Ashbury house and the one right across the street. They gave me the upstairs of the one across the street from them. It was a big hill, and one day Kelley and I were working on something in my studio, and we hear "clickety-clackety, clickety-clackety" getting louder and louder, and then there was this big boom and the whole house shook like there had been an earthquake. And we looked outside and it was Bear—he had crashed into the house with his Volkswagen! He was coming down the hill and his brakes went out, and he could either crash into the Dead house or the Dead annex house, and he chose the annex house. Just our luck!

ROSIE McGEE: At 710, they needed a bookkeeper; someone to open the mail, pay the bills, write the checks, keep track of the checkbook, and all of that. I was available, but Rock and Danny didn't want to pay me for that job. They said, "It's your contribution." I said,

"Well, you guys make a contribution and get paid for it. Fuck you."

Everybody who lived at 710 paid fifty dollars a week into the kitty for food. I think everybody was getting two hundred dollars a week, or maybe not even that much; the band members, Rock, Danny, and the crew. The working people were all getting paid. I wasn't asking for the same, just for however much an hour for the hours I actually worked. I went to Phil. Phil went to Jerry; "That's bullshit. Why shouldn't she get paid?"

Jefferson Airplane was the first of the major San Francisco rock bands to land a recording deal (from RCA). The Dead attracted some interest early on from record biz types, but were in no hurry to sign a contract and cut an album. Instead, they waited until the fall of 1966, when Joe Smith at Warner Bros. brought them into the fold of the L.A.-based label. A young San Francisco lawyer named Brian Rohan, who became a legal savior for many Bay Area musicians during the late sixties and beyond, negotiated the Dead's first deal with Warner's.

BRIAN ROHAN: I did not know fuck-all about music. I had a friend—we went to law school together, and he now worked for [jazz pianist] Dave Brubeck. So I called him up on the phone and I said, "The Grateful Dead want me to be their music lawyer." He says, "I hate musicians." How can you hate musicians? Later I found out that Paul Desmond, a brilliant sax player, just tortured this guy. I mean, a hundred phone calls a day. He had every ADD/alcoholic syndrome in the world. I said to him, "Tell me what I should do." He said, "Keep the copyrights." Dylan had given up his copyrights, the Stones had given up their copyrights, the Beatles had given up their copyrights.

The lawyers in L.A. would represent the bands, and then they would sell the publishing, the copyrights, to one of their clients. They just wouldn't tell the band that they were selling them to one of their clients. A couple of them had been dinged big-time—$14 million judgments against them—for conflict of interest. But in New York, it was just horrible. Kids didn't know about copyrights. They'd publish your songs—and what that really means is "you sign over your income to us for life, and we'll cheat you out of as much of it as we can."

At that time [Warner Bros.] was just this shit vanilla label, and they had no clue. So down [to L.A.] I go. I had my $109 wool suit on with my three-dollar tie, which was the top of the line at Brooks Brothers. And I go see Mo Ostin and Joe Smith, total height ten feet. They're in this little building which was screenwriters' cubicles, little tiny offices, very narrow hallway. Joe looks at me and he

says, "We're going to give you X and we're going to
give you Y, and we're going to give you Z, and we're
going to give you Z-plus," and then they stopped.
And I just got up and walked out of the room. I
didn't say anything. And I started walking down the
hall. Kesey had taught me this trick about leaving
the scene of the movie producers. You just get up
and leave, they think you're going to the bathroom,
and then you go home.

They come running down the hall, and I'm
walking down the hall. And I'm not a big guy, but
you know, under one armpit is Joe Smith, and
under one armpit is Mo Ostin. "What's the matter? What's the matter?" And the other one says,
"What's the matter?" So I turn in the hallway, which
wasn't even six feet across, and I throw up my arms
and I say, "You have insulted me. You have insulted
my client. You have insulted the music scene in San
Francisco. This is what the deal is." And I wave my
arm like Bill Graham used to wave his. "This is what
the deal is, for insulting me: you will pay all of the
costs of the record and not charge them against
their royalties. You'll give them [this amount of
money], and we will keep all of the publishing."

And there's this dead silence. And they say, "Okay,
okay." And I just turn around and I start smiling, and
I go, "Man, this is going to be fun!"

The record company always thought it was their
money and they'd dribble it out. Well, it's our money,
because if it wasn't for us, you'd fucking be an accountant somewhere. All I wanted was a fair shot for
everybody.

BOB WEIR: We're
legendarily dif-
ficult to deal with
for photographers.
This is the stuff that
legends are made of;
photographers quake
in their shoes at the
thought of trying to
do a Grateful Dead
session—and rightly
so, because nobody in
the Grateful Dead is
of a mind to sit still
for fifteen or twenty
seconds and have a
photo taken, not to
mention a twenty-
minute photo ses-
sion. [Linda Eastman]
figured, and rightly
so, that the only
way to photograph
us was to at least
get us all assembled
and started in one

Jefferson Airplane, the Dead, and Quicksilver played New Year's Eve 1966 at the Fillmore, and the next afternoon the Dead and Big Brother and the Holding Company were part of a free "New Year's Day Wail" put on by the Hells Angels and the Diggers collective in the park right below Haight-Ashbury known as the Panhandle. In those days it was easy to set up a band on the back of a flatbed truck and play for free in the Panhandle or in one of the small meadows in nearby Golden Gate Park.

On January 14, 1967, a magical event took place called the Human Be-In (aka the Gathering of Tribes). It featured several of the top local bands, including the Dead, along with various poets and other speakers ranging from Timothy Leary to Berkeley anti–Vietnam War activists and attracted 15,000 to 20,000 people—by far the biggest show of counterculture community and solidarity yet. It was sponsored and promoted mainly by the Haight's own psychedelic newspaper, *The Oracle*.

ROSIE McGEE: Many first-person accounts of the event point to one central theme: how astounding it was for each of us to see 20,000 like-minded folks, drawn to the Polo Fields that day mostly by word of mouth. The most common expression of that wonder was, "Oh, my God—look how many of us there are! I had no idea!" It was truly a revelation.

Sure, there was some publicity—posters in store windows, flyers on telephone poles, etc. But mostly, it was the neighbors saying, "Hey, are you going to the park today?" or seeing unusual numbers of people walking purposefully past your house in the Haight and shouting out the window, "Where are you guys

place. She figured if she used the stair steps at 710 Ashbury, where we were living, that we could only move in one direction. She got us all there and took one or two pictures of us all assembled, and then the confusion bomb hit and everybody started wigging out and getting weird. The only way we could go was down the steps, because I think she arranged it so the front door was closed so we couldn't get back in the house. So there are pictures of us crawling down the steps with whatever props were available.

going?" and then, once answered, "Wait up—I'll come with you!" There was an unspoken feeling of this being an event you didn't want to miss.

For those of us in the Dead's family, it was a call to do one of our favorite things: go play/hear/dance to music in the park on a sunny day. Grab your guitar, walk a couple of miles into the park, and there'll be a stage made from two flatbed trucks and a PA system waiting for you. When we left 710, we had no idea if there'd be twenty people there or two thousand. It certainly made no difference to any of us. It would be fun, no matter what. We lived for those events!

We got there early, and we started out behind the trucks—backstage, as it were—greeting all our friends from the other bands and their families, sharing a pipe, talking and laughing. A few introductions were made, to the Berkeley political activists, the North Beach beatnik poets, the Big Sur pot and acid dealers, Timothy Leary and his entourage—all drawn to this event by curiosity, high hopes, and for some, the potential to address remarks to a wider audience than they had previously known. That potential was met—not only by the 20,000 folks within reach of the PA, but by the media that was recording the event. That would have massive ramifications in the ensuing months.

After a while, I left the crowded area behind the trucks and walked out into the expansive Polo Fields, watching the people streaming in down the hillsides around the big oval. The place was filling up, and people were spreading blankets for picnics, playing with their dogs, greeting friends they'd arranged to meet there, having a great day in the park with or without anything going on from the stage. Owsley's runners were discreetly walking around through the crowd with baggies full of his recently minted White Lightning tabs of LSD, and it's rumored that well over 5,000 were accepted and ingested. I was one of those who did.

By the time poet Gary Snyder blew the ram's horn from the stage, signaling the start of the event, the grass was full of people; and I had come on to the acid, and had made my way back to the trucks. The spiritual folks chanted; the poets read poetry; the activists gave their high-octane speeches; and the audience listened, at least those in front of the stage did. But it was when the music started that the place came alive, all the way to the back. People got on their feet, crowded in closer, and danced and hooted, and hollered. It was a long, beautiful, glorious day, and culturally pivotal.

JERRY GARCIA: I'd never seen so many people in my life. It was really fantastic. I almost didn't believe it. It was a totally underground movement. It was all the people into dope of any sort, and like 20,000 people came out to the park and everyone had a good time. There was no violence, no hassles.

One of the things that happened was that somebody came along and cut the electricity. Some guys got together to repair it and then the Hells Angels guarded the wires. [The Angels] took care of lost kids; they babysat! You can hit on 'em to do that kind of thing. Like we're hiring a couple to guard our warehouse, now that [some of our] equipment's been stolen.

> About a week after the Be-In, the Dead caravaned down to L.A. to record their self-titled debut album for Warner Bros. Records, with producer Dave Hassinger at RCA Studios in Hollywood.

CAROLYN "MOUNTAIN GIRL" GARCIA: In early 1967, they went down to L.A. and I went with them. They were taking my diet pills at the time, and that's why there are accelerated tempos on that album. Their producer was this typical L.A. guy, with jowls, heavy tan, long, slick-backed hair—lot of Vitalis [hair gel]—white cardigan sweater with a gold wristwatch. They couldn't handle Dave Hassinger at all, but he was trying to be cool and they were giving him a hard time. He'd make suggestions and they would say stuff like "It'll ruin everything if we do it that way."

ROSIE McGEE: The record company had rented a furnished house for the band and crew to stay in, and we [the women] went along. The house had terraced gardens leading to a big swimming pool, and plenty of rooms for everyone.

Although I imagine wives and girlfriends were frequently present during recording sessions for other bands, I doubt the studio was all that ready for the long-haired, pot-smoking, make-yourself-totally-at-home gang that was the Grateful Dead family at that point in history. We stood in striking contrast to the buttoned-down record company folks who came by to observe the sessions, and who didn't stay all that long, mumbling excuses as they left.

It's not that there were that many of us, but studio control rooms tended to be small, and we spilled over all the couches and chairs that were available. So, after the first day of the four-day recording session, we took turns coming to the studio in shifts, some of us staying at the rented house and hanging out by the pool.

JERRY GARCIA: At that time we had no real record consciousness. We were just going to go down to L.A. and make a record. We were completely naïve about it. We had a producer we had chosen because he'd been the engineer on a couple of Rolling Stones records that we liked the sound of; that was as much as we were into record-making.

DAVE HASSINGER: Garcia played some guitar on [the Airplane's *Surrealistic Pillow*, engineered by Hassinger] and of course he was very good friends with them and just sort of helped them get some of their ideas into focus. Actually, though, they had been down there for quite a while before I even met him. I spent most of my time in the control room working on the sound. Finally, it came to me from [Airplane singer] Marty Balin, I think, that Garcia wanted me to work with the Grateful Dead. Shortly after this, I joined Warner Bros. full-time as a producer and engineer, and that's how I ended up working on their first album.

DICK BOGERT (Recording engineer): RCA Studio A was huge. I once did a Jerry Goldsmith score in there with ninety-three musicians, and there was room for more. It was like a barn, really, and back then it didn't sound that great, either. So we used a lot of baffles to try to close it down, contain the sound.

I liked the Dead as people; they seemed like pretty down-to-earth cats—especially compared to the Airplane, who I'd worked with. They were assholes. But you know, we were all working so much, a lot of it is just a blur. Back in those days you might be working a hundred hours a week, so you might easily do a commercial in the morning, a religious session in the afternoon, and then the Grateful Dead in the evening. A lot of my days were like that.

JERRY GARCIA: [The songs on the album were] just simply what we were doing onstage. Basically that. Just rock 'n' roll. Plus we wanted to have one extended cut on it ["Viola Lee Blues"]. But in reality, the way we played was not really the way that record was. Usually we played tunes that lasted a long time because we like to play a lot.

It was weird and we realized it. The first record was like a regular company record done in three nights, mixed in one day. It was done on 3-track, I believe—it wasn't even 4-track—[in] Studio A, an imposing place, and we really didn't care about it while we were doing it, so we weren't surprised when it didn't quite sound like we wanted it to.

DAVE HASSINGER: I wish I could have taken them someplace other than RCA; someplace where I could have engineered it. But at RCA Studios, once you started using their facilities as an outside producer, you had to use their engineers. It came out later that that upset the band, because I had primarily been an engineer and that's a lot of what the band wanted from me. I was new to production and the Grateful Dead didn't really need a producer to tell them what to play or how to play it. They needed someone to help them get the record to sound the way they wanted it to sound, and that's what I would have liked to have done.

BOB MATTHEWS: "The Golden Road (to Unlimited Devotion)" was recorded [after the rest of the first album], at the old Coast Recorders at 960 Bush Street [in San Francisco]. One or two nights, I remember being into the sixties on the number of takes. One of the unique little overdub things: if you listen to the intro and a couple of choruses on the outs, there's some funny little percussion stuff, which is Kreutzmann beating on Garcia's guitar with his drumsticks while Jerry was fingering the chords.

ALTON KELLEY: [The artwork for the first Dead album] was commissioned by their managers, Danny Rifkin and Rock Scully, who went around as Shady Management.

I put together the collage for the cover. The photos [of the band] were by Herb Greene. I cut up the pictures—the tubas came out of *Life* magazine, the Hindu god out of *Life* or *Look*. The sun explosion was also from one of those magazines. The broken glass behind Bobby was out of a photo magazine.

Right across the top there's a poem [lettered by Mouse] that says, "In the land of the dark, the ship of the sun is drawn by the Grateful Dead," but the group decided it was too much, so we just sort of obscured the lettering. If you look at it closely you can still sort of read it.

[Warner Bros.] was super-pleased because their in-house art department had been doing covers for Frank Sinatra and had no idea what to do with the Grateful Dead. They were thrilled. The cover worked real well, I thought. It was fairly avant-garde for its time.

BOB MATTHEWS: We waited for Mouse and Kelley to complete [the cover for the first album]. We were waiting to take it down to Hollywood to show it to the boys.

CONNIE BONNER MOSLEY: We had just enough time to get to the San Francisco airport for the red-eye down to L.A. They had to have it by eight in the morning.

SUE SWANSON: It was our excuse to get to go!

CONNIE BONNER MOSLEY: We volunteered to wait and fly it. It was a huge piece of cardboard that we had to hand-carry through the airport and through the aisle of the plane.

SUE SWANSON: And get it there safely.

BOB MATTHEWS: They were so happy to see us!

JERRY GARCIA (1967): I think our album is honest. It sounds just like us. It even has mistakes on it. But it also has a certain amount of excitement on it. It sounds like we felt good when we were making it. We made it in a short period—four days—and it's the material we'd been doing onstage for quite a long time. It sounds like one of our good sets.

PHIL LESH (1967): I think it's a turd. It's where we were at, at the time. The next one certainly won't be anything like that one, in any way.

CAROLYN "MOUNTAIN GIRL" GARCIA: The album came out and it's my favorite because that is the time Jerry and I got together and started living together.

DAVID CROSBY: [Back in 1965] I had heard of them playing down on the Peninsula. There was another name they went under first, the Warlocks. I had heard about 'em: "There are these guys down there who are really out there." That was like honey to a bee, to me. I wanted to immediately go and find out who they were and what they did. I didn't encounter them until they were full-blown as the Dead.

Paul Kantner [of Jefferson Airplane] gave me their first album, and I loved it. This wasn't Paul Revere and the Raiders—this was the real stuff! These guys were having fun, and that's my thing— I love having fun with music. I knew they were kindred spirits immediately.

I first met them when they were still living at 710, but we didn't play that time. I just hung out with them, talked, and liked them a lot.

JERRY GARCIA: We're getting into [electronic sounds and devices] more than we have been. We've been mostly just working on getting better at our instruments, and the electronic stuff is stuff that you discover playing at enormous volumes in the big auditoriums. Pretty soon your guitar is feeding back and there's this insane sound coming out of it and you find that by fiddling around the right way you can control it to a certain extent and that becomes part of the way you play. You can't not [use it]. If you ignore it, it just gets louder and louder and takes over the entire thing.

DAVID GANS: I think Garcia didn't really begin to sound like Garcia until somewhere in '67. There's a lot of stuff in the early days that is generic—it could have been almost any guitar player from that time. I remember hearing some Beau Brummels stuff in a movie from '66 and thinking, "That's the generic British invasion/San Francisco rock scene right there—a reverb-drenched guitar with hammered runs." Jerry was playing a lot of that, and some of the stuff in the early days had that sort of imprecise quality; he's playing the riff, but it's not really nestled into the music where it belongs. What Jerry developed later was a beautiful touch for putting stuff in the groove. There was a lot more precision and more connectedness to it.

You have to remember, too, that every single one of those guys, except Kreutzmann, learned how to play in that band. They were all novices on their instruments, basically. Pig was a rudimentary organ player before that. Jerry, Bob, and Phil all learned together how to play. I think that's a critical key factor in the evolution of their sound. They learned how to play this particular music with respect to one another's playing.

> During the spring and summer of 1967, the Dead went on a few key road excursions, including trips to New York the first two weeks of June—they played a pair of free shows there and also several nights at the famed Cafe Au Go Go nightclub—and, in August, Toronto with Jefferson Airplane, and the group's first shows in the Midwest. In between those was the three-day

Monterey Pop Festival, south of San Francisco, which brought together an amazing and eclectic array of American and British musicians—including the major San Francisco rock bands—and artists such as Ravi Shankar and South African jazz trumpeter Hugh Masekela. The Dead played on the third night, Sunday, and were barely noticed by the legions of writers covering the event, as their set came in between sensational, bombastic performances by the Who and Jimi Hendrix.

ROCK SCULLY: There was a lot of negativity about the L.A. crowd [Lou Adler and John Phillips, who were trying to put on the Monterey Pop Festival]—but we already had so many friends who were willing to go for it and wanting to go for it, and there was that whole thing about it being a benefit. "Oh, really? Where's the money here?" The fact is, at the [low] ticket prices, to book all those bands, it didn't make sense, so there was more money somewhere. They couldn't hire all of us.

It wasn't until Paul Simon got involved that we really would listen. Paul came and saw me, and I gave him a tour around San Francisco, to the park and all over. I told him about the scene. I then got him together with Bill Thompson, [manager] of the Airplane. Paul came calling because we weren't going for the Lou Adler rap. I told Paul, "Our fear here in San Francisco is that we're just being used and exploited. They're writing songs about us up here and making money off of it [Scott McKenzie's "San Francisco (Be Sure to Wear Flowers in Your Hair)," written by John Phillips]. That was released just prior to the festival.

JERRY GARCIA: That was the lamest version of [what was going on in Haight-Ashbury] I could possibly imagine.

BOB WEIR: [Monterey] was the first rock 'n' roll festival and it was wonderful fun, especially insofar as the San Francisco rock 'n' roll culture and the London rock 'n' roll [culture] got a chance to get together and mix it up a bit. The party backstage was pretty damned wonderful. I remember at one point I got involved with a jam—

myself and some other pretty good folks playing—and this guy I'd recently met, Paul Simon, he comes up and he wants to play. He's got an acoustic guitar and we're all playing electric. I had an extra jack where he could plug in. I said, "Paul, grab one of those electric guitars." He says, "No, I'll just play my acoustic. You'll feel the vibe." I guess I did. It was a fun jam. I had a lot of fun playing with him even though I didn't hear a damn thing he did.

ROCK SCULLY: I was thankful [the Dead] weren't filmed. The fact is, the Grateful Dead didn't play that well, the show was interrupted by [Peter Tork] of the Monkees asking folks not to storm the arena —which they did anyway—and the poor guys were sandwiched between the Who and Jimi Hendrix. God knows, the Grateful Dead were never one to do a show that way. They don't wear costumes, destroy their instruments, or burn their hair or anything.

BOB WEIR (To the Monterey crowd, before the Dead's opening fourteen-minute version of "Viola Lee Blues"): You know what foldin' chairs are for, don't you? They're for foldin' up and dancin' on!

PETER TORK (After "Viola Lee Blues"): People, this is me again. I hate to cut things down like this, but there's a crowd of kids— and this is to whom I'm talking mostly . . . and these kids are like crowding around over the walls and trying to break down doors and everything, thinking the Beatles are here . . .

PHIL LESH (To Tork and audience): This is the last concert, why not let them in anyway?

PETER TORK: Um, last concert, all right, except that they're trying to break things down, crawling over ceilings and walls, and like, they think the Beatles are here and they're not. . . . You, those of you . . . they can come in if they want.

PHIL LESH: The Beatles aren't here, come in anyway!

| The crowd cheers.

PETER TORK: Uh, yeah, there's great things happening anyway.

PHIL LESH: If the Beatles were here they'd probably want you to come.

PETER TORK: Yeah, except that just don't, you know, bring down ceilings and walls and everything . . . uh, carry on.

ROCK SCULLY: I helped arrange impromptu jam sessions at the free campground that we organized at Monterey College. We knew there would be overflow, so we let people camp there and we set up a stage, and after the shows various bands would put on jam sessions.
 [We had] Jimi Hendrix, Eric Burdon, Jerry Garcia, Phil Lesh, the Airplane. . . . At the time we hadn't met Hendrix and we didn't know the Who. We got to know them there. We all took acid together and played all night. Since Danny and I were doing free concerts up in the Panhandle, there was a sense that we couldn't go wrong. The equipment at the festival was free from Fender, who had just been bought out by CBS. After the festival, we managed to get the equipment moved up to San Francisco. With that equipment, we got Hendrix to play at the Panhandle.

PAUL KANTNER: Just for a while there, maybe for about twenty-five minutes in 1967, everything was perfect. They had reached the idealized state. Unfortunately, they hadn't learned how to maintain the idealized state, and mainly from heroin dealers, police repression, government repression, Charles Manson living up the street, speed. . . . Wherever you are, anywhere, there's always bad forces, bad people. That's why they have jails. So I don't think you can say everybody was wonderfully perfect. But the situation was very open and very Renaissance-like—a Leonardo Da Vinci kind of time, in the sense of just opening up all those arts and letters, and hedonism and sex-drugs-rock 'n' roll, and freedom. It's the American ideal gone bonkers. No real responsibility.

Utopian ideals usually break down in the face of human nature and human foible, and elements, and just life. But it was a noble experiment, and the repercussions will be felt well into the next century, I trust. Everything from the Sierra Club to not believing in government—rightfully so—and finding all this stuff out and correcting it, is a real positive example of that particular element. Correcting it, I don't know; just shedding the light of day on it is a first major step, being one of the earliest generations not to just accept the words. Question authority.

LSD is just one of the factors in the explosion. All these things happened at once. Who knows why? Why did Babylon become Babylon? Why did Persia run the world for a while? Why do these things happen? They do. It's a lot of random situations that combine in a certain volatile form and create a bigger-than-the-whole situation that nobody could have predicted. You couldn't have fed the fifties into a computer and come out with the sixties. No way. But somehow nature did. I don't think anybody—still—knows what went on or what happened, or what the true repercussions of the sixties will be.

ROSIE McGEE: I'm not sure there was a San Francisco sound. There was a San Francisco scene and a San Francisco vibe. But you can't take the Grateful Dead and Quicksilver and Big Brother and all of those guys and say that's the sound. What is it? Psychedelic space-out, some of the time, maybe. But they really weren't all that similar musically. I guess that idea helped to promote the individual bands over time, but it also led to things like the Summer of Love, which was a disaster. That was too many people and too much chaos. Too many people with no place to go and being taken advantage of. The streets got really, really dirty. It was just insane.

People came into the community looking to take. The real Summer of Love was [in 1966], when it was just this giant group of friends who loved each other and got along and helped each other and played music for free in the park. We had big dinners at each other's houses. I blame Timothy Leary for some of it, with his whole thing [at the Human Be-In] in January '67 with "Turn on, tune in, drop out." The media got a hold of it and started writing about it— "Oh, the San Francisco scene is so great. Come here and wear flowers in your hair!"

STEVE BROWN: What was happening in the Haight was scary to [the authorities] because it was a new thing they really didn't have any control of, like a virus spreading. They were going to see if they could nip it in the bud and lay down some ordinances and rules they felt they needed, to not let this thing get out of control. But we were harmless. There was civil rights going on and people protesting against the Vietnam War everywhere—not just the Haight. So to see a new culture of people representing yet another layer of the onion of new counterculture weirdness, it scared them.

The Diggers pushed their buttons even further: "They're giving away free food in the park! What kind of a store is this where everything is free?"

JERRY GARCIA (1967): We're moving to the Southwest. You know, we're concerned about our productivity. And what we're going to do is, like, get away. Get away from a lot of people and a lot of action and a lot of energy, and just go out and do our own thing for a while.

> Needless to say, that move didn't happen. However, Garcia's comment shows that the human inundation of San Francisco during the Summer of Love was starting to wear on the band. In late September, however, they made their first personnel change since their days as the Warlocks: Mickey Hart joined as second drummer.

MICKEY HART: I had the drum store in San Carlos [actually his father's store], and I had a band. I can't remember the name of it, but Joe Bennett was the lead guitarist—he was from Joe and the Sparkletones.

I met Kreutzmann at the Fillmore. Count Basie was playing, and I was hangin' out with [Basie's drummer] Sonny Payne. We were good friends. I loved Basie, and I featured myself as a big-band drummer then. Somehow, Kreutzmann and I met that night. I think someone pointed him out to me. I knew about the Grateful Dead.

Kreutzmann and I started talking about drums. We went out that night with a bottle of scotch and went around playing on cars. We weren't beatin' up cars or anything—we were trying to make music.

I had seen Grace Slick, but I had never really seen Janis [Joplin]. Kreutzmann said, "You want to see fire and ice? That's Janis and Grace." So we went to see Janis at the Matrix, and we took Sonny Payne with us. Sonny couldn't stand it, because it was too loud. I said, "I'm not going anywhere. This is great!" And [Big Brother's] James Gurley picked up his guitar and he raped it. I'd never seen anything like it. It was the best solo I'd ever heard. That amplifier was just pulsing on the floor.

[Sometime later, Kreutzmann said], "My band is playing at the Straight Theater on Haight Street. Why don't you come down and hear the band?"

I go, "Okay, cool." I went down, and the Grateful Dead were in the first set. It was just like an echo chamber, like half-full—maybe three hundred people there. All you could hear was Phil's rumble, and you couldn't hear Bill at all. And you could hear Jerry—Phil and Jerry, and that's it. It was amazing, and I thought "Wow!" I couldn't believe it. The echo and the reverb added to the effect, of course. It sounded like chaos. Obviously it wasn't chaos, but I was in the hall, and I had never heard the blues like that before. It was a blues band.

At the break, Kreutzmann said, "Do you want to sit in?" I said, "Sure!" But I had no drum set. He said, "Come with me." We went outside. He had a little Mustang, and we went somewhere; someplace that he knew. I don't remember exactly how it all went down, but he got a drum set, and he put the drum set in the Mustang. I always wondered, years later, How did he get a drum set in the Mustang? He told me that he took one of the heads off of each of the drums, and he put one drum inside the other drum, which was very inventive. It was all happening too fast for me. He set the drums up, and off we went.

We played for hours. I just put my head down—I had no idea what the music was about—and just played and played and played. It was really serious playing; everybody was really into the music they were playing. It continued for hours. And then, somehow, everybody ran out of ideas or something, and it just stopped. And everybody stood really still and just looked around at each other, and I saw the dust flakes coming down in the light, and no one clapped. I went, "Oh, wow, this is really bad. [I've got to get] out of here." And I started to get off my seat to move out the back door. I was gone! I was in total trance—I had no idea where I'd been, what I'd played, or anything. People normally clapped—I'd always seen music; when music ended, people clapped. I didn't realize [the silence] was a ritual; it wasn't about clapping and enjoying the music in that sense. These guys were actually moved to other universes, you know?

Nobody [in the band] had any expression—Jerry and Bob and Phil and Bill just all looked kinda blank. They just looked around in—I guess it was like—astonishment at what had just happened. I assume. Because they didn't smile or anything. And then all of a sudden the audience erupted and everybody smiled, and it was all wonderful. And we all hugged in the middle of the stage. Jerry said, "This is the Grateful Dead. We could take this around the world!"

It felt great to me. I don't know what it was. Next thing I remember, I woke up at Belvedere Street, in the closet. Bill and Phil and Bobby said, "You can have the closet." I was living in the closet. The next thing I remember, Bill was rolling these big joints made of chocolate paper. I was smoking a lot of good weed, and I was one of the Grateful Dead. It was just like, boom!—there I was. "Wow, where am I?" "You're in the Grateful Dead." "Okay. No problem, *mon*!" I never went back to the store. This was just too amazing.

ROCK SCULLY: I was there that afternoon [at the Straight Theater] when he came in. His temperament was so different. He was like a military drummer and a hard-hitting drummer. One of his gods was Buddy Rich, who was a real pounder. So he was into the straight beat, but willing to play with rhythms. Kreutzmann was like a swing drummer—really relaxed—and I think Jerry really appreciated Kreutzmann, because he had the ability to follow a rush: Jerry would rush sometimes and Kreutzmann would be right there making it seem totally natural—"Okay, this is where we're goin'."

Mickey helped by reminding the other musicians in the band that we were doing a certain beat. With the second drummer there was a foundation there that didn't alter—it was solid—so even if there was no agreement between Phil and Jerry and Pigpen, that second drummer—Mickey—kept that beat goin'.

BILL KREUTZMANN: I worked out with Mickey for a long time. We worked on all sorts of different drumming things and we did a lot of neat things together. One time he even hypnotized me, which was great, because you get real relaxed and into a total learning space. There was a lot of growing that got done by both of us.

During that period we really rehearsed a lot at the old Potrero Theater, and a lot of what we'd do was rehearse different times—we'd do [measures of] seven or nine [beats], and I think "The Eleven" came out of that stint. We'd play for hours until it was practically flawless. The drumming became really unitized, though. We'd lock into one time, and sometimes it would be hard for us to get out of it. We were locked into playing bar lengths instead of phrases; and a phrase is much better in my opinion.

It's funny—somebody once asked Coltrane what his favorite time was and he said 4/4.

CAROLYN "MOUNTAIN GIRL" GARCIA: [The Potrero Theater] was yucky. Every window was busted out of it and the doors were sort of sitting there chained to the wall. I hated going over there because I had Sunshine [her child with Kesey], and she would pick up paint chips and put them in her mouth. I think a lot of the equipment got stolen in that period.

ROSIE McGEE: [Phil and I] moved to Seventeenth and Belvedere [in San Francisco] in late '67. When Mickey joined the band he moved in with us in a little closet under the stairs. Bobby lived with us as well. I think he was sleeping in the attic at 710. When we got the place on Belvedere, Billy and his girlfriend Susula, Mickey, and Bobby moved in with us. It was from there that we started to migrate. There was a lot of shuffling before we left the city.

The one thing I noticed immediately was that Billy and Mickey spent lots and lots and lots and lots of time together, just the two of them. So Mickey and Billy had to go off and become one finger together, on the hand, and integrate.

DAVID GANS: Mickey joining the band introduced a new dimension. It broadened their sound and strengthened their foundation. I don't know how much of it was musical flavors that Mickey brought into it, because he was a military drummer and had been playing some jazz. I don't get the sense that he was a contributor compositionally at that time. But it made their thing bigger and more ambitious.

They were also starting to write songs more seriously. In the beginning they had a handful of pieces. They had songs that were repurposed jug band tunes, blues tunes, and things like that. They had briefly experimented with a bunch of short original songs like "You Don't Have to Ask" and "Cardboard Cowboy," which I personally think are really cool, but on a certain level are indistinguishable from Beau Brummels songs, except instead of being teenage angst romances, they were brochures for LSD. The form of them was very similar: they were short pop songs with twangy guitars.

Then they started writing these things that are frameworks for expansion, like "Alligator," "Dark Star," "The Other One," and "Caution." After a point, each set they did was going to be built around one or more of those things. I think they started doing that in a very ambitious way in part because Phil's consciousness was of larger compositions and songs as frameworks for improvisation. The notion of bigger structures and suites were ambitions from the start. I think they always had big plans.

MICKEY HART: The thing that made the Grateful Dead work was that everybody had the big ears, and they all listened to each other. Somebody could move slightly in one direction and other people would pick up on it. The band moved organically from one thing to another. So much amazing music was made in those days.

We were after a new cosmology. We kind of felt like circumnavigators, as opposed to performers. That was my thinking about it—the places we were going. Jerry was so fluid, Phil was so fluid, and Bobby was all over the map. He wasn't playing real rhythm guitar. Me and Kreutzmann were reinventing the rock 'n' roll rhythm section. There were no models.

Back then, sometimes you'd get so high you couldn't play. The music would just go down to a trickle. Everyone would put their instruments down, and eventually someone would go up and start to noodle on it again, and then another person would go up, and we'd start becoming a band again. It wasn't like you went on stage, the lights went on, and here's the Grateful Dead. Ideas would break down. People would stop playing and just watch the other person, or the ideas just went down to that place, and then it started to re-form.

So we learned how to handle this flow, this in-and-out. It became part of our cosmology. But it started because we were either so confused, or we went into this chaotic world of the unknown, and sometimes we just didn't want to add to the chaos so we'd stop playing until we had something to say, and then we joined in and it re-formed. It was a kind of odd way of creating our music, but no one seemed to mind. As long as something was happening; when nothing was happening, people would just walk around looking at each other, doing whatever they did, and then we'd get back and start playing. Phil or Bobby or Jerry would pick up something, and it would just re-form like that. Those were precious moments.

I remember Bill Graham standing on the stage, saying, "What are you going to do when you're twenty-seven? This band has no songs. You can't even hum a tune. This band will never make it. You'd better think about your future."

I said, laughing to myself, "This is the greatest thing that ever happened. This is paradise on earth. I don't know what you're talking about!"

He said, "You go on for hours, and don't even know what song you're playing."

Bill was wrong about a lot of things. But that was the spirit of the times, too, remember. Very culturally specific to the Haight—people were doing psychoactive drugs at the time, and we were all doing them together. It was very different. The rules were suspended. No one knew who we were. We used to get off the stage at the Fillmore, Jerry and I would walk to the back and grab a Coke from the little Good Humor truck back there, and nobody would bother us. Nobody would even notice. People were on the floor fornicating, you know? People were just making it on the floor all around the stage. It wasn't like a concert; it was more like a ritual, and we were supplying the juice.

In those kinds of situations, when you see people making love on the floor and writhing around, you don't feel the same kind of responsibility to deliver a clean show. You could go wherever you wanted, do whatever you wanted, as long as the feeling was there. If anything, back in the old days, we went for the feeling. The notes were secondary. The musicological impact was secondary. It was all about getting that feeling, and maintaining it for the longest time, and moving into trance.

We practiced hundreds of hours to be able to play together and get [to a] group mind. But the beginnings and endings? Naw, that was never really it. It was all about the middles, and the transitions. There were times when the whole night was a transition. That made it so much more enjoyable. Of course, the failure rate was quite high, but the success rate improved as we put in the hours.

On October 3, 1967, the headline on the front page of *San Francisco Chronicle* blared: "ROCK BAND BUSTED." A photo of Pigpen looking somewhat sinister accompanied the story, which began: "Two members of the Grateful Dead—the lively San Francisco group responsible for such rock hits as 'Good Morning Little Schoolgirl'—were busted on marijuana charges. The raid—on the Dead's way-out thirteen-room pad at 710 Ashbury Street—also led to the arrest of [three employees] and six girls variously described as 'visitors' and 'just girls.'" The only band members to be arrested were Bob Weir and Pigpen, who, ironically, was the one confirmed non-drug user in the group. The event was covered extensively by the local "straight" media and also became a page-one story in the first issue of a new rock magazine based in San Francisco called *Rolling Stone.* The band and their managers appeared at a well-attended press conference a couple of days later. Eventually, fines were paid and there were no other repercussions, other than making the band realize they were under the microscope living in the heart of the Haight.

ROSIE McGEE: I was not living at the house at the time; I was living up the hill with Phil, but I got my mail there. So I came down to the house, which was also the band office at the time, and as I was coming up the stairs, I saw Sue Swanson motioning me away—"Don't come in, don't come in!"—but it was too late, and they came out on the stairs and pulled me into the house and arrested me. The bust was happening inside at that moment. They put everybody in the tiny little kitchen while they were waiting for the wagon to come. I was pretty nervous because I had a giant ball of hash in my purse, which I had over my shoulder but under a poncho. So we were sitting in the kitchen and they had one cop watching us in the doorway, though his back was to us—I mean, we weren't going anywhere! Meanwhile they're searching the house upstairs. Sue Swanson asks me if I want some ice cream, so she goes in the freezer and ladles out these bowls of vanilla ice cream. So while the cop wasn't looking, I took the ball of hash, crumbled it in my hand, put it in my vanilla ice cream, and ate it; I ate the whole thing, because I didn't want it to be found on me.

As we were driving downtown, I started coming on to the hash, and I got very, very, very loaded; this was a lot of hash. I remember Sue Swanson propping me up on one side and Veronica [Pigpen's girlfriend] propping me up on the other as we sat on the booking bench, because I was threatening to slide onto the floor into a puddle. Miraculously, I made it through the night, we got out early the next morning, and they dropped the charges on me because I wasn't actually there when the bust happened. But I literally couldn't speak for three days, and I was stoned for about two weeks.

DANNY RIFKIN (Reading from a prepared statement at an October 5, 1967, press conference): The arrests were made under a law that classifies smoking marijuana, along with murder, rape, and armed robbery, as a felony. Yet almost anyone who has ever studied marijuana seriously and objectively has agreed that marijuana is the least harmful chemical used for pleasure and life enhancement. . . .

The law contains an even greater evil. It encourages the most outrageously discriminatory type of law enforcement. If the lawyers, doctors, advertising men, teachers, and political officeholders who used marijuana were arrested today, the law might well be off the books before Thanksgiving. . . .

The law creates a mythical danger and calls it a felony. . . . The result is a series of lies and myths that prop each other up. The people who enforce the law use it almost exclusively against individuals who threaten their ideas of the way people should look and act. . . .

Behind all the myths is the reality. The Grateful Dead are people engaged in a constructive, creative effort in the musical field, and this house is where we work as well as our residence. Because the police fear and misinterpret us, our effort is now interrupted as we deal with the consequences of a harassing arrest.

Even before Mickey joined the band, the group had started working on songs for their second album. Garcia's old friend Robert Hunter had

PHIL LESH (1974): I can't say for sure that the music would have been the same without the drugs. In fact, I'm not qualified to say. The thing about the audiences was that they were exactly what we were; we didn't even have to play good. It was like we were them, they were us, and when you're just standing there on the stage boogieing away and you can see five thousand people going up and down in a wave like the ocean, it tends to give you a feeling like you're doing something right. I guess that was where we got the idea that we could play whatever we wanted and it would still work.

sent lyrics for a couple of songs—"Alligator" was the first to be put to music—and in early September, Hunter got together with the group in Rio Nido, a small redwood-studded town a couple of hours north of San Francisco on the Russian River. The song that came out of Hunter's brief stay there: "Dark Star."

ROBERT HUNTER: That was the first song I wrote with the Grateful Dead. I heard them playing [the "Dark Star" figure] in the hall they were going to play. I just started scratching paper and got the "Dark star crashes, pouring its light into ashes" part, and I said, "Why don't you try this with it?" It worked well and then they wanted more verses.

Among the other songs the group wrote around this time were such complex numbers as Phil and Bobby Petersen's "New Potato Caboose," Weir's "Born Cross-Eyed," and a pair of songs that would become linked under the title "That's It for the Other One"—Garcia's "Cryptical Envelopment" and Weir and Kreutzmann's "The Faster We Go, the Rounder We Get" (later simply called "The Other One"). Bob's famous line from "The Other One"—"The heat came 'round and busted me for smiling on a cloudy day"—was based on an actual incident.

BOB WEIR: I was arrested for throwing a water balloon at a cop. He was conducting an illegal search on a car belonging to a friend of mine, directly below 710 Ashbury. I considered it to be an illegal search; the car had probably been parked there for quite some time, and probably was malfunctioning; he was probably trying to see if anybody really owned the car. But I thought this was an illegal search, and it incensed me. And besides, we were having a water balloon fight inside the house at the time.

I got him from the third-story window. I didn't actually hit him; I got it right next to him in a perfect bomb-burst pattern on the pavement. It probably got his shoes full of water.

They wouldn't have busted me, but after that I had to go out in the street and just kind of sit there and look at him and grin.

They had nothing on me. I beat the rap. I was abused, by the way. They beat me around a little bit at the station. They were not long on patience with hippies in the Haight-Ashbury precinct.

> Sessions for the second album began that fall at a couple of different studios in Los Angeles, but it proved to be difficult to get the new songs down in the studio. Nevertheless, when the band traveled back East for shows in New York and Boston in the last half of December, they carved out time to continue recording at a couple of studios in New York.

BOB MATTHEWS: We went on our first big East Coast tour. Dan Healy went with us doing the sound, and I was in charge of the equipment. Ram Rod came down from Oregon, as did John Hagen. We drove east in a Metro van and an International Scout.

We were recording in one studio in downtown Manhattan in the morning, and would finish in the late afternoon and then break down, and carry everything across town to Olmstead [Studios], on the tenth floor of an old building. We'd have to put everything in elevators and move it up there, and then take it back over the next morning. I don't know why. I wasn't privy to the booking of it. It was what the band and Warner Bros. had worked out, and Dave Hassinger, who was the producer at that point. I don't know, I just got told, "Be here, be there." At that point I was the head of the crew.

Mickey Hart had become a member of the traveling entourage. At the Village Theater [in New York], I was asked by the band to set up Mickey Hart's drum kit. I, being the eighteen-year-old that I was, and in charge of the world, said no. "We don't need a percussionist."

Phil came to me and said, "Bob, you're our equipment guy. We're [not] asking you. We're telling you. Please set him up."

I said, "Phil, I can't do it."

Phil said, "Bob, you leave me no choice." I was fired and sent home—which I thoroughly deserved.

MICKEY HART: Pigpen was the musician in the Grateful Dead. When I first met the Grateful Dead, it was Pigpen and the boys. It was a blues band, and Pigpen played blues harp.

He looked so hard, but he was a kind, soft man. That's why he had to look so tough, because he was so kind, he would get stepped on.

I used to room with Pigpen because I was the new guy. He smelled bad. He drank and I didn't.

If there was one black chick in the audience, he'd always go home with her. Somehow he'd always have her up by his organ; by the end of the evening, she'd be up sittin' on his stool. He just loved black women. That was his preference.

He'd get down on his knee, and he'd bring that audience right up. He'd talk right to ya, you know. He played so hard. But he played the blues, shuffle stuff. That was his medium. He was the blues; he lived it, and he believed it, and he got caught in that web and he couldn't break out. And it killed him. He was just living the blues life, you know? Singin' the blues and drinkin' whiskey. That's what all blues guys did. That went along with the blues.

The first person my grandmother met when she saw the Grateful Dead was Pigpen. We came off the plane in New York and she was there to meet me. She had never seen long hair—she had just read about the hippies—and then she realized that we were that. "Grandma, I want you to meet my friend Pigpen." And Pigpen goes, "Huh." He grunted. She loved Pigpen. He didn't scare her at all. She sort of grandmothered us all. She was there at all the shows. She and my grandfather, Sam, were our first old fans.

> Dave Hassinger, who had produced the Dead's first album, was retained to helm the followup. Continuing their tradition of on-the-job learning and feeling the expanding power of their collective creativity, the Dead decided to get ambitious with their second album.

BOB WEIR: Dave Hassinger produced our first record, and it was a mild success—critically acclaimed, mostly by *Downbeat* magazine and stuff like that. We went into the second one, and we were recording in New York. Things got kind of slow, because we were getting kind of crazy in the studio. The first record was recorded on a 4-track; with 8 tracks, the possibilities seemed limitless. So we started getting kinda nuts.

MICKEY HART: [*Anthem of the Sun*] was our springboard to weirdness. We thought, "Now we're not tethered by the engineers or the technology of the day! We can fly the lofty peaks, man . . . let us go together!" Of course, we knew nothing of the studio. It was very startling, it was new; it was invigorating . . . it was the edge.

ROCK SCULLY: It was an album we were really forced to do, by contract. We weren't ready to do it, but we took money in advance. That's one reason we had Hassinger: to have control of the purse strings a little bit. We did the first album in seven days. But [for *Anthem of the Sun*] the music wasn't really together enough to really have a focus. We weren't working the songs out beforehand very well. Our intent was good, but we were lacking in purpose.

Phil summoned his pal Tom Constanten to add some inspired weirdness to one of the two major suites that constituted the work in progress.

TOM CONSTANTEN: [Phil and I] had shared an apartment a block off the [UC Berkeley] campus. We had our tastes in music, and in a lot of other things, just jibe. They were not so congruent as to be identical—no doubt with any people who would think for themselves so strongly, there'll be little divergences here and there—but where we agreed, we agreed wholeheartedly, and quite emphatically: the music of [Pierre] Boulez, [Karlheinz] Stockhausen, John Cage, Edgard Varése, some of the others in that circle, as well as Americans like Henry Cowell—people who were doing revolutionary and exciting things at that time.

I had done some electronic and prepared-piano things with Phil; we did some concerts for the San Francisco Mime Troupe in 1964, and he and some others had an awareness of what I could do in that genre. Also, I'm not completely inept at the piano. It seemed that I would bring a measure of zaniness and "out-thereness" to the band that would be a shot in the direction that they wanted to move at that time. I was just a little bit more momentum to the flow, so to speak.

It was like a magic carpet that was there for me to step on, and I would have been a fool not to step on it. It was basically an invitation from Jerry, something like, "I think we can use you."

MICKEY HART: In 1967, Bob and I were high on acid and he said, "Let's go to San Francisco Zoo and record the animals on the full moon!" "Yeah, man, great idea!" Neither one of us knew how to record in the field. I went over to Owsley's house and told him I needed his mono Nagra [tape recorder]—it's amazing, thinking back on it, that the Bear gave me his Nagra and showed me how to use it: "Here, I'll put the tape on for you, and here's a mic," and he gave me about thirty feet of cable to do a two-foot job.

Constanten was in the Air Force during the *Anthem* sessions, so he wasn't able to join the band on tour until November of 1968. But he did participate in the recording sessions, doing new studio work and contributing a taped piece ("Study Number Three," 1962) that was spun into the middle of side one.

TOM CONSTANTEN: There was one part in the succession from "The Other One" into "New Potato Caboose" where essentially my function was to take this swirling maelstrom, whip it up into an explosion, and out of the rubble would arise the simmering springs of the next tune. At one point I used an effect wherein I took a standard gyroscope top, like a kid's toy, gave it a good spin, and put it up against the soundboard of the piano. The result was not unlike that of a chainsaw being taken to it. I'm given to understand that the producer, Dave Hassinger, cleared his seat by three feet when he heard it, because there was no line of sight, he couldn't see what I was doing, and he was really worried about the band by that time.

BOB MATTHEWS: We went to L.A. and got thrown out of Sunset Sound, where the Doors had recorded, for smoking pot. We never taped anything there. We went to American [Recording in L.A.] and did some recording. Hassinger was there, Dan [Healy] was there, and that's when the friction began. There was a lot of tension between Hassinger and Healy.

BROOKS ARTHUR (Recording engineer): That was my first experience with what I can only call pre-Woodstock Woodstock. I'd worked with Neil Diamond, I'd worked with Van Morrison, and I'd never seen anything like the Dead before. The Dead moved in [to Century Sound in New York] lock, stock, and barrel—guitars, drums, family and children and friends and roadies and breastfeeding ladies and people sitting on the floor. It was flowers, peace symbols, beads, bells; the whole thing. Pot was everywhere. There was so much pot the accountants upstairs used to get high from the smoke going up through the air conditioning system.

Although I was helping Dave Hassinger, I didn't really hang out too much with the group. What I remember most about those sessions was that everything took forever to do. I think Dave and I spent forty-eight hours just getting the cymbals right, getting the imaging right for those guys. That was their style. Normally I could get an orchestra recorded, I could get two albums done in the time it took to get a drum sound for the Dead. But I understood their logic. It was a different room for them and they wanted to get a certain sound that was a departure from their old sound, so they took time with their bass and drum

So we're lugging it there, and then Bobby and I are sneaking up; we start climbing the gate and the mic line starts getting tangled on the gate. Then my pants get caught, and we're laughing hysterically, and just when we get to the other side, a guard comes up with his flashlight. That was that. They opened the gate and we were escorted out. So my first recording in the field was a total failure. But it piqued my interest and made me realize maybe it wasn't going to be as easy as I thought.

sounds. Which microphone sounded better with this cymbal? What does it sound like when we stuff the kick drum, or un-stuff the kick drum, or pop a hole in the head of the kick drum? You try a microphone in-phase, out of phase. Then you take a long coffee break, get high, and then there's lunch.

ROCK SCULLY: I was pretty sure—and this is a psychedelic view, mind you—that it reflected how un-together we were to attempt recording this under the circumstances we did: Christmastime in New York, and hustling through snow and slush. It was weird and awful at the same time. So we kind of lost track of what was good about it and what was wrong about it, and basically we were sick of it before it was finished.

Meanwhile, the live stuff was getting better and better, and people were appreciating it. There were personnel changes [the addition of Tom Constanten], and Hassinger hadn't really done anything. We were becoming more and more convinced that live recording was where it was at.

DAVE HASSINGER: I was very straight, and it wasn't too easy for me to deal with people during that era. I knew I was dealing with people who were probably heavy into acid, and I knew that a lot of times our conversations weren't going to make a lot of sense. I always felt that it was hard to do real constructive work with musicians on acid, but I guess there were some great records made that way.

With that band, if you argued with anyone in the entourage, you were taking on the group—at least that's how they saw it. So that was the first big fracture. Basically, we just couldn't see eye to eye. They were all in on the decisions. Personally I preferred to communicate with Jerry because I got along with him very well. Actually I got along with them all pretty well except for Phil Lesh. He and I didn't hit it off too well. He's very, very opinionated. He would be worrying about the sound of his bass to the point where it got almost ridiculous, I thought.

ROSIE McGEE: Phil is a perfectionist, and he always has really strong ideas about what's right and how he wants something to be or how he wants it to happen. If he knows what he wants but he doesn't know how to get there, to him it's not unreasonable if it's going to take three hundred hours, and fuck everybody else.

The other thing about Phil is that he was also very seriously irreverent and he really did not have any patience for pomposity or pretension. He loved to goad people. If they couldn't take it, he'd do it even more. It wasn't meant to be mean or malicious, but it was definitely there, and if you got him going, he wouldn't stop. Hassinger was fair game, definitely. Anybody who was terminally straight, it was all over for them.

DAVE HASSINGER: I remember one time during the making of the record that I went into American Recording [in L.A.] and they had ordered so much equipment from Studio Instrument Rentals that you literally could not get into the studio. The whole album was that way. It was like pulling teeth until I finally couldn't take it anymore.

BOB WEIR: There was a great deal of confusion and hassling over just doing the songs—"No, I want it weirder"—and Hassinger wanted to get the record done within the budget, etc., like any good producer should.

I think we had Healy working as an engineer, at our insistence and Hassinger's reluctance. Healy and Hassinger weren't getting along particularly well. We were doing "Born Cross-Eyed." We'd more or less done the basic and some overlays.

There was a little bit of tension in the studio, but I was oblivious to that. I was on brown rice and pretty spaced at that point. I was describing how I envisioned the song going, and Healy and Hassinger were hassling over something. It got quiet at one point, and so I announced, "Right here, I want the sound of thick air." There was a break in the song, and I wanted the sound of thick air: a little bit of white noise, a little bit of compression. I was thinking about kinda like the buzzing that you hear in your ears on a hot, sticky summer day. I couldn't really describe it back then, because I didn't know what I was talking about.

Dave Hassinger throws up his hands and says, "Thick air. He wants the sound of THICK AIR. Thick air! He wants the sound of thick air!"—as he's walking out of the studio.

So we carried on without him.

DAVE HASSINGER: I just looked at him when he said it. He said it in such a serious way, I didn't really know how to react. Actually, a little later we did seriously look into trying to get into a certain quality of sound like I suppose he was talking about. We were going to take all the equipment out to the desert east of L.A. and record out there, but it never happened.

JERRY GARCIA: We started out by recording experimentally, in L.A., where we accomplished absolutely nothing. Then we went to New York to try some studio there, and we got our producer so excited that he quit. We got him uptight because we were being so weird, and he was only being human, after all, and didn't really have to go through all that, so he decided not to go through it and we decided, "Well, we can do it ourselves."

So we just worked and worked and worked—mostly Phil and I—for months, maybe as long as six months, at least six months. It was 8-track recording and we worked a lot in San Francisco. We assembled live tapes [recorded during the Northwest tour and in San Francisco], and we went through the most complex operations that you can go through in a recording studio. We had an engineer, Dan Healy, who is a real good, fast-on-his-feet, able-to-come-up-with-crazy-things engineer. And we worked and we assembled an enormous amount of stuff, and since it was all multi-track, it all just piled up.

CHAPTER 3
All Graceful Instruments Are Known

DAN HEALY (Sound engineer): I met the Grateful Dead via John Cipollina at a Quicksilver gig at the Fillmore, where the Dead were opening. I lived on a houseboat in Larkspur [southern Marin County], and Cipollina lived in the houseboat right next door to mine. Quicksilver used to practice on the houseboat pretty often. We became friends and he was always saying, "Hey, you gotta come see one of our shows," 'cause he knew I was into music and sound. So finally I went to that Fillmore show. It was during the Dead's set that we showed up, and the music had just stopped. There was no such thing as "spare equipment" for the bands in those days. If an amp died, it could stop the whole show. I think in this case it was Phil's amp that died, and it became one of those "Is there a doctor in the house" things. So Cipollina shoved me up there, and I fiddled with Phil's amp. And it started to work. At the end of the show, Phil and Garcia walked up to me and said, "Hey, thanks, man," and all that, and we introduced ourselves.

From working in a studio, I was used to pretty good sound. It wasn't great compared to what we have now, but for that time it was state of the art. The PA for rock 'n' roll shows, though, was almost nonexistent; it was just terrible. On each side of the stage, there'd be a little teeny box about one foot by two feet, and when the bands played you could barely tell the system was on. You could never really hear or understand the vocals, so singing was just kind of a joke. And so I remember making some crack to Phil and Garcia about how the sound system really sucked, and Garcia sort of challenged me, like, "Put your sound where your mouth is," or something. I said, "All right, you're on."

The next time they were going to play was about two weeks later, also at the Fillmore, so I went around to the three major places in the area that rented sound equipment and I got all this stuff from them, and I took it to the Fillmore a couple of days before the show. It was equipment from a few different companies, so I wanted to make sure it was all hooked up so that things were compatible. It was a horrible-looking monstrosity, but when the gig came—BAM!—you could hear the singing. That's sort of what launched it for me.

> Eventually, Healy replaced Owsley as the Dead's soundman, though the Bear would return in due time.

MICKEY HART: There was always tension between Owsley and everybody. The Bear had his way and he was very single-minded about his opinions, but the thing is, Bear was able to articulate things that nobody else could. He was the first one to actually teach me about a soundscape. He could talk about the sound field—depth of field, and right, left, and center, and he explained phase—things that we now take for granted. In those days he was like a philosopher. He taught me the physiology and geometry of the vibratory world.

He was so crazy! He would blame the machines for his failures. The machines would blow up or there'd be feedback and he'd be saying, "How could you fail me?" He personalized it way beyond rational thought. He was asking things of them and expecting results, and he took it personally when things didn't go right.

Phil and I had a special relationship with him. Jerry thought his madness was sometimes ruining our moment, whereas I thought it was in the name of science. I thought we had to go somewhere, and there were going to be a lot of mistakes on the way, and they might as well be creative mistakes. His ideas were often brilliant, and always at least interesting. But he was more of an idea guy; he had trouble actualizing them. Healy was a seat-of-the-pants guy who actually could make things happen. Everything Bear tried to make happen, he blew up.

> In January 1968, the Dead and Quicksilver Messenger Service embarked on a tour of the Pacific Northwest, hitting far Northern California, then bopping through Oregon and Washington over a two-week period.

BRIAN ROHAN: I got the Northwest tour together, which [started in] Eureka, at the Memorial Auditorium. Some kid had a bad acid trip, and the headline in the paper was, "Band Brings Acid"; it was all about LSD.

Then we go to Seattle. It was seventeen degrees in Seattle, the coldest day in the history of Seattle. Not that good a crowd. We go to Portland and play at the Crystal Ballroom.

We go down to Eugene. It snows three inches in the interim. The Grass Roots were a huge Top Forty group, and they had drawn forty-eight people three nights before; I thought, "We're dead meat." But there were a thousand people, two thousand people in the student auditorium. I thought, "At a buck apiece, we're going to be okay."

JOHN CIPOLLINA: We had some pretty wild times on the Northwest trek. There was no heat on us, because with Pigpen around it was like, "Oooh—look at that guy!" We all looked like businessmen in comparison with Pigpen!

When we first got to Portland, Dan Healy, who was working for us then, and I went into a pawnshop. Dan bought a 1956 Les Paul Special, and I bought guns and a bunch of blanks to continue the little cowboys-and-Indians game we'd been playing with the Dead for quite a while. It was snowing in Portland, and here I am with these guns and hundreds of blanks. I was taking "shots" at everyone in the group. And we had this rule that went along with the game we played, which was if you "died," you had to "stay dead" for a couple of minutes. If someone even shot you with their finger, you had to roll over and play dead.

One of the guns I bought was this little .22 caliber blank pistol that was easy to carry around. I remember seeing Pigpen, Rock Scully, and Danny Rifkin, and I think maybe one other guy from the group, driving down the street. So I went running out in the street making some kind of deranged weird noise—some anguished cry—and I emptied the gun into the car. The car came screeching to a stop. The doors flew open and Pigpen and everybody just rolled out of the car into the snow. They really looked dead. Out of the corner of my eye I saw this old lady with a shopping cart racing around the corner. I stood there surveying the "kill." Then they got up, we all had a good laugh, and we got in the car. About a minute later the place was crawling with police looking for the bodies. The whole tour went that way. I got a callus on my trigger finger from blowing people away.

The last day of the tour, we were all booked for a noon flight out of Medford, Oregon. We ended up taking a 10:30 a.m. flight, so when they tried their last big raid there was no one there except for the equipment guys, who never carried anything

JOHN CIPOLLINA: The funniest thing about the tour was the narcotics chase. The cops chased us from one end of California all the way through Oregon and Washington. The first show we played on that tour, the authorities found a couple of roaches in the building after the show, and that led to a big scandal in the local papers. They called the dance a pot orgy. The Oregon on them. The cops' warrant didn't cover the equipment truck anyway, so they drove away, leaving those poor guys cursing again.

Eventually, they got the correct search warrant and they stopped the truck out on the highway. The Dead have always carried a lot of equipment, and Quicksilver did, too. Plus we had Jerry Abrams's light show equipment in there. So the cops took every single piece of equipment out of the truck and spread it out next to the highway. It must have looked awesome to people driving by. The roadies didn't care—they sat there and made the cops do everything. After the search had failed to turn up anything, the roadies insisted the cops put everything back. The equipment guys wouldn't lift a finger. Now, when you go on tour for a few weeks with a big truck, you really learn how to pack it, but those highway patrolmen had no idea how to put all the stuff back in. They'd fill the truck completely and a third of the equipment would still be on the roadside. So they'd start again. It took them hours to do it.

CAROLYN "MOUNTAIN GIRL" GARCIA: That Oregon energy—it works hard, it drives long distances, it's a hard trucker. That early wave of roadies was impressive. They gave their lives up for the band. They were driving the equipment; it wasn't flying. And there were these long, awful rides. You don't have much time for your own life when this is what you do. It's taking you here and it's taking you there. On Friday you have to be in Sacramento and on Saturday you have to be in Bakersfield. That's not control over your own life; that's being dragged through life on a schedule. So it didn't feel very rebellious anymore.

And they were building all the speakers and sys-

authorities were informed, and they really dogged us everywhere—it was a real Keystone Kops caper. They were always one step behind us until Pendleton, Oregon; then they were a step ahead. They raided the hotel an hour and a half before we got there! We had no idea what was going on. As soon as we'd leave a place, it seemed like all these guys would bust in, tear up the bedding, check under the light switches.

tems. It was a devotional type of roadie-ism that was kind of neat to see. I think that feeling disintegrated [later], over cocaine.

KEN BABBS: Most of those guys came from the area around Pendleton, which has its own terrific energy because of the Pendleton Roundup and the cowboys and the Indians. Ram Rod and Rex [Jackson] and Johnny Hagen all had a real can-do energy. These guys didn't shirk any of the heavy work, but would always get it done, which wasn't always easy because in those days it was still a psychedelic journey, a true LSD-fueled thing. But they were all part of the same team, and they made it a better team.

> In the winter of 1968, a loose affiliation of hippies that included Ron Rakow, the Grateful Dead, and others leased San Francisco's Carousel Ballroom—once a big-band dance palace and later a spot for Irish music and dancing—as an alternative to Bill Graham's Fillmore and Chet Helms's Family Dog/Avalon Ballroom.

JONATHAN RIESTER: On January 17, 1968, we did a gig at the Carousel Ballroom. Nobody got paid; that was the war chest. From that day on we went after getting the Carousel Ballroom, and the deal was the Dead would own 10 percent, as would the Airplane.

BOB WEIR: We were young and strong and high on ourselves. At that point, Bill Graham wasn't the huge mogul that he became, and we thought, "There's room in this town for us, too!" We were also acutely aware that Bill was stealing from us, and he made no bones about it, but he also made no bones about the fact that we'd never catch him. That said, we probably did better working for him than we would've done working for someone who wasn't stealing from us, because he always managed to sell more tickets. He managed to get more people into the building and he knew how to get around the fire marshals and all that kind of stuff. So he was a crook, but he was a great one.

JON McINTIRE: What was clear from the outset was that Ron Rakow had signed a lease that was totally untenable. On the other hand, I'm not sure we would've gotten the Carousel without him. The landlord of the Carousel was Irish, lived in Dublin, and owned ballrooms all over Ireland. He had his representative in San Francisco—also Irish—who actually ran the place. He used to come around to these gigs we put on and there would be all sorts of outrageous behavior going on. It was just bedlam! It was like Babylon! He was a little uptight at first, but after a while he'd just come in, take a look around, and then get drunk and kind of smile.

The place could actually have made it if [we'd] had a better deal. I can't remember what it was, but it was something like 10 percent of the door with a guarantee of $5,000 a week. It was expensive, but then again, this was one of the busiest corners in San Francisco back then.

At either the second or third show, we had so few people show up that instead of charging admission, we went around Haight Street passing out tickets, and then when people got there we gave them free food and free ice cream. Free everything. We turned it into a party. That was Rakow's idea; I thought it was wonderful.

That was the kind of reputation you wanted to have. It was "Let's have a party. Let's have fun." And it was fun. It totally changed the atmosphere, and it was a gas. And it also gave us the proper reputation as being street people ourselves, which is what we were. Rakow had come out of New York and was different, but the rest of us were folks on the street. We had a great love for this place and gave our lives to it for a period of time. Everyone did. Everyone cared a lot about each other, and the care was genuine and it showed.

We didn't sleep. You'd finish one night and then come in the next morning and strip the wax off the dance floor and wax it again. We kept the place immaculate, so we were working our butts off all the time. But we were young and we believed in what we were doing fervently—with a great deal of love—so the fact that there was no sleep put it into a dream space, sort of.

MICKEY HART: The Carousel was our place. The familiarity of it was an asset. Doing one-nighters, there's an uncertainty to your existence. We were children in an adult world, and like children we were doing really desperate things—and it paid great dividends.

I used to hitchhike to the Carousel. There was a time when we weren't even getting salaries. It wasn't hardship; we were having fun, smoking lots of dope. All I had was an Alla Rakha record, a bed, and a candle.

RON RAKOW: We ran into a period of pretty bad business. I'm not saying this to escape blame for being an incompetent manager, if that's in fact what I am. But there was this period of thirteen weeks in which Bill Graham lost money for seven of them. The fact that there were two major assassinations [Martin Luther King and Robert Kennedy] didn't help very much at all.

JONATHAN RIESTER: We couldn't out-book Bill Graham. We did have an inroad to the Dead and we did have an inroad to the Airplane, because we were all a group of friends. We got the Dead to sort of be our house band, because they loved what we were doing—especially Garcia, who loved that idea of community and family. When we said "free," we meant free. We did all kinds of incredible stuff at the Carousel. I was in constant trouble with the chief of police in those days over our cabaret license because of the Hells Angels, the Free City Convention, Free News, the Diggers; you name it. We had one concert where you had to burn money to get in. Some people just couldn't do it. We got busted doing that. They didn't want us to be there, period.

Toward the end, the Airplane and the Dead kept us afloat for a little bit, but we couldn't use them all the time because of [over-exposure]. And the Dead weren't any great shakes in those days. I remember going into halls as the road manager the following year and there would be 5,000 seats and only 2,000 of them were full.

JON McINTIRE: [After the Carousel was bought by Bill Graham and transformed into the Fillmore West], I started working for the Grateful Dead. I started as a kind of office manager. They hired Jonathan [Riester] as the road manager, and Jonathan stipulated that in taking him they'd also take me and Bert Kanegson. The band was rehearsing in those days at the Presidio Theater and they had all the bills of the last couple of years in wastebaskets and paper bags, and Bert and I tried to put together the financial picture from this mess of papers. That took quite a while. I opened an office for us on the corner of Union and Fillmore, above a liquor store.

RON RAKOW: Garcia always wanted it to be successful. He came to me personally in '67 and said, "Listen, this is going to be a big thing. We could use someone who knows what the hell they're doing to sort of look over everybody's shoulder. We're sort of writing this book as we go along." Garcia was not impressed because I had Wall Street contacts. Garcia wouldn't know Wall Street if it landed in his lap. What did Wall Street mean to Jerry? He never owned a stock in his life.

In April 1968, Warner Bros. inexplicably released a single, a studio version of "Dark Star," backed with Weir's equally strange "Born Cross-Eyed," in a different mix than the one on *Anthem of the Sun*. It did not make a commercial splash, to say the least.

DAVID GANS: If you listen to the studio "Dark Star," all of the compositional elements are there: the lilting groove, the counterpoint, the intro, the outro. All the performances of it expanded one or more of those elements. They were huge openings, and they started growing. They didn't necessarily grow in length, but they grew in sophistication; you can trace the tropes as they enter and evolve. I think the idea from the beginning was to make it bigger, but it had to take its time to do that.

In the beginning there was a repetitive Pigpen organ figure, which got annoying after a while. When they stopped doing it was when "Dark Star" really started cutting loose.

ROCK SCULLY: When the band was going way, way out in "Dark Star," they knew they could listen to Pig and have some sense of where they were. So he was reliable in that way. You knew he wasn't seeing snakes. When Garcia's guitar neck turned into a snake, Pigpen saw it as a guitar; Jerry could rely on him to do that.

JERRY GARCIA: He was our anchor. We'd be out of our minds—just *YOWWWWGOINNGG!*—and we'd be tethered to Pigpen. You could rely on Pigpen for a reality check. "Hey, man, is it too weird, or what?" He'd say, "No, man, it's cool." Everybody used him on that level. He was like gravity. Hells Angels would sit around his room fucked up on acid and Pigpen would be taking care of them. It was so great. Pigpen was like a warm fire, a cozy fire.

MICKEY HART: We'd go back and forth, give and take on that stuff—one person laying on one part of the groove and the other laying on the other. It was very light. We tried to not have it broken up, stop and go. It was more of a flow. I played the gongs, all kinds of stuff. We were moving all around. I played guiro a lot; a lot of scraper stuff. Maracas, gong, drum set.

DAVID GANS: In the early days of "Dark Star" they were still more prominently featuring "Alligator," "The Other One," and "Caution" for jamming. "Alligator" is basically a bluesy jug band form opened wide up. Even "The Other One," as powerful as it became later, didn't have as much range. I think "Dark Star" signaled the band's turn into more subtle and sophisticated music, in addition to the balls-out insanity. It had a lot of compositional sophistication to it, even in its simplicity, and had this malleable quality to it. It became the place where they explored their more interesting and sophisticated ideas rather than the partying stuff.

TOM CONSTANTEN: "Dark Star" is a tremendously adaptable

piece—I can't think offhand of any other piece that is so comfortable to just ease into and work out for a while and leads to as many interesting places, and then you just ease out of it. It's simple enough to be malleable but complex enough to be interesting. It isn't like some of the jams . . . let's say, one that has just one or two chords that alternate. You get into this sort of generic jam, which might be nice for shifting gears or moving to another piece, but it doesn't engender as many ideas of its own. It doesn't suggest as many as the changes of "Dark Star" do.

Certain motifs were integrated over time, almost like an aural tradition. I viewed the piece not so much as something written out, but as a galaxy that would be entered at any of several places. That appealed to me from my aleatoric sixties days—John Cage and all. And naturally, in the sense that every performance would be unique, with one-of-a-kind moments that were completely spontaneous. We were just exploring the map—the dimensional, capillarious intestine of . . . cosmic goop!

STEVE SILBERMAN: It was "Dark Star" and "The Other One" that proved to be the psychedelic symphonies, and were designed by and for psychedelics. "Dark Star" is uncanny. The lyric seems like it has that Blake-ian compression of visionary experience, expressed with haiku-like simplicity. It's very acid-y and completely from that place. It's like a little key from that place, and Garcia wove around it a process of discovery each night. "Dark Star" became "Dark Star" not only for what was a given about it, but for what was not a given about it. I was fascinated when I was listening to the early show of February 14, 1970, because they had just played what many Deadheads consider to be the ultimate "Dark Star"—*an* ultimate "Dark Star"—the night before, and what you hear is the band arriving at the pivotal points they had arrived at the night before, and every single time Garcia would deny them a repetition of what had happened the night before. So you end up with a fragmentary and unsatisfying performance, because you hear everything drifting toward something and then Garcia will literally play over the other band members so they won't go there, but then they eventually get to somewhere else. I think Garcia, especially, was really firm that he never wanted it to become a reiteration of what they'd already looked at, what they'd already accomplished. That's perfect for psychedelics, because you can never have the same trip twice.

MICKEY HART: We walked into [Winterland] right as [Cream drummer Ginger Baker] was getting into his solo. It was amazing. I turned to Jerry and said, "They have to be the best band in the world," and he said, "Tonight, they are the best band in the world."

We invited them to play with us. We played Sacramento [March 11, 1968], and Kreutzmann and I really got up for it. We were the best band in the world that night. Ginger got crazy, and they blew out every speaker on the first note. They were trying to reach our intensity. We got our equipment guys to roll our equipment out. It was so clear, it scared the shit out of Clapton—they were used to feeding back through all their Marshall [amps].

PHIL LESH: [Using feedback as a musical element] was originally [mostly] my idea because there we were with these electronic instruments, and it was starting to be obvious to me that they could function in that kind of manner. Even though you can't control [the feedback] too well, they more or less end up being pretty tonal—tonal in the sense that the sounds that usually come out tend to have the harmonic structure of tonal notes. It was only two or three years that we did that. Weir was one of the absolute masters of that stuff, but he doesn't do it anymore at all. I can't imagine why, 'cause he would just come out with this incredible stuff, and it was absolutely off the top of his head, totally.

JERRY GARCIA: [In "The Eleven"] you're trapped in this very fast-moving little [A-D-E] chord pattern which is tough to play gracefully through, except for the most obvious shit, which is what I did on "The Eleven." When we went in to the E minor, then it started to get weird. We used to do these revolving patterns against each other where we would play 11 against 33. So one part of the band was playing a big thing that revolved in 33 beats, or 66 beats, and the other part of the band would be tying that into the 11 figure. That's what made those things sound like "Whoa—what the hell is going on?" It was thrilling, but we used to rehearse a lot to get that effect. It sounded like chaos, but it was in reality hard rehearsal.

PHIL LESH: ["The Eleven"] was really designed to be a rhythm trip. It wasn't designed to be a song. That more or less came later, as a way to give it more justification, or something, to work in a rock 'n' roll set. We could've used it just as a transition, which is what it was, really. It was really too restrictive, and the vocal part—the song part—was dumb.

CAROLYN "MOUNTAIN GIRL" GARCIA: The second trip to New York is when it really caught on. The difference was in the audience. They were so enthusiastic. Going to New York was like going to the Roman Colosseum, and you were the lions and the Christians. There was lots of cheering and shouting and all this whistling—that real penetrating New York whistling you don't hear anywhere else. We were like, "Whoa! What's with the audience? They're really lively." The audiences were way more electric—and starved for weirdness.

And the Grateful Dead were loose. They did all the things you're not supposed to do onstage—lots of tuning and discussions and smoking by the amps, and everyone's screaming "*Jerreeee!* C'mon!" There was a lot of repartee and banter with the audience.

Everywhere we went, there were always a lot of people who just didn't understand what we were all about. They'd come out scratching their heads, saying, "What the fuck was that?"—which we thought was really funny, of course. They'd play country-western tunes out of space tunes, and they really toyed with their audience a lot.

On May 3, 1968, the Dead played a free concert on the campus of New York's Columbia University during a student strike in protest of the Vietnam war.

BOB MERLIS (Columbia student): I was a junior, class of '69. I was a big music fan, and I had worked with the Board of Managers; we put on events, most of them in Ferris Booth Hall. I hired the bands, so I was somewhat versed in the world of rock 'n' roll booking. A friend of mine said, "The Dead are [in New York City]; you should call them." I was given the hotel number for Rock Scully. I picked up the phone and said, "Hi, I'm with the Columbia strike, and we'd love to have you guys come up and play, to show solidarity with the students."

He said, "Okay." That was it! We reserved the terrace in front of Ferris Booth Hall and sent out flyers. That's what you'd do—flyers were the way. "Grateful Dead for Free!"

The problem was, in the wake of the strike, only those with Columbia IDs would be let onto campus. I'm not sure if there were police lines at that point, but certainly there was very enhanced security and you needed a Columbia ID to get through. Outside agitators, y'know.

We put flyers around, and so it was a kind of a fait accompli when we went to the guy who controlled the student union. I said, "We've really got to get the Grateful Dead through the police lines. X thousand people are going to show up, and if there's no Grateful Dead it's probably not going to be a good situation." I wasn't really threatening the guy; I didn't know what was going to happen, but I pictured the possibility of a lot of disappointed people—who were already on campus because they were in fact holders of Columbia University IDs.

So they let the band in. I know there's this myth about them showing up in a Wonder Bread truck and us sneaking them in, but it just didn't happen. I don't think it would have worked anyway. Their equipment came in a Ryder truck. We loaded it in through 114th Street, in front of Carman Hall and around the corner, and plugged 'em all in.

I got to introduce them, which was the thrill of a lifetime. They played for an hour, hour and a half. It was a tremendous success.

It was peaceful. [It was] vaguely apolitical, but it [was] political by dint of the fact that they so represented the alternative universe that many of us aspired to populate.

We showed that the will of the people, the students, had an effect. The administration had to realize you don't have to draw a line in the sand every single time something out of the ordinary comes up. "Why is this not appropriate?" I don't want to say it was a salve; I wasn't in the business of trying to smooth waters. That was my come-on to the administration to let it happen. It wasn't much of an argument; they realized it was going to be a relatively benign thing. And everybody had a great time.

ALAN SENAUKE (Columbia student): I remember how completely thrilling it was, in the overall sense of empowerment that we had, from the beginning at Hamilton Hall, through the strike, of feeling that we were helping to create a culture according to the terms that we believed in, and the Dead were part of that culture—and here they were on our campus!

I think they had progressive identification, I think they believed themselves to be in empathy and identification with the revolution, whatever that meant.

BOB WEIR: We thought it would be nice for us to go down there and stir up some shit; nothing political, just lend some energy to the situation. As soon as microphones were turned on there was a mad rush for the microphones because everybody had "an important announcement." And I told five people in the space of one minute that "No, man, these microphones were for the music and not for politics." And from every single one of the people I told that to, I got "lame honky bastard" or "crass bourgeois son of a bitch."

Meanwhile, on the home front . . .

JERRY GARCIA: The Haight-Ashbury was coming apart. It was scary to be anywhere near it. That scene was over; it may or may not have been important, but where we were going was important to us, and what we wanted to do was keep doing what we were doing. Getting out of town was an effort to get ourselves together.

CAROLYN "MOUNTAIN GIRL" GARCIA: We were happy to get out of the city. They were throwing tear gas bombs down Haight Street and there was too much traffic, and people were stopping to look at the house all the time. [San Francisco Mayor] Joe Alioto came in, and he was really unpleasant. He was the one we had to fight with the most; he was a drag. He pretty much tightened everything down to where it became unpleasant. Kids were getting stopped all the time; there was a lot of harassment.

So we slipped away to Marin.

ROSIE McGEE: As time went on and we split up into different households, it became much more clear that even as we were in the middle of this insane Grateful Dead scene, there was a lot of traditional stuff going on. Especially when the band became a regular hard-working road band. Then it became the traditional rock 'n' roll world, which is: the women get left behind and there are groupies on the road and *blah-blah-blah*. The more well-known they became, the more temptations there were, and they were also gone for a longer time. I'm sure to this day, when you're talking about any band—or baseball players or football players on the road—there's a kind of boys' club, honor-among-thieves mentality: whatever happens on the road stays on the road, and that's the way it is.

Whether you marry a baseball player or a musician, most frequently in our society it's the women that make the change. Whatever the men are doing, I want to be with this guy so I'm going to be a motorcycle mama or a musician's old lady. You get what you get and go with it. Brenda Kreutzmann couldn't go with it. It was a pretty weird scene; "I'm a musician who takes LSD and is part of this group of freaks." I can't speak for her, but that's pretty obvious and clear. There was a kid, too. I might have done the same thing.

It had many levels of disconnect for me; partly the number of days in a year that I wasn't with Phil, the differences between our lives. His life on the road—a few days before and a few days after, you're getting ready to go or coming down from being on the road, so it extends that window to where no matter how much you love your wife, you're in another frame of mind. It takes a lot of effort to come back to the wife, kids, and bills.

It wasn't affordable [for the women to go along]. Whatever money the band made in the early years they put back into buying instruments and improving their sound system. There wasn't a lot of money.

I hung out at rehearsals a lot . . . to sit on the couch and roll joints. I was really good at rolling joints. I didn't dance until I was high during a gig.

The other piece of that puzzle is cocaine. The nature of its influence on people's attitudes and personalities, when they are doing a lot of it, exacerbated the separation and changed people. It got worse in the early seventies. It's not that the women weren't doing coke, too. The whole scene was coked out.

The home scene became more and more secondary to the road. Then [Phil would] get home from tour and go into the recording studio, or he'd have to write songs. That's the life of a musician. If a woman had her own shit together, which I didn't—I didn't have that much confidence, a passion, or a gig other than photography. I was lost in all of that. My passion was loving Phil and being with him. That was taken away from me in a bunch of different ways.

JONATHAN RIESTER: I was out in Novato and I made the mistake of letting Mickey move onto the ranch. Rock and I used to call it the "Ponderiester"; it became the Grateful Dead Ranch after I left. We had a nice big barn, and we converted the milking part of the barn into Mickey's apartment. Mickey was a good rider, and he had a horse. At one point Mickey and I had thirty-four horses. It was my hustle to feed them. Mickey and I once rode our horses across the freeway and all the way out South Novato Boulevard to the rehearsal hall. It was insane.

EILEEN LAW: People were in every room and out in the barn. You had to have seniority to [get a] bedroom. I'd sleep in haystacks sometimes, with the horses and all these other animals.

OWSLEY STANLEY: The Carousel closed in June. In July or August, Healy decided to go back to work with Quicksilver, whom he had worked with before. One day over at the Carousel, near the last shows in June or July, the Dead asked me if I would be their sound man again. And I said sure. And they were rehearsing in this gutted theater in the Potrero, and everything was primitive, so I went to work for them again and started improving the gear. They were in the studio doing *Aoxomoxoa* all during that period. I started working on the gear, trying to add the stuff I'd learned and bring it up to snuff. I was steady on with them from I guess mid-'68 till mid-'70, when they carted me off to the joint.

MICKEY HART: When we were at the Potrero Theatre, we used to go in every day and play. Hunter lived there, I think. That's when he was drinking. We'd push the door open and he'd be there on the floor with wine bottles. He was taking speed and drinking wine, and writing all that beautiful stuff. We would play, and Hunter would sit there and write. This was where we worked out "The Eleven," I believe.

In the old days, we'd wake up every day and play. That's all the band was there for. We played a lot. To do what we did you have to be in shape—not only mentally, but physically. You have to practice it. You can't practice the Grateful Dead, but you've got to practice playing.

BILL GRAHAM: From the early days on, when it

ROCK SCULLY: I had a bedroom out at the ranch. I was single at the time. I had an L. L. Bean sleeping bag on this elevated platform in this sort of glass-enclosed back house that was a kind of fallen-down kind of place. We'd gotten Stephen Stills's horses and some other horses, and some chickens. I don't know what we thought we were doing. The reason I was describing my bedroom is there were these French doors that opened up [to the outside] and my furniture was some bales of hay; the was business, I did business. If there was one guy that wasn't gonna go bananas that night it was always Bill. After a while it became, "Come on, Bill—loosen up! Get high! Take this, take that." And over the first few years it got to be a thing: "We gotta get Bill!"

I always said, "I'm working."

The first gig at the [Fillmore West] in the summer of '68, it had gotten to a point with them—"Don't touch anything." I knew they were up to something, so my wife at the time made me my food, put it into a pail, put some soup into a Thermos, and put the whole thing into a bag and put a wax seal on it so I knew they couldn't get into it. That was all I was going to eat that day.

They came in and set up, Healy and Ram Rod and the other guys. "Hey, Bill, you want a drink?" "No." "Want a puff from a cigarette?" "No." "Kiss me?" "I won't touch you!"

At that time, I used to drink 7-Up all day. I'd always go into their dressing room and rap with them, and take a can. They put a bucket of 7-Ups in ice—and they'd taken a hypodermic needle through the top and dosed them. They told each other not to touch them—and sure enough, I picked one up about a half hour before they were to go onstage. They were very friendly—"How you doin', Bill?" And I'm sitting there talking to them, and all of a sudden—"Hey, I feel great, man! How ya doin'?" And I just—*waaaaahhh*! And Mickey Hart said, "You want to hang out with us onstage? You lead the band; we'll play."

I knew what I was doing. I was totally clear. I saw many, many colors and shapes and things I hadn't experienced before. I walked out with them, and Mickey gave me a drumstick and said, "This is your baton." And for the rest of the evening, I stood in the middle

horses would come in and eat my furniture. The chickens loved my feather bed, and they'd come in and lay their eggs on there. It was really rustic. But we thought it was great at the time.

But we couldn't afford it, and [after a while] I didn't want to live there anymore. Mickey needed a place and was a band member and had the money, and wanted to build a studio in the barn. I was in love with Nicki [Scully's girlfriend] and we wanted a place and she was pregnant, so I moved out and Mickey moved in.

of the stage and conducted the orchestra. When he told me to hit the gong, I hit the gong.

MICKEY HART: Next thing I know he's hanging over the gong, and it's a ballad, and he's whipping the gong! Sweat was pouring off his face, he was playing the cowbell—he was as into it as anybody could be into anything. And he conducted the band. I gold-plated that cowbell.

After that, he understood a little more of what it was all about. He didn't want to get his feet wet, because he was an observer, not a participant. He was like a tavern keeper.

In the early fall of 1968, a meeting was held in which Pigpen and Bob Weir were fired from the band.

BOB WEIR: We were the junior musicians in the band, and Jerry and Phil in particular thought that we were sort of holding things back. The music wasn't able to get as free because it was hog-tied by our playing abilities, which was kind of true. I guess that what they were headed towards was fusion jazz, though that hadn't actually happened yet.

BOB MATTHEWS: Bobby was inventive in his mind, and that sometimes would drive Phil nuts because Bobby might not be able to perform it as he had conceived of it. But eventually, Bobby was able to pull it off and it had validity to it. It's just that sometimes it would be quite frustrating. Bobby, in his openness of looking at all possibilities, could be frustrating at times to a more organized creative-process person.

He did work very hard, and he was successful in his work. He showed his validity, and he had a place. He belonged there. Of course, as the years went by, it was a no-brainer. As a rhythm guitar player playing between Phil and Billy in the rhythm section, he did some phenomenal things. He's got an incredibly creative mind. Playing music, you've got to be right there that moment. It doesn't matter what you did two beats ago, it's what are you gonna do the next beat. And if you start getting good, you can start thinking about the next beat, and how it relates to 16 bars down the line.

ROCK SCULLY: [If the firing] had to happen, it came at a good time, because we were just sort of doodling in the studio. We weren't making any money. We didn't have any gigs booked, so there was really no loss, except emotionally. I was against it, but Jerry put it to me as the manager to do it. Phil was behind it, and so was Kreutzmann. But to fire nearly half your unit . . .

Pigpen took it very hard. It was horrible for him. He was crying about it later. I was really upset about it myself. I was upset with Jerry and Phil for making me do it—I thought it was something they should've handled.

I spent a lot of time with Pigpen through that period, because it was a number of weeks before they played with him again. What he did was play piano all day and all night. Bobby went off to practice, too, so they both took it to heart. I don't think it was ever meant to stick. I think they meant it as a warning.

GARY LAMBERT: I thought they were wrong then, and I think they probably knew they were wrong very shortly after they even considered it. A lot of Bobby's guitar playing was fully formed by then. If you listen to the guitar playing on "Cryptical Envelopment," Bob is playing this lovely little étude behind what Garcia's singing.

It speaks to what I'm sure were the various weird interpersonal dynamics in the band: why wasn't Phil being asked to play four-to-the-bar bass? I think 'cause Bobby was the junior member of the firm, and the Grateful Dead certainly had its moments of being like high school. Bobby got picked on to some extent.

The fact that Bobby stayed may have been the key to the survival of the band. If they had tried to get any weirder than they were at that point, combined with the cost overruns on *Anthem of the Sun* and all that stuff, they might not have survived as a band, period.

Now, Pigpen! That's almost more odd to me. I would have thought that they knew he was the only guy they had who could really get out front and captivate a crowd.

BOB WEIR: It wasn't the best time in my life. I kept working on guitar and singing. [I thought of trying to join another band] but I figured first things first—I oughta woodshed a bunch. I spent the time doing that and not thinking about what I was going to do next until I had woodshedded enough that I felt I had something fairly powerful to bring to whatever I was going to move into next. I never did get to that plateau.

I found myself back in the band; I don't remember how. After a while of playing without us, I guess they decided maybe it wasn't as full without us. I was into living it day to day at that point anyway, so it didn't much matter to me—hired or fired. Being back in the band, I more or less had nothing to lose. They could fire me again, but I'd seen that elephant, and it wasn't unthinkable for me.

JERRY GARCIA: My memory of it [is] that we never actually let [Pigpen] go; we just didn't want him playing keyboard because he just didn't know what to do on the kind of material we were writing. It seemed like we were heading [toward] some [musical] place in a big way and Pigpen just wasn't open to it. It's not that he couldn't have cut it; he actually could have dealt with it. He had the musicality to deal with it. He was a real musical guy; he was innately musical.

But the other thing is, we were off on a false note. We were doing something that wasn't really natural. We were doing music that was self-consciously weird. If we had paid more attention to Pigpen, it probably would've saved us a couple of years of fucking around.

ROCK SCULLY: Because of the fact that Pigpen never accepted LSD —he wasn't part of that consciousness—the talk about Pigpen was without Pigpen: "What are we going to do?" "Well, we're going to make room for him here, tell him to play quietly here." Then Jerry talked to him and said, "Look, we're going to do this and we want you to do this." Rather than yelling. It just became obvious, more to the band than it did to Pig, who just felt bad and didn't know why. And then he capitulated, actually—said, "I can't play on this," at which point we brought in backup and ended up with Tom Constanten.

TOM CONSTANTEN: [The "firing"] happened immediately before I joined the band full-time. It was stated at the time: the band was two bands, depending on whether Jerry was fronting it or Pigpen was fronting it.

Phil and Jerry could both be quite a martinet. Jerry could give you the look, and you knew that something that happened was wrong. He definitely had the power.

[Years later] Vince [Welnick] told me a story. Jerry said, "Do this . . ." Vince said, "But uh . . ." and Jerry said, "Don't argue with me!"

BOB WEIR: We were practicing a lot back then. We would practice seven days a week, many hours a day. We put a lot of work into the music, so the music was complex. That's one of the natural outcroppings of what happens when you take six or seven fairly bright young musicians and put them together for many hours a day for months on end. There's going to be a level of complexity you're not going to see from other groups.

We were all listening to a lot of North Indian classical music at the time, so we were borrowing from their rhythmic structures a lot; or the drums would follow the lead line and we did a lot of odd time signatures, placing them against each other. It was really heavy, mental stuff, real precise and real structured. That's part of what made it ultimately kind of limiting.

I can't say I'm altogether sad that era ended, because that complicated music didn't come off more often than not. Usually it was sort of, "Nice try, guys." It wasn't the kind of stuff that was easy to play and easy to lean into.

In the end, the so-called firing "didn't stick," as Garcia put it. There were no Grateful Dead gigs without Weir and Pigpen, though the others did play a few loose jam session shows at the Matrix as Mickey and the Hartbeats, with guests ranging from Elvin Bishop and Paul Butterfield to Airplane bassist Jack Casady. And when sessions for *Aoxomoxoa* began that September at Pacific Recording in San Mateo, Pigpen was not included; in fact he is not on the finished album, though he does appear on the musician list of who plays what as "Ron McKernan—Pigpen." Live, he continued to be a major force in the band, a showman extraordinaire.

ALLAN ARKUSH: In the winter of '69, I was working as an usher at the Fillmore East. I was walking down Second Avenue, and it was freezing. The theater lights were on, and that was unusual on a Sunday; the shows were Friday and Saturday.

I went up to the door, and there was the guy who was always at the door. "What's going on?" "The Dead are rehearsing." They were playing that week with Janis Joplin. I went in with my sandwich to watch.

They were sitting up on the stage on chairs. They had a big tub of beer and soda and they were rehearsing, hanging, and talking. It wasn't a very strict rehearsal. They would play the beginnings of songs, jam, noodle off, and then noodle back, but not for very long, and then play the ending.

I took out my sandwich, and I was sitting with my feet up on the stage, watching. They were locked in, playing. At one point, I got this Garcia stare, when he kind of sees you but he's looking through you.

In my mind, I was like: "Boy, I'd like a beer with this sandwich." When they were finished noodling, he went over to the cooler, grabbed a beer, and came over and gave me a beer. There was no conversation.

On the first night with Janis Joplin, they opened for her. They played, like, forty-five minutes. It seemed pretty tight. It was nice that the Dead were there, but all the focus was on Janis.

In the late show, she went on first. And in that late show, *it* happened. They did "Dark Star," with Mickey playing the gong. And it was clear that this was what it was all about. [Both sets were released in 1997 as *Fillmore East 2-11-69*.]

So now everyone was into the Dead: "When are the Dead coming back?" They came back in June. By then, I had listened to *Aoxomoxoa*, and we all kind of had a buzz: the Grateful Dead were really, really good.

> In the winter of 1969, Garcia, Mountain Girl and her daughter, Sunshine Kesey, and Robert Hunter and his girlfriend, Christie Bourne, were living together in Larkspur (southern Marin County). This marked the beginning of the most productive phase of Hunter and Garcia's songwriting collaborations, starting with "Dupree's Diamond Blues" and "Mountains of the Moon" from *Aoxomoxoa*, and encompassing most of the songs that would turn up on *Workingman's Dead* and *American Beauty*.

CAROLYN "MOUNTAIN GIRL" GARCIA: It was a charming house. It was on a couple-of-acre lot with great big redwood trees, shady, backing up on the creek. Janis Joplin's house was like a ten-minute walk at the end of Baltimore Canyon.

JERRY GARCIA: It was the basic thing of friendship, economics, and all that stuff. We had a nice big house that we could afford to live in together but probably couldn't have afforded separately at that

ALLAN ARKUSH: All I remember from the set was Garcia and the drummers. I remember the drummers going away and not playing, and Mickey playing the gong, and the music becoming completely without rhythm. And somewhere in there was "St. Stephen," into what I now know was "The Eleven." It flowed from one song to another, which was a huge revelation. That had not happened in that way, with that power, in any show I had seen of them before.

point. It was a nice place to be, and Hunter was kind of floatin' at that point.

ROBERT HUNTER: I was sleepin' on floors and stuff and he took me in.

JERRY GARCIA: Everything was fine until Babbs moved in with us. It was funny as hell. [Babbs] had the bus out front, him and Gretch [Gretchen Fetchin, of Acid Tests/Pranksters fame], and they had a couple of kids at the time; they were just starting out.

ROBERT HUNTER: I wanted to seriously concentrate on the forward thrust of my lyrical bent, but Babbs wouldn't have it.

JERRY GARCIA: Simply wouldn't allow it!

ROBERT HUNTER: He'd be playing his tuba, driving us crazy.

KEN BABBS: It was actually a baritone horn. In '68, folks from the Hog Farm came around to Kesey's [in Oregon], and when they left, Gretch and I spent the whole summer traveling with 'em. We ended up down in New Mexico [where the Hog Farm had set up a commune]. It was a good scene; there was a lot happening down there. While we were there, I met John Muir's grandson, who wrote that popular book about VWs [*How to Keep Your Volkswagen Alive,* published in 1969]. He had an Army-green bus he had bought at Fort Ord at an auction and I liked it because you could stand up in it—you couldn't stand up straight in our original [Merry Prankster] bus. So I bought it from him for about four hundred dollars. [That fall] I went to Ohio, where I had relatives, and then that winter we drove back to California, got to Larkspur, and parked outside of the house where Jerry and Mountain Girl and Bob and his girlfriend were, and that was a nice scene. It was a very creative environment. I felt very fortunate to be able to see how they worked together, bouncing ideas back and forth, Jerry always working on his guitar, and also Bob contributing to the music. They did a lot of [songwriting] on a reel-to-reel tape recorder. It was a 4-track, so they could add another track and you could see how the song was evolving.

The bus was parked on the street right outside their house. We slept in the bus but we'd use their shower and the bathroom. That bus was nicely laid out, with a bed and kitchen area.

CAROLYN "MOUNTAIN GIRL" GARCIA: Babbs was on his fifth and sixth kids. He always lived really close to the ground and made do with very little. We were living in the lap of luxury by comparison, with a fireplace and bedrooms, even though we didn't have much furniture to speak of.

KEN BABBS: Sometime in there, the Grateful Dead offered me a job. They had this warehouse, Alembic, and they wanted me to go up there and be the guy who stayed there all the time, park my bus there. It was fenced in and there was this courtyard, and the building itself was on the back of the lot. In the front of the lot was an office with a bathroom, so we could use that and then we'd cook on the bus. That was a great time. They were paying me; I even had health insurance.

Come about May, though, I was itching to leave. I knew I wasn't going to work for the Grateful Dead long. They're good friends, but I wasn't that kind of guy. So we headed out again.

OWSLEY STANLEY: Shortly after I joined back up with the Dead, they found a warehouse out near Hamilton Air Force Base in Novato and moved out there. During this period of time I had met [Ampex engineer Ron] Wickersham because he was working with the recording scene on *Aoxomoxoa*. I knew he was an electronic whiz, a tape recorder whiz, and an audio [whiz]. Along the way I'd met Rick Turner, who I knew was an absolutely beautiful maker of acoustic instruments. He knew how to do the wood and all that sort of thing.

I sort of stuck them together in the same pot and said, "We've got to build better instruments and get the electronics together." I thought that it should be called Alembic because [in alchemy] the alembic was the vessel in which everything breaks down, and then it's built back up. That's what we were trying to do: we were trying to take all of the technology and all of the experience and put it into a vessel. It was also the concept of a place of where it could be done: the warehouse was sort of thought of as the Alembic.

SUSAN WICKERSHAM: In March of '69 we moved up to Novato and shared the building with the Dead. Alembic was supposed to be, in Bear's idea, an extension of the Grateful Dead. Here's this arm over here, Alembic, where we have a think tank and wonderful experiments in audio. The Dead really weren't interested in doing that as part of the Dead, especially with [new manager] Lenny Hart. He wanted to cut off all the expenses. We never got a single paycheck from the Grateful Dead. Bear would give me five hundred dollars here, a few hundred there. It was not a paycheck.

I opened up the first Alembic bank account. My first invoice was to Lenny Hart for the amplifiers we had just redone.

RON WICKERSHAM: That big lab? The day we came up, Mickey Hart's father had that thing cleared out. All the lab components, all boxed up. We had to go out in the back into a tin shack. I put all kinds of gutters on because the thing leaked. It had inside gutters. You'd have to get out of there and roll up the great big door to go to the bathroom.

SUSAN WICKERSHAM: Bear was a catalyst to bring forces together. That's what he's good at. He recognized talent.

JONATHAN RIESTER: Owsley's an arrogant, egomaniacal motherfucker and I love him dearly. He's one of the most irritating people I've ever met in my entire life. I'm the only man who ever hit Owsley: I punched him out once at the Avalon Ballroom. We had our whole sound system set, and Phil and Jerry told me, "Don't let Owsley fuck with the sound system. It's perfect. We want it just the way it is." That was at a soundcheck, and when we came back in the evening to play, the whole place smelled like a soldering iron. It was horrible. He'd changed it all! I flipped on him and punched him in the chest really hard.

BOB MATTHEWS: I was hired by Brian Rohan on behalf of Mercury Records to do one-session demos for Bay Area bands that were being considered for recording contracts. I got experience recording at this studio called Pacific Recording [in San Mateo], owned by Paul Curcio, who was one of the Autumn Records people. I did the Santana demo that sold them to Columbia. Betty [Cantor-Jackson] went with me and she was my assistant.

I managed to negotiate a really sweet deal for using the studio; we got a lot of free time. We were gonna learn how to record ourselves. And of course, with [*Aoxomoxoa*], we learned everything not to do when recording an album. But we learned it really well, because the next studio album we did was *Workingman's Dead,* which was a demonstration of how to go into a studio, not take a lot of time, feel good about what you were doing, and when you were done with it be happy rather than never wanting to see it again.

The studio's chief engineer, Ron Wickersham, was also an engineer at Ampex. We came to work one day, and here was the 16-track. We had spent so much time with the 8-track trying to combine tracks, and make executive decisions about what made sense to do when. So this was a whole new day.

INTERVIEWER: I'm guessing there was someone at Warner Bros. who started tearing his hair out when he realized you were restarting the album on 16-track.

BOB MATTHEWS: Oh, yeah, his name was Joe Smith and he was the president of the record company.

I seem to remember that the final cost of doing that album was something like $150,000, which was a hell of a lot of money for a fringe band that had live performance popularity but sure didn't have any draw in the record stores. So yeah, they were tearing their hair out.

Aoxomoxoa was the first album they were allowed to do completely on their own. I think you have to give a little bit of credit to Warner Bros. for letting them pull off *Anthem of the Sun*. But this was our opportunity to get better at being recording engineers. [Betty and I] would be given a task—either a specific technical description or an aesthetic goal—and it was our job to realize that for them. Their ideas were as new to them as our solutions were to us; we were both finding our way. But it was very positive.

BETTY CANTOR-JACKSON: We did all kinds of experimental things. We miked close up; we miked way in the back of the room. The whole Grateful Dead scene was kind of an R and D thing for all sorts of areas, so we would try things out. Experimental! "Yes, we'll go for that, we don't care." "You're not supposed to do that?" "Yeah, let's see what happens."

BOB MATTHEWS: The 16-track enabled us to have one track for every input on the stage. Four vocals, the drums, two basses, rhythm guitar, lead guitar, and the organ. It provided the solution to the live recording problem I had previously isolated with 8-track, where we had to make decisions in the back of the truck about mixing. Once you made that mix, it was locked in stone. There was nothing you could do to change it. With the 16-track, we didn't have to make those decisions. We did the world's first live 16-track recording on New Year's Eve '68 [at Winterland].

TOM CONSTANTEN: The way most of [*Aoxomoxoa*] was put together is, we would put down the rhythm section first, then guitars, then keyboards, and the vocals last. On my part [for "Dupree's Diamond Blues"] I tried to simulate a sort of funky calliope sound on the Hammond organ. I also put glockenspiel on there. That was part of the mania when 16-tracks came in. We filled those tracks pretty quickly.

BOB WEIR: A lot of that record is gratuitous and complex for the sake of being complex. It's over-produced and -arranged. It was our first recording with 16-track, and we felt kinda obliged to use all 16 tracks—all the time! We'd get all the band instruments recorded on the first 8 and then wonder what the hell we could do with the rest.

TOM CONSTANTEN: Everything was essentially subject to Jerry's approval, and he would make recommendations, or ideas would be presented to him and he'd sound it out. Sometimes things would be tried just to try them, so we weren't doing the same thing all the time.

ROBERT HUNTER: I was doing background vocals for "China Cat Sunflower" during the *Aoxomoxoa* sessions, and Phil looked at me and said, "Can you ever sing the same line twice the same way?" and I said, "I don't think I can." So I bowed out and continued to offer my perspective on which takes were good and the like.

BOB MATTHEWS: We were finishing up *Aoxomoxoa* while we were doing the Fillmore and the Avalon recordings that precipitated *Live Dead*. We had it rehearsed: when a reel ran out, we had two people on the take-up reel—one to pick up the reel of recorded tape and slam down the empty and another one over on the other side, taking off the empty and putting a full one on, running it through the heads, around the [hub], and hitting RECORD and PLAY. We got to the point where we could do it in about thirty-five seconds.

They took time out from *Aoxomoxoa*, reviewed all the performances, selected the performances, made a mix of those performances, and put 'em on the shelf. Bear said, "You should go in and make a mix, because [theirs] doesn't represent the methodology of what you recorded." So I went to the management of PHR [Pacific High Recording] and called in a favor. I asked for time to work on this on off-hours. The band said okay, as long as it didn't cost anything.

Upon completion of those mixes, I submitted it to the band. The next thing I knew, it had a release date: November 10, 1969, my twenty-second birthday. *Live Dead* is a milestone. That was really my first—I'm reluctant to use the word—masterpiece. What the band was thinking at that time was, "We want to present an evening with the Grateful Dead."

JERRY GARCIA (1971): It's good. It had "Dark Star" on it, a real good version of it. We only recorded a few gigs to get that album. We were after a certain sequence in the music, in the sense of it being a serious, long composition, musically, and then a recording of it. It's our music at one of its really good moments.

CHAPTER 4

Psychedelic Americana

JOHN ZIAS (Musician): In 1969, they started bringing in something wholly unexpected. Cowboy songs and rootsy music seemed like a 270-degree turn. They were sort of an esoteric band, and they seemed to attract an esoteric audience that was there for some sort of cranial rearrangement.

When they play roots music, it doesn't sound like anybody else playing roots music. There's always a third eye somewhere, in telling the story, and it's elucidating a lot more than the surface. Anything they touched had some level of wisdom to it, and it was easy to forgive certain little transgressions—they're a little out of tune, or they blew an ending. In conventional terms, those are extremely important things, but in Grateful Dead terms it was secondary. Even in the shortest of tunes, they still took you to a place. It was a journey; it was always transportational.

Grateful Dead music never needed a conventional rhythm section; that would have destroyed Grateful Dead music. My ear gravitated a lot toward Lesh's sensibilities because he always kept their sound sort of on a rhythmic tilt-a-whirl.

GARY LAMBERT: I knew a lot of people who got off the bus around the time of *Workingman's Dead* and *American Beauty*, when everyone else was jumping on. Some of that may have been the Dead losing their patina of hip exclusivity, getting popular, and some people couldn't bear that. Other people thought they were becoming too conventional, too folky, too consonant. But it delighted me, and it seemed utterly natural, because if you knew their roots, if you knew where those guys came from as musicians—it wasn't just "Let's jump on the country-rock bandwagon" or "Let's jump on the Crosby, Stills, and Nash bandwagon"—it was something that was in all these guys. They were just incorporating stuff they'd loved all along. I think they felt, "Maybe we've taken weirdness for its own sake as far as we can. We can play the Matrix for the rest of our lives, or we can develop some survival skills that also involve making good music." I think those were both things they'd considered. They had to make some simple records after making these incredibly ornate and catastrophically expensive ones. Then, just by wonderful happenstance, they got really good at writing songs.

Those shows in '69 were plenty weird, too. And when they got weird, they fully committed to the weird. So the little sprinklings of country-rock were just little bits of lagniappe amidst the weirdness. But even then—*Aoxomoxoa* came out that year, and that was a little bit of a pull-back from *Anthem of the Sun* in that there were songs. "Dupree's Diamond Blues" and "Doin' That Rag" had that slight hint of their jug band heritage. So even by early '69, there were some intimations: Let's get . . . not less weird, but less exclusively weird.

It struck me that what the Dead realized about their presentation was kind of in macrocosm what Phil Lesh realized when he saw *A Hard Day's Night*: "I don't want to be this weird academic composer anymore—I want to make chicks scream." He didn't say exactly that, but just by virtue of the way they were drawing in ever-larger places, they were making popular music whether they liked it or not. So they had to figure out a way of reconciling those extremes of theirs, and they did it rather skillfully.

It wasn't to the detriment of the psychedelic stuff in the slightest. They learned how to compartmentalize, and I think it helped them learn how to pace the show. In that day, selling out the Fillmore East was a big deal for them, because they had been playing much smaller places or playing to half-houses. Once *Workingman's* was out and they were getting some real FM airplay, suddenly getting a ticket to the Dead show becomes a bigger deal. I think they had higher expectations of themselves, as well as wanting to cater to an audience's expectations. They wanted to do a coherent, exciting show but still leave room for all this exploration of terra incognita. They really managed to balance it beautifully. I thought to a great extent that they did that pretty well through their whole career.

ROBERT HUNTER: [The Western motifs and flavors began to come to the fore] through Jerry's and my mutual interest in folk and bluegrass music. Dylan came out with the *John Wesley Harding* album, and the Band came out with [*Music From*] *Big Pink,* and all of a sudden Dylan gave "permission" for areas that you just wouldn't think would figure into popular music.

> Jerry bought a pedal steel guitar, and soon found an outlet for it with his pals David Nelson and John "Marmaduke" Dawson.

DAVID NELSON: I remember going up to Jerry's house in Larkspur with John. We had Bob Matthews on bass. We practiced John's tunes, and then we thought, "Hey, let's get a gig! We can get Mickey to play drums!" We booked two or three nights at the Bear's Lair [on the UC Berkeley campus]. They said, "What do you call the band?" and Jerry blurts out, "The Murdering Punks!" Which was very

ROBERT HUNTER: I remember Phil once saying, "Can you write anything without cards, trains, and crows in it?" So I wrote a song called "Cards, Trains, and Crows," but I don't think I handed it over.

timely, because right around then the Manson killings happened. The guy wanted to call it Jerry Garcia and Friends, which Jerry hated, of course. "I'm a sideman!" he'd say. So we got down to thinking in earnest about a name, which is really hard, because once someone starts going funny, it gets crazier and crazier. It's hopeless! Fortunately we had Hunter there, and he's down to earth and serious. Or at least he can be, unlike the rest of us. He said, "How about the Riders of the Purple Sage [after the Zane Grey novel]?" And I said, "There's already a Riders of the Purple Sage band." So we became the New Riders of the Purple Sage.

MICKEY HART: Jerry wanted to learn the pedal steel. I wanted to learn about country and western music. We had Marmaduke, Bob Matthews, and David Nelson, and we set up in my barn.

Being in the Dead was like being in a space suit, and being in the New Riders was like wearing a pair of jeans.

The Woodstock Music and Arts Festival (August 15–17, 1969) became known as a monumental event in counterculture history. It was a debacle for the Dead, whose performance was not included on either films or albums until many years later, when a few tracks made it onto some fortieth-anniversary compilations.

ROCK SCULLY: [Woodstock producer] Michael Lang's people really went a long way to assuage [our doubts about playing there]. They went after Kesey and the Pranksters to be kind of overseers of security, and Wavy Gravy [then Hugh Romney of the Hog Farm collective] to help feed people and look after bum trips and all that kind of stuff, so eventually they met most of our demands and we believed it might run fairly smoothly. What went against all that, though, was they kept adding bands and making it bigger and bigger, which of course changes the equation of how you do things all the way down the line.

I don't remember offhand what we got paid at Woodstock [$15,000], but it was fairly hefty for that time. There were certainly other bands on the bill that were selling more records than us and could demand more money, but they really wanted us there and thought we should be there; even back then we were sort of a mythological, sociological movement rather than a musical one.

BOB WEIR: Once I got there I camped out about half a mile from the stage. I sort of drifted around. It was pretty filthy. It was muddy. And there wasn't enough food or facilities. If it had gone on for a month, it would have looked like a summer version of Valley Forge. On the other hand, everybody was pretty much into it. As long as they were there, they were going to make the best of it.

ROCK SCULLY: We were supposed to go on late Saturday afternoon, but everything was running so far behind from Friday that the revised plan had us going on right at sundown, which was a very difficult time to go on in the acid years because people go through a big transition from day to night when they're tripping. But we ended up going on later than planned anyway.

In order to facilitate the switching of bands, all the different groups' gear was sitting on large, movable pallets with wheels under them. Those pallets then slid together to form a riser, which the band played on.

OWSLEY STANLEY: The rotating "cookies" were built on furniture casters, not commercial units. Ram Rod and I took one look and begged that we be allowed to set up on the stage floor, because we knew our gear was so heavy it would collapse the casters. We were refused this option, and sure enough the setup had rotated only about a foot when the casters simply folded over, plopping the whole thing down on the spot. This caused a lot of strife, and somehow we were blamed for it.

ROCK SCULLY: So there we are at sundown, when we're supposed to be playing, scrambling to move all the equipment off one pallet and onto a new one, which already had gear from the next band on it. So that took an hour or even more. It was just one of those bummers.

OWSLEY STANLEY: There was a two-way radio that communicated with the helicopters ferrying people on and off the site. The radio was heard as leakage at a considerable volume in the PA and in many of the musicians' amps. No one from the venue seemed to know how, or care, to fix it. So when we finally got set up and plugged in, Phil's bass had the radio at a volume higher than his own strings.

ROCK SCULLY: After I don't know how many days of rain the week prior to the show, the ground was completely covered in mud. It had been decided there was going to be a light show behind the Dead, so there was this monster screen that they lowered while the Dead was playing. A gust of wind came up and caught the screen like a sail, and the entire stage—which was huge—started to shudder and slide down the hill. So all the crew and myself and a few others whipped out our Buck knives and started rending huge holes in this monstrously expensive screen, to let the wind through. Meanwhile, all the stage crew down below were shoring up [the stage] with wooden blocks to try to keep it from collapsing. It was outrageous.

TOM CONSTANTEN: We could hear the stage creaking and feel it shifting under us, which was pretty scary for everyone. Phil said he had visions of a headline in the next day's paper: "Huge Rock 'n' Roll Disaster: Thousands Maimed!"

ROCK SCULLY: All day long, Wavy had been making announcements: "Don't take the brown acid," and that sort of thing. Well, right in the middle of our first song, some guy came running out with a big bag full of that brown acid and started flinging it into the audience. I don't know how the hell he got onstage, but it completely freaked me out, and I had him removed immediately.

COUNTRY JOE McDONALD (To the crowd, a couple of songs into the Dead's set): Hello, people. A little pause here; I'd like to tell you something. My name is Country Joe. You know, all us people from the Bay Area, we're real LSD freaks. We take a lot of LSD, we've taken a lot of LSD, we know what LSD is. But I'll tell you one thing—the stuff they're passing out here today may or may not be LSD, but there's a chance you won't have a very good trip. Now, what you're supposed to do after you know that is you're supposed to stop takin' it. Now, if you've taken it already, don't worry, because you're not poisoned and you won't die, but if you haven't taken it, I'd recommend you don't take it and just listen to the music and wait till you can get some stuff that you know is good— if that's your inclination. That's called common sense. Right on!

BOB WEIR: It was raining toads when we played. The rain was part of our nightmare. The other part was our sound man, who decided the ground situation on the stage was all wrong. It took him about two hours to change it, which held up the show. He finally got it set up the way he wanted it, but every time I touched my instrument, I got a shock. The stage was wet and the electricity was coming through me. I was conducting! Touching my guitar was nearly fatal. There was a great big blue spark about the size of a baseball, and I got lifted off my feet and sent back eight or ten feet to my amplifier.

JONATHAN RIESTER: What I remember is being high on LSD for four days, and insanity. I looked at Rakow and said, "I've had it. I don't know about anybody else, but I'm leaving. I have one car and I know I'm getting out." I left five rent-a-cars behind. Garcia bailed, too.

It was the concert film *Woodstock* that made Woodstock into the pop-culture watershed, really, but there was a promising vibe in the immediate aftermath, too. Bill Graham observed in a 1984 interview that this event demonstrated that rock 'n' roll could be a big business. Huge music festivals began to be a Thing.

It all came to a different kind of head on December 6, 1969, in Northern California, when a free concert turned into a scene out of Hieronymus Bosch.

RHONEY STANLEY (Grateful Dead/Alembic employee): Rock Scully was pivotal in this idea about a free concert for the Grateful Dead and the San Francisco psychedelic bands with the Rolling Stones. Sam Cutler was the representative of the Rolling Stones. First we wanted to do Golden Gate Park. Bear kept saying the way the government was going to react against the psychedelic bands was to stop allowing them to have permits to do outside events, and that's exactly what happened—we couldn't get a permit to do this event in Golden Gate Park. We hired Melvin Belli, who had this fancy team of lawyers. Still, we couldn't get it.

JERRY GARCIA (1971): It was going to be a chance for all these various community elements to participate in sort of a party for the Rolling Stones. That was the original concept, but then we couldn't have it in Golden Gate Park, so that was really the end of the plan as it was supposed to have happened. That eliminated the possibility for any community scene in San Francisco because of the transportation problem—how many Chicanos, Chinese, or blacks are going to be able to get a bus to wherever-the-fuck? And then we began operating on sheer kinetic energy. Everyone was feeling good about it. Chet Helms was doing stuff, and Emmett [Grogan of the Diggers] and Chip Monck [of the Woodstock production team], and these solid, together, hard-working people, but somehow the sense of it escaped everybody.

RHONEY STANLEY: Finally, we got Sears Point Raceway, near Black Point in Novato. It was terrific because it was fifteen minutes away from Alembic. The Alembic team was Ram Rod, Jackson, Sonny [Heard], Hagen, and Bear. They were doing the sound and setting up the whole thing. They went out there and built the infrastructure, the stage, the speaker towers, and all that stuff.

Then Mick Jagger leaked to the press that they were doing a free concert. The promoters of Sears Point pulled the permit the day before the show, after they'd already set up the stage and the speaker towers.

We were on the phone all day. We had the Diggers helping plan this free concert. They were often involved whenever there was anything free.

The crew and Bear had to pull down everything they had set up at Sears Point and drive it all to this new place, Altamont, which was in the worst part of [Northern] California. There was a women's prison there; there was a high-security men's prison near there. And it was a racetrack. We had this vibe of negativism before we even got there.

They worked all night. I went over on the first helicopter to see how they were doing. They literally had the lights on all night. They were up for hours. The circadian rhythm was destroyed. It was hard. The setup was the hardest I'd ever seen.

Bear never got acid to give out. There was no free acid at Altamont, because he was too busy working on sound. I would say that was one of the reasons it failed: no LSD.

The Grateful Dead met at Altamont and decided they didn't want to go on. The vibes here were too negative. Mountain Girl was active in trying to get them not to play. "Shall we play?" I heard Phil saying that. Jerry said, "No way, man." He was wearing a poncho. "No way, man." They met maybe five or ten minutes and then headed for the heliport.

ROCK SCULLY: It was certainly a scary event, though about three quarters of the crowd had no idea what was going on and had a great time. There was nothing psychedelic about Altamont. That was reds and red wine and downers; it was fucked up.

CAROLYN "MOUNTAIN GIRL" GARCIA: We were in Jonathan's truck, hiding, as people were getting chased across the stage by Hells Angels. Pool cues were swinging and the crowd was surging back and forth. It was just an awful experience. We couldn't wait to get out of there, but unfortunately it was really hard to get out.

JERRY GARCIA (1970): There's no question that Altamont was a heavy trip. I've worked out the essence of the way it was that day, and it was so weird, man. I took some STP, and you just don't know. . . . Phil and I got off the helicopter and we came down through the crowd, and it was like Dante's Inferno. It was spreading out in concentric waves. It was weird . . . fuck, it was weird. It wasn't just the Angels. There were weird kinds of psychic violence happening around the edges that didn't have anything to do with blows. Shit, I don't know—spiritual panic or something. And then there were all these anonymous, borderline, violent street types that aren't necessarily "heads"—they may take dope, but that doesn't mean they are heads—and there was a lot of, you know, the Top Forty world.

Long hair doesn't work anymore as a distinguishing characteristic, but it never did in the first place. What there was in the first place was a loosely knit group of people who knew each other, one way or another, proximity or association, who were just getting shit on— makin' it a little easier for everybody, makin' new connections, getting some energy happening. Intelligent people, not drug sluggers.

RHONEY STANLEY: Jerry never met Mick Jagger. That was our other hope: that Jerry and Mick Jagger would get together. We were imagining what this would be like, but it never happened. It was a big disappointment.

Afterwards, I read about Phil saying that his decision [not to play] might not have been right, that maybe if they had played they would have changed the vibes. But I don't think they would have. They didn't want to be part of it. They didn't want to be associated with it.

At the end of the show, I went with Sam [Cutler, the Stones' tour manager] and Rock. We sort of hung out in this apartment in San Francisco, under cover. We didn't know what the ramifications were going to be. We had lawyers working on it. We thought we might be indicted for murder.

PAUL KANTNER: You never would have expected [Altamont] to happen. The bikers were the babysitters at the Human Be-In, [taking care of] lost children. . . . They didn't have an altogether bad reputation. But they weren't there that day; it turned out that most of them were having a big meeting in Oakland, and a lot of the guys who were there and causing a lot of the hassle were neo-phytes, young would-bes—early trainees, as it were. The older guys, who usually keep them in line—somewhat the way a road manager keeps a band in line when there's cops following them in squad cars in Ohio—weren't present that day. Had they been there, I think, just for their own good PR and survivability within the community, they'd have seen that that was a real artless way of handling the situation. It could have been handled in a much more admirable way, even from their point of view. They didn't have to get drugged and violent that way. It was just a day gone out of control, for a lot of ele-ments. I don't blame it on the Hells Angels. I blame it on the people who were there, but I don't characterize that as "the Hells Angels."

JERRY GARCIA (1970): I think the Angels behaved properly; I mean, they did just what they would do, so they were not out of character. Also, I don't think it was strictly a trip on the Angels. 'Cause the An-gels in California are surrounded by prospects—people who want to be Angels, and their way of showing they could be Angels is to come on bad. And they're the ones who are mostly responsible. Most of the Angels I know are into partying.

I think Altamont was a valuable experience for everyone who was able to learn from it, and I think that everyone who was supposed to did. . . . Obviously, it was something very heavy for us to see what we had initiated by just, on a good day back in '65, goin' to the Pan-handle and settin' up and playin' for free—we saw it turn into that. It wasn't lost on us, man.

CAROLYN "MOUNTAIN GIRL" GARCIA: Altamont made things dif-ficult for a while. It spoiled the joy. We couldn't say, "Oh, boy, let's do a free concert" anymore. It was like, "Oh, shit, we'll never be able to do anything free ever again."

In his memoir *You Can't Always Get What You Want* (2010), Sam Cutler describes being left behind by the Rolling Stones to deal with the cops and the Angels and the rest of the Altamont fall-out. He laid low at Jerry and Mountain Girl's house, and wound

| up going to work for the Grateful Dead.

ROSIE McGEE: There was this revolving door of road managers and secretaries, although Gail [Hellund] hung in there for a long time. [Cutler] first came in when the Stones left him to fend for himself after Altamont. Jerry and Mountain Girl took him in. He lived with them for a while. I don't know at what point he became the road manager. The management scenarios are very convoluted.

[McIntire and Cutler] were opposites; black and white, dark and blond. McIntire had 100 percent integrity, quite snobbish but lovable. He was really a solid citizen.

Cutler, at the time, I didn't know very well. My impression was that he was part of the Pleasure Crew, which was a bunch of guys who hung out together. They'd travel with the band, or show up. It was obvious when I visited a couple of them that money wasn't an issue.

SAM CUTLER: What the Grateful Dead needed was to learn how to be a successful band. It's a kind of ironic thing—until you can picture success, and how it works, and what you're going to do with it, and what's necessary to achieve it, it doesn't happen. So one of the ways you can make that happen in a band is to have somebody that already knows what organizing tours and all that is like.

The Grateful Dead, prior to my working with them, was basically like family. They didn't come from—if you like—a professional, music business background. They were all friends. And that's one of the charming things about the Grateful Dead; very special. When I joined them, the band was moderately successful in a West Coast sense, but they hadn't really cracked it in terms of a national presence in the United States. They were much better known on the West Coast than on the East Coast, except maybe in New York and Boston.

Jerry knew that apart from the fact that they had the sound together and the playing was good, the rest of it was chaos. Because, you know, everything developed by a kind of form of strange West Coast osmosis. Things weren't the way they were as a result of planning. They were almost like the way they were as a result of kind of a groovy California default more than anything else. Which in itself wasn't necessarily so bad, but Garcia was particularly interested, when we first chatted, in how the Rolling Stones organized things—how they ran their office, how did they do the bank accounts, who could sign checks. The Grateful Dead hated dealing with business, but it was forced upon them because they wanted to survive and they wanted to try and take as many of their people with them as possible.

In order to do that, then, they had no choice but to become efficient. Gotta pay the bills, gotta pay the taxes. All these things gotta be done, whether you like it or not. So they made a transition from being what you could not unkindly describe as a "hippie collective" into something else, which was a take-care-of-business, hardcore, stripped-down, lean, kind of mean, working band out on the road. Everyone is relying on you for their bread and butter, so yeah, the money has got to come from somewhere. Then, of course, the Grateful Dead wanted it to sound better: they wanted production values. They wanted their own light and sound on the road. Well, all of this costs money. It has to be paid for, so all these things tie into one another.

At that time, the only way they ever really made any money was by doing gigs. So the first year that I was with the Grateful Dead, we did 142 gigs. That's a lot of gigs with a big band; a lot of work, but everybody made the commitment to the work load. The first two years I was with the band, we worked our butts off. Hardest I've ever worked with a band, anyway. And the reason for that was simple: there was no other way the money was going to be forthcoming. The Grateful Dead were committed to that as a way of saving themselves economically. You want to play in Buffalo, you want to play in Philadelphia, you want to play in wherever it is, you need X amount of money to be able to get there. Before I joined them, they used to come back from tour and they never had any money. There's not really much point in going out on tour and coming back, having had a wonderful time, but no money, because you need money to go back out on tour. And you need money to pay the girls in the office, pay the office rent; it's endless. A rock 'n' roll band is a bit like a yacht. It's a hole in the ocean that you pour money into. There are always things to spend money on with a band.

It was a pretty hard time there for a while. There was no money; there was no money on tour. I remember when I introduced [the concept of] per diems. Nobody had ever heard of that before. That was a novel idea, that everyone gets ten dollars a day, so you could eat something. I asked Pigpen, "What did you do before that?"

He said, "Oh, you used to talk to Rock and Danny and get money off them."

"How much would they give you?"

"Well, that depended on what you wanted."

So if you had a good rap, you got lots of money, and if you had a shit rap, you got no money, and that was basically it. I said, "No, no, no, no! We'll all get the same. Everyone gets ten dollars." Of course, if you take twelve guys on the crew and six to seven guys in the band, the tour manager, and the girl that keeps the accounts on the road, all of a sudden it's twenty people—there's two hundred dollars a day. Being on the road, in and of itself, is an expense. It forces people that have been, let's say, a little bit cavalier about such things, to actually focus a bit harder on the reality.

In 1969, the band hired Mickey Hart's long-estranged father, Lenny, to manage the money.

RHONEY STANLEY: Jerry said that [Lenny Hart] could be no worse than what we already had—and maybe, given that he was family, he would be better. We respected him because he was a musician: he was a drummer who had played in big bands.

ROCK SCULLY: It's been insinuated that Danny [Rifkin] and I were mismanaging the band. Danny and I didn't really have a lot of experience in finances when it grew to the size it was growing to. We did whatever we could to try to save money with a machine that was chewing it up—and it was being chewed up by the makers of the music. They were spending their money on more equipment and a bigger and better sound system, and you couldn't argue with that 'cause we weren't selling records, we were selling tickets. We were desperate to please the crowds, make them happier.

We had a band meeting out at Mickey's ranch and he made this fevered pitch: "You guys don't know what you're doing with the money. My dad's a great guy with finances, and he can do the job." We had no beef with that, but we were going, "You sure you want your dad to be doing this? We don't know him. You haven't known him."

Then Lenny came in and told us what he could do and how he could do it, and it was all dealing with the IRS and getting us straightened out. But the IRS had nothing to do with renegotiating a contract with Warner Bros.—absolutely nothing. I [stressed] that Danny and I are doing the booking, and I've got the relationship with the record company. I was already talking with Clive Davis [about signing a new deal with Columbia Records when the Warner's deal was up]. He was to stay away from that.

[Then, while I was in England] the band goes to play in San Jose and Lenny's got all these papers and he says, "This is going to get you out of debt, because Warner Bros. is giving me this money. Can you sign this for me? We'll be ready for the IRS." Nobody sat down and read it; nobody knew what the hell was going on. Everybody signed it; it was like a three-year extension to the [Warner Bros.] contract—four more albums or something like that.

I was infuriated by the whole deal. Jerry said,

NED LAGIN: There were these softball games between the Grateful Dead and the Jefferson Airplane. I played in one, in Fairfax that summer [1970]. I forget who the Grateful Dead pitcher was; Paul Kantner was the pitcher for the Airplane. When they were ahead he was happy, and when they were behind he threatened to quit every five minutes. Jerry and I were next to each other in the outfield, I think Phil played second base. These games were remarkable for me personally because I found at least two people who were worse than me at softball. One was Phil, and by far the other was Jerry. A fly ball would come towards Jerry and he would run around in a circle with his hands up in the air like he was praying to God, and the ball would land—plop!— right on the ground next to him. He never got close to it.

"Cool out, cool out; calm down, Rock!" I said, "This is fucked up. You guys signed away everything we fought for. This is a disaster." He said, "We'll get to the bottom of it. Let's not blame anybody." I said, "That's not the way this is going to work, Jerry. You don't understand."

JONATHAN RIESTER: I wanted Bill Graham to be our business manager. Mickey overruled that because of his dad. We had just started to become successful, and Rock and I needed someone to deal with the money. All I wanted was credit cards to make it smooth on the road for the band. We thought [Lenny] was going to stay at home and take care of the money and give us a legitimate foundation.

The band was always wishy-washy. That was one of Garcia's bad character defects. He would go with the flow. Nobody wanted to hassle in those days. It was like, "What a bummer!" It's what we left our parents and the Midwest and started smoking pot for. We didn't want to deal with this shit.

BILL BELMONT: Lenny seemed to me to be completely out of place. But it's like with Rakow later: you embrace someone with what seems like a good idea, or someone who appears to be a guru or who can make it all happen for you. "He'll take care of the problems. We'll just go play music and have a good time"—which in essence is what happened. It's not really irresponsibility. You just don't always make the right choices.

RON RAKOW: The day I met Lenny Hart, I had an old lady, Lydia, who was pretty hip. We drove up to Mickey's ranch. I pull into the place with my old lady and there's this guy walking from the barn to the house wearing a sport coat, shirt and tie, and carrying a Bible in that way where the cross sort of sticks out above his heart. Lydia said, "Who the fuck is that crook?" She said, "Anyone who comes around this scene dressed like that, carrying a Bible like that, has got to be a crook." About three months later I went backstage to a gig at the Carousel Ballroom, I think, and Jerry said,

"Hey, Rak, you're going to have to come out of retirement and take us over again because [Lenny] is working us to death and there's no money." And the next thing I know there were major problems.

JERILYN BRANDELIUS: Lenny and Gail Hellund came to the Family Dog on the Great Highway, where I was working with Chet. Lenny was managing the Grateful Dead, and he came in and gave Chet this whole pitch about "We're going to make the Dead real famous and you won't be able to afford them anymore!"—all these grandiose things. He was like an Elmer Gantry kind of guy: the Reverend Lenny Hart!

RHONEY STANLEY: What Lenny was trying to do was book the Grateful Dead for gigs, but he came from this old era. He didn't understand that change had come, and that the places he was trying to book the Grateful Dead weren't right for the Grateful Dead. Whenever he got a rejection, he'd blame me. He'd say, "You didn't speak to them right." That was unpleasant.

Bear never trusted him. To Bear, the only reason that he was in it was for money. So where was he getting the money? We were broke. We didn't have any money. That was what made Bear suspicious.

ROSIE McGEE: I met him onstage at a gig; he was wearing a sports jacket and holding a Bible in his hand. Someone introduced me to him saying, "This is Lenny Hart, Mickey's father." I looked in his eyes and didn't like what I saw. I could see his resemblance with Mickey, but Mickey has intelligence and warmth. Lenny was shifty. I could tell right off the bat, and I didn't like that. I thought he was just visiting his son, but I became aware later that he had been hired as their manager.

When Lenny came into the scene they needed somebody trustworthy to be the secretary. I agreed to do it, but I could tell quickly that it was going to be a neutral job, answering the phone and opening the mail. There wasn't much to do at all. I didn't enjoy it, and I couldn't stand Lenny.

He was mostly absent—screwing the teller from the bank, we found out later. He was also lecherous, an unpleasant fellow. I went to the bank with him one day in his low-slung sports car. On the way to the bank he put his hand on my thigh and said something suggestive. It creeped me out. I said, "Just stop the car. You go to the bank by yourself." I got out and thought about it. I told the band, "I don't want to work for him anymore." That's when they found Rhoney, who was hanging around because the warehouse is where Alembic started. Bear and the Wickershams and Bob Thomas were all there. Rhoney was always hanging out with Bear, so they asked her to take over for me. She probably told Bear everything and was looking out for the band.

I don't know how long she did the job, but then they got Gail. That was the smartest move they ever made, because Gail had 100 percent integrity and nerves of steel.

GAIL HELLUND: I compare this to a normal person's fraternity and sorority days. That was our time when we were past being post-high-school whatever; we were developing a political consciousness; we all had our kids at the same time. It was a giant bunch of people who all really liked each other. I thought I had lucked into the best thing ever, to be working there. I could do the job with one hand tied behind my back. I would go to gigs at night, and be there at ten in the morning.

[Lenny] would try to dress less straight, and he would try to act like he was grooving to the music, but there was no way he was ever going to be one of us.

All Lenny did was be the accountant; he didn't do anything else. I interacted with [booking agency] Monterey Peninsula Artists. I took care of all the tour paperwork. I basically acted like a manager. Jon would do a lot of the setup for a tour.

The first thing Lenny said was, "You can't put postage stamps on the letters." At that time, the [recipient] would pay postage due. Bills, letters went out with no postage stamps. I said, "This is kind of iffy. These are big bills we're paying here. If they don't get there —"

"No, just do it." He pocketed that money. I would tell the band things like that. That just delineates the guy's character to a tee.

The band had rented this auto parts warehouse at Hamilton Air Force Base, just off the frontage road before Bel Marin Keys. You drove down this long driveway. There were two storefront windows. One was a store, and one was an office. There was another office in back, and that was Alembic. I was in the store part, and Lenny was in the other front office.

The band practiced in the back, and if they were working, I couldn't talk on the phone—"Whoever you are, you'll have to call back. The band is rehearsing."

Lenny decided to move us to Family Dog on the Great Highway, with Chet and Jerilyn. I said, "This is not a good idea." Everybody had moved to Marin; nobody wanted to go back to San Francisco.

The band was on tour—and this is when they got busted in New Orleans [January 31, 1970]. McIntire was the road manager; the crew was Ram Rod, Hagen, and Jackson. I couldn't get a message through. Finally, I got a call back, and I thought they got my message—but they were calling to tell me that they got busted!

By the time the band got back, we were back in Marin. The band was furious when I told them!

Lenny was smart enough to tantalize all of us. One of the things he did was let everybody take advances. If my car broke down, he'd say, "Do you need a loan to get a new car? I could set it up where I'd take so much out of your salary every week . . ." He would give you your check, and then he'd make another check out for the amount you had to pay back, and you had to sign that over to him. Nobody else was going to lend us money—we couldn't go into banks and function that way. So we were all complicit in that, without really realizing what was going on. We didn't realize he was cashing those checks.

Garcia, Mountain Girl, and Robert Hunter were living in Larkspur. Jerry did [some music for Michelangelo Antonioni's film] *Zabriskie Point,* and they were going to buy their first house with the check from that. Mountain Girl would call them every day: "That check come yet?" She had a house she wanted to buy, and she was anxious to get it. Every morning I would go to the post office and pick up the Grateful Dead's mail. I was not allowed to open it—I just put it on Lenny's desk. I saw the check from Warner Bros.—"Jerome J. Garcia"—put it on Lenny's desk, and called Mountain Girl. She says, "Oh, my God! I'll be right up!"

She comes up, and "Where is it?" "It's on Lenny's desk." She goes in, and Lenny says, "There's no check here for you."

She goes, "What the fuck? Yes there is. I know it's here."

He says, "No."

She comes into my office and says, "What's going on?"

I said, "I guarantee you, that was the check. I didn't open it, but let's call Warner Bros."

I called Warner Bros. They said, "Yep, we mailed it two days ago."

She goes back in and starts storming at Lenny. Lenny says, "That was something else. You're wrong about that."

She calls Jerry, and the word gets out. Pretty soon, every single member of the band is in my office, and Mountain Girl and I are telling the story. Mickey is standing there. It's a little rough. People are telling their Lenny stories, and it's going around and around and around—"What shall we do? How do we confront him?" It really wasn't even a lot of stories. It was a pretty subdued kind of thing—"I don't like the way he does this," you know. We didn't really have any evidence then. This is how naïve we were.

Finally Ram Rod, who hasn't said a word until this point, says, "I'll tell you what: It's me or him." Ram Rod was that kind of guy: He didn't say much, but when he did, it was important. Everybody loved Ram Rod.

Jerry says, "That's it, then. No contest: We fire Lenny."

Mickey is freaking out. He doesn't say a word, and people are asking, "Did you know this? Did you know he was like this?" Mickey was just numb.

Whoever went in—I'm pretty sure it was Jerry—told Lenny he was done. "Take your stuff and get out."

Then we, as a group, decided to go out to lunch. There was this great little place in Novato that had crab sandwiches that were out of this world. So we all went up there; must have been twelve of us. Left him alone in the office.

When we came back, you know what was in the office? My phone, on the floor. All the file cabinets were gone, the desk was gone, the chairs were gone. Everything was gone! He had a truck come and he said, "Take everything. Why go through her desk? Just take the fucking desk!" Took everything.

We came back in, and we all just stood there with our mouths open, going, "How stupid could we possibly be?" If there was any doubt about this guy!

I get on the phone and I call the bank. The bank says, "You are not a signatory on this account. The only signature on this account is Lenny Hart. Even though it says "Grateful Dead," has your address, your phone number." Jerry's on the phone, Phil's on the phone— "This is our money!" They said, "Nope, this account belongs to Lenny Hart."

We just are kicking ourselves like crazy. We go to the bank—probably me and McIntire. We start talking to this lady—and we found out later that Lenny was having an affair with this person. Lenny had two little kids, five and seven years old, and he acted like the most picture-perfect husband and father. He blew town on everybody! He started taking money from day one.

Pigpen was the nicest person. People took advantage of him. When the thing happened with Lenny, we found out that Pigpen had been having Lenny save money for him, and he lost everything. I think he took the biggest hit. All the money he thought he was saving, Lenny took.

ROCK SCULLY: Mickey was distraught beyond belief. He [eventually] quit because he couldn't face it. I'm in disbelief that he hung with the band that long after it was discovered his dad had absconded with all that money.

I hired [lawyer] Hal Kant, and we had to spend a lot of time negotiating with Warner Bros. because we hadn't paid any of the bills. A lot of time was taken up with lawyers, dealing with the effects that were caused by it. We had to go after it because we were left with no money and still owed the IRS. So we pulled in David and Bonnie Parker [to keep the books] and got down to brass tacks with that; he worked out just how bad it was—and meanwhile, where was Lenny? We got a detective on the case and then started negotiating with Warner Bros. to get out of the deal.

DAVE PARKER: It was a very traumatic time all around. They were broke. They were in debt about $150,000 just in unpaid bills, and they were in the hole even more than that to Warner Bros. because they had taken so much in advances on records that didn't sell very well. Warner Bros. was pissed off that they'd advanced all this money to this weird bunch of guys that weren't being responsible and turning out nice commercial hits. And then the band gets ripped off by Mickey's father.

I was relatively organized and responsible, compared to most of the people who were around, so Jerry asked me if I'd like to be their business manager. They had nobody else to do it and they wanted someone they knew and someone they could trust to handle this thing. So, since I was looking for a job and had nothing else to do, I said, "Sure."

Basically what they did was go on the road a lot and just played and played. I tried to work up a financial plan. I was dealing with creditors all the time—collection agencies and angry people wondering when their bill was going to get paid. At one point we owed American Express $17,000. I spent about a year and a half making deals with creditors. At the same time, though, the band and everyone had to have money to live on and pay the rent and eat, and what made all that possible was the band's ability to go out on the road and earn money. There was no money from records; that didn't happen until later. *Workingman's Dead* and *American Beauty* eventually allowed them to get back above even with the record company and pay back all those advances.

Salaries were low—a couple of hundred dollars a week for the band, although they would also get money for instruments and recording equipment if they needed it.

GAIL HELLUND: When Lenny was gone, McIntire said, "I'll be the manager." Sam Cutler was there. He wasn't pressuring anybody except Jerry; that's the only person you had to pressure in those days. Our sleepy little world just got turned upside down, and Sam was all business. He said, "I would take this band on the road." McIntire was sick of goin' on the road.

Sam's a hustler, man, from day one. The guy has more energy than you can believe. He is my good friend, but when he first came, he was hard to take. It was so different from how we all had been. He was really crass and rude and pushy. I didn't like him at all. He'd say things like, "What's the matter? Didn't you get laid last night?" You'd just go, "We're just not like that here."

RHONEY STANLEY: Lenny Hart disappointed us. The fact that he was blood family made us all realize that our tribal family was stronger than blood family.

GAIL HELLUND: [After that] we rented the house at Fifth and Lincoln [in San Rafael], painted it. I made curtains. It was a fun place.

Being busted in New Orleans cost Bear his freedom.

OWSLEY STANLEY: I had already been convicted [for LSD offenses] and been sentenced and was awaiting my appeals. The Dead got busted and I was busted with them, and that sent a bad message to the judge, and he revoked my permission to travel. The appeals went all the way through until the end of '71.

Another major change at the end of January was Tom Constanten parting ways with the Grateful Dead.

GARY LAMBERT: In the year when Tom Constanten was in the band, they had Pigpen mostly relegated to playing congas or maracas, hand percussion, tambourine. But whenever he stepped forward and took the mic, he commanded the stage in a way that was unlike anyone else in that band, for sure, and so odd because he didn't fit the physical type of the great front man. He didn't necessarily have the voice of a great front man, but there was something entirely metaphysical about Pigpen's mojo. It just was. It was in him. It was probably instilled in him by his R&B DJ dad. That music came out of him experientially, rather than like some young academic imitating a blues man or a soul man. He was magic! He was funny and present and commanding and just a blast. When Pigpen seized his moment, he seized it.

There was a faction for whom Pigpen was the guy, for whom he was really the draw, and who loved that part of the Dead that was still an electrified, psychedelicized blues band. [Constanten's] contribution was obviously much more subtle and much more in the background. I certainly appreciated it, because I was a fan of the avant-garde and loved some of the same people that had helped form his musical sensibilities.

TOM CONSTANTEN: There were a couple of tunes that Pigpen always played on—"Death Don't Have No Mercy," for instance. Pigpen, at that time, also became more of an out-front vocalist—as on "Lovelight," for instance—and he rather enjoyed not having to sit behind a keyboard while he did that. It worked out quite nicely. There were a couple of times when we both had a keyboard. I recall there was a gig in Cincinnati where there was one for each of us, although other times he'd play conga drums.

[In early 1970], I had an opportunity to write and direct a show in New York, *Tarot*.

BOB WEIR (1971): He's more or less found a better scene for himself. He's a composer, and as far as being a rock 'n' roll musician, he has absolutely no background. He has apparently no innate, and certainly no cultured understanding of the idioms that are responsible for rock 'n' roll, and so it occurred to us and him at the same time that he wasn't really a rock 'n' roll musician, and the whole group when we were playing with him sounded more like an experimental group than a rock 'n' roll band. More or less we all became homesick for rock 'n' roll and we all, T.C. included, decided that it was best that he either learn to play rock 'n' roll, or continue what he had been doing and had spent years working on.

ROCK SCULLY: His being a Scientologist bespoke one of his flaws as far as we were concerned. It wasn't a big deal; he didn't go around pushing it, but he was very proud of himself for being high up there [in the Church]. But he did not have the looseness musically for what we were looking for. We needed a guy who could go downtown—just get on the beat and be with the band. But not hearing himself could be a legit reason, because if you can't hear yourself, you're shit out of luck.

TOM CONSTANTEN: Keyboard technology could not amplify a Hammond organ to compete with four Jerry Garcia Twin Reverbs turned up to 10. It was very difficult to get a fix on my connection with the musical entity—which was frustrating, to say the least.

It was a mutual decision. We had a meeting in a hotel room in New Orleans, just before the bust. Jerry called me "an underachiever." I think that's a result of the frustration of not being able to find myself in the mix. Also, what was telling for me was that I didn't have a piano at home to practice on.

There's an ironic twist that a lot of the tunes on *Workingman's Dead* are numbers that I played with the band touring, although by the time the band went into the studio to record that album I was on the way with the next project. And interestingly enough, the band at that time was moving in the direction of shorter songs, more like song songs, almost country-ish. And rather than what some might think, from the point of view that I was coming to the band with, I wasn't resisting that. Rather, I was going along with it, and if anything, contributing to it in my own way. It was a style of music that I was not at all uncomfortable with, and didn't feel any reason to try to say, "Hey, let's play more Varése!" I was quite at home and comfortable with all those types of music.

BETTY CANTOR-JACKSON: They got into writing more tunes, Jerry and Bob Hunter. There's always been something very old-world, old-school about Bob, and he thinks that way. They were kind of concise tunes. They had an obligation to get [a record] done, so they just thought, "Let's just do this." And they looked at Crosby, Stills, and Nash and how they were singers, and they did those kind of songs. Our whole live performance thing was going on for five hours or so. That was their thing. So this was a departure. It was definitely focused that way: they were trying to make a record that would sell, that people would buy. This is what the record companies wanted, this is the obligation we are trying to fulfill.

They were trying to get their vocals together. They wanted to sing like their buddies, like David [Crosby]. Crosby, Stills, and Nash set a standard for vocals, so they wanted to do stacked vocals. And they wanted to get it done fast. They said, "Let's just get in there and do it and get this thing done."

DAVID CROSBY: They had listened to us a lot, and they liked what happened when three-part harmony went over a good track. It's very generous of them to credit us with it, but we never sat down with them in a room and said, "Okay, now, you sing this, you sing this." That never happened. Those guys are brilliant. They knew exactly what we were doing, and they evolved their own version of it.

BOB MATTHEWS: After the experience of *Aoxomoxoa*—so much time, so much loss of direction, so many hands involved—on *Workingman's Dead* we went into the studio first and spent a couple of days rehearsing all the tunes and recording them on 2-track. "Before we even start, let's have a concept of what the end product is going to feel like." We learned from *Sgt Pepper's* [*Lonely Hearts Club Band*] that every album had a beginning of side one and an end of side one that segued mentally into the beginning of side two and out through the end of side two.

I gave copies of the proposed album sequence on cassette to each of the band members, and they went back to the rehearsal studio in Point Reyes and practiced with that concept in mind. So when they came into the studio, there was a vision in everybody's mind about the continuity and the emotional feel of this project, ending up with the next to last one being one of my favorites, "Black Peter."

BETTY CANTOR-JACKSON: Bob would handle the board most of the time, and I would do all the setup, handle the room, set up all the microphones, and I would run the machines. I got to do my first solo mixing on it, and it was the first record I got to master by myself.

BOB MATTHEWS: When I delivered the *Workingman's Dead* reference lacquers to Joe Smith at Warner Bros., he gave me a hug and said, "I can hear the vocals!" He was also very pleased with the fact that we did the whole album in less than twenty-eight studio days, delivered. And he loved it.

ROCK SCULLY: That was a different Grateful Dead, really, from what it had been before. It showed how tight they were getting with Crosby and Stills, and Jerry playing pedal steel and working in the same studio as them [Wally Heider's in San Francisco]. Nash is the one who brought in that English thing of stacking vocals—building out the harmonies on top of each other and keeping the songs short and simple. That's what Hunter was writing and it translated great to that. Jerry liked it simple, and he liked that presentation. He liked singing together, those harmonies.

ROBERT HUNTER: It's what Garcia and I wanted to do. It gets back to our folk roots. It's what the first album was supposed to be, actually. A lot of the songs on that are really just folk tunes rocked up. "Viola Lee," "Cold Rain and Snow"—those are folk songs. Garcia and I knew we could write better songs than that; we knew that idiom cold. It shocked the public [when we turned in that direction], but they were just songs to us.

JERRY GARCIA: We didn't mean for people to start taking a lot of cocaine when we put out ["Casey Jones"]. It's clearly an anti-coke song. The words aren't light, good-time words—it's just the feeling of it. We were manipulating a couple of things consciously when we put that song together. First of all, there's a whole tradition of cocaine songs, there's a tradition of train songs, and there's a tradition of Casey Jones songs. And we've been doing a thing, ever since *Aoxomoxoa*, of building on a tradition that's already there. Like "Dupree's Diamond Blues."

BOB WEIR (1970): You try to make an album as good as you can and hope it will be salable. *Workingman's Dead* came out with ten cuts on it as opposed to three or four [like on *Live Dead*].

[In the late sixties] we got into more extended improvisational stuff. Then, after a couple of years of that, we found sort of a happy medium, where we could do both extended improvisational stuff and songs. From a record company standpoint and the way the media's set up these days, it's easier to sell songs than it is to sell improvisational long pieces. That's one of the restrictions of the art of making a record [that] encompasses the music, how long the piece is going to be, how appealing and how accessible it is to the audience. By accessible I mean easily understood. As opposed to John Coltrane, who played some dynamite music—I mean some really fantastic music— but he was never any superstar. And he had not much of an audience, because not many people could understand what he was playing.

It bugs you if you are playing music the best you can play it and not many people are listening. And just because you're a performer, a performer wants people to listen. Generally, you might consider changing your material or finding a new sort of material that more people will be interested in listening to and at the same time you will be interested in playing it. That's kind of where we settled down, at least with *Workingman's Dead*.

[*Workingman's Dead*] was a sudden change for the record-buying public, but it was a gradual change for us, because over the period of months before that, inasmuch as we've been hanging out with David Crosby and Stephen Stills, particularly, and listening to them sing together, and just blown out by the fact that they really can sing together; and we began to realize that we had been neglecting our own vocal presentation for instrumental presentation. And so we started working on our vocal arrangements, and choral arrangements. As it turned out, the next record we did had a lot of that on it. And it represented a marked change from the way we had sounded in the past, though none of us had really given it any thought. We were just going straight ahead and doing what we'd been doing. It was a lot of fun to make that record. It happened very quickly, and there was a spontaneity about that record that was just beautiful.

In mid-April 1970, the Grateful Dead headlined a show at the Fillmore West with Miles Davis.

BILL GRAHAM: With a Miles Davis and the Dead situation—just like the Who and Woody Herman or Ten Years After with Buddy Rich—people would say, "Aw, we've got to sit through this," and I would stand on the side of the stage and watch the conversion. There was even a better one: Love, and the Staple Singers. The Staple Singers went on and people started going toward the concessions. Then Mavis [Staples] started . . .

It was always the axiom of "We know you came to get the ice cream," like with children, "but you've got to eat the meat first." You had no choice—there was Miles Davis. You had to eat that. And sometimes you'd say, "My God! Give me some more of that!" And if you have a choice of getting the ice cream right away, "No, let me finish this meat."

At the end of the first night—and Miles was exceptional that night—they go streaming out after the Dead set, two in the morning, and these two guys are going down the steps. They said, "Hey, Bill—great, man, great!" And as they go past me, this one guy taps the other guy and goes, "Are you hip to Miles, man?"—as if he were in Harlem with the black cats. He couldn't spell Miles Davis when they walked into this place. It was great! When someone says, "Why do you do those strange [combinations]?" That's why. If five people that weekend bought a Miles Davis album, we've that much more of a cross-cultural awareness of where music comes from.

MILES DAVIS: [Playing with the Dead at the Fillmore West] was an eye-opening experience for me, because there were about five thousand hippies there [over the four-night run], most young, white hippies, and they hadn't hardly heard of me at all. We opened for the Grateful Dead, but another group came on before us. The place was packed with these real spacey, high, white people, and when we first started playing, people were walking around and talking. But after a while they all got quiet and really got into the music. I played a little something like [from] *Sketches of Spain* and then went into the *Bitches Brew* shit, and that really blew them out. After that concert, every time I would play out there in San Francisco, a lot of young white people showed up at the gigs.

Jerry Garcia and I hit it off great, talking about music—what [the Dead] liked and what I liked—and I think we all learned something. Jerry Garcia loved jazz and I found out that he loved my music and had been listening to it for a long time.

PHIL LESH: We had to follow him at the Fillmore West. He only played for forty-five minutes, and it seemed like a year. We had to follow that, and it was pretty difficult, I can tell you. We were both influenced by the same things, but it came out in different ways.

Grateful Dead music, like any kind of popular music that arose about that same time, was influenced by the blues, and by jazz, and by just about every kind of music that was available to us on record and on the radio, through tapes and through people playing and traveling around. But jazz music was kind of a latecomer to the mix in the Grateful Dead, as it were. I guess I'm as responsible as anybody for bringing it on in. The thing that I wanted to show the guys in our band was how these people would interpret in different ways the same changes to a tune—they do it in sequence, and what we do is we sort of do all the same things that jazz players do, play different solos, but everybody's playing their improvisations at the same time. Whereas in jazz music everybody takes their turn.

At the end of June 1970, the Dead signed on to be part of a grand musical caravan, dubbed the Festival Express, that would travel across Canada by train, playing gigs in various cities. The initial show of what was formally called the Transcontinental Pop Festival was in Toronto (June 27, 1970), a twelve-hour show featuring the Dead, New Riders of the Purple Sage, the Band, Delaney and Bonnie, Ten Years After, Traffic, Buddy Guy, and a number of other acts. Unfortunately, it was marred by unruly protesters who loudly argued that the festival should be free. (Several of the acts did play a free show the following day in Toronto's Coronation Park.) Some, but not all, of the musicians then hopped on the train and headed west, playing shows in Winnipeg and Calgary, but the Festival Express never made it all the way to Vancouver on the West Coast. Still, it was an incredible experience for the Dead and all the others who made the trek. Hunter and Garcia later wrote a song about the train trip, "Might As Well," and a fine documentary called *Festival Express* was released in 2003.

DAVID NELSON: Sam Cutler was telling us that he was going to set up this big tour of Europe. It was going to be the Dead, the New Riders, the Jefferson Airplane, any good San Francisco bands he could get, and we were all going to go over on a big ocean liner. There were all these meetings, like a big one at Jerry's house in Larkspur, where we talked about getting our passport photos taken and all. There were all sorts of changes, though, and it ended up being all these bands going across Canada on a train. We were disappointed we didn't get to go to Europe then, but the train was just fabulous. It couldn't have been any better.

BOB WEIR (1970): When we played in Toronto, there was a big manifesto being handed out that was saying there would be guns and violence and a lot of people were going to get hurt because there wasn't free music and free dope for everybody. You know—"Because I'm here and I deserve free music and free dope and every indulgence that I want." And sure enough, just as they promised, there was violence. A lot of people's heads got busted.

JERRY GARCIA (1970): I think the musician's first responsibility is to play music as well as he can, and that's the most important thing. And any responsibility to anyone else is just journalistic fiction, or political fiction. Because that bullshit about "the people's music," man—where's that at, what's that supposed to mean? It wasn't any "people" who sat with me while I learned to play the guitar. I mean, who paid the dues? I mean, if "the people" think that way, they can fucking make their own music. And besides, when somebody says "people," to me it means everybody. It means cops, the guys who drive the limousine, the fucker who runs the elevator. Everybody.

GAIL HELLUND: On that train, it was pretty tight. There weren't a lot of extraneous people, because there was a finite amount of space. The Grateful Dead was in the first sleeping car, as was Janis, who was with the Full Tilt Boogie Band. And Flo and Eddie, Mountain, Eric Andersen. That's who was in the first car. Every car had somebody! Buddy Guy; Delaney and Bonnie and Friends, the Band—that was an unbelievable thing.

Normally, I didn't go on the road with the band, and if I did, there was no special dispensation because I was a female. I had to share with whoever would share with me: Ram Rod, McIntire; whatever. We didn't have enough money. But they said, "You gotta go on this one."

Hunter and I were very close. I always told him that he needed to go on the road. I said, "If you're writing their songs, you need to live their

GAIL HELLUND: Mickey had a barbecue at the ranch and he had buried a whole pig. The whole band was there; everybody was there. It had to be 1970. Somehow we all had guns. I don't know where they came from, but there were guns everywhere. Mickey had a poster of Ronald Reagan on a big bale of hay. We started shooting at that poster of Ronald Reagan. It was hysterical. What we didn't know was all the barbecue sauce had been dosed. I remember shooting and doing really well, and thinking, "Man, life. You need to know what it's like." So this was Hunter and me on the road with the band. There were hardly any females on the train—Bonnie Bramlett, Janis, me, this chick named Tosca Gazer who worked for the promoter, and Sylvia Tyson [of Ian and Sylvia].

We got on the train and everybody was congenial and glad to be together. We had an electric bar car and an acoustic bar car. Everybody started playing together. I can remember Garcia teaching Bonnie Bramlett "To Lay Me Down." I was mesmerized by that. She was so good, so powerful.

The filmmakers weren't on the train the first couple of days. It was band-only, and their immediate crew, for the beginning. It was awesome. Then, at the first real stop, everybody called their old ladies and everybody else and said, "You gotta come out here," and they all flew into Winnipeg. The film crew got on about there, too. [After] all the old ladies showed up, it changed dramatically. It was still really fun, but not as fun as those first few days. We played this gig in Winnipeg that was so windy! Everybody's hair was sideways. You're watching everybody sing, and the wind took their voices away. It was a weird, surreal gig.

DAVID NELSON: There were two band cars with equipment set up so you could play, and of course everyone would go down there and jam. Everybody had his own little room with a window and a little bed that folded down. Traveling through Canada and then pulling into these little stops that seemed like they were in the middle of nowhere with the band playing—it really seemed like

I'm doing well for someone who can hardly see." Then you start realizing that you're coming onto acid and you haven't eaten anything that you could possibly—then you realize: the barbecue sauce! And Mickey is laughing his head off. You're standing there the whole time going, "We're all high on acid and we're shooting guns. This is stupid." And you're just sort of thinking, "Is this really happening?" Garcia, everybody, was shooting guns. It was crazy. "What are we doing? Wow, we don't do guns!"

a circus. All the townspeople would come around and see what was going on; they'd look at the band playing through the windows and be totally amazed.

JOHN COOKE (Janis Joplin's road manager): I guess it started with Janis, but I remember aiding and abetting her: the goal was to get Jerry to drink. I have a picture in the footage that I shot on the train—sometime after we left Calgary, going through a patch of rain, of Jerry sitting at a little table by himself and looking out the window. Then he turns his head, and you can see him in profile, and on the table in front of him is what looks like a Bloody Mary. Janis might have bought him some drinks.

In Saskatoon, Tom Rush and I collected $350 in about fifteen minutes because there was a rumor—which proved not to be true—that the bar cars were running out of booze. It seemed entirely reasonable, because the Canadian National Railway no doubt stocked the train as they would stock a normal train. They didn't expect to be descended on by, I don't know, 150 or however many of us were on the train. People were drinking morning, noon, and night. I had this idea that we would collect money for the People's Bar.

When we got to Saskatoon, we got a car and a driver and took all of this money, and at least three or four of us went to the liquor store and just pointed at things until we had, I think, about four cases. As I recall, we did not buy any beer; we were interested in distilled spirits. We came back to the train, and then we had the People's Bar, and it was free.

DAVID NELSON: I think someone counted four hundred bottles of booze. I remember at one point I had two quarts of tequila, one in each hand, because there was plenty more to go around. I was out of it. Left to my own devices, I just took my two bottles, went into my compartment, and played my mandolin until I couldn't see anymore.

ROCK SCULLY: The Festival Express was a ball! There had never been anything like it. Of course none of us were used to drinking that much. To see Jerry and everybody with hangovers—you've never seen anything so sad in your life.

JOHN COOKE: Rock Scully says in his book, *Living with the Dead* [2001], something about getting off the train in Calgary. He says he remembers all of us totally hung over sitting on the tracks waiting for a taxi. We had hotels waiting in Calgary. But before we got to Calgary, we discussed hijacking the train. We thought it would be a good idea. We didn't want to leave the train, and thought we'd take it to San Francisco. That didn't prove practical.

When we got to Calgary, they disconnected the engine. Guess what? The engine is the source of all electrical power on the train, so once they disconnected the engine—it was morning, seven or eight o'clock, and people were not nearly ready to get up—the train started getting pretty warm. As the train got warmer, people stumbled out onto the platform. There were taxis waiting, and they took us to the hotel, and that was the end of that. More's the pity.

But Calgary . . . we only played the first night, and [Janis and band] had to fly out the next day because we had a concert in Seattle. So the first of those two nights, our guys said that somebody spiked a bottle of tequila with acid. And Clark Pierson and Richard Bell, our keyboard player, both got dosed. Richard said he was flying like a Chinese kite. But they played the gig without trouble. I think that was maybe the best one on the tour.

BOB WEIR (1970): You can go "out" at any given point [in a song] and then come back and there's that flash of recognition. That's a ploy where the audience gets off a whole bunch and respectively you get off—where you've gone out for an extended improvisational period of time, shall we say, and you flash back in on the song and everybody says, "Wow!"

We've been doing that pretty consistently on "The Other One," the song with the "tiger paws" rhythm that Billy and me came up with. The other night it was getting slowed down and convoluted, and there was really direction toward which it was headed, and all of a sudden I had a flash of inspiration and I kind of half-remembered a Coltrane riff from *Africa/Brass* [a groundbreaking 1961 album] that I was particularly fond of, but I couldn't remember it all, so I made up my own tonal structure for it, and I came [at] it with a rather slow, lazy African shuffle. Phil picked up on it real quick and underneath it all the time was the ["The Other One"] rhythm, because they were synchronized.

We're playing one thing and suggesting the other, and then intuitively at one point we both made Garcia feel it; Garcia was playing in between the two. So me and Phil, and I think Bill, came crashing back with the other rhythm and the crowd, of course, stood on its head. That's a great feeling, because I look over at Garcia—before all that went down, everybody was tense, trying to get it on, nobody was smiling much, and at the point that we came back into the other rhythm, the bottom half of my face about fell off—and Garcia, well, he was more grin than beard, which is unusual.

JERRY GARCIA (1970): After all this time we've learned to work very well together, generally speaking. We've all learned to leave room for each other in the development of an idea or playing. I mean, it has to be a cooperative trip or it ain't music. We're a band, that's where we are; it's evolved that way because we stuck it out. We never worked at it. What we used to do is rehearse a lot; we would take weird ideas and rehearse a lot—every day, six hours a day—and you could keep that up for so long, and then everybody starts getting at each other's throats because you start getting more and more detailed, where finally you're defining musical feelings to such a razor's edge.

> The Grateful Dead went back into the studio in the summer of 1970. Many of their teammates were out of town on another traveling festival, the Medicine Ball Caravan, which the Dead had decided at the last minute not to do. The band was assigned a young engineer from Kansas City to record their new album, *American Beauty*.

STEPHEN BARNCARD (Recording engineer): In 1969, I joined the staff of Wally Heider Recording [in San Francisco] as an assistant engineer. Some of the acts I worked with and assisted were Crosby, Stills, Nash, and Young; the Jefferson Airplane; and Steve Miller. At the same time, I was doing some spec work with this troubadour, this player named Chet Nichols—he worked in interesting guitar tunings; he sang and played tunes similar to some of the darker, deeper, more interesting songs of David Crosby. That gave me a chance to experiment with acoustic guitars a lot. We'd do sessions on weekends, and I would perfect some microphone techniques, including some stereo ones with mics I had available at Heider's. When the main first engineer at the studio left to work with Creedence Clearwater Revival full time, I basically became the number-one guy for the studio.

One day, the studio manager came in and said, "We have a chance to get the Grateful Dead to record here. All you have to do is get a great bass sound." Phil was using the exact same rig as [Airplane bassist] Jack Casady, and I was familiar with Jack's rig. He had a big amp for the low end and thud, and then a little amp for the buzz in the middle. So between the two amps and a direct input, I was able to make a bass track that worked for him. My audition for the Dead was a song called "Till the Morning Comes." A wonderful thing that happened on that track, at least from my perspective, was they didn't insist on using two drummers, so it was Jerry, Phil, Bill, and Bobby—the quartet. Nice, clean tracking session. We did it live and then added the vocals later.

I was worried [going into the sessions with the Dead] because I had read the stories about the

JERRY GARCIA: Our trip is really analytical when we get into rehearsing. We'll take one figure and play it over and over again for two hours, and stop it, and slow it down, and write it out, and invert it, and do every sort of variation with it, and look at it in every respect 'til we understand it perfectly. Then we'll go into the next level of it rhythmically, and then about three levels into an idea, we'll start to have differences of opinion because of the differences of our nervous systems that perceive time subtly different, and perceive pitch subtlety different, and so it gets into that extreme and tiny subtlety where you start finding differences, but around the big open center which we're all a part of, we can all agree perfectly well.

"blue air" [sic] and the stuff with Hassinger. I had read this stuff in *Rolling Stone* for years, and thought these guys have got to be freaking acid-head weirdos. So I was ready for anything, but I was eager to try it because they were interesting.

They really knew what they wanted, and they laid down everything as fast as you can imagine. *American Beauty* is a very live record, and it was fun all the way through. There was not a whole lot of experimentation. They had rehearsed, so they were ready to go when I got them.

Some records sort of assemble themselves: You do a take and everybody says, "Yeah, that's it. Let's move on," and everything falls into place. There was hardly any working out of anything in the studio, unless it was a guest musician—[like David] Nelson or [keyboardist] Howard Wales. Those guys required a little more time, but everybody else left the room. I think we cut the tracks in a week and a half. Bill would play with brushes on most of the tunes, which made the dynamics work. Because he played down in the acoustic space, that matched the acoustic guitars. And I put the two guitar players, usually Bobby and Jerry, facing each other.

Garcia ruled the vibe territory in the room, although he didn't say much. Phil and I really did most of the work on the record. And Phil was pretty much getting people lined up for overdubs and so on. Jerry was always there, they were kind of working together, but Jerry didn't say a lot; maybe didn't have to, I don't know. Maybe things just went that well.

"Attics of My Life" is choral magic. I don't know where it came from, except they were so harmonious together and just made it work. Going three-on-a-mic [for the second pass] really helped, too, because then they could do an air blend and perhaps make up for or subtract from what they did before [on three separate mics].

I was skeptical [going in about their vocals], but they were brilliant. They walked in and just did it. People don't believe me when I say this. I used three mics [for Garcia, Lesh, and Weir], then doubled it. The pitch is fantastic on this record. I was listening to it on headphones and Garcia was spot-on, Phil was spot-on, Bobby was spot-on. We did not tweeze over these vocals or pitch, and we didn't try to do any tricks.

Mixing was all done in the afternoon. I was doing the mix of *American Beauty* at the same time I was working nights with Crosby [on his solo album, *If I Could Only Remember My Name*]. So I would get in about 11:00, have a can of something for lunch, and then I would do six hours mixing with the Grateful Dead. Then, at 6:00 p.m., I would take a break, go out and get a can of something else, and at 7:00, or whenever David felt like coming in—he would show up with an absolutely stunning, gorgeous woman, or maybe alone, or maybe with a bunch of people. I never ever knew what he was going to do any night. There was no plan.

JERRY GARCIA (1970): The first four records were us trying to make records, seeing what works and what doesn't; we were learning how to do it. The last couple were us doing it—and they're simple records, really.

Workingman's Dead, which has turned out to be our most "significant" album, was the album we worked the least on; I think we spent nineteen or twenty days and finished the whole album. And while that was going down, that whole being-busted scene in New Orleans was hanging over our heads. It was like the record was an afterthought. With *American Beauty,* there was this rash of parent deaths where everybody's parents croaked in the space of about two or three months. It was just Tragedy City—bad news every day, really.

ROCK SCULLY: I think that's what got them through all that— they had those songs. It was a tough time. I know Bobby was very affected by it, and so was his sister. Phil was kind of stoic about it all. But they had this music and they had that excitement and they really settled down and did it. This was a monumental effort for them. It was a project that fed itself. Garcia really came into his production wizardry there.

| "Friend of the Devil" started out as a New Riders tune but

| wound up in the Dead's songbook instead.

DAVID NELSON: John Dawson had all these great songs, but Hunter is an old friend of mine, so he said, "They ought to have one of mine, too." So he comes over to the house one day and says, "I've got a song for you guys."

We said, "Great. Let's try it." I had to take the time to get the tape recorder together; meanwhile, John Dawson and Bob Hunter are doing these phrases—"I lit out from Reno," and all these verses that never saw the light of day.

So I get all the levels right, and I'm ready to play, and I get my guitar out. They're already playing. I notice they're in the key of G, so I play a [descending] G scale. Hunter goes, "Yeah, yeah! That! Play that!"

I'm goin', "Bob, no, no! I was just tuning up! I wasn't playing anything."

He goes, "No, no, no, I want you to play that. That is the opening lick for the song." It was maddening, because "Hey, I can make up a good lick. Let me play the song awhile. It'll be a real thing." No, he wanted that.

The question is, if he brought it around to the New Riders in 1970, how come we didn't play it? It never was a New Riders song. Here's what happened:

We played it, we taped it, we did the development of it, but it was just the verses. There was no bridge. Hunter goes home—he happened to be living in Larkspur, sharing a house with Garcia. And Garcia's up, looking out the curtains as Hunter comes home.

"Where have you been?"

Hunter goes, "I was over with the New Riders, writing a song."

He says, "What is it? What is it? Let me see it."

Hunter goes, "I'm tired, I'm gonna go to bed."

Garcia says, "Just play it for me once." Hunter plays it for him and goes to bed. Garcia stays up all night. In the morning, we had such a beautiful bridge, man! ["Got two reasons why I cry . . ."] It just tops the song off. We all heard that and went, "Okay, it's yours! Go ahead!"

BOB WEIR: "Truckin'" is kind of a tongue twister. Hunter wrote it that way out of spite! He just put it together so it's impossible to sing. It's not a matter of not remembering the words so much as not being able to get 'em out sometimes. This was way back when I hadn't learned to stick to my guns or rearrange things or anything like that. I took what I was given and worked with it.

ROBERT HUNTER: ["Sugar Magnolia"] is a song that went through a lot of transitions. [Weir] just worked to death on it. And Weir's a hard taskmaster—he wants everything to be just the way he wants it. We went around and around and around. He'd go off and work on it some more, and bring it back and demand more lyrics or better lyrics. And then, when it was all done, he wanted some extravaganza to cap it all off. So I wrote that "Sunshine Daydream" thing for it right in the studio. I just went out and wrote it down. [Weir said] "That's just fine," and tacked it on.

JERRY GARCIA [1988]: It's a good-time song, a good song. Still good, still fun to do. I contributed the "Sunshine Daydream" part, the chord changes at the end.

ROBERT HUNTER: The first time that song ever came off was in Chicago. They had been playing it a lot, but the audience had only reacted very mildly to it. Bob Matthews was at the soundboard at that time, and he went off into the audience or backstage or something like that, and there was nobody there at the sound booth. So I zipped in there, and Weir starts singing it, and I just cranked his vocal up. There was a thing that everything should be at the same level—including the voices, which tended to get lost—so I just cranked it up, and the audience just sat up, and then they had the reaction to it at the end that they've had ever since.

ALTON KELLEY: They called me up and said they had an album coming out, and they were going to call it *American Beauty*. Immediately the rose came to me. At the time I was experimenting with some techniques, and that rose is actually etched into a mirror. I etched it into the glass from behind with a sandblaster, so I had to do it all backwards. I had to put in the shadows and highlights first and work it inside out. [Fellow artist] Wes Wilson was working with glass and had a sandblaster, so I went out to his place and used his sandblaster and then set up my airbrush and painted it, in a chair in his kitchen.

The frame is an actual piece of mahogany that has the mirror laid into it. Then we photographed the whole thing, which was kind of hard because it reflected so much. Finally, we ended up putting up a gray sheet and standing the camera at a little angle so you couldn't see the camera in it. [The photo on the back cover] was shot on my bedroom table. I just put a lot of stuff on the table and Mary Ann Mayer took the photo.

JERRY GARCIA (1970): A long time ago, we were sort of incidental music at the celebration of life. Which was super cool. Now, however, we're in the position of being rock 'n' roll stars, which is not anywhere near so cool and takes a lot more from you in the sense of . . . well, you get in a very wired place. You're playing music, you're up, you're excited, you're on, you leave the stage . . . and there's a backstage full of drifting shadow forms and peculiar show-biz vampires. I've never been competent to deal with that to my own satisfaction. I always like to feel that any encounter between myself and another human being is going to be some free exchange of energy. I try not to hang anyone up. But there are a lot of scenes in rock 'n' roll where people are looking to hang you up and put you through weird trips and shit like that. Who needs it?

I feel essentially functionless. I'm not a contributing member to society in any real way—I'm a musician. A long time ago, I decided not to play games, but to play music, and I feel kind of outside of it all. But at the same time, I feel that what I'm doing is a service. I think music should be put in that category, rather than in the business category. Like, people get high from music, and everybody should be able to get high.

The rest of it has to do with dealing with the externals, like what's there to work with. What there is to work with is a theater here, a multi-purpose room there, this PA, this approach to advertising and economics, all that shit.

But there's another trip. When we play at the Fillmore East, the place is set up as a theater. So instead of being the incidental music, or the house band, you're there delivering something else. And you begin to think in terms of structuring your evening a certain way. That's how we came up with the idea for the Evening with the Grateful Dead. I'd like it to go as many ways as possible, but it's getting so fuckin' weird that . . . it's so weird when music lovers break down the door of a place.

Also in the fall of 1970, Garcia met Merl Saunders and started on another parallel musical path.

MERL SAUNDERS: Mike Bloomfield had a great blues band— [saxophonist] Ron Stallings, Bill Vitt on drums, John Kahn on bass. I used to run out there and play organ. Doing that, I met Nick Gravenites, who was doing a lot of sessions. He would hook me up with this guitar player. I only knew his name was Jerry. Jerry and I clicked. It reminded me of certain players that I had in New York. Jerry was, in a way, like Eric Gale: anything he does is magic. Anytime I had a session I would call him up. I never knew his last name. This went on for about four or five months. My girlfriend says, "Who's this Jerry guy?" because I had been hanging at the Matrix with this Jerry. I said, "He's a wonderful guy. We're really hitting it off great." I was still wearing shined shoes and these three-hundred-dollar sweaters. I believed in big cars. I started hanging out with Jerry, and pretty soon my beard started growing and I started wearing tennis shoes. My parents thought I had gone crazy.

We were doing all these sessions and playing at the Matrix. When we first started playing it was Jerry and [me] and Bill Vitt on drums. I was doing organ pedals [for the bass]. About thirty people each Monday or Tuesday would come to hear us. I knew of the Dead because I used to live about four blocks from them but I never put together that this was Jerry Garcia.

That's how it really all started. We started building from there. We were playing at the Matrix for about twenty people. That was a great place because even Carlos [Santana] used to drop by sometimes. We had all kinds of sessions: Armando Peraza [of Santana] would jam with us. Vince Guaraldi would come play keyboards sometimes. At intermissions they would show classic cartoons that you'd never see at the movies. This was a great place.

After seven or eight months playing there, we began to pack the place. People would start flying in from New York.

> Mickey Hart left the Grateful Dead abruptly on February 18, 1971, the first of a five-night run at the Capitol Theater in Port Chester, New York.

JERILYN BRANDELIUS: Everybody knew that Mickey had nothing to do with [Lenny Hart's malfeasance], but he was devastated that everything his mom had ever said about the guy had come to pass. And in good conscience, I guess, he couldn't be around the band. We never talked about it very much. But it broke his heart and he felt he was responsible for all this trouble that was brought on the Grateful Dead, because it was his dad.

That changed Mickey. Mickey is a very trusting person, generally speaking, and when that happened to him it really broke his heart. It broke his trust in people. He couldn't imagine how someone could do something so underhanded and horrible to his own child. He loved the Grateful Dead.

GARY LAMBERT: At the [February 18, 1971] show, there was something that seemed agitated about Mickey. He left the drum kit several times during the course of the show.

Even though the rest of that run at the Capitol was terrific, it felt like Billy took a little while to get fully comfortable with it. Obviously, by late '71 and into '72, he had no problem with it at all. The band became, obviously, leaner and more spare. It's interesting how that seemed so compatible with where the music was going. I don't know which was the tail and which was the dog in that case, but because they'd already done *Workingman's Dead* and *American Beauty,* it seemed to me that if you're only going to have one drummer, this is a good time to do it; so much of the music demands knowing where to leave stuff out. It became as important an element of the music as what to play. That's always a good thing in music—that sense of restraint, that sense that you don't have to play every note you've ever known in the next eight bars.

Whatever happened, it just seemed to provide the space for the band to develop in a different direction. God knows, 1969 and 1970 were such massively important years for the band, musically, and what Mickey brought to them may never have happened without him—the polyrhythmic sophistication they developed.

BILL KREUTZMANN: It was okay with me, frankly, because I felt at the end of that period we weren't really gelling that much. It's hard to explain what was going on. Those were real complicated times for him, and real private times.

[After Mickey left] I had the sense that the music became a little more clear. The rhythms and the grooves had a clarity you can hear on tapes from the period.

JOHN ZIAS (Musician): I remember being a seventeen-year-old at the Princeton show [April 17, 1971], talking to Lesh, 'cause it was pretty easy just to talk to people then. "What's your feeling of it?" Lesh said, "Before, it was like riding two horses, one leg on each. Now it's like riding one sure-footed one."

DAVE PARKER: In those days, Garcia and the other band members used to come hang out at the office fairly often. People would be smoking joints all day long. That was one of my problems. I tried to get things done that had to be done, and there was always some-one showing up with a joint. I finally learned how to work that way, although it never got easy. To me, they're two different things—being stoned and doing work with numbers and money and papers don't go together that well. I had to be the guy who dealt with the straight world—bankers and insurance men and accountants and lawyers. It kept growing and growing and getting more compli-cated every year. But before the end of '71 we were completely out of debt and things were going okay.

JERRY GARCIA (1971): It looked like [Warner Bros.] was going to be the loosest of all the record companies, and it turned out they are. No pressure, really, and they gave us unlimited studio time. What we were looking to do was learn how to make records. We didn't feel pressured to sign with a record company, because we didn't care if we made any records or not. But we were enthusiastic about getting into the studio and seeing what it was like. They paid for our education. All that studio time came out of our royalties, but since we never had any royalties. . . . Our Warner Bros. debt was pretty high, but it's all figures that don't mean anything to you. It was no more real the times we were heaviest in debt than it is now that we're almost out of debt. So what? What debt? I'm really delighted when I have like thirty bucks cash, you know.

> In June 1971, the band was scheduled to play a festival in northern France, but things didn't work out as planned.

JON McINTIRE: I kept trying to set up tours in Europe. Like when we did that festival in Newcastle-Upon-Tyne [May 24, 1970] and then the Chateau D'Herouville in France [June 21, 1971]—that one was supposed to be a free three-day festival, but it was rained out. Both times I tried to mount tours, but neither time could I get the money needed to offset the costs. We thought it was okay to at least break even on something like this, because you're breaking in a new territory, but it was not okay in our position at that time to lose money because we were just getting out of debt.

BOB WEIR: The second time we went to Europe, we went over to play this rock festival that this guy Michel Mann had put together. He had this chateau in Herouville, which is about two hours out of Paris, and the place is allegedly, and quite apparently, haunted by the guy [who built it]; you can still see him walkin' around there late at night and stuff like that. Kinda melancholy.

We got there and the whole deal was rained out. But then it stopped raining. It was a beautiful, gorgeous day, and we figured, "Okay, we came all this way, what're we gonna do? Well, we've got our equipment, let's just set up and play."

So we set up at the chateau, on the lawn, and all the townspeople from Herouville came—and the fire department, the police department, all their wives and kids and stuff like that, and we had a big party.

PHIL LESH: With the best wines that Michel could find, and the best food. We played for free for the people, complete with psychedelic light show [by] Light and Sound Dimension.

> In July 1971, Jerry Garcia went into Wally Heider Studios in San Francisco to record a solo album. The working group was tiny: Bob Matthews and Betty Cantor engineered; Bill Kreutzmann played drums; Ram Rod saw to the equipment and protected their privacy; and Robert Hunter worked on the songs.

ROBERT HUNTER: "Deal" and "Loser" [which debuted at the Capitol Theatre in February 1971] were both written about seven o'clock one morning when [Jerry, Mountain Girl, and I] were all living in Novato. Back in those days, I was chipper and feeling wonderful, and I dashed those two songs off. Garcia got up a little later and he was reading the newspaper at the breakfast table and I laid these two lyrics on him. "*Awww,* drat!" Off I went to town to do my business, and I got back a couple of hours later and he had them both set. He generally showed a great deal of resistance to lyrics, but once he liked one and set his mind to it, he'd get right through it.

BILL KREUTZMANN: We did a lot of music pretty fast. All of the main recording was done in a week, I think. Hunter was sitting in the control room listening and watching us and writing the words to the songs as we were playing, trying to get the rhythm ideas to work.

BOB MATTHEWS: *Garcia* [the solo album] took, I think, twenty-one days from beginning to end. Jerry would play the guitar or the piano, with Billy playing drums. The majority of the overdubs were played by Jerry, too.

"The Wheel" started as—I wouldn't call it a goof or a lark, but it was Jerry and Billy just jamming, playing some ideas. Betty and I were in the control room, and I turned around and said, "Start the tape. This may be something." It got to be a groove, and they realized it was a tune to be recorded. As the takes were occurring, I remember Bob Hunter up against the wall with a piece of paper, writing the words as they were playing in the studio. It was very short, from the time Billy and Jerry got into the groove of the jam, realized that it was a tune, and continued to record it. Suddenly it was a song, a very good-feeling song.

ROBERT HUNTER: I believe they were jamming in the studio and as would sometimes happen, I'd be writing in the studio like a madman trying to stay on the beat, hoping they would keep playing for a while.

[With "Sugaree," also from Garcia], I was living up at China Camp [a rustic part of San Rafael]. I was lying on the couch and I just got this little song going in my head: "Shake it, shake it, Stingaree . . ." And an old friend of mine, who was a criminal, once said, upon leaving the room, "hold your mud and don't mention my name," and whoever would say that kind of thing became my central character, who I picture as a pimp. Then, when I was done with it, I handed it over to Jerry. I used to write full songs [with music], but after a period of time I got to where I wouldn't go through the musical phase of it; I'd concentrate more on lyrics.

I wrote "Sugaree" probably within a couple of weeks of writing "It Must Have Been the Roses" and "Yellow Moon" [which eventually turned up on Hunter's 1975 album, *Tiger Rose*]. "Must've Been the Roses" I came home, picked up the guitar, and I think I wrote that song in about ten minutes—one of those wonderful times when you had a song and it wanted to burst out, and there it was.

I think I had a bit of [William] Faulkner's story "A Rose for Miss Emily" in mind when I wrote it, which is a rather morbid story. There's more than that, but there's a touch of the deep emotionality of "A Rose for Miss Emily" in it.

CHAPTER 5

Let It Grow

The Grateful Dead toured as a quintet without Mickey Hart for about six months during 1971. A number of shows in the winter and spring featuring this lineup were recorded on multitrack, and the resulting live album—simply called *Grateful Dead* but more popularly known as *Skull and Roses* or *Skullfuck*—came out at the end of August and was an immediate commercial success. The two-disc set included three new original tunes—"Bertha," "Playing in the Band," and "Wharf Rat —as well as concert favorites such as "Not Fade Away," "The Other One," and "Johnny B. Goode."

BETTY CANTOR-JACKSON: Warner Bros. had a big problem when we wanted to call the live album *Skullfuck*. We had a big meeting about that at the Continental Hyatt House [in Hollywood]. It was wild. "We want to call it *Skullfuck!*" "Then we're not going to call it anything! We're not going to put anything on the cover!"

SPENCER DRYDEN (New Riders of the Purple Sage drummer): The Dead always had a very big scene. Everything was always done in large groups, and it always seemed that whoever was around at any time could be involved in the decision-making. We were pretty democratic in the Airplane, but the Dead really took it to extremes. Roadies, girlfriends, everyone got involved.

I was one of the people at the famous meeting in Hollywood when the Dead met with the heads of Warner Bros. to tell them they wanted to call their album *Skullfuck*. There must have been thirty-five or forty people from the Dead, or who were just part of the scene, in this conference room in a big hotel. People were sitting around this giant table, and then there were a whole bunch of people sitting on the floor, standing against the wall, just everywhere. This was very typical of Dead meetings. They looked unwieldy and they were, I guess, but things would get done. I saw meetings where things got real emotional, like when somebody got let go or something, and there would be tears and everything—very heavy. But this one was funny because everyone sounded very rational. It was like almost everyone in the room took a turn in trying to explain to these straight guys from Warner's why it made perfect sense for the record to be called *Skullfuck*. People had these long explanations, explaining the word on all sorts of different levels, totally serious. And the Warner's guys were very polite. They listened to what everyone said and then tried to explain why they just couldn't call it *Skullfuck*, 'cause how were they going to sell the records in Korvettes [a defunct New York–area chain akin to Walmart] and places like that? Somebody would say, "Well, we don't want to be in those kinds of stores," and the Warner's guys would just kind of smile.

This went on for hours, it seemed, and I knew going in that there was no way they were going to let them put it out as *Skullfuck*. You might be able to do that now, but we're talking about 1971. It just wasn't going to happen. I think a lot of people in the room believed it would happen, though, because, like I said, everyone had their reasons, and they all sounded like good ones. But that's the Grateful Dead. They were never exactly in tune with the real world. Of course that's one reason they're great, too.

JERRY GARCIA: Oh, we wanted to use it so badly! We had a big meeting with Warner Bros. They were horrified! They were shocked! They were so serious about it: "Don't you understand? We won't be able to distribute to drugstores and supermarkets and Woolworth's and all that!" They fully believed we were going to do something awful they didn't [agree to], that we were going to insist that they call it *Skullfuck*. So we finally backed down, but it was more of a joke on our part. And also, aesthetically, it would have been so perfect. It was really a perfect name for the record.

> Pigpen played organ only sporadically during this period, and by the end of summer the band was hungry to augment their sound with a more proficient keyboardist. Miraculously, an unknown piano player named Keith Godchaux, prodded by his wife, Donna (a singer herself), came along at just the right time.

DONNA JEAN GODCHAUX: I grew up in a situation where a new sound was originating. In the early sixties, the whole Muscle Shoals [Alabama] scene was just beginning to get big. My first recording session was with Ray Stevens, right after "Ahab the Arab." Felton Jarvis was producing, and one day one of the background singers couldn't make the session. I was fifteen, a cheerleader at Sheffield High, and the whole bit. I remember I'd had cheerleader practice, so I ran down to the studio in my little uniform. That was the beginning.

[I was into] rhythm and blues, people like Otis Redding, Solomon Burke, Sam Cooke, Joe Tex. Amazingly, I ended up recording backgrounds with all those people, except for Otis, because Muscle Shoals became such a popular place to record R&B. It had really started with Percy Sledge, who was an intern at a local hospital. He had a little band on the side, and my best friend, who sang with me in a vocal group called Southern Comfort, had a husband who produced Percy's first big hit, "When a Man Loves a Woman." Us girls were the background singers for his first records. I still remember the day it hit number one on the charts.

After Percy's record, we were on other black records. The black artists who would hear us didn't know we weren't black. Most of them, when they got down to the studio, would see four white girls aged eighteen to twenty-three, and they'd flat-out lose it. There were a few who refused to use us when they found out we were white, but most of them were excited [that] there [were] white girls who sang like them.

I remember always wanting to go to California. I just saw myself there, for years and years, even when I was a relatively little girl. It came to a point where even though I was doing music, I wanted a new adventure in my life.

In California, everybody was into the Grateful Dead. I didn't get it, because I had come from a pristine, arranged studio situation. I had never really heard improvisational music, especially rock improvisation incorporating every kind of music you could imagine, with this adventuresome "It goes wherever it goes" attitude. But just the fact that it wasn't produced and arranged, I thought, "Do they really know how to play music? What are they doing?" I was listening to some of the records and I thought, "These guys must be really good-looking or something," to have that kind of impact, this hold over people. Somebody showed me the back of an album, and I go, "No, that's not it!"

Finally, [my friends] made me go to a Grateful Dead concert [October 5, 1970]. The New Riders were playing, Quicksilver, the Airplane. I said, "You guys just like this band because everybody's on drugs. You're out of your minds. I'm not going to take anything, I'm not going to smoke anything. I'm not going to be stoned." I was in the back row of the balcony of Winterland, and the Dead were spot-on and magical—quintessential Grateful Dead. I just got my little pea brain blown right there. I didn't understand it, but I dug it, and I knew that it was something unique that I had never heard before. I said to the people next to me, "When I sing again, it's gonna be with that band."

I had met Keith. He was so quiet—we never really talked until we fell in love. I'd never heard him play the piano and he'd never heard me sing when we decided to get married. Keith was still in college—or was supposed to be. I didn't realize that when he was supposed to be going to college he was at home trying to learn how to play rock 'n' roll. He had never played rock 'n' roll; he grew up playing classical and jazz.

[One day] we were in our apartment and my friend Carol said, "Let's listen to some Grateful Dead," and Keith said, "I don't want to listen to it anymore, I want to play it." We had gone to some shows, and he just felt a real affinity for it. It was kind of jazz-oriented, and it was improvisational.

I said, "Well, okay, let's go get in the band." We got the [*San Francisco*] *Chronicle* and looked up where Jerry was going to be playing next. He was playing at the Keystone Korner in San Francisco— maybe it was with Howard [Wales]. This was probably early '71, or mid-'71.

We did go to Keystone Korner, and we were sitting at a table right along the aisleway where the [musicians] would be going backstage. Jerry walked right by me, and I just tapped him on the arm and said, "My husband and I have something we need to talk to you about."

He looked me really intently and said, "Okay, come on backstage." He went backstage, and Keith and I were just too nervous. We were scared shitless. We just sat there at the table trying to figure it out. Garcia—he was really perceptive. He knew something was up, and he came from backstage and sat down at our table. Keith was sitting where he didn't see Jerry come up and sit. I will never forget my words. I said, "Honey, I think Garcia's hinting that he wants to talk to us. He's sitting right beside you." Keith turned around and looked at me, and then he looked at Jerry, and he said, "You'll have to talk to my old lady right now. I can't talk," and he put his head down on the table. He was just nervous; he was shy. We weren't high on anything.

I said, "I need your home number so I can call you and we can make arrangements to get together." I said, "Keith is your next piano player." We didn't know that [the Grateful Dead] were looking for one.

Jerry said okay and he gave me his home phone number. And he gave me the office number, and I said, "I'm going to try to call the office first, and if for some reason I can't get through to you,

I will use the last resort and call you at home."

For about a week after that, I called the Grateful Dead office and I said, "This is Donna Godchaux, and Jerry said to call," and of course they never gave him the message. And that's when I called him at home. He said, "We're having Grateful Dead rehearsal on Sunday. You guys come on down." I can't even describe how easy it was.

Keith and I went down there, and Jerry was there by himself—the rest of the band had forgotten to tell him that the rehearsal had been called off. Keith and I had written some of the material that eventually turned out to be on the *Keith and Donna* album. [Jerry] heard me sing, and then he and Keith were playing together and they just hit it. Jerry called Kreutzmann and asked him to come down. Then the three of them played, and it was just meant to be, and they knew it, and they said, "We're having a rehearsal tomorrow, come on down." So Keith played with the whole band on Monday. And if I'm not mistaken, they asked him to be in the band on that Monday.

Jerry asked me to sing, too, and I said, "I want Keith to get to do it first," and that's why I laid out for a couple of tours.

JON McINTIRE (1973): In this scene, when you need something, you just hang on until somebody comes to fill the space. [With Keith] I saw Garcia and asked him what it was all about, and he shook his head, very amazed, and said, "Well, this guy came along and said he was our piano player, and he was."

BILL KREUTZMANN: I loved his playing. I remember when we auditioned him, Jerry asked me to come down to our old studio and the two of us threw him every curve ball we could, but he was right on top of every improvised change. We just danced right along on top. That's when I knew he'd be great for the band. He was so inventive—he played some jazz stuff and free music that was just incredible. He had a heart of music.

DONNA JEAN GODCHAUX: When he rehearsed with them for that first time, he had never played one of their songs. He'd listened to them but never sat down and tried to play them, learn the chord changes. Bobby will tell you they tried every way they could to trip him up, but they couldn't do it.

ROCK SCULLY: It happened pretty quick, obviously. They didn't even try anybody else out, and there were some really good piano players lookin' to join up. I remember I was expecting them to be auditioning people.

PHIL LESH: He was a fine player. He was the perfect guy for our music at that time. It's like he came forth fully grown. He didn't have to work his way into it.

GARY LAMBERT: Keith was a real cool drink of water. He refreshed the sound of the band, and he made everyone else play in a really nice, economical, responsive way to what he was doing. I was an instant Keith fan.

Keith had this wonderful terseness to his playing. He is exemplary of the guy who knows that what you leave out is as important as what you play. His sensitivity to the context and his ability to adapt to the various idioms—he could do those little Floyd Cramer trills on the country tunes with the best of them, but then when they got into something like "Playing in the Band" he was comfortable with that, too. Robert Christgau reviewed [Bob Weir's solo album] *Ace* and said that Keith sounded "like a cross between Chick Corea and Little Richard."

> Keith's first tour with the band began in Minneapolis on October 19, 1971, and it was clear instantly that the Dead had made a good choice. He was surprisingly assertive, and he seemed comfortable on both short tunes and long jams. That first night, the group introduced six new songs: "Tennessee Jed," "Jack Straw," "Mexicali Blues," "Comes a Time," "Ramble On Rose," and "One More Saturday Night."
>
> Touring with the New Riders (now featuring Buddy Cage on pedal steel guitar in place of Garcia), the Dead traveled extensively that fall, hitting the Midwest, Southwest, the East Coast,

and California. Almost everywhere they went, the demand for tickets far exceeded the capacity of the mostly small venues they played, so to mitigate the ticketless hordes coming down to sold-out venues, the Dead arranged to have their shows broadcast on local FM stations in many cities. This also gave them plenty of exposure to new fans and helped give rise to the Grateful Dead taping scene, as excellent quality show recordings from the tour became widely traded and occasionally turned into bootleg albums.

JERRY GARCIA (1971): Texas was great. Yes, amazingly enough, it was. Atlanta was a bummer. I mean, that was kind of like the old days—it was a police scene. It was a civic center, public-owned building. They always have a lot of police there, to protect the property, that sort of thing.

At one point, one cop jumped up onstage and started goin' after Phil. In their mind, there's a riot happening, because everybody's standin' up. With us, we know that isn't happening and are capable of handling it in a way where nobody gets hurt and nobody gets uptight, either. But the police always have to try and do it their way—at least in the places where that's what's happening. Lots of places we've had a cooperative scene going with them.

Albuquerque was a nice trip. In fact, they want to us to do a gig and have the sociology department of the University of New Mexico come and observe it, and also the police, to see how we handle a crowd. Just in terms of how to avoid hassling, and how to avoid busting people, people getting hurt, and all the rest of that stuff. I don't know what they think they'll see.

SAM CUTLER: Rock Scully was really the only guy in the Grateful Dead who understood the centrality of FM radio to what the Grateful Dead were doing. There was a way in which FM radio could be used to reach markets that hadn't been touched.

So, for example, in Pennsylvania, you wanted to do a gig at the Spectrum in Philadelphia, which holds 18,000 people. The promoter would say, "We'd love to put you on at the Spectrum, but you aren't even going to sell eight hundred tickets." So how do we get this exposed to enough people that they can sell out the Spectrum? One of the keys to that was FM radio and college radio stations. We took Pennsylvania as a market area, and worked on playing at different colleges where there were 15,000 to 20,000 resident people, and used the FM radio station in that market to reach more people. You play in the state universities of Pennsylvania in order that when you play in a Pittsburgh or Philadelphia, people actually come to you. They're drawn to you, and they know about you. Then you broadcast live [concerts] for free. That just snowballed. The band, in those four years [1970–74], went from not selling very many tickets to being very successful.

JERRY GARCIA [1971]: The Grateful Dead has become incredibly popular and we can't play a small hall anymore without having 3,000 people outside wanting to get in. Our classic situation the last six months has been people breaking down the doors and just coming in. We have to play 7,000 to 10,000 seats to be able to get people in at a reasonable price. Just to do it. It's weird.

Here's what we're wondering: Do we really want to do that? When it comes down to it, we're just heads. We're not interested in creating a lot of fucking trouble and being superstars and all that shit. We're just playing, getting off, out to have a good time and giving it all a chance to happen. And all of a sudden there are all these problems making it more difficult to do, and it's getting to be where it's not fun. We have to play shows like some military campaigns just to make sure the equipment guys don't have to be fighting thousands of people to save the shit.

> Beginning with the Dead's seven-show residency at New York's Academy of Music at the end of March 1972, Donna was added to the group as a backup singer on a few tunes. Then, a few days after those concerts, nearly the entire Dead family headed off

to Europe for what would be one of the band's most storied adventures. Since the beginning of the Dead, not a year went by without some plan being formulated for a big overseas tour. But these "best laid plans" always fell apart for one reason or another—money, logistics—until the spring of 1972.

JON McINTIRE: Sam Cutler did a magnificent job of putting the Europe tour together. He really, really did. It was like pulling a rabbit out of a hat. He did it better than anyone could have. Kudos to Sam for putting that together. It was really spectacular—getting the bookings and making it financially possible to do. Along with Warner Bros.' support . . .

ROSIE McGEE: I was brought along as part of the promise that was made to all of us in 1967 that whoever was around from this original group would get to go if we got to Europe. We made a list with twenty-five people on it. I was on that list. Five years later they went, and kept that promise. The list had grown to fifty by then because of the crew, but I was still on the list—partly because I spoke fluent French and demonstrated how important it was to have an interpreter. Sam organized and put together that whole tour; booked it, fronted it, road-managed it, etc. When I went to Europe, at first I wanted to be of more help. I was working for Alembic so I was listed on the recording crew. They had to put me somewhere in the program book.

DONNA JEAN GODCHAUX: I could've been on a poster for "a fish out of water." Arriving in England was like you're stepping into a history book. For a little girl from Sheffield, Alabama, who had never really been anywhere, it was a very intense experience. It was hard enough just trying to take it in that I was singing with the Grateful Dead, for one, and then here I was in Europe!

JON McINTIRE: I adored Keith and Donna. I don't think Donna gets overwhelmed by anything. She's classy and she's extremely musical, so she wanted to ease her way in and learn what it was she could give, rather than finding out from her mistakes what she couldn't give. Keith was the same way when he began.

Donna Jean was adored by everyone. She was a musician, so she got treated better than any woman who had ever been in the Grateful Dead scene. She was treated as a goddess. Everyone was looking out for her and helping her. No one would be mean to Donna Jean.

ALLAN ARKUSH: When the Dead came over to Europe in '72, they hired us [Joe's Lights] for the London shows. They were supposed to go to the Rainbow, but it closed, so they got Wembley [arena]. It sounded just like playing in the shower.

The tech guys came up with the idea of hanging curtains the length of this place, which ended up not only working soundwise, but looked fantastic. They basically rented every curtain in London, and every parachute. It looked like you were watching them in a giant tent.

JON McINTIRE: This big, boomy warehouse with a steel superstructure was an acoustical nightmare, so Rock came up with the idea of getting a whole bunch of parachutes and folding them in half, so they were festooned down and hanging from the rafters in nine tiers of three each, or something like that. It was a brilliant stroke. The sound wasn't great, but it was handleable in comparison to what it would have been.

BOB WEIR: Magically, one by one, these parachutes were coming down from the ceiling. The heater was put on full blast. The next night when we came back, the place was full; the parachutes were all up, and the sound was beautiful. We really had a good time all night playing, and the audience was really dynamite—really appreciative, enthusiastic, warm. It really blew my head.

DONNA JEAN GODCHAUX: It's a boon anytime you get to play a real concert hall that was built for music, rather than a hockey rink. The acoustics at the Tivoli [in Copenhagen] were just so beautiful, and the musical expression from row one to the end of the theater was the same. It was made for music, so to play places like that and the Olympia Theatre in Paris was a dream. To this day, those are my favorite kind of places to play, by far.

JON McINTIRE: Jahrhunderthalle in Frankfurt [April 26, 1972] was a modern concert hall with absolutely magnificent acoustics. It's meant for symphony orchestras. In that hall there was a stepped-up, pumped-up recognition [among the musicians] of the nuances.

I do believe that the spectacular acoustics of that hall, and the wisdom with which it was built, did affect them. I believe they were able to hear themselves better than they normally could. Phil was totally stoked on it because he knew exactly what was happening there. It was right down his alley, you know.

BOB WEIR: We would take the first few songs and feel out the band that night—but we would also feel out the audience, see what they were responding to. We did that pretty naturally with the first set by just playing a bunch of tunes, and toward the end of the first set starting to develop them a bit—take them for a walk in the woods. By the second set, we had the audience with us and we could trip out. It was different from town to town; we would try to come out of the chute kind of tight and polished, just so that we didn't put them off. We needed to have them on our side. And then by the time we were warmed up and they were warmed up, we could let fly.

We had to chip away at preconceptions, because most of the writers who had submitted pieces to the local papers had never been to a show and didn't really know what they were talking about. So the folks who showed up didn't know what they were walking into, and we had to take a step back and say, "Here's us playing a regular song, or two or three. Now we're gonna step out a little bit . . . now we're gonna step out a little bit more . . . and now we're gonna have at you!" That was the approach, but at the same time, [it was] the original mindset—"We need these guys on our side"—that stuck with us throughout the tour. We were trying to leave no child behind.

Pigpen had missed performances sporadically in 1971 due to deepening alcohol-related health problems.

JERRY GARCIA: We were so delighted when [Pigpen] was able to come to Europe with us, 'cause he'd been so sick. And then when we were there he played and sang real good. He had a great time. He wasn't as strong as he had been, certainly, but he was there.

ROCK SCULLY: He couldn't drink but his temperament was good. He loved Europe; he really loved it. He rode on this Danish bus, which was sort of like the crew bus. It was the quieter of the two buses, usually. Pigpen lived on the back bench of that bus. He got knocked off that bench five or six times. He rolled off that bench and a couple of times he really hurt himself—I could see it; he really hurt his kidneys and bruised himself.

DONNA JEAN GODCHAUX: Pigpen was very, very, very sick, and they knew that his days were pretty much numbered. So Pigpen did what he was physically able to do on organ, and Keith played piano. That was the situation throughout Europe.

When the alcohol was drained out of his life, he got to be more reflective and began to touch a deeper space of who he was. It was very interesting and sweet. Keith and I had a really, really wonderful time with him. We were in Germany and we had a wonderful whole day just rapping it down with Pigpen. That is absolutely sealed in my heart, just having that time with him. But I think he did know, and he was alluding to or going toward another place.

JON McINTIRE: The equipment guys could be a problem because they were . . . emotionally willful. But really, in general, they were on their best behavior; everyone was. Going from country to country to country and all these different languages being spoken, and almost every night is a hall you've never played before and it has its own things, different cultures, what's allowable and what's not—everyone had to keep it together to an extent and look after each other.

STEVE PARISH: On that tour, we were screwed up out of our minds on these beautiful psychedelics. We would go all over the continent as free Americans seeing this world we had learned about, and we got to be there and play in great places. And that was some great music, too.

On that tour, what we usually thought was our medication level was stronger than it usually was from what we took at home. In other words, we were getting out of our minds laughing. On a day off, we all ended up in Heidelberg. There was this old castle, and in this old castle was this souvenir shop with these rubber skulls. When you pressed down on them, they just started laughing hysterically. So we took those on the bus, and we walked around town with these skulls laughing hysterically. We didn't stop laughing for two days.

We also went to the greatest cathedrals, and stood in those places and whispered and heard our voices carried around. Phil Lesh was a great master of architecture of these European cathedrals, and he'd explain things to you. And trips! On the top of Notre Dame, hanging on to a gargoyle. I don't know if you can still do it, but in those days you went right to the top of the place.

In the hotels in Europe, everybody puts their business shoes out, or their beautiful ladies' pumps, and the night porter will polish them all and put them back in front of your room in the morning. I was going to bed about three in the morning, I saw Sonny Heard. He put his finger up to his lips, and he was walking up the back stair-

DONNA JEAN GODCHAUX: I was so stoned during one of the [Paris] shows that at one point I found myself under Keith's piano. And I remember thinking, "Wow, this is really fantastic music, this Grateful Dead!" Then, "Oh, my gosh, I sing with this band!" I don't know how in the world I pressed through, but when it was time for me to sing again, I was up at the microphone.

way with his arms bulging with shoes. He methodically went up and down the stairs and mixed everybody's shoes up.

The next day, the hotel was in chaos. They were screamin' and yellin' and people were at the desk holding up ladies' beautiful, delicate shoes—a big businessman. And ladies with men's Oxfords. It was chaos.

PHIL LESH: [While we were in Germany] we went down to the hall to check it out. I'm looking at all the busts of the famous composers in the foyer, and everybody else has gone in. Mountain Girl came back and said, "You gotta see this, man!" They took me up to the balcony; we're lookin' down at the orchestra. "Look at the solo cellist." The solo cellist is my double: he has my hair, he has my build, my eyes, my movements. When they stop and take a break and the guy gets up and walks around, he looks like a clone of me.

After the rehearsal, I went down there looking for that guy, and it turns out there was another orchestra in the bowels of the building doing something. It wasn't the same orchestra that we had just seen. But all these other musicians are wandering around down there, and I'm down there in cowboy boots, a Pendleton shirt, a Levi jacket, jeans, and everything but the cowboy hat. They're all lookin' at me like I've just done a costume change. "Wait a minute —Hans! You look so different!" And they're all lookin' at me like I'm a really weird person. But I never found this guy to come face to face with him.

It turns out in every German city there's at least fifty Leshes in the phone book, so this guy could conceivably have been named Lesh, and I never did know.

JON McINTIRE: The audiences in Paris, although they were Parisian and spoke a different language, were like the audiences in New York. It was just thrilling, absolutely thrilling. And of course it's the Olympia, which was Edith Piaf's home, and all the incredible things that have happened there over the years. France was very high-energy, like the Fillmore East in New York.

191

> One movie-worthy episode that occurred on the Europe tour
> involved a near-riot at a show scheduled to take place in Lille,
> north of Paris near the Belgian border.

BOB WEIR: It started in Paris, where this Communist decided that
everybody should be able to go to the show for free—in stark igno-
rance of the economics of the matter. He got shown the door. That
didn't pretty up his mindset any, so he decided what he was gonna do
was piss in the gas tank of our diesel truck.

PHIL LESH: He didn't do that until after the show, when we went back
to the hotel. Rex and Sonny and I were up on the balcony, and somebody poured chocolate ice cream on his mauve velvet jacket. This is a
Communist wearing a mauve velvet jacket. It was very, very chic. He
got a little miffed. That was, I think, the final "trigger" that caused him
to piss or put water in the diesel fuel tanks of our trucks, so that our
equipment couldn't go anywhere.

BOB WEIR: The next morning, the truck headed out of town, bright
and early, and then we all got on the bus and headed to Lille. The
truck made it about eight miles out of Paris and broke down, but
we didn't know this [until] we arrived at the hall in Lille to a mob of
irate Frenchmen shouting anti-American stuff. Since it was deemed
that my French was the best in the group, I was awarded the oner-
ous opportunity to go out and tell a howling mob, "Hey, folks, no
show tonight. And not only that, the promoters bolted with your
money."

PHIL LESH: Which wasn't true, though. The guy hadn't bolted with
the money. I don't think he could get it that night, to give them
their money back for their tickets. I think he later gave them back
the money. And if he hadn't done that, we wouldn't have gone back
to play [the following week]. But we're getting ahead of ourselves.
We retreated—

BOB WEIR: —To the dressing room. We spent about thirty seconds in there wondering, "What the Sam Hill are we gonna do now?"

PHIL LESH [In mock fright]: Do we have to go out there and talk to them again?

BOB WEIR: Meanwhile, the door started to go thump, thump, thump and bulge a little bit, and we could see that that was gonna hold for, oh, maybe a minute and a half. We had one avenue of escape, and that was out the window and down a drainpipe, just sort of climbing, holding onto the drainpipe down three stories.

PHIL LESH: Actually, it was only a story and a half, Bob.

BOB WEIR: Really?

PHIL LESH: You could have jumped it, but it would have hurt when you landed.

BOB WEIR: Yeah, we would have had a lot of broken ankles. Anyway, so we were out of there, out the back window, down the drainpipe, and a quick sprint for the bus. We left a little rose on the windowsill there.
We came back about two, three weeks later [May 13, 1972] and played in the park for free.

PHIL LESH: The promoter was in tears, because he'd given all the money back and he had promised that we would come back and play.
It was a beautiful day, too. The light in France, there's nothing like it. It's understandable why it's produced so many great painters. We played in the park and there were real French working people, the kind that Van Gogh would paint. There they were, sitting down in front.

BOB WEIR: It was wonderful, a sublime experience.

DENNIS "WIZARD" LEONARD (Alembic recording crew): We canceled the gig [in Lille], a near-riot happened, we scrambled and eventually got back to the hotel, and then at five o'clock in the morning I get a call from [Sam] Cutler saying, "Get your ass down to the lobby, we have to go into the town." We got in some cabs and got into this little teeny town outside of Paris, which is where the truck was still broken down, and the pressure was on because we had to make a specific ferry to get across the channel with the gear in order to make Bickershaw [a festival in England], which was a big payday. We would have been in real trouble if we hadn't made it. So we get down there and there are two mechanics working on the red truck. Cutler's smoking three cigarettes at a time—not literally—and running in and out of this little cafe making phone calls, and he says, "Okay, I've got a trailer coming up; it's coming with a tractor and we'll get a trailer."

The truck was like a traditional English lorry, with a big box that was over the cab itself and we used that for spares and people's personal crap, and after we got most of the gear into the trailer, I think Parish said, "Hey, Wiz, go up there and hand me the shit." He had a couple of cardboard boxes. So I was gathering stuff and I grabbed a pair of jeans that were up there and I feel moisture and I reach into the pocket and there was a brown glass bottle with an eyedropper [containing liquid LSD]. I found that out a little too late. It was a very concentrated little thing. So I tighten up the top and lick my hands off and lick the bottle off. I was a really experienced voyager so I was thinking, "Okay, nice ride to Calais." Ram Rod sees me and says, "What did you just do?" I said, "This thing was leaking so I tightened it up." I said I might've gotten two or three drops worth and he said, "Wiz, it's concentrate."

So we're pedal-to-the-metal and we're going through northern France on the way to Calais, and Barry, the English driver, seems to be taking amazing chances passing people, and we're having a hard time keeping up with him [in the recording truck]. I'm really high by this point and I feel like I'm on a roller coaster; the road is undulating and Joe [Winslow, who is driving] and I look at each other and we realize, "Oh, shit, he's driving like that because we might not make it!" So the trip across France was breakneck. We pull up—we're the last two vehicles in the queue for the last ferry—and there had been so much energy and tension that I was basically straight. Suddenly, Winslow looks like a deer in the headlights: "What's wrong, Joe?" "I can't find my passport!" I said, "Joe, just get in the back and hide behind the 16-track; fuck this shit—we're going to England!" So we sneak out, get him in the back, we're inching onto the ferry, and all of a sudden I hear BOOM! BOOM! BOOM! It's Joe in the back—he's found his passport!

We make it onto the ferry and then, to add insult to injury, we get to English customs and we hand them posters and all this shit we hand out to try to smooth things, and this one customs guy wants to see something. The one object he picks is this fake amplifier that has a stash in it. So we pull it out, show him the serial number, and he says, "All right, boys, thank you very much!" It was a sigh of relief, and then we drove from Dover up to London.

JOHN "MARMADUKE" DAWSON (New Riders of the Purple Sage): When everyone went to Europe in '72, we really didn't spend that much time together. The New Riders went to Europe independently. We went to London, where we caught a bus that took us up to the Bickershaw Festival. It was really rainy and horrible—typical English weather—and the *New Musical Express* called it "Bickerswim."

DAVID NELSON: There was a report right before we got there that some English guy had been electrocuted somewhere near there when he touched a wet microphone, so we were totally scared. Even though there was a canopy over the stage, the wind was blowing really hard and the rain was all over us. I don't know how people in the audience stood it. But we'd look out and see people sitting in the mud on little pieces of plastic.

After more than a month gallivanting around "the Continent," the band returned to London, where the tour had begun, this time playing four nights at the Strand Lyceum. The ever-affable

Bob Weir was again available to try to explain the Grateful Dead to a radio interviewer.

BOB WEIR (1972): If Garcia sings the first one, I sing the second, Pigpen sings the third, and then we go back around in that sequence again and again.

During our plunges through the innermost and outermost regions of space or whatever, if we get to a region that has a rhythmic and a tonal mode that suggests a particular song, one of us will start playing and everybody will fall in behind it.

When we're playing free, and we're drifting from key to key, from feeling to feeling, mode to mode, Garcia and Phil are generally playing single lines, and any combination of two notes suggests a chord. My role, and a piano player's role, is to intuit what that chord is going to be, the next note they're going to play, the combination of those two—and be there with that chord and maybe an augmentation on that chord which will either suggest staying there and building that, or suggest going to a new passage, a new mode, or a new key, or whatever. It's quite a chore sometimes. It takes a lot of concentration. Sometimes it just rolls out really easily, and sometimes you get a combination of people just guessing that comes up with some inspirational new idea which is—well, it's worth living for.

Sometimes we know what we're doing, sometimes we're completely lost in what we're doing, and maybe it just grabs us and takes us there, too. It's a tenuous art, trying to make form out of chaos. As we get better practiced at it, we can get looser and freer in our associations, and let the music more or less move us in a given direction. Sometimes, if what we're doing just really wants to go somewhere and the air is just pregnant with it, it's undeniable, we'll just go there. On a really good night it'll happen a succession of times. No one will even play a cue, yet bang, we're off.

BILL GILES (Fan): The Lyceum Ballroom was a beautiful place. No seats downstairs, just the dance floor. At the back of the hall there were tiered balconies; on the lower ones there were comfortable seats grouped around low tables and low lights. The New Riders opened the shows, and for the two I attended [May 25–26, 1972], I watched them mainly from the back. Then down to the front for the Dead. Plenty of people were there in front of the stage, but not too crushed.

My most striking memory is of the hand-clapped intro to "Not Fade Away" at the end of the first set. They had just finished "I Know Rider," and somehow the crowd got into clapping the Bo Diddley beat. I remember all the band laughing and looking at one another with some astonishment, and knowing there was only one thing they could do. That was amazing—band synchronizing with audience.

PHIL LESH: [On that tour] Keith was just coming into his own, really. And I gotta say that Billy played like a young god. I mean, he was everywhere on the drums, and just kickin' our butts every which way, which is what drummers live to do, you know.

DONNA JEAN GODCHAUX: Billy was so there with what the Grateful Dead's music was all about; he was always postured to play anything. He never set down a 2 and 4 that you couldn't get away from; Billy's left and right arm were always postured at any millisecond to take that rhythm anywhere that it needed to go. That's the beauty of Billy Kreutzmann's playing. He played like a dancer.

BOB WEIR: *Europe '72* [the triple album, released in the fall of 1972] was the answer to a whole lot of questions, like "How the hell are we gonna be able to take the entire staff and crew and all of us on a European vacation?" So somebody said, "Let's make an album over there and that'll pay for it." And through a great deal of hassling and haggling and that kind of stuff, it actually came to pass that we went to Europe, recorded an album over there, came back, and, lo and behold, the album has paid for our European tour, which was a real nice way to do it, I thought.

RON WICKERSHAM: They came back from *Europe '72* and they were disappointed with the vocals. Rather than just listening with headphones and redoing the vocals, which would have been artificial, we set up the whole sound system in 60 Brady Street [Alembic's

San Francisco headquarters]. The microphones were all spaced out just like they were on the stage. We reproduced the guitar tracks through the guitar amps. All the leakage into the mics was the same as the live performance.

> Although from outward appearances the Dead and Warner Bros. seemed to be getting along fairly well—after all, they had scored bona fide hit albums with *Workingman's Dead, American Beauty, Skull and Roses,* and *Europe '72*—the band was not-very-quietly looking into breaking away from the record business establishment and starting their own independent label. Ron Rakow was the one who pushed a vision that allowed that to happen. By the end of 1972, the decision had been made, much to the disappointment of Warner Bros.

RON RAKOW: It was divine inspiration. February '72. It was the rainy season. I was riding along Highway One [California's Pacific Coast Highway] and I got a picture of us really being able to nurture our people. Instead of people who actually abhorred our lifestyle—the executives I met at Warner Bros.—I saw the entire structure of what became Grateful Dead Records in one complete picture.

I ran into the Grateful Dead office that day and explained this vision to Jerry and McIntire at the same time, and they both seemed to love the idea. So I got a separate letter from each of them that said essentially, "Introducing Ron Rakow. He's doing some work for us. Any help you can give him would be greatly appreciated by us." And I used that to go around the record industry and gather data, which I then used to augment this vision I had and create a series of cash-flow charts to explain different scenarios that might come up if we had our own company.

On July Fourth, 1972, I presented the "So What Papers" to the Dead at Billy Kreutzmann's house. I put a big chart on an easel and on the top, with the arrow flowing into Grateful Dead Records, was the word MESBIC [Minority Enterprise Small Business Investment Company]. [It was a] government agency; I had hippies declared a minority! And $300,000 was written on that arrow, which meant we only had to put in $1,350, and by using the MESBIC law, we would lever that into $350,000. It was an anomaly and it was not designed for Wall Street–trained hippies. When I explained it, Garcia went nuts. He thought it was the greatest thing. Phil went nuts. But Bonnie Parker was saying, "No government, no government!" She had worked for a small business investment company and the government came in to investigate them once in a while. She was so upset that I pulled out my pocket knife and I cut the chart right up, and I cut the MESBIC out of it. Now I had to find $300,000. So I went to Jerry Wexler [of WEA—Warner-Elektra-Atlantic, a distribution cartel] and offered to sell him the Grateful Dead's foreign rights for $300,000 for a period of years.

ROCK SCULLY: I really didn't want to see that happen. I just knew it wasn't going to be worth the trouble. I said, "We don't really want to be in that business." I liked Warner Bros. We finally got a working relationship with them and things were going well. I especially liked it because they hooked up with [Atlantic Records'] Ahmet Ertegun and Jerry Wexler—"Man, now we've got some beef here; these guys are great and understand what we're doing."

JERRY GARCIA (1973): There are a lot of people on our payroll, and we can't really count that much on record royalties to take care of business. The live shows we do are the main source of income for the band, and we've been playing an awful lot to pay off our overhead.

We've planned for over a year to form our own record manufacturing and distributing company so as to package and promote our stuff in a more human manner. A large benefit from that will be our capability of getting away from the retail list price inflation while still keeping more of the profits. We have nothing against the way Warner Bros. have treated us. They've never interfered with our music. But if the records cover a larger share of our overhead, then we can pick and choose on our live shows. We can experiment a little bit and play the really groovy shows.

> At the first show of 1973, at Stanford University's Maples Pavilion, the Dead introduced seven new songs, each one something of a stylistic departure for the band—"China Doll," "Eyes of the World," "Loose Lucy," "Here Comes Sunshine," "Row Jimmy," "Wave That Flag" (a forerunner to "U.S. Blues"), and "They Love Each Other."

DAVID GANS: The songs that came up in '73 at Stanford began a transition out of the Americana good-time country stuff into a different direction. I think their charge to each other was to bring in a new song that opens up a new space. "Eyes of the World" opened up a new harmonic and rhythmic direction. "Weather Report Suite" did the same thing. Pretty much from "Eyes of the World" on, every new song was a new groove or a new harmonic space.

ROBERT HUNTER: I hadn't intended to stay in a cowboy space forever. It was a passing . . . well, it was more than a passing phase, certainly.

JERRY GARCIA: It was just another voice you could use.

ROBERT HUNTER: I'm pretty sure "Eyes of the World" was from Larkspur. I remember I'd practice my trumpet out there in the shed all the time—blow my brains half-out until I got psychedelic, and then I'd go write. I finally had to quit it—I was afraid I'd blow a blood vessel in my brain if I didn't give it up.

JERRY GARCIA: I don't remember writing "Eyes of the World," but I do remember that basically it wanted a samba feel, which it still sort of has. It was kind of a Brazilian thing.

ROBERT HUNTER: I can sort of see a piece of paper in a notebook at that time, and then it became the introduction to "Eyes of the World." And I guess the image of "Eyes of the World" is something I just lifted off a [Paramount]-Pathé newsreel—"The Eyes and Ears of the World."

DAN HEALY: The Grateful Dead has always been really supportive of the various things I've wanted to do. There have been many
times I've gone to them and said, "Hey, you guys, I need . . . " and
it involves huge sums of money. A lot of times when it's been an
absolute risk and there really wasn't much proof that the suggestion was going to be viable, they've gone out on a limb with me. The
band has never said no to me, and I've had my share of faux pas in
the past.

Hometown gigs are where you experiment a lot because you're
near the shop and so on, and you want to iron things out before
you go out on the road. I had gone to the band in late '72 and gotten $10,000 or $12,000 to work on this idea I had. Now, in '72
that was a lot of money, especially for the Grateful Dead. So I went
out and got these super low-distortion tweeters and all this other
stuff. Just prior to that, the band had bought me this other piece
of equipment that reads out the amplitudes of the different musical notes called a real-time analyzer. The upshot was that I equal-
ized the system, got it all flat, and then about three seconds into
the Stanford show, the tweeters were so out of balance that it just
blew them out. I smoked $12,000 worth of speakers just like that!
I thought, "Oh, God," but I think the most that was said was, "Nice
going, asshole."

DAVE PARKER: They wanted to develop the sound system, and an
enormous amount of money went into that. In those days the state
of the art hadn't developed to the point where you would have good
sound in arenas and stadiums. They wanted to play smaller places,
but it was tough to make any money doing that because their travel
expenses were so high.

Bear was the one who helped inspire them to what could be done.
There was a sense of going for the best. They could have taken more
money for themselves if they'd chosen not to, but [they spent]
hundreds of thousands on sound equipment. It was driving me nuts,
because Bear was very good on the conceptual, but I thought a lot
of money was being wasted. Bear and I were sometimes at odds
because he'd have a vision of some fantastic thing he'd want to do—

"Replace all this!"—and I was trying to deal with the resources that were actually available. But maybe my perspective was too limited to really pass judgment on that.

> Meanwhile, development of the Dead's record company had kicked into gear.

JERRY GARCIA (1974): It's dumb to complain about all that record company bullshit. I mean, if you're enough of an asshole to stick it up where they can shoot at it, you can't complain for getting shot. It was our blunder and we've been living with our mistake all these years. Now, hopefully we're free to make our own mistakes.

DAVID PARKER: If it were up to me, I wouldn't have gone in that direction. But it wasn't up to me. It's what the band wanted to do—particularly Jerry, and Rakow had inspired him with this idea: you could have your own record company, and independence was an idea that spoke very loudly to all those guys; they loved that idea. They'd had the usual hassles with record company people who didn't appreciate and understand what they were trying to do. This looked like an ideal vehicle to be free. I think the plan presented to them was overly optimistic and not really workable, although it did hang together for a few years. By '76 it all came crashing down. But they did get to have the exhilaration of saying, "Hey, we have our own record company." It introduced a lot of complications and difficulties into the work that had to be done. And I was really kind of glad when that phase of things was over.

RON RAKOW (1973): The record company appeals to people like Jerry Garcia for two reasons. One is that it's dangerous, and therefore exciting. If there's anything in the world [Garcia] hates, it's security. The second is that in every industry they're getting larger and larger and more concentrated. This represents a step away from concentration. We think that's very important.

JERRY GARCIA (1973): Why should we be providing juice for the Kinney Corporation [Warner's parent company]? We thought it would be groovier to do it ourselves and take a lot of the money the record company made and use it to put out a better product. And we also felt that even if we fucked up real bad, we could still sell as many records as Warner Bros. did.

RON RAKOW (1974): This company represents a very intense sociological statement. A whole bunch of freaks take over; one year later we have a $3.5-million to $4-million record company—and we're still freaks.

STEVE BROWN: I had been in radio and the record business from 1961 until 1972 in various forms. So my experience in both record distribution and marketing and promotion was pretty solid at that point—I was the head buyer at this chain in San Francisco called Mighty Fine Distributing; we had the Record Factory stores.

The Dead's contract with Warner Bros. was ending and Rakow had been pushing some kind of machinations of real-world domination, trying to turn them into their own scene of being their own record company, by hook or by crook, and with Jerry's help. Rakow was able to convince Jerry that this was a good idea, and Jerry was able to subsequently sell it to the band. There was a certain amount of risk, obviously, but it's the Grateful Dead.

When I got word from somebody at Warner Bros. that they were going to lose the Dead and that they wanted to start their own label, I put together a proposal. I knew if I delivered it to 1330 Lincoln, San Rafael, their main office at the time, and Rakow took a look at it, I might stand a chance of being able to change from being the head buyer for a record distributor to working for a really cool band, and working for their record company. I got a call back and they said they saw what my credentials were for having been around the scene and the industry, so I went for an interview with Rakow and Jerry. That was November or December of 1972. I didn't start working with them until February of 1973.

[At the meeting] Rakow went over the structure of what he

thought this would entail and how we would structure it personnel-wise, and distribution-wise what his ideas were—the primary markets and the secondary markets and so on.

That only went on for a few minutes, and then I wound up alone with Jerry for a few more minutes and the record business talk dissolved into a memory lane trip: "Where did you grow up in the city?" "The Excelsior." "Oh, you were in Ingleside near the El Rey Theater." "Remember the Barts and Pachucos?" We started talking about the gangs we knew in each of our areas, the bands we'd seen, influences we both had. Then Rakow came back and he was saying, "We're going to be setting up down the street at Fifth and Lincoln," and he went out again and Garcia said, "Well, see ya!" and I caught up with Rakow and he said, "I heard from Jerry: you're on."

Rakow and Jerry were really the record company, the two who were talking the most about stuff. At the band's meetings, the other guys would bring up stuff, but I wasn't privy to those. They would also come to the office often and talk with Rakow, especially Phil. But Jerry was definitely there the most.

Some of my fondest memories of all my Grateful Dead experiences were being out in the front office and hearing Jerry in the kitchen playing. One day David Bromberg showed up and the two of them went for a whole afternoon just playing together and laughing. "Oh, man, where's my recorder when I need it?" They were rehearsing in the kitchen, with French roast and pastries.

Pigpen made what turned out to be his final appearance with the Dead at the Hollywood Bowl on June 17, 1972, but he did not perform. Over the next nine months, he worked hard trying to regain his strength, but his liver disease kept progressing. The band learned to work around his absence, with Weir, particularly, stepping up to take on some of Pigpen's showman role. Pigpen died at home, alone, on March 8, 1973.

BOB WEIR: Pigpen had been slowing down and gradually getting sicker, and his musical output was tapering, so by the time he had to stay off the road, he hadn't been contributing that much so it didn't have that major an impact. Coincidentally, I started to hit my stride around the same time, and with Pigpen sick, there was a need for me to do more.

LAIRD GRANT: God knows what kind of emotional shit he went through near the end, between trying to keep up with the band and keep up with that alcoholic jones that he had. When it got down to where he couldn't drink, that really knocked him for a loop, because then he had no place to hide. He didn't smoke weed, he didn't take psychedelics, he couldn't drink. It was like being shuffled off to the side track and watching the freights go by.

ALAN TRIST (Management): During that period when he wasn't on the road with the band, he was working on an album, working on songs. Around that time the solo album thing really took off—Jerry was the first, then Weir, and Pigpen was right in there, too. I remember going over to his house [in Corte Madera, Marin County] a couple of times and hearing odd tapes that he played. His way of projecting the blues through his singing was so soulful and authentic, whether it was with the Grateful Dead or by himself at home.

ROCK SCULLY: I don't think it was really going to be a solo album. I think the way he looked at it was it was going to be part of a Dead album. He wanted three songs on a Dead album. He didn't have enough for a whole album; he wanted to be a significant part of a Dead album again. A couple of them were beautiful. Pigpen was supposed to come back. All the reports I had were very positive that he was getting better. He didn't do anything to fuck up; it's just that his body gave up.

SUE SWANSON: I was at home [when I heard the news of Pig's death]. Jon McIntire, Danny Rifkin, and I shared a big house up in Novato, and I remember sitting around the table early that morning trying to remember to call everyone, because poor Mountain Girl had read it in the paper. We hadn't called her early enough. We were all completely in shock. I mean, even though everyone knew he was really sick, it still seemed sudden. I think everyone wanted to believe he'd make it in the long run.

ROCK SCULLY: For Pigpen to die alone—that was one we really beat ourselves up about for a long time. We had somebody looking after him and everything, but she wasn't around when it happened.

JON McINTIRE: I chose the booze for the wake and we bought cases and cases of stuff. I mean, what are you gonna do, man? A favorite thing in Pig's life was drinkin', so what are you gonna do if you throw a party for Pig? You're gonna drink a lot, and we did, and we told lewd and rude stories about him all night—and there were lots to tell. It was wonderful. It was a great party because it was loose and desperate and it was full of love.

SUE SWANSON: [At the funeral] I was in complete shock. The Kesey people came down from Oregon. All I remember about it was not going by the open casket. We were sitting three or four rows back, and I was on the end and I just turned and walked out. I didn't want that to be my last view of him. I couldn't handle it.

ROCK SCULLY: I just remember the funeral as totally depressing. I was just totally brought down. I've never seen Jerry more unhappy, ever. God, he was devastated; we all were. Right from the get-go after Pig died, Jerry stated it out front: "This'll never be the same again. It'll always be something else. It's just a whole different thing."

BOB WEIR: We'd been getting used [to Pigpen's absence] all along, so it wasn't a sudden change when he died. It was a very gradual change that became formal when he wasn't here anymore at all.

JERRY GARCIA: We played without him for almost a year [before he died], but still, after he died, you'd go out there [onstage] and it'd be like, "Where's Pig?" And we missed all those songs. It was like operating with a broken leg. So we went with our next strong suit, which was kind of a country feel; the American mythos, the Hunter songs. And our other strong suit was our [musical] weirdness. So we went with our strong suits that didn't involve Pigpen.

DONNA JEAN GODCHAUX: It was heavy, but I think everybody in the band sort of said, "Okay, we've gotta move on." Everybody sort of took it on the chin and pressed forward.

JERRY GARCIA: He was genuinely talented. He had no discipline, but he had reams of talent. And he had that magical thing of being able to make stuff up as he went along. He also had great stage presence. The ironic thing was he hated it—it really meant nothing to him; it wasn't what he liked. We had to browbeat him into being a performer. His best performances were one-on-one, sitting in a room with an acoustic guitar.

Out in front of the crowd he could work the band, and he'd really get the audience going. He always had more nerve than I could believe. He'd get the audience on his side, and he'd pick somebody out—like a heckler—and get on them. He'd crack us up. Sometimes he'd just kill me!

You had to be there for Pigpen. He's a guy who's tough to talk about, like Neal [Cassady] or any of the other people who are not here, and what was special about them was themselves. He was special because he was special, you know? The way your friend is special. The way someone you love is special. Pigpen, for me, was more than a performer. He was a very dear friend. Really a dear friend. We had a lot of crazy times together, and Pigpen was always on the side of crazy times, although he and I were not always on the same side. But he could always be trusted.

CHAPTER 6

Independence

JERRY GARCIA: ["Dark Star"] was incredibly different every night and sometimes it was so utterly unrecognizable. "Dark Star" had no form, no real substance. The only thing it had was a snatch of melody and a few words, and everything else was open. It was meant to never be the same way twice.

STEVE SILBERMAN: Sometimes in shows in the early seventies, you'll hear an "Eyes of the World" in the first set where the jams are ten minutes, or there will be an "El Paso" in the middle of a "Dark Star" and there's this funny shuffling of the cards. It was like driving the Starship Enterprise, and you come out of warp and you're in this little bar and then you would warp out again.

What I love especially about the versions of "Dark Star" from '72 to '74—and this is present in the early [versions] too—it's as if the music is already going on in this parallel universe and they just take you to where it's always going on. That's a psychedelic thing, too, because oftentimes when you take acid, you would arrive in a place that seemed familiar, if you'd tripped before, and seemed ancient, even. Once you got there you knew that the Aztecs making designs of lizards and whatnot in pottery were in that same place that you were at right then. In your mind you'd associate the musical exploration and that psychedelic place, and after a while you'd start to think that the Grateful Dead owned that place, or were the music of that place.

There was something about the jamming process that was inherently psychedelic—starting with a melody and then expanding that melody until you were perhaps in a new place where you no longer recognized that place as being within the melody, and then coming back to that melody, or moving on to another. You're not constantly reminded of the place you've left. You're allowed to forget where you were.

> In the summer of 1973, the Grateful Dead joined forces with another of the most popular bands of the day, the Allman Brothers, for a pair of marathon concerts at steamy RFK Stadium in Washington, D.C. (June 9–10, 1973) and a one-day festival (July 28, 1973), also featuring the Band, at a Grand Prix speedway in the tiny upstate New York community of Watkins Glen. Though the event had none of the cultural impact of Woodstock, it was actually much larger, attracting more than six hundred thousand people—the largest musical gathering in U.S. history at the time.

JIM KOPLIK (Watkins Glen promoter): When I was a student at Ohio State, I was putting on shows in Columbus, but when I came east to go to law school, it got too hard to do shows in Columbus any longer, so I looked for a [concert] market that was in its infancy. Bill Graham was in New York, Don Law was in Boston, but there was nobody in Connecticut of note, so I started booking there. The first show I bought was the Allman Brothers, but Duane [Allman] was killed so I had to cancel. I partnered with Shelly Finkel and we got the Grateful Dead to play at Dillon Stadium in Hartford [July 16, 1972]. I remember getting my first Grateful Dead contract, how excited I was. And then Dickey Betts and Berry Oakley [of the Allmans] came to the Dead show and jammed with them. They were artists who had a similar audience and I got a call from the road manager of the Allmans, Bunky Odom, asking, "Do you mind if we come up and jam with the Dead?" I loved both acts, so I said, "Oh, my God, that would be great!"

JERRY GARCIA (1973): [Playing with the Allman Brothers] is kind of like playing with us the way we were five years ago. Musically and setupwise, they're kind of similar to the way we used to be. They especially sounded like us when they were the original Allman Brothers. They had two drummers, two guitars, organ, and bass—exactly the instrumentation we had [from 1968–70].

Dickey and the guys had flashed on our music when we played a festival in Florida about five or six years ago. We really inspired them and they patterned a lot of their trip after us. They're like a younger, Southern version of us in some ways musically. I really enjoy playing with those guys; they're fun to play with. They're good.

JIM KOPLIK: After I saw them onstage together in '72, I started talking to the managers about putting them together for a big show, and they were all for it. Shelly actually came up with the Watkins Glen site and we showed it to [the bands] and they loved it.

It was a really quiet little hamlet until we had all those people there. We thought we'd bring in about 150,000 [people]; we got a permit for that. The people who owned the track were looked upon very favorably in the town, and after Woodstock, the state had enacted a mass-gathering law we had to meet. They required a certain number of toilets and water. The state came in and counted the toilets and the water bottles.

We ended up agreeing to hire Bill Graham to build a stage and bring the sound, so we had the goodwill and the education of Bill Graham helping us, because Shelly and I were twenty-eight and twenty-three years old. We were not really fully capable of pulling this thing off without his expertise. We advertised it and right away we knew it was hot, because it took off very strong. Of course, we had no idea it would end up being what it was. We were two babes in the woods who got lucky.

It sold out in advance, basically right before the show, but back in 1973 it was hard to get the word out. We kept ten thousand tickets to sell at the door, because we knew people would come to the door. We didn't think 450,000 more would come to the door.

BILL KREUTZMANN (1973): We were talking to Bill Graham before the concert and we figured there would be about 130,000 people. But Graham said, "Haven't you been reading the papers? There's gonna be a lot more than that." You should have seen it from the air, man.

People were very nice. They moved out of our way and handed us beer and things. About a mile from the motel, we couldn't go any further and we got out and walked. Cars were all stopped and nobody could go anywhere. I remember there was this guy and this chick on the roof of their car, huggin' and kissin'. It gave me a migrant feeling.

BILL GRAHAM (1973): By Thursday night, there were already 80,000 to 100,000 camped outside. I said to the promoters, "Let's open at dawn [Friday] and do a soundcheck in front of a hundred thousand people." Everybody agreed. My theory was that rather than have a stampede, open at dawn, and those that were up could come in, and those that were sleeping could sleep, then get up, and not be in the middle of a crowd.

So they came in Friday. At noon on Friday the sound was set. The Dead played two hours. It drove the kids crazy. The Band came on and did an hour. The Allmans did two hours. By Friday night, 150,000 people had gotten a five-hour show. They'd gotten a taste—an appetizer—and they knew their heroes were there.

JIM KOPLIK: I thought the Dead's soundcheck set was much better than the show set. The funny thing about the first day is it was only supposed to be a half-hour- or forty-five-minute soundcheck, and they played something like two hours. I was sitting backstage with Dickey Betts and he was saying, "Oh, shoot, now we have to play two hours!" So they ended up doing a long soundcheck also. I remember going over to Shelly and saying, "Why wasn't today the show? I'd like to go home."

People just kept coming and coming. We couldn't believe what was going on. We knew we'd lost it the night before the actual show started. It was around one or two in the morning and we lost the gates.

It got so crowded I couldn't drive a golf cart through. We had radios and a helicopter, and I would go up and look at the crowd. We'd fly down the road and [see that] it was ten to fifteen miles of cars, and we realized, "We're totally screwed!" Then I heard the state police were closing the Thruway, so I thought I'd have to give everybody their money back. I thought I was out of business and wished I was back in law school. About an hour later they reopened the Thruway, so I knew we were safe at that point. I really thought it went off quite well considering we had 600,000 people there, of which 450,000 were uninvited guests.

The next day, at the real show, it was pouring during the Band's set. It was so great having the Band there. That was the Dead's choice. We had actually agreed to put on Leon Russell as the third act on the show. But then the Dead or Jerry or somebody really wanted the Band, because that was their home territory. I remember having to pay Leon Russell money to not be at Watkins Glen.

The Band was excellent and I thought the Allmans were great, also. I thought the Dead were a little flat. We knew [the Dead and the Allmans] wanted to do a closing jam. I wanted to get them to rehearse it [on the soundcheck day] but it was too crowded. And there was no way to make it look like it was a surprise jam, so they decided not to [rehearse]. I don't remember the jam being particularly memorable.

We had an agreement with the bands that none of them would record audio or video of the shows, per the Dead's wishes, and then everybody did.

The Dead got paid $117,500, and then I had to give them a $25,000 bonus because there were so many people. I was not a happy guy. But we made money. The only extra cost we had was cleanup, and it went from $5,000 to $50,000.

BOB WEIR: There were numerous injuries, but none that involved violence—no stabbings or shootings. But when we got back here [to the Bay Area] everybody was saying, "It was a bummer, wasn't it?" The concert apparently got bad press on the West Coast. There was definitely a spirit of cooperation there, like Woodstock. But this was better than Woodstock because this time people knew what to do, what to expect.

The cops were more or less indistinguishable in that they carried no visible weapons. I remember a few dances in Redwood City [south of San Francisco] when we used to go down there to hear Buck Owens that were a lot rougher.

> As 1973 progressed, the Dead continued to assert their independence, putting various structures into place to keep the responsibilities (and profits) in the "family."

RICHARD LOREN (Booking agent and manager): Sam Cutler was a real businessman, a shrewd West End London kind of guy. He grew up on the streets. Very, very ambitious. He became the point man, because Rock and Danny weren't really businessmen. They were hippies trying to deal with business. Cutler knew the buttons to push with promoters and heads of record companies and all that, and he did that with a great deal of self-aggrandizement. He forms an agency. It becomes the Sam Cutler trip. He signed the New Riders and this one and that one. He was the one who worked closely with the big sound system. He'd intimidate the promoters and he got the Dead more money than they'd ever gotten before, which they needed for the sound system—and of course he was taking [the standard agent's commission]. So he was the first guy to make them play the big gigs. But he took it too far, and eventually they let him go.

JON McINTIRE: His worldview was entirely different. He was an empire builder, which eventually other people became too, but at that particular time, my whole emphasis was community building and preservation of the community and sharing. I remember one time being in Sam's office and he had a big poster of a Jensen-Healey [sports car] on the wall and a yacht; he wanted all those things. I said, "Sam, this isn't the place to get those things," and he literally leaped over the desk and ran out into the office and shouted, "McIntire says I can't have a Jensen-Healey! McIntire says I can't have a yacht!" What I was saying, though, was, "This is not the type of community where that can happen." Of course, eventually it became that, with everybody having BMWs and Ferraris and whatever else, but that was not what I felt the mandate was, and it certainly was never part of Jerry's vision of things.

> Shortly after Watkins Glen, the Dead went into the Record Plant in Sausalito to cut their first studio album in three years, *Wake of the Flood,* which was also the debut release for the band's new label, Grateful Dead Records. The album contained a broad range of material, including a few songs the band had been playing for a while such as "Mississippi Half-Step Uptown Toodeloo," "Stella Blue," "Here Comes Sunshine" and "Eyes of the World," and a couple of freshly minted tunes: Weir's ambitious, three-part "Weather Report Suite" and the Keith Godchaux-Robert Hunter track "Let Me Sing Your Blues Away," which Keith sang. Those tracks were also notable for including horns for the first time on a Dead record.

JERRY GARCIA (1973): We're recording close to two albums worth of material, and [will] distill it into one record, leaving the rest in the can. It's funny, you know, but I can't really pin down what kind of album it's gonna be. I never have been able to tell with past albums, either. When I get the final copy home and listen to it, then I'll be able to look back and see what it is. Right now, all I know is that the tunes are all good. The tunes that me and Robert Hunter wrote are the best we've ever written. They're a little more sophisticated in terms of structure than our other ones. But they're Grateful Dead all the way. I mean they sound like the Grateful Dead. I can't really look at them objectively, but I feel that they're better. It's hard to tell what direction they're moving in. All the tunes are very different from each other, and the ones that preceded them as well.

BOB WEIR (1973): We made this record in the month of August. We recorded day and night for thirty consecutive days, and this is the product. We all had a lot of fun making it; it sounds just like what was happening. We were all working on doing this kind of music, and this is what came out. I don't think you could call it country-rock and I don't think you could call it acid-rock. It seems like a logical extension of what we've been doing all along, but then, we've been changing gradually and we put out a record every year, so what seems to us to be a gradual change seems to be a big, cathartic one to everyone else.

JERRY GARCIA: "Stella Blue" is a mood piece. It's lovely and it is also unique—it's not like any other song. It doesn't owe anything to anything else. When Hunter gave me the lyrics, I sat on 'em and sat on 'em. Then, when we were in Germany [in 1972] I sat down with an acoustic guitar early in the morning, and the song just fell together. It was so effortless writing it that I don't feel as though I wrote it. It's also one of those songs that I was born to sing. Every time I do it, I find something new in it, like a little thing in the phrasing or in the sense of it. And the way the Grateful Dead plays "Stella Blue" is just gorgeous. At times it seems like a moment freezes on one of those chord changes, and I have to go a long way to find where I am and where the lyric is. The song brings out a certain delicacy that only the Grateful Dead is capable of. Those guys will follow my lyric. If I change the tempo inside a phrase, they'll be right there in the next bar. It's amazing.

STEVE BROWN: The first production we did with the new label was *Wake of the Flood*. Which was a real family production all the way, like most of the previous records. For the artwork, we got Rick Griffin to do the cover and he came up with that nice image [a hooded figure holding a sickle and a sheaf of wheat, with the ocean and a skull-shaped cloud in the background], which was real different for him and real different for the Dead.

We went out of our way to come up with the best materials we could find and tried to get virgin vinyl, which was the best material available for the actual pressing. So we put all the time and effort into making the whole thing as good as we could make it and then— BANG! About a week after it came out, bootlegs started to show up. Goddamn bootlegs!

If you really knew the record, you could tell the difference. The color tones [on the cover] were a little different, and the sticker on the back, instead of having rounded corners, had square corners. And, of course, the bootleggers didn't use virgin vinyl, so a lot of those copies don't sound that good. But they really did go to great lengths to duplicate it, and the casual buyer didn't know the difference.

We didn't really have any idea how to deal with it, so we did what most regular companies would do: We called up the FBI! I'm sure when the FBI called up the Grateful Dead file at headquarters they must have been saying, "What? These guys want help from us?" The FBI found out that it was the mob working out of New Jersey, and so a cease-and-desist order was put out, and that pressure—the pressure that the FBI was actually on the case—seemed to stop it. But we have no idea how many counterfeits got out there or were sold. For years they turned up in used record stores all over the country.

The shock to us was that no sooner had we gone independent than we became highly vulnerable, and we didn't have the kind of protections that big record companies have—armies of lawyers who you just don't fuck with. We were, unfortunately, little and very fuck-withable. But the FBI came to the rescue, and we never had any subsequent problems. Having the FBI working for us helped, but I also think the bootleggers realized that we had a pretty limited market and that they weren't going to be reaping the rewards of an *Abbey Road* with *Wake of the Flood*.

> In addition to having two record companies—Grateful Dead and Round (for solo albums and projects attached to the different band members)—the Dead also handled their own booking, travel, and publicity in-house, and they made a major outreach to their fans. Ever since the gatefold of *Skull and Roses* trumpeted "DEAD FREAKS UNITE" and asked Deadheads to join their mailing list, the band had been communicating with

them regularly through a typically idiosyncratic (but totally cool) newsletter, and folks on the "Dead Heads" list were also sent seven-inch samplers of new Round releases and other promo items.

ROBERT HUNTER: Looking back on those old "Dead Head" newsletters—I'd just get stoned and draw that "Hypnocracy" stuff [the pseudo-philosophical musings of St. Dilbert]. So, I'd do that and then we'd add a little information in there about what was going on, most of which I wrote, and which Alan Trist would sometimes write. Jerry would maybe add a drawing here and there, and then we'd send it out. It was fun to do and very low-key. Our fan club was at a fairly low ebb, probably just a few thousand people. And the Deadheads and the Dead were a close, symbiotic unit at that point. But looking back on them—whew! Those things are very intimate, like the clippings you might paste up on your own refrigerator.

I don't think it was something that was marked to continue, and I'll tell you where I got off it. When we formed Round Records, Ron Rakow took the mailing list and sent out these horrible little promo postcards signed "Anton Round," and I thought it was the sleaziest looking Hollywood bullshit you'd ever want to see. I was outraged at this. "How dare you use this for commercial purposes?" I was told that the list was now to be used for this sort of thing and basically that the list had been taken over. I said, "Count me out."

ROSIE McGEE: Frankie Weir, who was Bobby's girlfriend at the time, wanted to find a more affordable way for the women to accompany their spouses on the road more often. She hatched a plot to open a travel agency, which was a brilliant idea because not only would the business get the commissions that would otherwise go to the other travel agent, but they would get some free tickets for having these huge groups, while making money. It worked really well.

Frankie lured me away from Alembic to be the primary travel agent for the band for Fly By Night. Travel agencies are very heavily regulated: in order to get a license, you have to pass a bunch of rigorous tests from the government. You have to have an experienced agent as the lead agent, which I was not. You also had to be open to the public, with advertising. [We needed] somebody who would not only fulfill the government requirements but would be able to deal with the craziness of who she was working for and the people that would come and go through the office. It was a total zoo all the time. We found a straight housewife travel agent lady in Novato named Wilma. She took it on with a great sense of humor. She and I became very tight buddies. She taught me everything I needed to know to open the agency.

We were booking travel for the Dead, the New Riders, Boz Scaggs, Steve Miller, Jesse Colin Young. We had this ridiculous workload. This was before airlines had computers and fax machines, so we did everything on the phone and on paper. It was really a hard job.

I've always been a gypsy at heart, so when Frankie invited me to work in the travel agency, I saw it as an opportunity. In those days you could get a free around-the-world ticket and only pay the taxes on it, if you became a travel agent for a year. You'd get one a year if you wanted it. I did the job. I took a lot of bennies, drank a lot of coffee, and did some cocaine for a while. I didn't like the person I became with coke, thank God. I met the man who would become my husband and father of my child, who came into my office at Fly By Night in 1974. We fell in love and I left the scene to go to Taos, New Mexico.

The Grateful Dead's vaunted sound system had been in flux since . . . oh, early 1966! It's true it had been a work-in-progress since the days of the "Owsleystein System," with Bear and all the sound techs who followed in his footsteps, from Dan Healy to Bob Matthews and Betty Cantor, and all the people who cycled through Alembic, constantly making suggestions for improvements, large and small. This magnificent obsession with the Holy Grail of "perfect" sound culminated in the development of the Dead's "Wall of Sound" system, which at its peak in the summer of 1974 consisted of more than six hundred loudspeakers of varying sizes stacked thirty feet high behind the band.

BOB MATTHEWS: I would go out to promoters who wanted to do a show; I would arrive with a two-inch-thick rider, walk into their office, toss it on the desk casually, and say, "So, you think you're ready to do a Grateful Dead show?" I would go through all the things, review the hall and the crew and how their union relations were and all that.

One of the places I advanced was the Boston Music Hall [November 30–December 2, 1973], which was one of those nice proscenium theaters like the Fox in St. Louis. It was a great theater, but the problem was that at that point we had an eighty-foot-wide stage presence [and this] was only a sixty-five-foot-wide proscenium.

They were playing Pauley Pavilion in L.A. [November 17, 1973]. I flew in, and I was in the backstage area—which was the coaches' room—and when they came in between sets to get an update I turned the coaches' whiteboard around to the chalkboard, and I drew it out. I said, "Here's where we are. We're this far out, and here's the width of the stage. We can do this show if we take these wings and put 'em back in common ground with the amp line."

That was the birth of what became the "Wall of Sound."

A singer has to hear himself. "Turn up the monitors!" You turn up the monitors, and you get an earful of feedback. That's been the battle since day one. Bear and Wickersham and Healy had come up with the out-of-phase microphones for the stage; noise-canceling microphones is what they were properly called. They allowed us to put energy behind the microphones, to have more presence without leakage.

The Boston Music Hall was utilizing all the components we had previously used for the monitors, band line, and PA towers, arrayed in scaffolding behind the band. It was a challenge, because not everything was designed to do that.

We started late that first night in Boston. There were a whole bunch of people wanting to get in, and they were starting to get a little upset, as Grateful Dead fans can be—mainly when they're not told what's going on. I went out with the promoter and started grabbing people. "Look, the band's come up with a new improvement. It's taking some time. Please be patient." The audience was very supportive—they appreciated that something was being done for their benefit, as the band had always done. They cared about the quality of the sound they got.

RON WICKERSHAM: We couldn't support the weight [of the rear system] in the center of the [stage] floor, but at the proscenium we could. They took the first eight or nine rows of seats out and built the stage out there. [The sound system] was a straight line behind the band.

OWSLEY STANLEY: When the Dead said, "We want to go to bigger shows," I said, "From my conversations with Wickersham and [engineers] Rick Turner, John Curl, John Meyer, and others, I believe that, based on what speaker-makers tell us now, we can build an integrated system where every instrument has its own amplification, all set up behind the band without any separate onstage monitors.

RICK TURNER: It's easy to underestimate Bear's contribution because everyone thinks of him as the Acid King. Yeah, he was the Acid King, but he was so much more than that. A lot of it was conceptual. I very clearly remember going out to the Novato warehouse in 1969, before I was officially part of the whole thing, and everyone's hanging out and smoking joints, and Bear suddenly says, "The PA system has to be behind the band." Everyone looked at him like he was out of his fucking mind. "No, it's gonna feed back, it's gonna do this, it's gonna do that . . ." And he says, "Nope, it has to be behind the band." And by God, he was right! Of course, we didn't know how to do it then, and I'm not sure we even trusted that it was doable. But he did. Bear always dreamed big.

The Wall of Sound made its formal debut at what was billed as "The Sound Test" at the Cow Palace on March 23, 1974—a show that also featured the first live versions of two Grateful Dead classics, "Scarlet Begonias" and "Cassidy." Because the sound system was so enormous, the Dead had to play larger venues that could accommodate the Wall, and because setting it up and tearing it down was so time-consuming, the band couldn't play two shows on consecutive days in different cities, and the expanded equipment crew actually had two stages out on the road, with one being set up in the next city while the band was playing on the other one. When the group started touring with the Wall that May, they learned what a logistical quagmire their dream system could be. However, it did achieve its main goal, which was to deliver crystal-clear sound in large spaces.

JERRY GARCIA (1974): On a normal stage, it's up to the sound crew to decide what everybody's going to hear. Our system, it's up to the musicians. And we're hearing the real balance, not a product of vocal monitors or any of that stuff.

Our other system was okay. It was a step towards this direction, just like this is a step towards another direction—more, better. That's our trend, to make it as good as can be made. What that means is we're probably going to manufacture the components of the thing, because we're at the point now where what's available in the market is not good enough anymore.

RON WICKERSHAM: Bear would walk around the hall and listen everywhere and see what was working and how the sound was covering, and the like. He would buy exotic hi-fi gear, set it up, and either it would burn out because it couldn't take the signal levels, or maybe he didn't like the sound of it, so it would be discarded. He was always testing things, trying to find the next better step. We got into making speaker cabinets that were made out of this denser wood that would travel better and be more durable.

Everything that went on in the sound system had to be paid attention to. [Bear] was hyper-critical about building mic cables, how to coil up the mic cables; every detail. You respected every piece of gear.

PHIL LESH: [The Wall of Sound] allows us to play super-loud without killing ourselves or frying those in the front—to get loud, clean sound at the back of the huge hall, and supreme musical control, because we run everything from the stage. For me, it's like piloting a flying saucer. Or riding your own sound wave.

STEVE BROWN: We did the Wall of Sound at the Cow Palace, and then the next place we went was Reno, outdoors, at the University of Nevada. This was the first time to put up the Wall of Sound [outdoors] and it was like a hurricane! I thought it was going to collapse: "This is really bad!" I was scared. It was untested—607 speakers being put up with University of Nevada stagehand help. But we survived it.

BILL KREUTZMANN: It was really hard to hear because there was so much sound pressure coming off all these speakers. The very first day in Reno, too, it was sort of windy, and the whole center [vocal] cluster was blowing around—not a lot, but enough, and I had to sit underneath it. At first they had the drums right underneath it and you couldn't hear anything. It was like being in a tunnel with a bunch of hot-rod cars roaring on both sides of you. You were supposed to have some monitors [behind you] that were going to help—ha-ha-ha! It was not my favorite time. They had done the phase-canceling microphones, and those sounded terrible. Things can look good on paper but not be so great in reality.

RON WICKERSHAM: Another thing that interfered with keeping the sound system is we needed extra time to set up and tear down. A lot of the cities were involved in getting money to build these sporting

STEVE PARISH: We'd start at 8:00 a.m., and it would take two hours just to get all the equipment onto the stage. By noon we'd have the speakers stacked and we'd take a half hour for lunch. Then we'd wire it and get all the amps running by 4:00 p.m. for the soundcheck. The show would start around 8:00 p.m., and in those days the band would play until 1:00 a.m. We left the hall around 4:00 .a.m. The next day we'd travel all night and start again.

223

event multi-purpose [arenas], and they wanted them rented out. So they would do things like send more fire inspectors around to the old buildings that you could otherwise perform in; they were being zoned out of existence. You now had these multi-purpose rooms that weren't available for rent long enough to build the system. Sometimes we'd need two days to set up the stage.

You can't put those speakers on the floor of a hockey rink. They have a basketball wood floor that they put over the ice, with insulation. You've got a protective covering over that so you're not messing up the basketball finish. If you put the sound system on top of that, it would crush the Styrofoam insulation. So we had to have a scaffolding company build a bridge out to the sides. How are you going to do that when you've got a basketball game one day before?

> That spring, the Dead recorded a new album, *From the Mars Hotel*, at CBS Studios in San Francisco with veteran staff engineer Roy Segal. Songs included "Scarlet Begonias," "U.S. Blues," "Ship of Fools," the searing ballad "China Doll," and Phil's first songwriting contributions since "Box of Rain": "Unbroken Chain" and "Pride of Cucamonga," both written with poet Bobby Petersen.

DONNA JEAN GODCHAUX: Imagine walking into rehearsal thinking about recording a new album and hearing "Scarlet Begonias" for the first time. Jerry really had a full notion of what he wanted the song to sound like. And the band was so used to playing with one another, and at that time especially, the camaraderie and the listening to one another was so attuned, to where everybody just got what Jerry wanted to hear and played it.

It was [like], "This is what I hear right here," but it wasn't, "This is what I want you to play." He would talk about the feel, the groove, the overall intent, dynamics—like going from a verse into a chorus, how he wanted it to be expressed differently. He had kind of a producer's ear when it came to his own songs and how to get across what he wanted to hear.

ROBERT HUNTER: ["Scarlet Begonias" is] about my wife [Maureen]. It was called "Bristol Girls" at the time—"Look all around this whole wide world / You'll find nothing stranger than a Bristol girl." In the song the character flees—"As I was closing the door . . ." But it didn't end [in real life] the way the song ended; I'm still with her. I have to say, that's her special song. [It was written in England] for that girl, really. I was pretty much commuting to England, going over three or four times a year.

JERRY GARCIA: [Musically] it has a little Caribbean thing to it, though nothing specific. It's its own thing. I wasn't thinking in terms of style when I wrote that setting, except I wanted it to be rhythmic. I think I got a little of it from that Paul Simon "Me and Julio Down by the Schoolyard" thing. A little from Cat Stevens—some of that rhythmic stuff he did on *Tea for the Tillerman* was kind of nice. It's an acoustic feel in a way, but we put it into an electric space, which is part of what made it interesting.

We really worked on it a lot. That record, we rehearsed across the street at SIR [Studio Instrument Rentals] before we'd go into the studio every day, so we had them pretty fully arranged.

STEVE BROWN: The sessions started every night with a meal from Original Joe's—meat and fries and spinach and salads and French wine that Phil would bring. "Okay, now we're ready to record!" We'd get there at four-thirty or five in the afternoon and go until one or two usually, depending on what we were doing.

They came into those sessions pretty fully rehearsed, so it was a pretty smooth project on that level. The basic tracks went down pretty quick, but the overdubs took a little more time, because it was a matter of making it really perfect.

Because we were able to sync up two 16-track machines, we had all these tracks to work with. [Engineer] Roy Segal was a really nice guy and easy to work with. We'd sit at the board, and when the other guys in the band would do tracks, Jerry would make comments and I'd write down notes. Then you had Phil in there listening to "Unbroken Chain" and "Pride of Cucamonga" a million times and changing this and that. There was often a long list of stuff with Phil.

Jerry would often use visual identification with the sounds he was trying to describe, and they were an interesting insight into how he "saw" music. Sometimes he would actually draw it—he would have a celeste with these lines going out to these sparks and stars—he wanted it to burst. "That's like a carousel sound." "That should sound like it's a cold place on Saturn, very cold and hard." Weird stuff.

ROY SEGAL (Recording engineer): I always got along very well with Jerry. He's the reason the Dead recorded *Mars Hotel* [at CBS Studios]. He liked the studio and thought it had a good sound, which it did. It had a more "live" sound than some of the other rooms around at that time. They had played most of the material live before they came in, so they were pretty tight, surprisingly tight. "Unbroken Chain" was very difficult; we worked on it in sections. Still, it came out very well.

PHIL LESH (1974): The first step we made towards [exploring electronic textures with the Dead] was using Ned [Lagin] playing synthesizer on "Unbroken Chain," which I thought was extremely successful. It blew me over, I must say. Even though I had thought of using synthesizer in the beginning, what happened in the middle part when he started playing it like it was drums—that really made it.

DONNA JEAN GODCHAUX: I loved making those first couple of studio records with the Grateful Dead [*Wake of the Flood* and *Mars Hotel*] because the studio had been my home, so I was in my element. I loved every minute of it. During *Wake of the Flood* I was pregnant with Zion; he was a baby during *Mars Hotel* and I was nursing, so I was balancing two very important things in my life. He's that little creature I'm holding on the [back] cover.

Singing live, to me, was the hardest thing to get used to, so I had a blast any time we were in the studio. And Jerry and Bobby were so funny. It seems like every time we would get to the microphone— the three of us—it would dissolve into a comedy routine.

STEVE BROWN: It was a congenial scene. Everybody was still healthy enough. There wasn't that much cocaine around; it wasn't that abusive a scene. Mostly it was smoking dope and Jerry and his Tia Marias—coffee with Kahlua.

JERRY GARCIA (1974): We're not the band that makes our albums—that's just a guise we adopt to get by in the studio. As soon as they invent a means of putting five hours of music at a time at some kind of realistic price, we'll release all of our shows.

I've always felt the Grateful Dead is a pretty bad recording band. We don't put that much energy into developing as a recording unit. It's difficult, because as a live band our dynamic range goes far beyond what can accurately be got down on vinyl. We can play down to the level of a whisper, and we can play as loud as twenty jet airplanes. So the expressiveness of our music is limited by recording.

Recording is always a compromise and I don't enjoy it very much, and I think that lack of enthusiasm is evident in the albums. Right now I'm trying to develop as a studio musician, because I feel it's something I ought to be able to handle. But, quite honestly, I've never recorded a solo that's worth a shit. Not on a Grateful Dead record, anyhow.

PHIL LESH (1974): Before we were into doing tunes with a whole bunch of lyrics and very little instrumental, and a beginning and an end, I always felt that I was able to bring into the rock 'n' roll medium a kind of highly structured symphonic flow to the music, which has been sadly lacking in rock 'n' roll music for one thing, and especially in our music since we started trying to focus it all down into tunes; that is, songs with lyrics. You can only go so far with them.

In other words, all it is is the melody and a chord change, and if you're going to have a tune that's comprehensible, you have to more or less be musically repetitive. I personally have never been into that kind of music. The part of playing when we get off the best is the part that's not structured like that, that is not repetitive over and over. Some kind of structure is necessary in music if it's gonna be communicative at all. It just seems that tunes don't go beyond a certain level. That's just a personal opinion. There are some people who do tunes very well. As far as I'm concerned, I don't think our tunes are that great. I think what we do best is improvise, with some kind of spontaneous structure occurring at the time of the improvisation.

> Beginning in the summer of 1974, Lesh and Ned Lagin started to perform duets of completely free-form and often dissonant electronic music—dubbed "cybernetic biomusic"—in between the Dead's sets. Based on music they had developed in the studio and later released on the album *Seastones* (Round Records, 1975), the duo's mini-sets visited many challenging and highly unconventional spaces in the realm between music and noise. Lesh and Lagin unleashed their sonic weirdness at twenty-three Dead shows that summer and fall.

PHIL LESH (1974): Ned Lagin, Mickey Hart, and myself were involved in experimenting with electronic music, but Mickey's since dropped out so there's just the two of us. We perform it at the intermission at concerts. Ned has a very involved instrument that consists of a modular synthesizer with keyboard, and electric piano, and a computer. The computer is like the score in a way—he lays out certain functions that'll go down in the course of the music, and he programs it into the computer, and then when he starts the computer, the changes all occur automatically within a certain time period.

He's got under his control virtually an infinite range of sounds and music, and I've got a very limited range. There's no possible way that one guy with two pedals and a ring modulator [i.e., Phil] can possibly compete with an entire computer/synthesizer system. I don't personally think that the middle of a Grateful Dead concert is the best place for this music, although in some places the response has been amazing. [At the Hollywood Bowl, July 21, 1974], for instance, people were all pretty crazy 'cause there were some security people who were getting pretty violent, so we went out and did our thing—everybody was pretty high in Hollywood [and] they just sort of relaxed, got into the zone, in the space of long, slow changes, which, if you're pretty high and feeling like killing, it just might change your thinking. I really don't know exactly what it will do to a person, but the vibe was totally different after we finished.

JERRY MOORE (Taper and co-founder of *Relix* magazine): After about a minute and a half [at the June 23, 1974, Miami concert], I thought, "Okay, well, I guess it's music," so I turned the tape recorder back on. They were playing in the dark. I kind of enjoyed it. I mean, whatever its purpose or why they were doing it, I don't know. I guess they were enjoying themselves. Maybe they were looking to baffle people. I guess it's music, but it doesn't partake of most of the requirements. It didn't have a melody. It didn't have a beat. It didn't have a theme of any sort. Well, maybe it had a theme, but not a very musical one.

NED LAGIN: I was told frankly by the Grateful Dead management that they wanted to make sure that I didn't make the Grateful Dead too strange and weird. There was a real desire for the long stuff to get shorter and the short stuff to get more popular.

When I started with the Grateful Dead [in 1970], the direction they were going was *Workingman's Dead* and *American Beauty,* not towards bigger jams and longer stuff. And instead of staying in that direction, they integrated that back into what they had been doing before.

It was a sort of rounding some edges, doing some shoehorning, and hoping for the best. And here I come, saying, "We can open the door and step out into the Twilight Zone, or empty space, or go up five stories, or down five stories." I'm not taking credit for this: Garcia was ready to do that, and Lesh was ready to do that.

I am very proud to have been on the '74 summer/fall tour, and the [1974] European tour, because monumental things occurred. You cannot judge those second sets without knowing that the Phil and Ned stuff happened in between. The experience has taken place in your body, in your soul, in your mind. You're playing to an audience who sometimes was very appreciative, and sometimes was very hostile. And you have to remember that when Debussy performed stuff that would be considered syrup today, chairs were thrown at the stage, and less than a generation later, the same thing happened with Stravinsky.

When we were jamming, it was an excuse, in a way, for anybody who was playing with me to get as far out as they could. And when you're in a performing situation, you can't start doing something else when somebody is way far away. Sometimes there were some performances that I think were very beautiful, and subtle, and rhythmic, and melodic, or at least quasi-rhythmic and quasi-melodic. And there were times where we were way out intentionally. And there were other times, I'm unhappy to say, that we weren't on the same page when we were performing.

We now had a very big stage that, for the most part, was way above the audience. Huge stacks of speakers were filling a very large space. Anything that could go wrong could be very catastrophically wrong; it wasn't swapping out a Twin Reverb anymore. The difficulties of hearing one another were eventually resolved, but they weren't resolved the day they started using newer and larger equipment. Their ability to control the equipment grew over time. There were a lot of frustrations and a lot of anxiety involved in that. There was a sincere desire to put on the best show they could for the public.

I had a discussion at this time with Garcia, and we talked about this issue a couple of times during our friendship. Could you ever end a concert basically not on an incredibly high, you know, "One More Saturday Night" / "Johnny B. Goode" extravaganza? Could you leave it in a contemplative, meditative, happy state? Could you ever end a concert with "Dark Star," for example? And the answer ultimately came back: No, you couldn't.

The band returned to Europe, Wall of Sound in tow, for a relatively short tour in September of 1974.

STEVE BROWN: They had this tour planned to make some money and promote the album [*Mars Hotel*] somewhat—as much as you can in Europe—England mainly, and Germany to a certain degree. But it wasn't as successful on most levels as '72. It was a little more perfunctory—"Let's go do Europe." Amsterdam would have been cool, but it got canceled at the last minute. But that gave me a couple of extra days to travel with Phil and Ned and Healy in a rented Mercedes through Switzerland.

The Wall of Sound in the Alexandra Palace [in London] was remarkably far-out. You're in this historic building that never would have seen this kind of thing coming, and the people there were really nice. I thought the English crowd was the nicest of the tour as far as enjoying the music. It was a hip crowd.

In Munich, the people came to the Olympic Hall with a lot of good energy, but they were rather disturbed by Phil and Ned's performance. I was on the arena periphery there with the [information/promotion] booth, and it seemed to me that Phil and Ned were sort of re-bombing Berlin, and apparently the people there weren't that far away from remembering their parents' stories and their own world of understanding, that this was not a good thing. The whistling started, and then shouting, and pretty soon this beautiful interior, which I'd shot some film footage of before the show, looked like a riot had occurred. Chairs had been thrown, stuff was scattered all over the place. Even though the Dead were able to come back and do a second set and seemingly retrieve the goodwill, people were really upset.

NED LAGIN: By the time we got to London, everybody was clearly doing too much drugs. Everybody had a lot of cocaine, and everybody was sharing it. At least Phil and I were also doing LSD. Phil did not do cocaine. I can't speak for Weir; I didn't hang out with him. But I knew the habits of all the rest, and of the crew.

There was a meeting [in London] that included everybody who was on the road. We agreed that everything was fucked up, and part of it being all fucked up was cocaine. And so we all agreed to flush our stashes. We all dutifully did—with, as it turns out, the exception of Jerry. I can't say everybody, because I didn't go into everybody's room and watch them. I certainly did, and the people that I knew did. Cocaine became very un-apparent: you can tell when people—if you knew them—were doing it, and they weren't doing it.

I believed that Jerry had flushed his stash, too. And maybe he did, but twenty minutes later he had a new stash. It became evident later that he hadn't flushed his stash.

This took place, as I remember it, on the afternoon before the third show. The audience at Alexandra Palace was like the dream Grateful Dead audience. These people had eyes that had opened up to, like, three inches in diameter. And they were dancing and moving and swaying, and they were all so blissfully happy. They looked like we felt and played. And it was just a magnificently beautiful moment.

That launched us into that European tour. It took what started out as a very downer, negative, going-in-the-wrong-direction experience and turned us in the right direction.

PHIL LESH (1974): I do [acid] all the time. I love it. I think it's one of the greatest tools for learning about yourself. It's my quality knob. I take a few drops of acid and I turn up my quality knob. Listening back to what I've played later on tape—because the drugs can't have any influence on the tape—I find that generally speaking, the quality is just what I thought it was. Especially about what I, myself, was playing.

The relationship between what I was playing and the whole band is not always on the same plane, or on the same trip. I've seen some people take acid and just get bombed out horribly. It all depends on your state of mind. But as for the drug influence now, I would say it's a lot lighter than it was in the peak [in the late sixties]. It's like we're coming off the other side of the mountain, and besides, the quality of available acid has gone down to such an alarming degree that you just can't get good shit. [Plus] there are all these other new drugs around whose names I don't need to mention, I'm sure. Most of which I don't care to use. Cocaine, for instance, makes me evil and makes me hate music. I hate music when I'm under the influence, so I can't use it; it's just impossible.

NED LAGIN: The whole band went to Zurich and then everybody

went their separate ways, and we were supposed to meet up in a few days in Dijon. Phil and I got a Mercedes, and for some reason I thought that it would be a good idea to get a big bag of peanuts—like five pounds—which I proceeded to eat, and fill up the entire rear floor of the Mercedes with. And it was decided that Phil and I would just do a good deal of LSD every day and drive around the high Alps. We ended up in Geneva, where we picked up Dan Healy and Steve Brown. Healy had a bunch of pot in his suitcase.

We got in the car in Geneva and were driving towards France. And you get to this sign, "Welcome to France." And then, eighteen or twenty kilometers inside France, there it is: the border crossing and customs. And you're looking at these French soldier-police-army-customs types in uniforms, and we have to stop the car and they have to go through our bags. Healy is now going, "Oh, fuck! I've got all this pot in my suitcase." Steve Brown was sweating bullets. Phil is like, "I'm just going to be above all of this, whatever plays out." Because remember, we're on LSD.

Steve Brown has vacated the premises, and Phil has vacated the premises; they're off standing by the guard house or something, acting like if there's anything in this car, they don't know about it, and it might not even be their car, and they might not even be here. And the police have now opened up the trunk, and they have these suitcases. We get to Healy's suitcase and he unzips it. Healy starts talking to the guy and the guy looks up, he's got his hands in the suitcase. I put my hand into the other side of the suitcase and find the plastic bag. And there are now two hands in the suitcase. Healy keeps engaging this guy in conversation while he's feeling around. Healy has eye contact with the guy, so while he's talking to the guy and the guy's feeling around in the suitcase, I'm dragging the plastic bag just out of reach of him. The guy never looked down at the suitcase while he was feeling around. As I said, we were on LSD—not huge amounts, but we were cruisin'. It was just engaging in the magic of the moment. The guy was not gonna look, his fingers were never gonna touch the bag, and when he pulled his hand out, in the same breath, the same gesture, I pulled my hand out. He looked to turn around and zip it, and my hands were at my sides.

We got back in the car and drove away, and all those guys—it was one of the few times that I got total, full love and support from the group of pirates that I was with.

STEVE BROWN: A few more miles down the road, we pulled off the side of the road, opened up the trunk, and pulled it all out and laughed and laughed and laughed. But it was one of those moments we could have ruined the whole tour then and there. You lose your soundman and your bass player. It was an ugly possibility, but we somehow magically were able to see our way through.

By the end of the European tour, the band had decided to get off the road, maybe even for good. The Wall of Sound had become an expensive albatross, the group had been playing shows almost nonstop for ten years, and everyone in the band was interested in pursuing musical activities outside the Grateful Dead. A series of five "final" shows was booked for October 16–20, 1974, at Winterland. For a while, Garcia had been interested in making a feature film of the Dead concert experience, so for the Winterland shows, a crew of seven cameramen and director Leon Gast were brought in to shoot the concerts and also capture what went on in the crowd, in the hallways, even outside the venue. Everyone agreed the Dead played very well at those shows, and the last night (dubbed "The Last One" on the tickets) took on a special glow when Mickey Hart—out of the band since February 1971—showed up and played a number of tunes with his old mates.

BOB WEIR: That was the last night, as far as we were all concerned. There was a chance that we might reconvene at some future date, but we weren't looking towards that. We were looking at that night as being the last night.

We had pretty much roped ourselves into an unworkable situation.

We had this huge PA that we were carting around, we had a crew of, God knows, about forty people, and we had to work too hard and too much to support it all—to the point where every time we played somewhere we lost money, but we had to keep working just to pay everybody who was on salary. All the money that we'd make from records would go into supporting this whole organization, and it was still in the red. It was just millions and millions of dollars that went into that. It wasn't any fun after a while, not having enough time to really get loose and get creative, having to stay on the road all the time. So we decided that we had to knock off.

Mickey came on down figuring, "This is the last night—I'd better get my drums down there." He didn't want to miss out. When he showed up at the back door with his drums, "Oh, Mickey, that's right! Set 'em up!"

JERILYN BRANDELIUS: That night when [Mickey] played Winterland, it was supposed to be the end of the Grateful Dead. Mickey was working [in his barn studio] with the Fairfax Street Choir—I called it "torturing the sopranos," because he was making them cry: "No, no! Do it again!" He was being a tyrant: "C'mon, you can do it better!" But the phone calls kept coming in from the roadies—Jackson and Ram Rod mostly. I said, "Mickey, they want you to come down and play."

"I don't want to go down and play. None of the band members are calling me."

Finally, and I don't remember exactly how it went down, we had a conversation and I said, "Look, if it's really the last night of the Grateful Dead and the roadies have been asking you to go down there and play, why don't we just go?" So he decided to do it and he and I went down in the Porsche and loaded all his drums into Jim McPherson's old green 1945 Chevy, or whatever it was, and we went off to Winterland. We left the cars parked downstairs in the garage and went inside the place, and when [recording engineer] Billy Wolf saw Mickey, he told us years later, all he said was, "Where am I going to get the microphones for this?"

In Winterland, you walked in the back door and then you went up this ramp to the first dressing room, which was this long rectangular room, and the band was on break after the first set. Mickey said, "I've got my drums . . ." "Oh, hi, Mickey, you've got drums," and Billy was saying, "Well, I don't know—he doesn't know a lot of our new songs . . ." And Mickey got up and started walking out the door. Jackson went after him and Billy, and they got about halfway down the ramp and Jackson grabbed both of them by the back of the head, shoved their heads together, and said, "You guys are gonna play together tonight. Got that?" "Okay!" So we ran and got the drums out of the car and got all set up while the set break was going on.

PHIL LESH (To the audience, October 20, 1974): Some of you might remember our old drummer, Mickey Hart, who's playing with us tonight.

BOB WEIR: Fresh out of a mental institution and a brand-new man!

JERILYN BRANDELIUS: At the end, they were all in the dressing room saying, "Wow, that was really fun, man. I don't know why we haven't done that." They were blown away.

JERRY GARCIA (1974): We haven't broken up, we've just stopped performing. We're going to keep on recording, and we probably will get back into performing, but we'll wait until we've had a chance to define how we want to do it. Our whole development has been "going along with the changes." It's not as though we've plotted to get to a certain level. But just not thinking about it, or not making conscious decisions about what we were doing, we ended up in that place of stadiums, coliseums, large civic buildings, high ticket prices, enormous overhead, in an effort to fulfill the requirement of whatever the level change was.

For example, we changed from playing theaters to large places.

The reason we were doing it was because there were more people who wanted to see us. The obvious thing was to go to bigger rooms. We can only go to bigger rooms if we sound good in them, and that led to our whole PA thing, which is expensive. Our rationale was, "We'll divert the income into developing the resource," because, really, we have a relationship with our audience. And we're only interested in keeping that straight.

DONNA JEAN GODCHAUX: I don't remember there being talk of not having the band anymore. I remember that Phil wanted to linger in Europe, but if they were talking about not playing anymore, I was unaware of it or I don't remember it.

> Once the hiatus began and the steady flow of touring income stopped, there were a number of layoffs among the expanded Wall of Sound road crew and in the office. Eileen Law lost her job for more than a year, and Sam Cutler and the band parted ways at the end of 1974.

EILEEEN LAW: I never understood why they let some of us go, because it all seemed to be peaking then. The mail got really voluminous around the time of *Wake of the Flood* and *Mars Hotel*. I could understand why the band wanted time off, but we were swamped.

GAIL HELLUND: Rakow was in charge of Grateful Dead Records and Round Records; Sam ran the booking company [Out of Town Tours]. Frankie did Fly By Night [travel], but that was pretty haphazard. She was always gone. We had the New Riders. We had that other building, 1330 Lincoln, and we had all the Courtenay [Pollock] tie-dyed covers for all of the fluorescent lights. When the elevator doors opened on the second floor, regular people would go, "I think I'm on the wrong floor." You'd see them look around, and they'd start hitting the buttons. We were on a delivery system with Nancy's Yogurt, which was Kesey in Eugene: they came and delivered yogurt once a week for us to eat. It was a big thing. We had everything. We did everything.

It worked really well. It was sort of everybody that had ever worked there, still working there, in different offices with a more defined scope. The band was making a lot more money. When they did Watkins Glen, they pulled in some bucks for that gig. Frances and Sam would come back and we had this huge conference table. They'd be counting the money out on this huge table, going, "Wow, this is really different." Just a ton of money.

That changed things. But I think it was a welcome change for most of the time I was there.

The band got mad at Sam. I don't know what happened, but they fired him. He came back in and he said, "We're closing up. Frances and I are leaving. Take care of everything. Take care of the taxes. You can have everything in the office, we're taking this and this, and you deal with it." He didn't tell me he got fired. He just said the band has decided to stop touring for a year. Could be that's what they told him initially, but he knew he was getting fired. He just took off.

It took me a while to get everything cleaned up and get out of that office space and get everything ready for taxes and all of that stuff. I got all of that done, and sent them the rest of the money, and that was the end of that. It was just over. We worked right up to the end of '74.

And so the Dead's twenty-month performing hiatus began. Except the band actually played four gigs during 1975—none of them publicly announced—in wildly different surroundings: Kezar Stadium (as part of a star-studded benefit concert), Winterland, a small San Francisco club called the Great American Music Hall, and a free concert in Golden Gate Park with Jefferson Starship. The Dead recorded one album during the hiatus, *Blues for Allah,* and the individual members kept busy with a slew of projects and side bands.

STEVE BROWN: No one ever said, "We're done forever." It always seemed like, "We're taking this year off."

We knew we were going to have to sell records and get product out there, so the Round Records thing was going on and Jerry was working on things like the Good Old Boys [an all-star bluegrass ensemble featuring David Nelson and the legendary mandolinist Frank Wakefield]—the *Pistol Packin' Mama* album—and trying to keep a certain amount of cash flow to cover these projects, and at the same time get the things processed and printed, get the art done, pay the artists, and all that. So the promotions stuff with the stations and the advertising and all that stuff was filling up the time for me.

JERRY GARCIA (1975): We've been a group in the most real sense for ten years with zero breaks. We've gotten so into functioning as a gestalt personality, at times it's all the same person. It's the Grateful Dead, whatever that is. And in the interest of keeping that thing colorful, 'cause it's groovy—and comfortable enough so we could easily be that way forever—it's time to go out and do our things. Because the Dead incorporates the musical viewpoint that it's none of us particularly. We each have our own particular interests, and what we can agree to do together is something different than we would do individually.

BOB WEIR (1976): Branching off into separate bands was an extremely healthy step for all of us. We were suffering from being inbred, and the only way to deal with this was for each member to go out and seek a new endeavor.

It's fun to play music with [Garcia], but it's also fun to do other stuff. With the Grateful Dead, I could fuck up immeasurably and Garcia could pull the whole thing out of the fire. I can't afford to have Garcia be a crutch—I'll never get anything done that way. For my own personal development, I must be involved in a situation where nobody can help me out.

DONNA JEAN GODCHAUX: The hiatus allowed us

RON RAKOW (1975): I would rather fail than be moderately successful, and the only way we can ever score a dramatic success is to have a hit single. I identify very strongly with the music I represent and it would make me feel very good if a million people would agree that anything I offered was worth having. I want to sell a million records, not only because of monetary considerations, but because to get a million people to agree with you about anything is something to be proud of.

239

to make the *Keith and Donna* album happen; it's something we had wanted to happen for a long time and something we initially came to Garcia with when we met him. So by the time the hiatus came, we were ready to rock 'n' roll in our recording studio in our house in Stinson Beach. Jerry was out there, of course, and Ron Rakow, too. I hung out with Mountain Girl a lot. We recorded the album there, and did a few overdubs at the Record Plant, I think.

JERRY GARCIA (1975): The Grateful Dead is coasting. We were anxious to get out of the huge coliseums and to get back to a situation where the level of communication is better and it's more comfortable for us as humans. Yet the Grateful Dead can't play a club; it would be pandemonium. So we got into different situations.

Now we can voluntarily come together as the Grateful Dead when it feels right, when it motivates us, and because it's fun. We don't want to do it because we have to or because it's our living.

BOB WEIR (1976): [*Blues for Allah*] was done at my place. A studio is an instrument that I would dearly love to know better. It is really expensive to rent a studio, and you have to know what you're doing or you're wasting your money. Having your own studio allows you to be more relaxed.

JERRY GARCIA: We had a formula [for working on *Blues for Allah*]: we were not gonna develop anything outside of the studio. We were gonna get together every day at Weir's place, and anything that came out of that we were going to use. We weren't gonna go home and write songs and bring them in. It all got written there at Bob's, but a lot of songs went through tremendous convolutions. "Crazy Fingers" started off as a power-rock raver and turned into something completely different by the end of it.

STEVE BROWN: They started recording *Blues for Allah* in February

'75, doing some basic stuff up at Weir's—woodshedding, basically.

As much as I enjoyed working on the *Mars Hotel* sessions and sitting there in the control room next to Jerry doing the listening and taking notes and keeping track of stuff and taking care of everything I was assigned to do, for the *Blues for Allah* sessions [because there was no separate control room], you're in the room with them and you're sitting in the room while they're creating and coming up with things they've never done or heard before, and you're hearing it for the first time—it was a very special and magical situation. It was a dream-come-true kind of experience. That let me understand the process even more than before. These weren't songs they'd been doing on the road; they were working them out.

Steve Barncard gave me a line that ran from the studio to Weir's living room and I set up two cassette recorders, and I would put in tapes and just let them roll. [That let me] preserve their process that way, and the various stories and other extraneous stuff that goes on in there—talking about Rakow, talking about Charlie Manson. There were also people who would drop by—like when they were rehearsing for the SNACK [Students Need Athletics, Culture, and Kicks—an all-star benefit for San Francisco schools organized by Bill Graham] concert. Merl [Saunders] was there and [John] Cipollina would come by. David Crosby spent a lot of time there. Crosby made them do a whole basic track for his album. Van Morrison came up and hung out a few times; that was neat.

JERRY GARCIA (1975): We're trying to explore, in the woodshed, to develop other forms that can have instruments and vocal stuff, but things that aren't necessarily based on verse/chorus/bridge structures. We're doing stuff that's kinda scary, kind of weird.

The Dead have been eclectic in the extreme, since we've done all kinds of styles of music up to the point where in our own minds everything we do is something we've done before. So we're trying to create new realms, things we haven't gone into before. And the only way for us is to do that. It's just inventing systems of music, inventing scales, saying, "Okay, we're gonna play consistently in this mode, we're gonna create this aesthetic not based on any of our old clichés."

DONNA JEAN GODCHAUX: Bob wanted me to do some kind of solo work on "The Music Never Stopped." I think in a way he wanted to get me out there a little more, which I really appreciated, and I appreciate to this day.

We had fun coming up with that. I think I came up with my part and he came up with his part. He gave me kind of the basic melody, and from what I remember, I think we just got on the microphone and did it.

JERRY GARCIA: *Workingman's Dead* and *American Beauty* is one kind [of songwriting]. *Wake of the Flood* and *Blues for Allah* was on a different level— harmonically they're more dense, more a combination between experimental music and pure songwriting craft.

MICKEY HART: We miked a box of crickets, and throughout the second side of *Blues for Allah* there are crickets on the basic track. We slowed them down, sped 'em up, played them backwards at half speed—they sounded like whales, and they sounded like chirping birds. After we were finished, we let the crickets go on Weir's mountain, and for years after, Weir had exotic crickets outside his house.

Mickey Hart, having reappeared at the last show in October '74, was invited to participate in these sessions.

MICKEY HART: We made this [track] called "The Desert." Garcia was engineering, and I was in the studio. I played all my little percussion things— bells, metal, glass. We made about a twenty-minute track. And he gated it with a vocal gate. He was saying "Allah" but you don't hear a voice—you hear the desert saying the word in place of his voice.

STEVE BROWN: When Phil Garris, who was from San Diego, came up with the artwork for what became *Blues for Allah,* he originally had the skeleton figure pretty much the way you see it on the album, except that it had green sunglasses. And what having those glasses be green did was make the entire figure look very insectoid. When I showed it to the band up at Weir's studio where they were working on the album, they rejected it for exactly that reason: it looked too insectoid and weird.

So I took the original artwork home, because I was responsible for it and I didn't want anything to happen to it, and I hung it in my bedroom right at the foot of my bed. For a couple of days I just stared at the thing, until I got the idea that if Phil changed the color of the glasses to match the robe on the figure, it might seem a little warmer. So Garris actually made a red overlay [for the glasses] and after a few weeks of not being able to come up with anything better, I decided to show it to the band again, and this time they loved it. Garris won a national illustrator's award for that piece.

PHIL LESH (1975): It's the first of our albums that's really grown on me. I've always been happy with our albums but I've rarely listened to them after they're finished. This one's different. It indicates a new point of departure for our music. We wanted to free ourselves from our own clichés to search for new tonalities, new structures and modalities. I think we succeeded. We'll still play a lot of our old stuff, of course, but we're all pleased with the new areas to explore.

DONNA JEAN GODCHAUX: It was an extremely creative time in that band, and a lot of the good songs—"Franklin's Tower," "Slipknot"—were written at that time. I have real fond memories of Garcia introducing those songs at band rehearsal and watching them come alive as we would begin to rehearse for a recording. It was tremendous, it really was.

> During the summer of 1975, Garcia, looking for a new direction for his solo work, formed the first Jerry Garcia Band with British piano great Nicky Hopkins, John Kahn on bass, and Ron Tutt on drums. The music lost the jazz feel that Merl Saunders and Martin Fierro had brought to the previous ensemble, but it gained a certain stately elegance and some interesting new contributions to the repertoire, including "Mission in the Rain," "Sugaree," "All By Myself," and Hopkins tunes such as "Pig's

Boogie" and "Edward (the Mad Shirt Grinder)."

Given serious health and drug issues, Nicky Hopkins wasn't up to the rigors of touring. His last gig with the Jerry Garcia Band was December 31, 1975, at the Keystone Berkeley. After a brief dalliance with New Orleans legend James Booker—who also had some issues—Garcia and Kahn re-formed the Jerry Garcia Band with Keith and Donna Godchaux.

DONNA JEAN GODCHAUX: Jerry, Keith, and I were together a lot in Stinson Beach during that period, so the proximity probably influenced us joining that band. Garcia was at our house all the time and we would take out old gospel records and listen to them for days and days, and decide which ones we wanted to do. Like "Who Was John?" [an obscure black gospel song originally recorded by Mitchell's Christian Singers in the thirties]. That was totally spooky; what you call a deep spiritual. But there was a spot in [Jerry] that was reserved for that. He had a little pocket in his heart that was opened up to that. But he had a lot of pockets! The old-time gospel stuff by real people who were really into it was incredibly soulful.

[The music in that band] was more deliberate; things weren't quite as all-over-the-place as they were with the Grateful Dead. Even though there was still a tremendous amount of jamming, it was more structured in where it went and how it went where it went. Between John [Kahn] and Jerry and Keith, they figured an interplay that worked with just three musical pieces. I think it turned out really well.

That really slow stuff [that the band played] is only effective if you can command it. You really have to be in command of slow songs or people will think it's boring and fall asleep. But if you're really on top of each note, and the intent is to have some authority, then it will go over, and Jerry was a master at that. Jerry was up to the challenge of that kind of music, and in fact it wasn't a challenge—it was a real joy to him. He loved bringing as much expression into one note and one measure as was humanly possible.

CHAPTER 7
On the Road Again

After twenty months off the road, the Grateful Dead returned to touring at the beginning of June 1976, with Mickey Hart firmly back in the fold. For their first tour back, they decided to play smaller venues exclusively; the much-in-demand tickets were offered first to people on the Dead Heads mailing list, then through conventional outlets. The group rehearsed for a significant period before the tour, rearranging many old songs (including "St. Stephen" and "Cosmic Charlie," neither of which had been performed for years), dropping several that had been played up until the hiatus ("Dark Star," "China Cat," and "Sunflower") and introducing a bunch of new songs that fit the revived double-drummer format and the new emphasis on harmony vocals (such as "Samson and Delilah," "The Wheel," and a new disco-influenced arrangement of "Dancing in the Street." Additionally, most of the songs from *Blues for Allah* found their way into the live repertoire.

RICHARD LOREN: I thought the hiatus was really good for the band, for the people, for the energy, because they came back and we booked this tour in small theaters for extended runs. They made less money. They said, "Let's not look at the money, let's look at playing a lot."

DAN HEALY: When we went back on the road we decided: no more albatrosses. We had a year to get to miss touring, and we had time to reflect on what a truly valuable, precious thing we had. And we wanted to keep it economical, so that it would survive. After we all came back, at first nobody got any salaries and the consciousness was, "Let's separate them that is from them that ain't." And, by God, some people did leave our scene, but the core nucleus stayed. We cut off the deadwood. We all knew who we were: it was the same people who were there originally, no more, no less.

We went through a number of different [sound] systems when we came back. I spent a lot of '77 working out how to have good sound using equipment you haven't really seen before. You can do it—you just have to learn not to expect too much. At the same time, though, equipment did get better throughout the industry, so there wasn't as much risk involved.

JEFF MATTSON (Guitarist, Dark Star Orchestra): When they came back, even the regular songs were different and rearranged, and had better vocal parts. You could see they had done their homework. It was one of the only times in my experience where you really felt like, "Wow, this band has been rehearsing!"

DONNA JEAN GODCHAUX: In smaller places you can be more nuanced. Getting back together after a separation of sorts, there's greater appreciation, and you can kind of start from a new beginning in a way.

STEVE SILBERMAN: Jerry once said that before the hiatus they felt they were caught up in this machine that was much larger than they were. They were playing these big gigs and carrying the huge sound system, and they felt like they no longer had control over this thing they had created. Garcia talked a lot about wanting to get back to what they had originally liked about being in the Grateful Dead, and that that wasn't about constantly touring and it wasn't about this gigantic sound system. They wanted to search their souls to figure out why they had embarked on this enormous project in the first place, and the way they were able to succeed was by downsizing in many different ways—not only the sound system but also the scope of the music, in a way.

I think they wanted to build a new structure that was more narrative, so you didn't have these expansive, "vista-cruiser" versions of "Dark Star" and "Playing in the Band," which were amazing, but you had these very precisely structured sets, and even within songs you had these inflection points. Take for example something like "Lazy Lightning" and "Supplication" [Bob Weir songs introduced in 1975 by Kingfish, and by the Dead when they came back in '76]. You have these moments in the music when they can leverage the structure of the jam in order to produce an ecstatic release; another level of music. What I loved about "Supplication" is that it was like lightning in a bottle, because it had a very contained structure—after "Lazy Lightning" they'd bring it way down to this quiet beginning of "Supplication," but within minutes it was exploding.

I feel that what they did was take all the new material they had from the grand experiment of doing Grateful Dead Records and they used the new songs from *Blues for Allah* and elsewhere to build a new kind of set structure that ended up becoming the set structure for the rest of their career, really. Even "Fire on the Mountain" came from *Diga* [from the instrumental track "Happiness Is Drumming"].

ALLAN ARKUSH: They were playing at the Shrine Auditorium [in Los Angeles], during the baseball playoffs in [October] 1976. Jerry said: "Oh, you gotta go say hello to the band. They're right down there, on the right." I walk there and I see these old guys playing poker. I said, "I thought you said that's the band."

Garcia says, "Yes, that's the band." Then he told me this thing about the Shrine Auditorium. If you were a rock band coming into their place, the union rules said that you were usurping the job of the house band. You had to hire the house band and pay them off, because you were taking their jobs. He thought it was endlessly funny.

247

They also brought in these great covers, like "Iko Iko" and "Jack-aroe," so they had all these resources available to them to reinvent themselves on a scale that was much smaller but sort of had more bang for the buck.

The other thing about that time period was how much, if you were a Deadhead, you felt like you were in on this secret thing, because the Dead had sort of fallen off the radar—they'd "broken up," and suddenly you could go to these smaller venues and be part of this really committed, really informed audience. And in a sense, after the hiatus every show felt like this luxurious opportunity.

BOB WEIR (1976): We have been rediscovering that intimacy is a musical dynamic. When you don't have it—and in those huge [venues] you don't—you lack an important facet.

Musically, the band is rediscovering itself. We're still adjusting because we are working in a second drummer. The gigs have been wildly different. But the returns are getting better the more we play.

As far as the crowd situation goes—well, on the first night in New York, we had more people than we could get into the hall, and there was the threat of trouble. That was sobering. Fortunately, nothing happened.

Frankly, I don't think there is much danger of any trouble in the rest of the country. But if it turns out that to avoid problems we have to play the big indoor places again, we just won't do it. We won't go out on the road. We'll just stay home and make records.

In fact, the Dead returned to large venues for their fall 1976 shows.

JEFF MATTSON: I remember taking a date to a Dead show in '76. She had never seen the Grateful Dead. I said, "What did you think of the show?" And she said, "It was great! Except for that weird part." That was kind of it for our relationship. I was like, "That was the whole point!"

JERRY GARCIA (1975): Music has a place in society. Music is one place where freedom is available on a communication level. It talks to a person individually, based on his personality. Music is freely open to different interpretations. It's not locked in like language. The people who come to Grateful Dead concerts come in the spirit of celebration, to get high on one level or another. That's always been part of life. It's fulfillment on as many levels as any one person believes it to be.

DONNA JEAN GODCHAUX: Kreutzmann was the timekeeper in that band. He didn't really need anybody else. He was like a clock-work fixed in the Grateful Dead. In his mind and his spirit, he was always postured to go anywhere, anytime, not a nanosecond late. He was always there, and that was part of the synchronicity and the beauty and magic of the Grateful Dead. Kreutzmann was the guy.

When you have two drummers, you've got a bigger sound, you've got more sound, you've got all the extra things going, but it's harder to pull off the finesse. When it gets down to nuts and bolts, I think the one-drummer thing is where it's at for me—no slight against Mickey.

BOB WEIR (1977): We've had to do a lot of conscious work on dynamics, simply because with the reintroduction of Mickey, he missed out on years of tacit agreements and understandings, so we finally had to start talking about it, because otherwise he'd go banging and crashing through the quiet parts, or he wouldn't know when that sudden sucker-punch is coming. We had to tell him, which means we had to be thinking about it, which means while we were thinking about it, we might as well rethink things in general.

JEFF MATTSON: I wouldn't necessarily blame it on Mickey Hart per se, but any time you have two drummers, it just makes it really hard to turn a corner. Even if one guy breaks it down, the other guy can still keep going. Whereas when Billy was playing the drums, and he just went to the cymbals or something like that, it just opened up immediately: BOOM! You could do anything.

ROB EATON (Guitarist, Dark Star Orchestra): It limits you to where you can go and how quickly you can turn. With Billy in '72–'74, they could spin out and do what they wanted, because it was one integrated thing of the five of them. As soon as you added the second drummer, it was more regimented. They didn't have the flexibility of just all of a sudden swinging into a different groove, because most of the time the drummers wouldn't be able to do that—not together, anyway. Mickey's skill set wasn't Billy's skill set. Billy's a really good jazzy style drummer, really deep swing, whereas Mickey was more of a beater and a basher. Billy had to dumb down his stuff, in a way, to play with Mickey.

DONNA JEAN GODCHAUX: I don't know whose idea [the new arrangement of "Dancing in the Street" was], but disco was very happening. Mickey was so into *Saturday Night Fever.* Oh, my God—what the band would have to put up with in the hotel room; Mickey had his tape player going full blast with the door open, playing *Saturday Night Fever.* But also, Garcia, God bless him, was into all kinds of music, provided it was really good. Bobby and I had to really concentrate to get the phrasing [on that song] really sharp and staccato.

> The Dead's decision to play small halls when they came back was certainly an aesthetically pleasing one for all involved, but it didn't do much to help the band's precarious financial situation, which had deteriorated considerably without the income that touring brought. The Grateful Dead Records and Round Records experiment proved to be a voracious money-eater. Over time, the organization jettisoned some of the logistical headaches associated with running their labels, such as manufacturing and distribution (they signed a deal with United Artists to handle those). Nineteen seventy-six was the first year

the Dead put out an album with no new material on it: their lone release that year was a poorly received double live album culled from the October 1974 "retirement" shows, titled *Steal Your Face*. Further adding to the group's fiscal woes was Garcia's *Grateful Dead Movie* project, which also turned into a time-consuming money pit.

Ron Rakow tried many different avenues to raise funds for the various projects—even borrowing money from a network of drug smugglers at one point—but in May 1976, he abruptly left the organization, taking with him a hefty check from United Artists. He claimed the band owed him money and had ripped him off, and that some of the money was to pay off shadow creditors. Whatever the reality, the group, following Garcia's wishes, chose not to go after Rakow legally, and the Dead were once again in desperate financial straits.

RON RAKOW: We got stretched out making the movie and we couldn't be an independent record company anymore, and I made a deal with United Artists. The deal was a domestic deal, and then at the end of the deal I said, "If I could get the foreign rights, what are they worth to you?" And [United Artists president] Al Teller said, "I'll give you two hundred grand for them." So I went back to Atlantic [which held the foreign rights to the Dead's records] and I said, "You haven't done very well with these foreign rights." They said, "No shit!" I said, "Well, I'll buy them back for fifty grand." So I bought them back for fifty grand cash and sold them to United Artists for two hundred grand. We made a hundred fifty grand on that deal.

Until the movie broke us, Grateful Dead Records made a lot of bread. Our pennies per album went from $0.41 with Warner Bros. to $1.46. So while we didn't sell many more than Warner Bros.—maybe an 8 percent increase—there was a 400 percent increase in the per-record yield.

STEVE BROWN: The movie was taking a lot of money and we needed to get those funds. We were juggling the movie and records coming out [*Diga,* by the Mickey Hart–led Diga Rhythm Band, and *Steal Your*

Face], so those were putting pressure on Rakow to come through. Mickey was remixing and remixing *Diga*. United Artists was expecting the live record and Rakow was not happy. It got to be a pressure situation Rakow took advantage of as an excuse to write himself out in a liberal financial way. Things between 1330 [the building where the record company was headquartered] and Fifth and Lincoln [the Grateful Dead office] became extra ugly at the point Rakow ripped off the band. Jerry had the mark on his forehead for a while there. You could see him wearing it. I felt bad for him. But they had been kind of pushing the way they wanted to do things.

RICHARD LOREN: Rakow was executive producer of the movie, and then he split. Here was an enterprising Wall Street mind. Quick bucks, a little shady, willing to push the envelope, an early Michael Milken–type character, attracted by a love for Jerry and the excitement of the music business. I respected his expertise. But we had different styles. What he was able to do was infuse capital into the Grateful Dead scene after Cutler had left; the money I brought to the band was through gigging, which was finite. So with the record company, he saw a way for the Grateful Dead to make money in other ways, too. Rakow came in with panache. And he went out that way, too, richer.

DAVE PARKER: I got splattered with the mud as Rakow went through. I had been the guy who was trying to keep their finances straight and keep them from getting ripped off—that's how I came into their business [after Lenny Hart's departure]. And then here was this guy who gained the confidence of Garcia and basically took over, and I was kind of relegated to a sideline role. Then he walked with the money, which the majority of the band felt he was not entitled to. Garcia felt that he was. Garcia was basically on his side at first. Then he kind of changed. He was in between somewhere. He had been very tight with Rakow during that period and had a certain amount of gratitude toward him because he felt Rakow was the guy who made it possible for him and the band to do this thing of having their own label. The rest of the band was concerned about getting ripped off and there were some very heavy meetings where there was a lot of arguing about this, and there were a couple of meetings where Rakow showed up with his lawyer and there were some very tense exchanges. And this went on for months and months. During this whole process, Garcia became more sympathetic to the way his fellow band members were looking at it, whereas before it had been a sort of adversarial thing.

JERILYN BRANDELIUS: When Lenny [Hart] disappeared, that was different. That was an out-and-out rip-off. He took the money and ran. With Rakow and Round Records, that was too big a can of worms; that's what Garcia said. I don't know what went on exactly, but I know it was Jerry's decision to let him get away with it, because he felt like it was more trouble than it was worth.

DONNA JEAN GODCHAUX: Rakow was bright and charming. Our house was right above his in Stinson, and we got to be such good friends that I was really shocked by that. I think I've even blocked some of it out of my memory. He was always a little bit of a shark, and I think he just couldn't help himself, and convinced himself that he deserved it and went from there. Jerry and Keith and I and Ron were probably closer than the rest of the band and Ron.

DENNIS McNALLY (Grateful Dead publicist and biographer): The movie was a classic Grateful Dead thing where they didn't think about it in advance. But it became Jerry's personal project, so nobody was going to interfere with it. On the other hand, he almost had to steal money from the Grateful Dead to get it done. And there's Rakow, who's Jerry's guy, and Rakow burns everybody. It's a sort of a perfect storm of negativity, and what does Jerry do? He starts self-medicating [by using heroin] to stop the anxiety, if nothing else.

It wasn't much of a surprise when, not long after Rakow left, the Dead returned to the mainstream record business by signing a big-money deal with Arista Records' Clive Davis.

RICHARD LOREN: I thought Clive was the best person they could be with. Arista was hot and Clive Davis is probably one of the best record company executives that ever was. Why? Because he never wanted to be a film producer. He liked being a record company executive. He liked being with artists and he was very well suited to his job. He seemed stable—he wasn't going to run off and do something else. He liked Jerry, and whether or not he really understood what the band was all about—and I can't say one way or the other—he believed in them and thought he could take them from being a band that sold a couple of hundred thousand albums to a million-selling band.

JERRY GARCIA (1976): The independence we had with Grateful Dead Records really isn't that important. I felt as though it was something we tried to do, but the time it happened was just the worst possible time to do it. It was the time when there were incredible vinyl shortages and all that stuff. And here we were, starting our own record company in the midst of "the collapse of the record industry." It was like swimming upstream.

But it doesn't bother me if some plan like that doesn't work. They have lives of their own after a while. If they work, they deserve to. If they don't, the heck with it. No sense in worrying about it.

And now we have somebody else to push around. When we had our own record company, the only people we could turn on were ourselves. This way we have a parent company we can turn on and snarl at and make outrageous demands of.

We proved to ourselves that we don't want to be in the record business. Making records is something that in the past wasn't really that relevant to what we do. We made records because, well, what do you do with music? One of the things you do with it is record it. Records have never been appropriate to our music because our work has always been longer than our records are.

> When the Dead signed their deal with Arista, they agreed to
> Clive Davis's request that they hire an outside producer for
> the first time since Dave Hassinger left at the end of 1967. The

lucky guinea pig this time was Keith Olsen, riding high after turning Fleetwood Mac into a hit-making band. Could he do that with the Dead? It seemed like a long shot, but at least the band had worked up some strong new material, including Weir and Barlow's off-kilter reggae-ish tune "Estimated Prophet," and Hunter and Garcia's ambitious and magnificent "Terrapin Station" suite.

ROBERT HUNTER: There was something more than uncanny about the way ["Terrapin"] happened. That song is very meaningful to me. I wrote it in front of a picture window overlooking the storm-lashed [San Francisco] Bay. There was lightning in the sky. It was one of those moments when I just knew something was going to happen. I was sitting there in front of my typewriter, just very, very open to this. There was no furniture in the room; it was a bare room.

And I just wrote "Terrapin Station" at the top of the page, and said, "Well, what's this about?" And I said, "Let my inspiration flow," and so actually the beginning lines describe the invocation. A name occurred to me, and then the beginning is an invocation to the muse to deliver further information on this, and make it something. Give it "sense and color."

Jerry had written some changes, and I had just written "Terrapin," and we met, and his changes and my lyrics went hand in glove. I think we were both approaching "Terrapin Station" from different directions and met in the center and there it was. A magical moment, and the Dead carry it right on into what they do, and the performance of it. I'm amongst those [who are not fans] of the record, but the live performance of it—*Mmmmmm!*

KEITH OLSEN: In November or December of '76 I had a meeting with Clive Davis, and at one point he said, "You know, I've signed a band that I've wanted to have for years and years, ever since I was at Columbia." I said, "Oh? Who's that?" He said, "The Grateful Dead." I said, "That's interesting." He said, "I need a commercial record out of them." I said, "*Nawwww!* No way!" Clive said, "Give it your best shot," so I said I'd go talk to them.

JERRY GARCIA (1978): Of the guys that were around, we thought that he got the best general sound on the records we heard of his. Weir went and hung out with him a little bit and reported he was an okay guy.

[Then], when we were rehearsing and he came up to hang out at the rehearsals, he showed up and he was right there. He's a good cat. He doesn't really belong in L.A., even though that's where he makes his living and all that. He could have more fun somewhere else. But he's a good guy to work with; he's the pick of the litter, as far as they go.

It's helpful to have an objective ear—somebody who's there who cares about the music and knows what it's supposed to do and all the rest of that stuff. In a way, it takes us off the hook and it doesn't hang us up as much. We can hang ourselves up for months and months and months. Not that we don't dig it, but it's just the way it is.

KEITH OLSEN: They played a couple of songs for me which were frankly better than I had expected—I can't say I really knew their songs that well before this—and then Garcia and I started talking. He said, "I've got this weird thing called 'Terrapin Station.'" "What's a terrapin?" "A turtle." "Oh, okay." And he started telling me about it; just sitting with me and telling me the story of it. And I got completely swept up in it and my mind started going: "Why don't we put it together like a suite, like a concept record?" During this first meeting we even talked about orchestrating it. Garcia thought the song would be "theatrical," which appealed to me.

JERRY GARCIA (1977): I think [Keith Olsen] has a really excellent ear, and he's worked really well with us. It's an indication that he's a pretty good man. It's hard to work with us. And he's a good enough musician and astute enough—pays enough attention, and really did his homework. It really worked out well. We're all really happy with it, especially on the level of the sound and everything. The drum sound is the best we've ever had. The performances are really amazing, much better than we're able to flog out of ourselves when we're in there producing ourselves.

KEITH OLSEN (1977): The band had to break a lot of bad habits and they also had to learn that in recording, less is more.

Garcia has amazing color in his voice if you place it just right, bridging the gap between Donna and Bob. He has a George Harrison quality to his voice that makes an incredible blend if you voice the parts correctly.

I remembered what they sounded like when I heard them play live once, several years ago, and they blew me away, they were so good. I always wondered why they couldn't get that on record.

I listened to just one record. I listened through *Blues for Allah* once, and I think I gave it away to a friend. It wasn't very well done. I told them. It seemed like they rushed through it, and then I found out afterwards that they spent five months recording that album.

Five months, really? Then Garcia said, "Let me rephrase that: we spent four and a half months trying to figure out what we should do first, and then the last two weeks recording." Garcia's so great.

I'm really pleased with the outcome. There were some trying moments, when we really had to grind away to figure out if what we were doing was right. It was a fine line. I didn't want to dictate to the Dead, 'cause I would destroy a rapport. I didn't want to let them dictate to me what was going to go on the record. I wanted every performance to come out of them, but be open to ideas like Tom Scott doing a [saxophone] solo on "Estimated Prophet."

BILL KREUTZMANN: Everybody told me he was a real motherfucker on drummers, and he made me do some stuff I didn't want to do. Like playing with big sticks. I think he wanted me to be some Top Forty drummer. He was kind of a megalomaniac, which isn't the kind of person who should be working with the Grateful Dead.

KEITH OLSEN: We learned a lot at section rehearsals. When everybody went off to get a bite to eat, I asked the drummers and Phil to come back. I said, "Okay, let's run down the tune."

"What? No guitars? No voices?"

"Sure. You all know where you are." All of a sudden they had to start thinking. Billy's going [whispers], "Mickey, how many bars 'til the bridge?" I said, "Don't worry about it—don't count the bars—it's got to be a unit." So in the section rehearsal, it just clicked.

Phil was the instrument that had to play the chord changes. Phil is a very inventive bass player, and he's also a super-intelligent person. Duty called! [Phil realized], "My God, it's me! I'm now the rhythm guitar player; I'm holding down the bottom of this tune; I'm also setting the internal rhythm of this tune—any focus on where the chord change is going is all focused on me." He just fell right into it. It allows Weir to do a more inventive guitar part, where he doesn't have to be down there at the bottom coppin' the bass note on the low E string all the time to make sure there's a good fundamental; the fundamental's there, or it's passed through in a passing tone, always leading to what the next chord is, without any doubt in the listener's ear.

Working with two drummers took a long time at first. When you have a drummer who's naturally on the back side of the beat and one on top of the beat, something's got to give. You have to pick the person who's got the right feel of the tune—which drummer's going to be the most solid. Have that drummer be the pulse and let the other drummer be the color. I used Billy for snare drum and pulse, pretty much the entire album, and Mickey as the color; that's what Mickey does best.

During the cutting of the basic tracks [for the *Terrapin Station* album] it was pretty hard to get every member of the band in the studio at the same time, because there were always places to go and things to do. So I told Steve Parish, "As soon as we get 'em in, lock the doors." Sound City [recording studio in Van Nuys] didn't have door-knobs on these two studio doors, so Parish went out to the hardware store and got these giant nails and a great big hammer and as soon as everybody was in, he hammered the door shut from the inside, leaving the nails still sticking out on our side so we could pull them out to get out at the end of the night. We had a bathroom and a coffee room. You couldn't get anywhere else. After he started doing this, we didn't have drifters from the other studios coming in to listen. We didn't have people leaving to go screw around elsewhere. We started getting work done. I thought, "This is great—Steve Parish, my hero!"

DONNA JEAN GODCHAUX: Everybody, at least in the beginning, was excited to work with Keith. But as it turned out, Keith was very much the producer, and the Grateful Dead weren't necessarily into being strongly produced. I think they wanted help in coagulating ideas, but Keith is a very much in-control producer. I think Keith was more than they bargained for, and he did things without consulting them. For instance, there was a lot edited out of the instrumental parts of the "Terrapin" suite, and Mickey was furious.

MICKEY HART: Keith Olsen was a good producer and a good engineer, but he had a problem: he didn't know the Grateful Dead, and he wanted to mold the Grateful Dead in his own image.

He did one of the most disrespectful things that has ever happened to me, musically. On the second side of *Terrapin*, "At a Siding" and "Terrapin Flyer" are mine. The "Flyer" was supposed to be me and Garcia doing duets, timbale, and guitar. Olsen erased one of the beautiful timbale tracks and replaced it with all these strings. He played it for me, and my mouth dropped. He didn't ask—he erased it off the master and replaced it all with strings. I put my timbale solo back on.

BOB WEIR: We had nothing to do with [the orchestrations on the album]. We went on tour and Keith went to London. The [British] pound was at an all-time low and [the Martyn Ford Orchestra] was cheap. Wish we could have had a little say in it, because we probably would have been a bit more ambitious.

The first time I heard it, it was mixed way, way more prominently than it is now, and I was—not pissed off, but concerned that all the orchestration and choral stuff was gonna be given too much prominence in comparison to the band. So we began the long negotiation, as it were, to put it in a more reasonable perspective. Keith was real stoked on what he'd done. He'd gone over to England and gotten these parts. They're kinda nifty parts; anything but 101 Strings [an easy-listening orchestra]. It's off in a peculiar direction. I think what it sounds like is English court music, but it serves the song well, that particular grandiose conception of how the orchestration would be done. I didn't mind the parts—there were a couple of lines that I would have spent more time with, but it's real expensive to do a sixty-piece orchestra.

JERRY GARCIA (1978): On "Terrapin," Olsen went hog-wild. He had this less-is-more approach to producing—all that clean, uncluttered crap—and then he comes back with a gazillion fuckin' strings and counterpoint you can't hear. It made me mad. He and [orchestrator] Paul Buckmaster had an erroneous rhythmic sense; they changed it from a dotted shuffle to a marching 4/4 time. . . . It should've been a loose shuffle. They screwed up the feel.

MICKEY HART (1984): There was something about him that I liked. He knew how to make good sounds, and he had good ideas. It's just that he was an egomaniac. He didn't know the Grateful Dead; he had no simpatico. He was in business; it was just bucks. He would have liked to make a great Grateful Dead record; it would have been a great feather in his cap—no one's done it, you know?

I have a soft spot for him in my heart, and I'd also like to ram my foot up his ass.

DONNA JEAN GODCHAUX: It's a shame that that feeling is out there about *Terrapin Station* [being overproduced], because it's such an incredible composition and I thought the album was very good.

When the chorus kicks in [at the end of "Terrapin"], that takes it over the top—but that doesn't take away from the grandeur of that composition. "With nothing to believe in, the compass always points to Terrapin." Hunter's lyrics are transcendent, and they can be whatever you want them to be.

> Shortly before *Terrapin Station* was released, Garcia and company finished work on *The Grateful Dead Movie*, which opened in a few theaters around the country in June 1977.

JERRY GARCIA (1976): For me, the movie is just so much raw material. It's a piece, like music. It has rhythm, it has peaks and climaxes and slow places. It's a long form that represents flow the same way a concert does. It's like a journey.

DONNA JEAN GODCHAUX: The reason Keith and I don't have a little interview segment in there like everyone else is that our interview took place on the last night of the Winterland shows [October '74, pre-hiatus] and we were absolutely flying on acid. I was not in this world. I was out in the zone! The camera crew came with us back home to Stinson Beach and they were all loaded on acid, too. So none of the interview really turned out. All I remember was a lot of staring at the table. I went into the film editing room later and saw some of it and just said, "Oh, no!" Nobody could relate to it because we weren't on the planet. Later, they wanted to shoot some new stuff but we weren't into it. Keith was a very low-profile kind of guy. That wasn't his scene, and I wasn't into it, either.

ALLAN ARKUSH: Whenever [Jerry and I] saw each other, we talked about movies. In the mid-seventies, whenever he was in town and had the night off, he'd come over and we'd watch movies together. We watched [Fellini's] 8½. He had never seen *Hellzapoppin'*, which he thought was just about the greatest, weird-ass movie. But it was always like: "What movie do you want to show to Jerry?"

I went out and watched them mix *The Grateful Dead Movie*. He came to me a lot for advice about the movie—structure and editing. He and [producer] Eddie Washington and I would talk about sound, and the mix, and "would this work?" They were trying to break barriers, as always. We would have technical discussions. I didn't give notes; I gave opinions.

Then they were worried about selling the movie. I was doing trailers [for Roger Corman], so I said: "I'll cut you a trailer." I think I borrowed the New World Pictures editing room. They were very happy—they had somebody who had actually done a trailer, who understood the Dead, doing it.

SUSAN CRUTCHER (Film editor): We chose to mix the sound down at Warner Bros. in Burbank because on their biggest stage they had a great Neve [mixing console] and it was a formal feature [film] stage.

We had three mixers, all of whom were very brave to work with us. We brought in a ton of outboard gear and hooked it into their board, which actually they had never had done. It was music processing stuff that you'd commonly find in a recording studio, but never on a film soundstage in those days. We were mixing, and it was all going fine— long hours and tedious, but good. We got to the last night of the last day—Jerry was going on the road for the weekend and didn't want to have to come back on Monday. We were already in overtime, heading for "golden time" [triple time]. We were trying to get the last reel done, which was going to be really hard to do in one day.

When we made that decision at midnight to go for golden time, everyone hit the coffee. There was also some tequila around. Anyway, a person who shall remain nameless decided that since we were all exhausted, it might be even more exciting if we were dosed, so he dosed the coffee and the tequila but didn't tell anyone. About one-thirty, one of the union guys in the loading room had to be carried out. At that point I didn't know what was going on; I was paying attention to the work. I knew things were weird, but I thought everyone was just tired. It wasn't until I was driving back to the motel with my three editors that I started to notice that I was hallucinating. At one point my friend Pat mentioned she wanted an ice cream cone, and I turned around and looked at her and I saw an ice cream cone on the end of her nose and it was dripping down her face. That's when I felt, "I must be really, really tired." It wasn't until later at the hotel, when I started laughing uncontrollably, that I realized, "Oh, fuck, we've been dosed!" I'd never taken acid before so I didn't know what to expect. I spent the next two days laughing. It was intense. In the end, Jerry came back on Monday and we finished [the mix] then.

JERRY GARCIA: The movie works for me. I can watch it and get a pretty good buzz—"Hey, far out. That's an interesting thing." In terms of the flow of it, the first part [after Gary Gutierrez's opening animation sequence] has a roughness—it's a little fuzzy, a little hot, and not really gathered. Then, later on, the whole thing composes itself, until finally the cinematography is really incredible. In the second half, the clarity comes in. And that's a way of expressing that thing: when you go out there and play, at first things are confusing. It's noisy, you're still trying to tune up, and the whole first half is settling into something.

Around the time the film was launching, the band got a double dose of bad luck. Donna had to go into the hospital for surgery, which took her out of commission for a while, and, more seriously, Mickey was in a bad car accident. As a result, the Dead had to cancel what was shaping up to be a very lucrative summer tour at a time when many agree they were playing some of the best music they'd ever made.

JERILYN BRANDELIUS: Mickey and Rhonda [Jensen] had gone down to Half Moon Bay [a coastal town south of San Francisco] to see Norton Buffalo play at some little club and to do a little work with his good friend Valerie and her horses—she has a horse ranch, and Mickey loved to go down there and ride. So [Rhonda and Mickey] were coming back around midnight in [Mickey's] Porsche and driving up Tunitas Creek Road, which is this big, curvy, winding dirt road that goes up to her property. They came around a curve, Rhonda said, and Mickey was going too fast and the Porsche swung out in the back and slid off the road. Where it slid off the road is the deepest canyon on Valerie's property, but there are all these huge eucalyptus trees that grow from the bottom of the canyon, and the car rolled down the hill and landed on this branch that was sticking out, on Mickey's side. Rhonda managed to get out. But it caved in Mickey's door and nearly cut his ear off and broke his shoulder and collarbone and some ribs. His ear was hanging on by a little bit of skin.

I was at home. Rolling Thunder [Native American shaman and friend of the band] was in town; he was giving a lecture at Indian Valley College, so I was awake and waiting for those guys to come back from his lecture. The phone rang at about two in the morning and it was Rhonda and she was really upset. "We've been in an accident. They're taking Mickey to a hospital in San Mateo. Come right away." "How badly is he hurt?" "Oh, it's not that bad. Just come to the hospital right away." So I called Cookie [Eisenberg], who was his ex-ol' lady, and said, "I need somebody to come to San Mateo with me, because I don't know what I'm going to be looking at when I get down there." So I picked [her] up in San Rafael and drove down there. As a joke, I put on my nurse's uniform I'd worn to the premiere of *The Grateful Dead Movie* at the Zeigfeld Theater in New York. (We'd all dressed up in costumes—Donna wore a Scarlett O'Hara dress, I wore a nurse's uniform, Mickey wore a referee's shirt, and some of the others wore masks.) I walked into the emergency room just as they were wheeling him in, and Rhonda and Valerie and her partner Kathy were sitting there with terrified looks on their faces, and Mickey is grey; he looks dead. His ear is huge and swollen—it looks like hamburger and he's got blood all over him. I said to Rhonda, "You said he wasn't hurt that bad." "We were afraid to tell you." So I followed the gurney in my nurse's uniform and they start cutting his clothes off, and this and that.

I had told Rolling Thunder when we left. I woke him up and said, "Mickey's been in a horrible accident. Can you guys start praying for him?" Immediately they got up and started chanting and praying and drumming. I came back to the ranch later, and as I was getting things together [to go back to the hospital], the phone rings and it's Cookie, and she says, "You won't believe this. Mickey woke up and they're going to put him in a room." "Really? Unbelievable!" "Hey, Rolling Thunder, it's working!" It was good we had him, because we needed him.

Rolling Thunder went there the next day and did a healing ceremony at the hospital, burning sage and all this stuff. He also gave me an eagle feather for my nurse's cap. He had me stand outside the room to keep people out. "Hey, we smell smoke!" "That's okay, it's part of the ceremonial thing." [That wing of] Mills Memorial Hospital had beautiful rooms that were like suites. We decorated it with posters and tie-dyes, and Bill Graham sent this huge plant; it was really nice.

Mickey was there for about two weeks, and it was horrible for him. It was a long recovery—all summer long. He really worked hard at the rehab—he had a great therapist—but it was really difficult. He's a very determined person. There's nothing that will stop him if he wants it.

It was a huge financial blow to the band to have to cancel a whole summer tour.

DENNIS McNALLY: I do wonder what might have happened if they had maintained their rhythm and hadn't been interrupted by Mickey's car accident. It was so fantastic early in '77.

> The band returned to the stage on September 3, 1977, for a concert at Raceway Park in Englishtown, New Jersey, with the New Riders and the Marshall Tucker Band opening.

MICKEY HART: I had just come back from an incredible accident. I had totaled my Porsche and I was all broken up. My ribs were broken and my shoulder was dislocated, and this was my first gig back in five weeks after an operation. I was working for this one gig and it was for 175,000 people [actually, 107,000 paid]. I didn't know if my shoulder would hold together, 'cause we hadn't rehearsed, and I hadn't opened it up. It was the hardest gig of my life. The adrenaline, the excitement, the wonder if I could make it through the night with that many people was like an out-of-body experience for me. I remember everything. I can remember all those railroad boxcars ringing the perimeter.

JOHN SCHER (Promoter): We had outgrown Roosevelt Stadium [in Jersey City] and they'd played both Woodstock and Watkins Glen. Depending on who you talk to on what day, those experiences were either awful or they were great. There's revisionist history going on even now—guys in the band have said, "Well, maybe we weren't as bad at Woodstock as we thought we were." Anyway, we always thought they could draw a hundred thousand people, which was pretty much an unprecedented thing at that time, for anybody. But if they did something that big they wanted to do it on their own terms.

The people in the neighboring town [close to Raceway Park] freaked out when they heard about this show; it was your classic hippie-versus-the-straight-community conflict. We were in court virtually every day—the townspeople were trying to enjoin us. Ultimately we prevailed, and the interesting thing was, one of the neighboring towns defied a court order and essentially closed down one of their main thoroughfares by ripping up the street. All that did was it made people park their cars there and walk.

It was one day, no camping or anything, and it went very smoothly; it was a pretty extraordinary show.

PHIL LESH (To the Englishtown crowd before the band's "Terrapin" encore): And now, ladies and gentlemen, we'd like to perform a little ditty from our newest album, at your record stores currently. . . .

BOB WEIR: We had worked up the [never-played-live "Terrapin Flyer" section of the "Terrapin" suite] for the Englishtown show. I even put on the double-necked twelve-string and I was gonna play it. But then Mickey decided at the last moment that it was too hot and he was exhausted—that "Flyer" section requires a whole lot of energy from the drummers, 'cause they're doing 32nd notes at a pretty good clip, and he has to hold one arm up and do 32nd notes on the cymbal all through the section. So we scrapped it.

STEVE SILBERMAN: I think a really important element of this era is that Jerry was looking to expand beyond the normal sonic vocabulary of an electric guitar player—the most obvious example being his use of the Mu-Tron [envelope filter] on "Fire on the Mountain." If you listen to something like the "Playing in the Band" from May 17, 1977 [in St. Louis], at one point he's using some sort of effect that sounds very much like the "flute" sound he would get with MIDI years later. He was looking for ways of creating new kinds of voicings within the tighter structure that really expanded the sonic palette of the music. Nobody sounded like Jerry on Mu-Tron. It was so great because it was almost like there was a new member of the band with this sort of hornlike tone, and I think that was a boon to the experience for Deadheads.

The sound was so crystalline during this period; I really love both

Garcia's and Weir's guitar tones. Also, by learning how to leverage new options in the more contained structures, Jerry figured out how to make a room explode, like in that fantastic "Sugaree" from May 11, 1977 [St. Paul, Minnesota] or the "Scarlet–Fire" from February 5, 1978 [Cedar Falls, Iowa]. It's like he figured out that because there was more definition within the jamming, more structure, he could exploit that structure to really bring the tension in the music to a kind of frenzy. What's nice is you get to hear the band immediately pick up on when Jerry was going to do that. He would start going off in his solo, and the band would catch up to him and then they would collectively drive the energy in the room to a peak. It's something they got to be very, very good at. And then you could almost hear everybody sigh and relax after one of those peaks.

In the late sixties it was almost universally powerful in any song they did, but by '77 they'd learned how to sculpt that waveform so they could create bigger and bigger peaks.

MICHAEL NASH (Writer): I saw 1974 as the end of an era with the Dead. I had been at that last show at Winterland, and that was the end of a certain complete world. I thought it took them a while to evolve to a place that I really found compelling, and 1977 was that year. Towards the end of that year, I think they got real brawny.

To me [December 29, 1977, at Winterland] was just the biggest. There were lots of things about that show. There was an overarching quality to the playing that was incredibly muscular—larger than life. It had a swagger to it. It was certainly not a perfect show; it was kind of rough-and-tumble, but it had its own universe of strength. It was very loud, but in a great way: clear and loud. There was this urgency to everything; everything seemed like it was about to explode. I knew it from the moment "Jack Straw" lifted into its takeoff space.

The factors that add up to making a Grateful Dead show a unique experience, which they all are, are not something that lend themselves to words; they're emotional and visceral. There are things you can single out that are cool—for instance, they played "China Cat" for the first time in three years at that show, and that was high drama. "Playing in the Band" was just brilliant, a caldron of alchemy, things

JESSE JARNOW (Writer): After the jamming, the main reason I listen to the Grateful Dead is Garcia's voice, which, at its peak, I rank somewhere near Ray Charles as one of the most expressive, beautiful, heartbreaking, comforting instruments in the history of American music. I need to hear it every day. After the Persian years [Garcia's heroin addiction] really start, it really depresses me to hear Jerry sing, regardless of the emotion and pain and everything else being communicated. He (or any of them) might have been better musicians in the eighties or nineties, but I don't think anyone would ever make that case for Jerry as a vocalist.

just coming and blossoming, and blue and dark and powerful—that big sea of dreams that they would create with that song. It kind of [settled] into this wash of cymbals and piano tinkling. Jerry had moved over to the left side of the stage [stage right]. I saw him lingering in the wings, and at a moment where everything just quieted down, he hit the opening notes to "China Cat" and walked onto the stage. There was a roar that lifted from the audience. It was theatrical in the grand sense: something no one expected to happen. Weir hit that little filigree figure there and everything just took off.

They messed up lyrics, messed up this and that, but every instrumental took off, just electric, crazy, huge. It was larger than life in the best of ways. You'd look around and everyone just had that same look on their face like, "Is this really going on?" There's that thing that just takes over, the whole "music plays the band" phenomenon, and that happened this particular night, where the music takes you somewhere else completely. When we walked out of that place afterwards, we were all just completely stunned.

For the Dead's second Arista album, *Shakedown Street* (1978), the band chose Little Feat leader Lowell George to be their new producer. This time, the sessions took place at the band's newly completed Le Club Front studios [aka Front Street].

JERRY GARCIA (1978): We chose Lowell George because we wanted someone who understood band mechanics. Really, it's better to work without a producer at times. I'm not happy with all the basic tracks on this—but I'm never completely happy. I think it's a modest album, like *American Beauty,* simple in design.

BOB WEIR (1978): George produces us with a feather touch. Mickey is strong-willed and inflexible, so he lets him alone. And Garcia can do it on his own pretty much. With a twenty-four-hour schedule, Garcia often ends up working alone, too.

RICHARD LOREN: Lowell George was different. He was a freak and a fellow musician—a brilliant musician at that—and a really funny guy; a truly unique man. Along with Jerry and Pete Townshend and David Grisman, he's one of the more intelligent musicians I've ever met. I think the problem [he had working with the Dead] is that he was a little too susceptible to the drugs that were pervasive at the time. It made for a lot of long nights and unproductive sessions. By the same token, it made for some interesting social and musical interchanges. So I'd say it was positive overall, whatever you may think about the album that came out of it.

MICKEY HART: Lowell George was mad. We wrote a great song one night, but we never recorded it. It was called "My Drum Is a Woman." We snorted miles and miles of coke and wrote this song about all my instruments and what I thought about them, how I address them. Lowell played good guitar, but he was no producer—certainly not for the Grateful Dead. He did too much coke. There's no way for him to have any kind of rational judgment.

BOB WEIR: It's really a pity with *Shakedown Street* that Lowell had to go out on tour pretty much in the middle of it, leaving us. Then we went to Egypt and then came back and finished it rather hurriedly [without him]. That could have been a much better record than it ended up being—if Lowell had stuck around and there had been some overview all the way through, or if Lowell had not been involved at all.

The most spectacular Grateful Dead adventure of them all— playing three nights in the Egyptian desert at the foot of the

Great Pyramid and the Sphinx (September 14–16, 1978)—interrupted the Dead's *Shakedown Street* sessions. No one complained.

MICKEY HART: Phil and I said, "Let's go to Bill [Graham]. We'll get him to take us there." At that time we wanted better gigs, and we wanted Bill to buy us a PA. So I made placards that said, "MORE GIGS, BETTER PA, EGYPT OR BUST," and we went to Masada [Graham's home in Corte Madera, California] at around eleven o'clock at night and started shining flashlights in his windows.

Bill comes out. "What's happening!? What's happening?!"

"Okay, Graham! Back in the house! We're going to talk business!" We went in the house, and I took his phones off the hook, and we told him we wanted to go to Egypt. We talked for hours, maybe all night.

The next day he called up Zippy [Richard Loren, the Dead's manager] and said he loves us but he thinks we're irrational. He said he was going to do it, but he really didn't want to do it, because he didn't think we should go. There was a war on [in the Middle East].

I said, "That's why we have to go over there. We have to be part of this, and this is a way we can do something." Bill didn't see it like that; he thought it was dangerous, and he thought it was just another Grateful Dead acid trip or something. So we said, "Fuck you, we'll do it ourselves." We practiced saying that different ways: "Fuck *you*, Bill—we'll do it ourselves." "Fuck you, Bill—we'll do it *ourselves*." Which, of course, we eventually had to say to him.

So we did it ourselves. And after it was all together, Bill said, "Wow, what a trip!" So he bought some tickets, and he and his boys came over and enjoyed

BOB MATTHEWS: I was Jerry's engineer and Steve [Parish] was his equipment guy. [During the making of *Shakedown Street*], Jerry sat at the piano, and made Steve sit at the drums, and he got a bass out and handed it to me, and said, "We're gonna play some music." We started out playing "Werewolves of London," and then we did "Accidentally Like a Martyr." I believe Jerry got [demo tapes] from Warren Zevon. Steve and I like to talk about how we performed on a Jerry Garcia record [their version of it with us. They were the Pleasure Crew [friends, hangers-on, ne'er-do-wells]. No producing—he was just a guest and a participant. I've never seen Bill higher than this.

RICHARD LOREN: In the late sixties, I was a rock agent in New York, and I represented the Doors and the Jefferson Airplane, and a bunch of other rock bands. During that time, I befriended Marty Balin, the lead singer of the Airplane. When I moved to California in 1970, I lived with Marty for a little while. He is an avid reader, and had an astonishing collection of books on Egypt. It was he who turned me on to the wonders and mysteries that Egypt had to offer. After being there with him and talking and listening to all his stories, I thought to myself, "Man, I've got to visit this place the first chance I get." This was before my involvement in the San Francisco scene at all. [Shortly after that] I was working for Jerry as the manager of his non–Grateful Dead groups like the Merl and Jerry band, Old and In the Way, and so on. In 1974 the Grateful Dead asked me if I would be their booking agent.

That was kind of an interesting year. Ken Kesey was commissioned by *Rolling Stone* to go to Egypt and to write a piece, which turned out to be "The Search for the Secret Pyramid," which came out in a couple of issues [in November and December '74]. The Dead had just completed their filming of *The Grateful Dead Movie* in October, and then decided to go on hiatus. [I thought], "Hey, this is my opportunity—I'm going to go to Egypt!" So I went with my wife at the time and Goldie Rush, a friend of ours and a close member of the Dead family. It was during this trip to Luxor, in Upper Egypt, that I met a man named Abdul Atee, a boatman who later

"Martyr" is on disc six of the Garcia boxed set *All Good Things*].

Another tune that we played during those sessions was "Shakedown Street." Before the band got it, he worked it through with us. During the *Shakedown Street* recording sessions, Phil came to me, in front of several witnesses, and said, "Bob, one of the licks you used is one that I used and like. I just wanted you to know. I'm not stealing it—but it's a good one, and I've incorporated it." That's quite a validation!

271

took four band members and fifteen or so other family members on a four-day trip on the Nile from Luxor to Aswan. I was so enamored and overwhelmed by the country that when I got home after that trip I decided to return the next year. I took another two weeks off in January 1976. And after I was there a few days, I was riding a camel around the pyramids and the Sphinx when I suddenly looked over to my left and I saw a stage. I mean, it all kind of hit me at that time. A light bulb kind of went off in my head, and I thought, "God, the Dead should play here!"

During this trip, and the previous one, I had come to know the [Egyptian] people a bit, and as Phil Lesh put it succinctly in his book [*Searching for the Sound*, 2006], he said he saw a connection between the loose, laid-back style of the Egyptians and the spirit of the Haight. And it was exactly that. The Egyptians and our counter-culture at the time shared a nonlinear concept of time. And I knew the band and the friends would get along just fine there. It was also politically a propitious time. Anwar Sadat, the president of Egypt, had recently expelled the Russians, who had been Egypt's financial and military benefactors, and had recently begun to ally themselves with the United States and the West. So, I thought, here's an opportunity for an authentic cultural exchange, like a "hands across the water" event.

I called Atee and I told him about this idea that I had. I said, "Could the band really play here? You think there's an opportunity?" He said, "I know some people in Cairo. Let me introduce you to this tour director I know." I met with him, and he made me feel that this was something that could be achieved. I couldn't have been more stoked. I was just out of my gourd. I returned home, I immediately informed the band of what transpired, and, as expected, they were totally jubilant at the possibility of playing at this site. We had a band meeting and decided to embark on a serious feasibility study to determine whether we could do it, and what it would take to pull it off. An Egypt committee comprised of Phil Lesh, Alan Trist, and myself was formed. We were nicknamed "The MIDS"—the Men in Dark Suits—because in order to accomplish our goal, we had to dress the part, so we sheared our locks a bit, bought these dark suits, and off we went to Cairo via Washington, where we met ambassadors of each of the countries, along with an untold number of bureaucrats and dignitaries, before we finally got a signed contract for three shows on September 14, 15, and 16.

When we got back to the States, we really had our work cut out for us. Our travel agent arranged for charter flights and hotels for band and crew, as well as flights for Deadheads from San Francisco and New York. The logistics alone of moving the equipment [and] fifty people halfway across the world was really no small obstacle. We didn't want to move all of our [sound system] from San Francisco to Cairo, so I got in touch with the Who's management [in London] and they were generous enough to rent us their PA and recording equipment. In order to get it to the site, at the foot of the pyramids, [the gear] was driven from London to Genoa, where it was put on a cargo vessel. It was then picked up in Alexandria and driven to the pyramids site in what I believe were maybe the only three semi-trucks in Egypt.

BILL GRAHAM: There was talk between [the Dead and me] about me [putting on the shows], but it was one of the few times, I must admit, I didn't think it could happen. I didn't take the time to make it happen because I didn't think I had the time. Eventually, they took it on themselves and were able to do it.

RICHARD LOREN: Then, of course, when the event happened, Bill came to Egypt with [his Bill Graham Presents lieutenants] Bob Barsotti and his brother Peter. They came and threw a big party, and it was great having them there. It was great having Bill there not as the impresario, but as the party-giver.

BOB WEIR (1979): That had always been a grand dream of ours, really. For as long as I can remember, our most cherished dream was to play at the pyramids. They represent the grandest enigma of them all. We're curious; we're naturally drawn to stuff like that. We don't know much about the pyramids, but we do know they represent something pretty far out.

JERRY GARCIA (1978, before the first show): This is kind of like giving ourselves a present or taking a vacation. Frankly, we're amazed we're getting to do this. If we had asked to play the Washington Monument, we know damn well what they'd say.

JERILYN BRANDELIUS: We went over a few days before the gigs and everybody was so paranoid about "Don't take any dope" and this and that. Because Mickey is who he is, and because we planned to do a tour of Egypt after and do recording, I packed four footlockers full of stuff, including protein powder, toilet paper, film. I ended up being like the commissary. But no dope at all. We figured we'd let the Deadheads do that. Then we get to the airport and we saw all our stuff get loaded onto carts and go right past customs. Our stuff never went through customs. They said Madame Sadat arranged that. We went straight from the airport to Madame Sadat's house for a garden party she threw for us. The weekend the Grateful Dead played there was the same weekend as the Camp David peace talks [between Egypt and Israel] which was totally cosmic. So [President] Sadat wasn't there but Madame Sadat was at the shows with her mother.

CAROLYN "MOUNTAIN GIRL" GARCIA: You know a desert is going to be hot, but nothing quite prepares you for the way it really is. When we left Marin it was a foggy afternoon, probably about 60 degrees. When we stepped off the plane in Cairo, it was at least 110. We'd hit Cairo in the middle of a heat wave, if you can believe that.

The charter flight over there was just wonderful, really crazy! We just had the greatest time, but the stewardesses were about ready to quit by the time we'd flown from San Francisco to New York. They were so freaked out at how we were behaving that when they reached New York they took all the alcohol off the plane. That was the great blow. We're taking off from New York ready to resume the party and the Pakistani stewardess suddenly announces, "So sorry, but due to the rowdy element on the plane, we have removed all the alcohol. That's our prerogative as an airline. Goodnight." Boy, after that you could cut the gloom on board with a knife—New York to Paris with no booze! Fortunately, on the leg from Paris to Cairo there was alcohol on the plane, so everyone was happy again.

Getting off the plane was weird. You taxi through this desert and every hundred feet or so there'd be a small brown man in a ragged, torn uniform with bare feet and a rusty machine gun. This was during the Camp David talks, and Egypt and Israel were still worried they were going to bomb each other or something.

The cover for the whole thing was, of course, this very respectable thing: We were doing benefit gigs for Madame Sadat's favorite orphanage. We were into it, but we were definitely looking to have some good times, too. The first night in Cairo, a bunch of us were just milling around telling stories about what we'd been doing that day and evening. What I didn't realize is that in the group was an infiltration of a couple of journalists from the wire services.

Unfortunately, I shot my mouth off, as usual. Earlier I had been down in the deep, dirty part of Cairo going after hash and having all these terrific adventures along the way. So I was telling someone about it that night in my typically loud voice and I said, "Cairo is so great! It's like Disneyland for dopesters!" And it really was, 'cause there we were with the Sphinx, the pyramids, this golden desert, the colored lights, and the Grateful Dead! A reporter overheard this and the very next day an article appeared in the San Francisco paper headlined "Disneyland of Dope." It was pretty embarrassing a few days later when a copy arrived in the mail. We were afraid the Egyptian government would see it and get scared. Then it was like, "Look at this, M.G. Keep your mouth shut from now on." I was a little better about it from then on.

JERILYN BRANDELIUS: Those Egyptians thought we were the weirdest tourists they'd ever met in their lives. We were in their houses, we were dressing like them. They thought we were crazy because we smoked hashish without mixing it with tobacco. They thought that was insane. The roadies figured out a way for you to take Coke cans and punch holes in them and make pipes out of them; it was pretty ingenious.

BOB WEIR (1979): It was a blast for us to play to a sea of black and tan faces. The crowds were Nubian and Arab.

JERRY GARCIA (1979): When we were in Egypt, what you heard on every street corner was "Stayin' Alive." Everywhere! In the darkest bazaars in the middle of Cairo, there's the Bee Gees' "Stayin' Alive" blastin' out of the bazaar. It's definitely happening all over the world.

JERILYN BRANDELIUS: Billy [Kreutzmann] fell off his horse and broke his wrist before he got [to Egypt]. After the first show he was having trouble holding his drumstick with that hand because of the cast, and he says, "Jerilyn, you've got to help me! Cut this away." All I had was a steak knife, so with Shelly [Billy's wife] kind of keeping a lookout, I cut his cast away from his thumb so he could hold the sticks better.

JOHN CUTLER (Sound tech): In 1978, I was not yet on salary with the Grateful Dead. I had my shop at Hard Truckers [speaker cabinet makers] with [Grateful Dead roadies] Joe Winslow and Sparky Raizene, and I was doing all the electronics repairs and design but I was an independent. When the band decided to go to Egypt, they decided to record and had a 24-track truck the Stones used to use brought over from England. Somebody got the bright idea we should try to wire up the King's Chamber in the Great Pyramid as an echo chamber. Lucky me, it was decided that I should come and this would be my job. I was, of course ecstatic. I'd been working under Dan Healy, and working in the studio on some of the records, but I was just an electronics tech.

The band was on tour and I was preparing for this. Back in those days, things weren't quite as technically advanced, and I remember saying to myself, "The stage is going to be this far away from the base of the pyramid, and then we have to go up inside the pyramid a long ways to get to the chamber." So we telexed the band and I told them I wanted to buy a mile of cable to bring with me. I waited for days and I got this answer: "No, just come."

When I got to Cairo, there wasn't enough wire, so Alan Trist and

I-don't-know-who-else hooked me up with an engineer from Cairo TV and he and I went in a cab to the back streets of Cairo, all over the place, to all these little shops, and we'd find one reel of cable and we'd buy it; then we'd go down some other street and find another one. Most of the cable was World War II surplus stuff that had been sitting there for thirty-five years. It wasn't good anymore. Dan Healy and Ram Rod [had] read books about the pyramid and there was supposedly a little shaft inside the King's Chamber that went out to the outside, not all the way to the top, so those two guys climbed the outside of the pyramid trying to find this hole, and they spent a whole day at it but never succeeded.

The recording truck was down at the Sphinx Theater, and we got a little wireless transmitter and put it up on top of the recording truck, beaming a signal up to the top of the pyramid, where we had an antenna and a receiver. We had a long cable going from the top of the pyramid all the way down to the entrance, and then way up inside to the King's Chamber. In the chamber, I had a little battery-powered amplifier I'd made, and a speaker, and we had a microphone and a pre-amp I'd built. The cable had to go all the way back out of the King's Chamber, out of the pyramid, back up to the top, and transmit it back to the truck. It never worked. Sometimes I could hear the signal from the truck getting to me, but the shielding was broken on the cable and it was like an antenna and it was picking up Egyptian radio stations.

When the concerts came, I was feeling totally inadequate that they'd sent me all the way over to Egypt to hook up this whole system and I never got it to work. It was [still] wonderful for me, though, because I became Mr. Pyramid. I had private access to the Great Pyramid; at five o'clock, the tourists were no longer there and it became my place, and I had one of the Mohammeds—one of the famous guys who work there; a tall skinny dude—with me. When Jerry and Bobby and everybody got there one day after five o'clock, I got to bring them up into the pyramid and show them the King's Chamber. It was Mountain Girl and Jerry and Bobby, and we had a great time.

BERNIE BILDMAN (Friend of the band): They found out there would be a total eclipse of the moon on the third night. One of the first two nights, Donna was walking around backstage with the lyrics to "Dark Star," trying to learn it. And Jerry took his guitar and went in a back room with her to teach it to her. And I was thinking, "All right!" Everyone thought they'd play it because of the eclipse. Needless to say, it never happened. So she learned the lyrics for nothing.

The third night we were dosed on crazy acid, and the band was into mushrooms, I think, because of the naturalness of it. Billy had fractured his arm two weeks before the shows and had played one-handed the first two nights. But on the third he couldn't stand it anymore, and despite what the doctor had told him, he just got into it with both hands.

The first two nights, a group of Egyptian singers had opened the show. On the third night, the band started the show, and they had the singers come out after the break because they wanted to watch the eclipse. When the eclipse started happening, I walked out on the part of the stage where Jerry and Ram Rod were. Jerry was sitting in a chair, and Ram Rod and his kid had laid down flat. We just laid there tripping, watching this eclipse come on. David Freiberg was there taking pictures, documenting the whole thing. Then, as [the moon] started coming out of the eclipse, the band took the stage again and opened with "Fire on the Mountain."

JOHN CUTLER: I never even got to hear the music, dammit! I was up in the pyramid trying to get that echo chamber working all three nights. Finally, the last night, I think I heard the end of the last set because I finally just gave up and said, "The hell with it. I'm all the way over here in Egypt. I at least want to hear the music." So I came down and hung out on the stage, and I remember I felt like a total failure. I had some pride in my work. I remember coming down there, and I think I was in tears, and I remember Jerry came up to me at some point, maybe it was between songs, and he gave me one of his great big bear hugs, which made it all better. He was just laughing about it.

CAROLYN "MOUNTAIN GIRL" GARCIA: One of the highlights of the trip for me was this great camel ride we took across the desert after the final show. It was real late at night, and Bill Graham rented every camel and horse he could find, and we went in a huge caravan across the desert to this big tent village a few miles away called Sahara City. I gather it's sort of the Las Vegas of Egypt. It was really fun. It was a full moon and we had just about everyone—at least a hundred people. As I remember, Graham and Mickey led the procession, with Mickey on his fabulous white horse. It was huge, and it could dance and prance because it was really a show horse. It was this impossibly macho horse, and Mickey just had the time of his life galloping around on it. He looked like he was in some movie or something.

DONNA JEAN GODCHAUX: Most of the people who went to Sahara City got either a camel or an Arabian stallion. I'd ridden a horse earlier in the trip and had the life scared out of me. I'd never done it before, and the second I got on, mine bolted. I was thinking, "My God, after all this I'm going to die in Egypt." But just as I convinced myself I was going to die, I got into the flow of it and it was just wonderful. Still, I was happy to get a camel for the night trip.

It was funny, because if you're an American woman, the Egyptian men all assume you're loose. The guy who owned the camel I rode told me he wanted to marry me and he wanted me to have his kids and all that stuff. But the real trouble started when we got to Sahara City around sunrise. This Egyptian guy who was sort of like the caretaker for one of the ladies' rooms there just wouldn't leave me alone. He actually chased me all the way out to where Keith and all the other people from our group were. He was pawing me and everyone was yelling, "Leave her alone! Leave her alone!" He was serious. He was going for it! Finally, the only thing that succeeded in getting him off me was Ken Kesey stepped out of the crowd and poured a bucket of beer on his head.

RICHARD LOREN: After the concerts, Jerry, Bobby, John Kahn, Keith and Donna, Ram Rod, Alan [Trist], Mountain Girl, myself, and a bunch of friends piled on to Abdul Atee's felucca sailboat and we all went down the Nile on a three-day voyage from Luxor to Aswan. We had, like, twenty-five people, and we all had a little space, [each] with a cushion, and that's where we kind of stayed, except when we had to go to the head. We ate right there; the food was brought to us. It was like a timeless place. What we saw—looking at the fishermen and looking at the banks of the Nile—was probably not much different than it was two thousand years ago.

JERILYN BRANDELIUS: We called it the Ship of Fools. Sue Stephens [from the Dead office] came into the hotel in Aswan and she says, "We thought we were going out for like a three-hour cruise—we've been on that ship for two and a half days, with all these people sleeping under scratchy packing blankets. I jumped off upstream and took a cab here, but they'll be here any time, so make sure our rooms are ready." They were *done*. Garcia was the first one off the boat.

JOHN CUTLER: I was drafted by Mickey and Jerilyn and [sound tech] Brett Cohen, and the four of us went on a trip with Hamza [El-Din, Bay Area–based Nubian musician and friend of Hart's]. We flew down to Aswan and went around recording and filming Egyptian musicians—local people in various cities in Egypt. Mickey put out those records from it: *Music of Upper and Lower Egypt*. I had known Hamza pretty well before, from working at Mickey's barn—I was a "barn slave" for a long time in the old days.

JERILYN BRANDELIUS: Hamza was like the Nubian ambassador to the world; he was like the King of Nubia. We went all over the place recording people. Mickey gave his tar [Nubian drum] to a blind man, and he couldn't believe how smooth and well-made it was. It was beautiful.

JOHN CUTLER: In Hamza's village, at night we'd go out there and sit in the dirt on blankets, and the guys would be playing tars and other instruments and we'd all be passing around a bowl of hash and everybody would get really stoned. I would just fall asleep out there, and they'd cover me up. I remember waking up one morning and all these little boys were poking at me. It wasn't like I was the first white person they'd ever seen, but they weren't used to hippies in their village, sleeping on the street. They woke me up and took me swimming in the Nile with them. It was a wonderful, exotic experience.

MICKEY HART: I also went up and down the Nile recording music in the cafes. It's great stuff—all these indigenous instruments playing this amazing music for the tourists and the locals. Playing double-reeds; third-eye music, man! People were drinking and having cups of coffee and smoking hash and this wild music was going down. You hear the clinking of glasses and laughter. These guys were really going after it musically. I always had my Nagra [recorder] with me no matter where I went. If I went into the shower I had my Nagra. If I went to eat I'd have it at my feet, because you never knew where something cool might be.

JOHN CUTLER: In Cairo, Mickey liked the echo in this mosque we went to, and he [especially] liked the echo in the men's room of this mosque. So he somehow convinced this Imam guy to go down in the men's room and chant while we recorded it.

BOB WEIR (1981): We stepped out of the twentieth century for a good few days, and that was wonderful.

JERRY GARCIA (1981): It was a wonderful adventure, to play the Great Pyramid. It totally blew my mind. Totally. For me it was one of those "before and after" experiences. I mean, there's my life before Egypt and my life after Egypt. It expanded certain levels. The Great Pyramid itself is such a wonder, it completely burns out your concepts of things like size and the realm of possibility.

RICHARD LOREN: We were hoping to recoup all the money we put into it from a live record. I thought for sure we'd get a live record, but the piano was out of tune and there wasn't a single song the band was happy with. Jerry in particular was very unhappy with it musically because of the piano. The piano tuner got pissed off with the crew because they wouldn't let his mother onstage at the Giants Stadium concert in New Jersey [before the trip]. "Fuck you guys, I'm not going to Egypt." So the band arrives in Egypt and there's no piano tuner. Where are you going to get a piano tuner at the eleventh hour? So the piano was never tuned.

JOHN CUTLER: Obviously we wanted to put out [an album] of this show when it was timely, but it was always deemed, "No, no, the piano's out of tune, we can't do this." I wasn't involved in making the [thirtieth anniversary CD release for Rhino in 2008, *Rocking the Cradle, Egypt 1978*], but when I spoke to [mixer] Jeffrey Norman about it, he said that when all was said and done, when he put up the multitracks and started mixing, [the piano] wasn't that bad at all and it wasn't a deal-breaker by any means. But somehow it had risen in mythology to "Oh, no, the piano's out of tune, we can't use these tapes!" and they sat in the vault for thirty years.

BILL GRAHAM: If we had nine hours, perhaps we could tap into what it was about for me. The music and that place and that ride across the desert after the last show . . . I mean, seeing Kesey and Bill Walton [basketball star and the world's tallest Deadhead] having a camel race is not exactly an everyday occurrence!

[The Dead] didn't think they played well enough to put the tape out, but for me it was the most moving musical event—and there've been New Year's Eves where they played great, and jams at the Fillmores and Winterland where they were great and jammed with all these people. I can rattle off maybe twenty great gigs—but the first night's show in Egypt . . . Mickey had met this Nubian tribe. They started to play, and I was on the side of the stage feeling no pain—there were goodies all around—and then very gently came all these notes, and it was Jerry's picking, like this bird that was flying over the stage, amongst the tar playing. Then there was a bass line! And one by one the guys picked up their instruments and they just tapped into what the Nubians were doing. And they were as one for twenty minutes, and then the Nubians left the stage and the Dead played. That twenty minutes can never be equaled for me. It has nothing to do with musical content. It was everything. Here's the Sphinx and here's the pyramid. And here I am. I can't begin to describe it. If you said to me, "Based on the experiences you've had in life and what you imagine would be pleasurable, and you're going to the electric chair the day after tomorrow—what do you want to do tomorrow?" I'd want to be on that stage with those players in that situation, to feel that way again.

But if the Dead gave me the highest experience of my life, they also gave me the seventh, nineteenth, twenty-sixth—so many separate experiences with the Dead are part of my top fifty or one hundred experiences.

JERRY GARCIA (1979): [The Egypt trip] came right at the end of making *Shakedown Street,* so it was also a bit of a relief. We were hustling to get the record down [and finish] the sucker—going to Egypt was an amazing change and perfect refreshment. To come back and do the slight amount of finishing we had to do on the album and feel really "up" for everything. [Egypt] did cost a lot and took a while to do, but boy, was it ever worth it! It was an utterly plus experience. Most of us haven't really gotten back yet.

RICHARD LOREN: My thing with the Grateful Dead was I always wanted to take them to new places. I was ready to take them to China. I took them to Alaska [for a pair of summer solstice shows in 1980]. That's the stuff that made it so great. That's why I wanted to be with the Grateful Dead. I got sick of them playing tours and the same thing over and over again. I wanted to see them on Lake Titicaca. I wanted to see them at the Great Wall. But I wanted them to be there more than they wanted to go, and I think that's in part because of the financial failure of the Egypt trip, and because they weren't rich then.

When we came back from Egypt, that's when the pain began.

Egypt might have been the coolest gig the band ever played, but they were seen by a helluva lot more people when they made their debut on *Saturday Night Live* on November 11, 1978. For the first time, they played for an audience of millions

TOM DAVIS (Comedian and *Saturday Night Live* writer): Lorne Michaels [producer of *SNL*] was standing next to [*SNL* bandleader] G. E. Smith. They're both my good friends. This is 1978, in the spring. Nineteen seventy-eight was a great year for me—probably the peak of my career, really, or certainly of my influence at *Saturday Night Live*. I thought it was the right time to pop the question: "Hey, Lorne, can we book the Grateful Dead? I think they should be on the show."

Lorne goes, "*Hmm,* weren't they big in the sixties?" He turns to G.E. "G.E., do you think we should book the Grateful Dead?"

G.E. goes, "They're not happening."

I said, "Lorne, they sell more tickets than anyone else."

"Tom, this is television. No one knows who they are."

That week, I wrote a sketch with Gilda [Radner] and Laraine [Newman] giving testimonials in some commercial parody. Gilda was "Candace Brightman" [name of the Dead's lighting director] and Laraine was "Donna Godchaux." I always used real names.

It got on the air, and the following Monday I was summoned to the boss's office. "Davis, did you use real Grateful Dead names in that thing you wrote?"

"Yeah, I always use real names."

"Don't do that again, 'cause I got all these phone calls."

I said, "Lorne, you told me nobody knows who they are!"

He goes, "All right, I'll book them. But I'll book them in the fall." And true to his word, he booked them in the fall. And that's how they got on. Thanks to me!

[The week of the show], the Grateful Dead are in that hotel on Central Park that Bill Graham owned [the Navarro]. I go over there in the afternoon on Monday to meet my heroes. The drummers, I discover, are the ones who are *Saturday Night Live* fans, and they've been hanging out with [John] Belushi. They were the gung-ho guys about getting on *Saturday Night Live*. Jerry didn't want to do TV, but he went along with it because the drummers wanted to do it.

They chose "Casey Jones." I think it went right over NBC's head, somehow. I didn't go and ask them if they had a problem; it just sneaked on the air. I was ready with answers like, "It's an anti-drug song, it's a cautionary thing," wink-wink, nod-nod. But that wasn't necessary. People were so concerned about the Grateful Dead sound crew and the union guys killing each other that they were all distracted long enough that it just went on the air.

The music is blocked at eleven in the morning on Thursday. Our director, Davey Wilson, was an old-school director. He likes to know where you're gonna be at what part of the song. He was in the control room, and they were rehearsing, and of course Jerry was doing it differently every time. Sometimes his back was to the camera.

"Jerry, where are you going to be when you do your solo?"

Jerry goes, "I don't know."

"Don't you want to be on camera?"

"Not particularly, no. I don't give a shit."

When they got on the air, it was like Jerry was shot out of a cannon. He played every camera; he knew when every camera was going on; he looked right into the lens; and he articulated every word perfectly, like, "I'll show you how to do it." And you could see him having fun. He loved it. After giving everybody trouble, who enjoyed it the most?

After they did that first show, we went up to my office and started partying. I had this doll of a cowboy, about a foot-and-a-half high, that had a photosensitive thing over the heart and a six-shooter that shot a light beam. I thought I was really good at it, 'cause

TOM DAVIS: The whole band's in this hotel room, and they're rowdy, and they go, "Hey, Tom Davis, Tom Davis!" And they picked me up and put me on the bed like I was on a pedestal.

Kreutzmann goes, "Davis, what song should we play?"

I said, "How about something where Jerry plays pedal steel? Because pedal steel sounds so good on TV."

Jerry said, "Get him off that bed!" That was the last time they ever asked me anything.

it was way across my office, on top of a file. Weir, after he did the last line on a mirror, picked up the mirror, turned around backwards, aimed into the mirror, and shot the cowboy in one shot. That was the last time I ever played that game. One shot, facing backwards, into the mirror. That impressed the hell out of me.

We left the office and went downtown to the Blues Bar [the notorious John Belushi-Dan Aykroyd hangout], and we watched the sun come up.

> Meanwhile, things were rough within the band's ranks. Keith and Donna were not getting along well, and the band members were increasingly dissatisfied by Keith's playing and Donna's singing.

DONNA JEAN GODCHAUX: We started to take out our problems in dealing with all this pressure on each other. By the time we got to be making enough money to afford the drugs of our choice, we did the drugs of our choice and that made matters worse. It was like everything that we'd gotten married for and loved each other for was getting ripped off. There's no blame—it's just what happened.

I got egotistical and selfish there for a while. I'm not saying Keith was an angel—he wasn't—but I acted really badly quite a lot. There was one night we had Grateful Dead practice and it was during a time we were trying to stay separate from each other a little. He wouldn't leave me alone this night, so I took my new BMW and backed up and rammed into his new BMW. I backed up and rammed into it again, and then I did it again. I hit his car as hard as I could three times and completely totaled his car. Then I took mine and totaled it into a pole and took a taxi home.

Along the same lines, if the hotel we were staying at didn't get my silk blouses back in time so I could wear the one I wanted onstage, I would simply demolish the hotel room. I remember one time I did a spectacular job on a hotel room in Detroit, and Phil and Bobby and the road manager came up because they'd heard it was the worst they'd ever seen. I was notorious for it.

All was harmonious when the Dead played at Winterland on New Year's Eve 1978, the final night in the aging facility's long history; it was to be torn down and replaced by a condo development. The New Riders, the Blues Brothers, and the Dead sent the ol' place out in style with a marathon show that was televised live on the local Public Television station (and released on DVD in 2003 as *The Closing of Winterland*).

As 1979 dawned, the Grateful Dead were not exactly considered to be on the cutting edge of what was happening in music. Punk and new wave were all the rage, and disco was hanging on and evolving. But the Dead's popularity continued to grow, largely from word of mouth, and as they always had, they attracted legions of college students all over the country. Though Arista hadn't landed a hit single from either of the Dead's first two albums with the label, relations between them remained cordial.

JERRY GARCIA (1979): Arista is a different kind of record company because there's a personality involved: Clive Davis, who more often than not likes to be involved in his record company's projects and who cares [and] is involved and actively participating in career guidance and all that stuff—selecting material, production, everything. He's left us completely alone, completely autonomous. They aren't always interjecting their presence into our scene.

BOB WEIR (1979): I don't know [why the band has lasted this long]. It's karma. What can I tell you? It brought us together. There's an alchemy that happens with us that's done us a real good turn. It's given us something to do for the last few years and given us no end of stuff to work on. There's no end of challenge, at least that I can see, for this group. If challenge is what it takes, then challenge is certainly a vital ingredient in keeping a band together and going, as far as I can see.

PHIL LESH (1979): When I started with the Dead, I said, "Look, guys, I don't want to be doing this when I'm thirty." Well, I'm thirty-eight now, and I'm going to be doing it when I'm forty. It may turn out that

I'll just go gentle into that good night, you know? I may just become a country squire and forget my musical ambition. Because I've seen what musical ambition can lead to for people who are incapable of handling success or failure, or frustration, or whatever: loneliness. I would love to be able to contribute something to the culture. I don't know whether I can at this point. It remains to be seen.

JERRY GARCIA (1979): There's a certain amount of liberation in being a successful musician. Even making a living at it is a big score. Everything that happens after that is just a gift.

The fact that we ever had [an] audience is incredible. The fact that we still have one and, further, it's still dynamic and changing—all those things are very surprising. 'Cause even if you're only remotely successful, the indeterminacy factor in rock 'n' roll is tremendous. I mean, bands are famous for not living very long or not lasting very long. The fact that the Grateful Dead exists after all this time is remarkable.

BOB WEIR (1979): In the early and mid-seventies, the audiences took a turn for the more staid. They were into the "entertain me" stage. It seems that now they're starting to be more reflective of the audiences that I seem to remember from the late sixties. They are more participatory. The ambience is getting a little more charged these days and so the band is playing hotter. That could be because practice makes perfect, and we've been getting a lot of practice of late. For some reason we've come up with a curious sort of chemistry that creates an energy bubble—the way we relate to the audience and the way they relate back to the band, and to each other. It creates an atmosphere, a great ambience to be playing music in.

> Keith Godchaux continued his long, sad slide in the winter of 1979.

ROB EATON (Musician): Englishtown '77 was the first time Keith didn't have a grand piano. It was a Yamaha CP-70, which sounded like a toy piano. It didn't blend as well, didn't have the same vibe as the other one did. By May of '78, he was pretty much taking a backseat to everything. Towards the end, he'd sit there with one hand in his lap, playing two or three notes over the course of a minute, it seemed. He was really not in a good place. It was pretty depressing to see. He was in the middle of the stage at that point—maybe they put him there to get him more involved, I'm not really sure. But they moved him closer to Garcia. I can see why they decided to get rid of Keith and Donna; the drugs were having a huge impact on the music, in a negative way.

BOB WEIR: [Keith] got wedged somewhere, is all I can say. He really didn't like it here. He was really bored with life in general, and would freely tell anybody that. The madness, or the darkness, came upon him and that was it. He was just not interested in living, and it was reflected in his music and everything else.

DONNA JEAN GODCHAUX: We were really wasted. You get a husband and wife on the road, and that is a prescription for you-name-it. It was really hard on us. Coming into such a huge scene, like we did, and being thrust into such a monumental and extended musical expression. It's not only musical expression, but you get the whole Grateful Dead dynamic. It's just a huge thing. And all of the elements that were in place during that time—it was a pretty hefty prescription for Keith and I to be "in demise," you might say.

We realized that we had to get out of the band. We talked about it; we said, "We're not quitters. We don't know how to quit." But we knew that we needed to be out of the band. It was nobody's fault; it's just what was happening. And never would there be any blame there in any way. Everybody's responsible for their own actions. But we knew we needed to be out of the band. They did, too. I get questions: "Did you guys quit, or were you fired?" And I say very honestly, it was very much both.

I had left in mid-tour once [fall of 1978]. I just said, "I can't do this anymore." Keith and I did one more tour. And there was a meeting at our house, and the whole band came, and I believe it was Bobby who said, "We think you guys need to do your own musical thing, and it's time for you to go and do what you want to do." And we said, "We agree." That's where we were at. So it was a very mutual decision. It was never real strained or weird. Keith and I just went about doing what we needed to do, and so did they.

BOB WEIR: First we decided that Keith and Donna just weren't happening. Then we decided whether we'd replace them, and we decided, yeah, we would. And in that case, who? Everybody in the band at one time or another had gone to hear my band while I was on the road, and they all were impressed by Brent [Mydland]. So Garcia suggested, "Hey, what about that guy you've been playing with? What's his name? Brent?" He was in from then on.

CHAPTER 8
Hungry for Color

JERRY GARCIA: What we always wanted was somebody that would produce color. The thing of having another percussion instrument in an all-percussion band was really too much of the same thing. The effect that the piano had on the ensemble was something we could accomplish with guitars, so what we were really looking for was that sustain. You know, we were all hungry for color. Real hungry.

BRENT MYDLAND: I was born in Munich but came back to the States before age one, early enough that I don't remember anything of Munich. We moved to Antioch [Northern California; east of the Bay Area], lived there until I was three, then we moved out to Bethel Island. My last year of high school, I lived in Concord. I've lived in Concord ever since, except for three years in L.A.

I started taking piano lessons when I was around seven or eight. I got into my first band [while in] high school in Concord. I don't know whether you'd qualify it as a band—I got together with some friends and started playing around. We had a drummer, sort of, a bass player, sort of, and a guitar player, sort of. It was pretty much whoever wanted to play at the time. We never really made over ten bucks a head.

I started working steadily in about '75, in L.A. I moved down there with the intention of breaking into the biz. I worked with Batdorf and Rodney for a while, after the last of their three albums was made. We made one single, but not much came of it.

Then John Mauceri, Greg Collier, and I got a band together called Silver. We had a semi-hit called "Wham Bam"—"Wham bam shang-a-lang and the sha-la-la-la-la-la thing." It was embarrassing. It was written by somebody outside the band. We made an album that did fairly well for a first album. The single was in the Top Twenty. We got dropped a year later. I kicked around in some other bands down there, but never came up with anything I was satisfied with—somewhere I could express my own ideas. In Silver I was part of the band as a writer and lead singer as well as keyboardist.

There was work in L.A., but I got into a slump and came back [to Northern California] because I knew more musicians personally, and thought maybe I could get something together.

Within a couple of weeks of moving back here, I got a call from Mauceri about Weir's band. Mauceri's connection was David Lindley. John played with Jackson Browne on one tour, and when Bob went to him looking for a drummer, Lindley mentioned John.

We rehearsed for about a week and then went to work. It's a little hard to cop three keyboard parts [from the tracks on Weir's solo album, *Heaven Help the Fool*]. I tried to take whatever seemed best, whatever seemed the most prominent.

[The Bob Weir Band] was a lot more structured than the Dead, but it was a lot closer to the Dead than Silver was. Silver was like every other band that comes out of L.A., or most bands, period: this is what we play, this is how we play it; that's it. It's tight and easy to listen to and definitely not offensive.

With Bobby, at first, I'd say to him, "Well, should I play this instrument on this song, or this other instrument?" and he'd say, "I don't care. Why not play one this time and the other the next time if you feel like it?" It loosened me up a lot and got me more into improvisation, which there hadn't been a whole lot of in Silver. I liked it a lot.

Mydland had been with the Bob Weir Band for about a year when the invitation came to try out for the Grateful Dead.

BRENT MYDLAND: Bobby gave me a call out of the blue and said, "Would you be interested in being in the Dead? It's not for sure, but Keith and Donna might be leaving soon, so you ought to check out some stuff." He gave me a list of some tunes—fifteen or twenty songs.

I knew quite a few of them. I'd liked the Grateful Dead when I was younger, though I kind of lost track of them in the early seventies. In fact, when I first met Bobby I didn't even know they were still together. When I started playing with Bobby I started listening again.

So I listened to those songs, and then Bobby gave me a call back and told me that Keith and Donna were leaving and he asked me to come in and play with the band. I came [to Front Street] and we jammed on some blues and stuff. We didn't even go over the stuff I'd learned! It was really just seeing how we played together. And the thing with jamming like that is, it shows more the natural way that you play than doing a song you've learned.

I learned [the songs] twice, actually. I picked them up off records at first. When I came in the first time to play, I told them I'd learned them from the records and they said, "Uh-oh." So they told me, "Well, this song doesn't go there anymore. Now it goes here." It was like, "Now you're going to learn them for real." That took a little getting used to. I probably would have been better off not learning from the records at all. We rehearsed for about two weeks before my first show with them.

The day before [my] first concert I asked what tunes we'd be doing, so I could concentrate on those songs, but no one would tell me. It freaked me a bit, but then when we got on stage, I realized that nobody knew what we were going to play. Keeps you on your toes.

MICKEY HART (1984): He had the chance of becoming one of us. I wondered, for a while. I was the hardest critic, in a way. He didn't have the passion at first. Then his attitude and his playing changed, and he relaxed.

God, he must have been intimidated, playing with the Grateful Dead. He was seeing so many inconsistencies around him in the music. He was used to playing music that had a beginning, a middle, and an end, that repeated, and had bridges and stuff. And people wouldn't forget lyrics, and they'd play it the same way every time. He probably thought every bar was another mistake or two. Until he saw the beauty in it, I couldn't see the beauty in him. He knows now, and I really like him. I think his playing is really nice. He's a better player than when he started with the Grateful Dead, and he's doing more with what he has. But it was strange at first.

BRENT MYDLAND: The Grateful Dead is already full of rhythm instruments, so a lot of times it's better to lay back, let the rhythm happen, and just color it. A lot of people kind of put me down for it, but I feel like I'm pretty much there to color, more than paint the picture to start with. Sometimes I feel like it's open enough to do both, and I should do both. But I like doing the color with sustain and this and that.

Now and then I'll use some of Keith's licks, because it seems like a natural part of the song, but more often than not I'm just playing myself, just jamming.

JERRY GARCIA (1981): Keith had a thing with the piano that was truly remarkable. You could play him a record of something he'd never been exposed to before stylistically, like Professor Longhair, and a minute later he'd have the whole idiom. It would blow your mind. But what we wanted was a keyboardist who wasn't a pianist.

BOB WEIR (1980): Our textures are more varied. The singing has gotten a touch tighter, because Donna never did learn to inflect the way Jerry and I grew up inflecting together. Brent does it more naturally, and it's just more natural with him there.

I never thought having a female vocal in the band—not just Donna, but any female—was exactly right for the band. I'm not being a male chauvinist or anything, but it's just a matter of taste. For this band and for the kind of tunes we do, it didn't work well. It sounded askew to me.

JERRY GARCIA (1980): I think Brent is a real great addition. He's got a real great voice, just the right register we need, so he blends in real well with Weir and me. We've been having a lot of fun singing together, and old tunes sound real nice with him singin' on them. And he's a nice aggressive keyboard player, and imaginative, too. I think that his presence is really going to start being felt. It'll probably take another year for him to start really being absorbed and for him to start influencing us in the way I know he's going to be able to. But he's real talented and we like him a lot.

ROB EATON: There were a lot more notes coming out of Brent than there were coming out of Keith. I'm not talking about '78 when Keith was pretty much unconscious. In '73, '74, Garcia would play a phrase and Keith would somehow extend it and make it make even more sense. He was very tasteful.

Brent, when he came in, was all over the place. That [Fender] Rhodes [electric piano]—he was filling in so many notes that Weir had to change his style from the sort of hammer-on and single-note stuff that he would do back in the one-drummer era. He started playing more chords and less of the thing that he was focusing on when he was really creative. I think it was because of Brent's—I don't want to say overplaying, but Brent's aggressive style. And tonally, too—Weir's bright tone and the Rhodes were in the same zone in terms of tone and placement, and I think Weir dumbed down his style a little bit to accommodate that.

BETTY CANTOR-JACKSON: When it came to [making] *Go to Heaven* I had to fight with our producer, Gary Lyons, who wanted to have a control room put in [at Club Front]. I was adamant about not having a control room. I didn't want to divide the room up.

When we first had [Club Front] as a rehearsal studio, we just tried to deaden the space and control it a little bit. It was a big cement box with a big, high, wooden ceiling and some skylights. We had it partitioned off. Half was for storage, and the other half was pretty much our studio. I fought to keep it that way because I liked the openness. I didn't want to change the sound of what I was hearing coming from the speakers. I just turned the speakers off when I was recording the band and listened on headphones to make sure I was getting everything.

BRENT MYDLAND: I was thinking that Bobby might use ["Easy to Love You" and "Far from Me"] in his band. I figured Bobby was into some off-time signatures, and "Easy to Love You" had a little twist to it that was interesting. Clive [Davis] didn't like the lyrics to "Easy to Love You," so John Barlow and I got together and worked on it. I think we ended up with the same song, anyway. I can relate to what Clive was saying now more than I could then. The stuff I write, I feel, isn't necessarily lyrically Grateful Dead. The stuff I write is a little tight to the vest, as opposed to painting images in your mind, which is what most Grateful Dead songs are real good at. My songs don't really go in that direction.

BILL KREUTZMANN: We can get that magic [we have when we perform live] on a record—just cram five thousand people in a studio with us while we record!

BOB WEIR: The idea [for the cover of *Go to Heaven*] came up somewhere on the road, I think. "What are we gonna call the record?" I think we'd been thinking about *The Grateful Dead Go to Egypt*, *The Grateful Dead Go Here, Go There*—just as various adventures, not as record titles. And "Why don't we call the record *Grateful Dead Go to Heaven*?" "Yeah, great—we could have pictures of us as angels, or something. Put us all in white suits." And on the back we'd have *The Grateful Dead Go to Hell*, and have us all in red suits—or in the same white suits, but have them tattered, with us all sleeping on some door stoop.

Well, the back picture never got took. It's unfortunate, because it should have been *Grateful Dead Go to Heaven* on one side and *Grateful Dead Go to Hell* on the other—a two-sided record. Or it could have been a sequel.

JERRY GARCIA: We wanted to play around the idea of "go to hell," because the Grateful Dead really is like a visit to hell; a very entertaining hell.

BOB WEIR: My major reservation with that record had nothing to do with [producer Gary Lyons]. I just felt that we didn't have good, mature material when we recorded it. Some of it we'd never even played live.

Our material isn't like a lot of popular groups' material. We develop our songs in different ways from most groups, and the kinds of music we play, the stuff we sing about and the whole aesthetic is a little different. It takes us a while to find the heart of a song, even after it's been written, whereas with most pop songs it's a finished product by the time it leaves the pen, and it then becomes a matter of just getting a good rendition. With us, songs tend to evolve more. So it's a good idea for us to let our material evolve so we fully understand the heart of the song before we record it.

JERRY GARCIA (1981): Nobody was very happy with *Go to Heaven*. We had kind of a good time making it. It wasn't a total bust, but personally, I don't believe I've written any real great songs lately—with the exception of "Althea." I don't think our records have ever been much to scream or write home about, actually.

In 1978, Mickey Hart and Bill Kreutzmann filled Club Front with hundreds of percussion instruments to create audioscapes for Francis Ford Coppola's film *Apocalypse Now* (some of which were released on an album titled *The Apocalypse Now Sessions:*

Rhythm Devils Play River Music). This project birthed "The Beast," a large metal frame that held up an assortment of very large drums, which became part of the Dead's touring setup. And beginning in the spring of 1978, an extended percussion interlude became a permanent feature of the band's second sets. The guitarists and keyboardist would leave the percussionists onstage, and after "drums" they would return to jam while Kreutzmann and Hart rested. Thus, "Drums and Space."

BILL KREUTZMANN: We'll start out [on the solo] and I'll play a complicated pattern. Mickey will get off the drum set and go to the Beast and play lines over what I'm doing. I'll stay playing metronomically.

MICKEY HART: It repeats, so it's something I can grab onto.

BILL KREUTZMANN: It's like a carpet, a foundation. [And then] the line will change.

MICKEY HART: We're more interested in seeing what will happen than actually working something out beforehand and making it happen. That's our magic. That's what I like to do with Billy. It's what we enjoy about each other more than anything else. We're not afraid; chances are taken onstage.

BILL KREUTZMANN: One thing I really like is being able to bend the drum note [with a talking drum]. Because the trap set has fixed notes, I've always wanted to bend the notes. I wasn't satisfied having to use the same notes all the time.

MICKEY HART: It's his need to become melodic. If anything has changed over the years, it's our excursion into tuned percussion. Also, we're checking into all kinds of different materials and the sounds they create: woods, metals, skins, bone. See, he gravitated to the talking drum at the same time that I went for the tar, which is a great combination. They've never been used together like that. Besides our music you'll never hear those two together.

JERRY GARCIA (1979): In the Grateful Dead, things work dynamically. They aren't a result of somebody's point of view made into policy; rather they're the other way around. Things happen, and we try to figure out what they were. We arrive at decisions as a result of necessity . . . or luck. Just like anybody. Any idea has to make allowances for what everybody believes. The idea is to preserve the sanctity of the individual, so to speak, however warped it is. What's interesting about the Grateful Dead is that we don't share a common point of view about anything.

We're disorganized with a purpose. It's a way of going about things that yields a certain interesting result in the music that we would like to have reflected in the business and everything else.

JERRY GARCIA (1980): Since we've been in the studio and haven't done that much touring yet this year, this one has taken a little adjustment. It so happens that the three weeks before this tour—after we did *Saturday Night Live* [for the second time on April 5, 1980]—I was just planning on not doing anything. And I succeeded, too; didn't play at all. And my musical chops declined so enormouslyc that I'll never do it again. That's like the longest period in the last ten years I've gone without playing, and it's taken almost the whole tour just to get myself together again. So that was a big mistake.

MICKEY HART (1980): Getting in shape is a big part of my playing. I didn't like to spend that much time warming up before shows. I found that by breaking down my activity into its basic parts, rather than just grabbing two drumsticks and a pad, I shortened my warmup period.

I've developed a Zen kind of exercise. I address each finger, each hand, each foot when I get up in the morning. I verbally greet them. Then, as I'm verbally addressing them, I begin to work them independently, then together. I'll end up playing drums in the air. It's kind of fun because I can play drums without bothering anybody. Sort of isometric drumming. And I warm up in one-third the time.

I'm getting more of a connection to my extremities. They used to be things that just hang out there. Now I'm trying to make my hands and feet more a part of the instrument. It's a yoga. Preparing to play the music is a yoga.

> In the middle of 1980, it occurred to somebody that maybe it was a big deal that it was the Dead's fifteenth anniversary. It became a hook in press stories about the band for the rest of the year.

JERRY GARCIA (1980): It doesn't feel old at all. It certainly doesn't feel like fifteen years to me. Although if I start to go back and remember individual events, I realize there are whole years missing from my memory.

I wasn't really aware that we were in our fifteenth year. I'm not that aware of the passage of time. I realized it was over ten and under twenty. But for me, fifteen years doesn't have any more significance than ten years or twelve years. Time is a totally subjective experience in the Grateful Dead flow.

BOB WEIR (1980): As hard as we try to trash the mystique, I guess we can't. I hate to be chained to a mystique. I'm too close to it to know what it is. Everybody has a different notion. I don't think it has anything to do with a period of time. It's not much to do with hippies or flower children. We were among the first longhairs, but I never felt like a hippie or a flower child. We're a band. We felt free. We still do.

JERRY GARCIA: We cling to each other in moments of horror. But we've learned to go with the flow; that there's always something going on that's worth the hassle and all the bullshit. Even things like taking a chance and forming our own record company. Basically, we feel so lucky to be in the position of doing what we're doing that we feel it's our responsibility to fuck with it. It's an experiment and it's only pure fortune that's taken us this far, and that fortune has a lot to do with taking chances. We abandoned the whole concept of a game plan early on. As soon as things started happening better than we could plan, we decided to trust that instead.

MICKEY HART (1980): In 1990, we'll be absolute killers! We're pretty good now, but if we keep it healthy, we'll go on. Look at Count Basie and [Duke] Ellington. There's no reason we couldn't be one of the dance bands that last thirty years.

JERRY GARCIA (1979): I think there's maybe a certain percentage of people that can dig the Grateful Dead at any given time, and they can dig it for as long as five, six years, maybe longer than that depending on who they are. It's an additive factor that's useful in some people's lives. Every three or four years there's a whole bunch of new people who can dig the Grateful Dead.

I've always been on the trip of, like, I'd sure hate to mislead anybody with this. It'd be a drag to have people believing weird things because of what we're doing. But our old psychedelic experiences always pointed out the possibility that the best thing you can do is to do what you're doing the best way you can and hope for the fuckin' best. Because psychedelics suggest, I think, that there are bigger and better things as far as human consciousness is concerned. There's some place to go, something to look for. I think of our audience as people who are out lookin' for something. We've sort of gamely stuck to those initial possibilities and maybe they pick up on that and it gives us some kind of validity.

I go to science quite a lot, in trying to figure this out, because science has the best consensus. I also go to astrology and the I Ching and random input—you know, people stop you on the street and say, "Hey, man, there's a big flood coming next week, and your car has four flat tires." Prophecies. You learn to just let things happen to you because it's just random input. You've got science with its world of structure and legitimacy, and the intuitive and the occult with their nonlinear relations to primal questions and philosophy and religion. They're all addressing the same thing in a lot of ways and we're addressing it in another way, which has to do with getting a lot of people together and playing music and having energy of some invisible kind that's nonetheless real for everybody involved with it.

In the fall of 1980, the Grateful Dead played and recorded extended runs of three-set shows—one acoustic, two electric—in San Francisco and New York City, with a stop (not recorded) in New Orleans in between. The last show, at Radio City Music Hall, was Halloween 1980, featuring a live simulcast to theaters in various cities. Comedians Al Franken and Tom Davis of *Saturday Night Live* were recruited to host the simulcast and pre-produce some comedy bits for the occasion.

JERRY GARCIA (1981): We thought that on the East Coast, where we have a problem of sort of too large an audience, maybe it would be a good way for us to be able to play fifteen places in one night. It was really an experimental idea from top to bottom. We did it mostly as a gesture to our audience to see if there was something we could do apart from living on the road—something that would maybe allow us to be a little more selective, and also to see if the experience would have any value to the concert-goer. So it was an interesting experience for us and it paid for itself. It wasn't something that made money, but it paid for itself and it yielded not only the simulcast itself, but a Showtime special, which is coming out of the tapes.

LEN DELL'AMICO: (Video producer-director): I had shot the band as [video] director at the Capitol Theatre [in Passaic, New Jersey] and other bigger venues, many times before I met them. And because I directed multitudes of acts, week in and week out, for [promoter John] Scher, I became an expert at live switching [of cameras] without rehearsing. So when the Grateful Dead decided to do a pay-per-view to theaters, they needed somebody who could do that. Scher told me about it and said, "I'm going to send you out to San Francisco to audition." I had just done the Meters and the Neville Brothers, with high production values, in New Orleans for another producer, so I sent that tape ahead. This was September 1980.

Of course, how you come across and how the Dead feel about you is actually more important than the tape, though I didn't know that then. Garcia was in charge. At the Warfield Theatre in San Francisco [the first night of the group's fifteen-show series there in late September to mid-October] Steve Parish leads me backstage to a door, swings it open, and kind of pushes me in; it's thick with smoke. I'm in the doorway and Jerry's sitting in there and he says, "How ya doin'? Here!" and he hands me a fatty. I'm talking a joint like a little cigar. They had women back there who spent hours making these things. I thought, "Okay, this is clearly step one—you must get stoned with these people," which I normally wouldn't do for a meeting; maybe later. But he was so warm and welcoming. "Hey, relax!" There was a Hells Angel there, Steve Parish, two other people, and no place to sit. This is twenty or thirty minutes before the show. So Steve says to the Hells Angel, "Barry, give your seat to Len!" I'm this little nerdy guy from New York! He did give me his seat, but eventually I was able to maneuver him back into it, because I didn't mind standing. There had been other directors through, I guess, and Weir came in and made a joke to Jerry, "Oh, is this your latest toy?" Me. Eventually, everyone else left and it's Jerry and me, and it's almost showtime, and I'm aiming to leave. "No, no, sit," he says. And he's practicing his runs on this big Martin [acoustic guitar] and I'm thinking, "What am I doing here? I should go now." The door swings open, Steve says to Jerry, "Now, now!" and the door shuts, and I'm sitting there by myself. That was the meeting. Then I went up and had the best seat in the house, front row of the balcony in the Warfield, and I watched the show.

Probably later that night or maybe the next morning someone in management said, "You're going to stay here for a while, so cancel everything, relax, we'll pay you . . ." So I figured they were either narrowing it or I got the job.

A music pay-per-view on such a scale had never been done before. The Who did one within Chicago to four theaters, but as far I know, the Dead were the first to really embrace this technology. It was in sixteen theaters. They were fearless and didn't care about money, because they were making money. With them there was always a willingness to see where it went and not worry about money first—that was my experience with them all the way through the years I worked with them.

A couple of days later, Franken and Davis come out, and they started writing [comedy bits to fill holes for set breaks of the Hallow-

een simulcast]. We decided the Warfield would double for the backstage of Radio City, which was a good choice, because Radio City may
be the best and biggest stage in the world, but not the backstage.

TOM DAVIS: Long before I met the Grateful Dead, I was a Deadhead. I remember being very high at Winterland once and talking—I
thought it was to God; I'm not sure. I said, "If there's any way I can
work with these guys, I want to do it. It's the most important thing
to me."

That came true in 1980. It started with a phone call from Jerry.
Jerry didn't call very often. "Would you guys like to host us on a
closed-circuit broadcast on Halloween from Radio City?"

They did a [run] at the Warfield, which is a very nice venue to see
the Grateful Dead. They flew us out. Everybody had rooms at the
Holiday Inn right nearby.

We knew we were going to pre-tape some stuff. We had to write
something and pre-record it there. But the first couple of days, we
were just wandering around the venue going, "Ooh, ah, oh boy, they
sound good, isn't this great!" What we did there was, "Hey, it's Franken and Davis. We've got our laminated, access-anywhere passes.
Come on along with us; let's go hang out with the Grateful Dead
backstage!" Which, of course, is the dumbest thing you could say.
That was always our formula: What's the stupidest thing we could do?
"Come on back with us." The camera starts following us, and we go
right to the buffet table—a mock buffet table that was supposed to
look elaborate. Al picks up some ribs with his bare hand, and I pour
myself a beer. Ram Rod comes up and says, "Hey, you guys, that's for
the band!"

We point to our laminated passes. "We're with the band. Come on,
everybody!" So the camera follows us. We went and visited [the band
members backstage]. Bob Weir was using a hair blower to make his
hair pretty; we had an actress playing Kreutzmann's wife, and I hit
on her. Brent comes up and I don't recognize him, and I ask if he can
go out and score some beer for me. Just all the worst things that you
could say to the Grateful Dead.

LEN DELL'AMICO: We'd shoot these bits at the Warfield as they were doing their shows. There was one where Davis, in his tuxedo, is up on the mezzanine saying, "We understand that there are drugs being done here. And I've been told some Deadheads do drugs in the men's room, so let's go into the men's room!" So they go in there and there are real people in there, and the smoke is coming out. And we had Dan Healy back in a stall. And God bless Dan for wanting to do this—he's such a character, at least as big a character as anyone in the band. But he comes out of the stall and Davis says, "Can I interview you? Were you doing drugs in there?" And Healy pukes all over him. It was barley soup we used for that. It was so realistic that a lot of people got really upset. That was a roll-in that went out live [to the theaters], but never made it into any of the products that were made from those shows.

The band got into it, too. You're dealing with non-actors, and the thing that was so great about these six guys was their gameness. Since then, I've never met artists as game to do anything, and I've worked with the Stones and everybody. Most of them have a thing they do and they don't want to step out of that. But with the Dead, if you could sell them on it—"Oh, okay, I get it." We'd rehearse it a couple of times. They took direction really well.

The Radio City experience was probably one of the most mind-altering of my entire life.

JERRY GARCIA: [The fall 1980 acoustic sets] had the effect of sort of galvanizing the whole evening. Really, the proximity had a lot to do with it. In our acoustic setup, the band is set up very close together. We're close enough to hit each other. We could reach out and touch each other if we wanted to. That's kind of refreshing. The acoustic music gets so quiet that the audience also got to be very receptive and responsive during that first part. So it also changed the nature of the electric sets that followed—they started with a little more delicacy and so forth; they were also a little more relaxed than normal, so the whole evening was actually really nice. It wasn't at all tiring; in fact it was refreshing.

LEN DELL'AMICO: We edited the videos [from Radio City, for *Dead Ahead*] partly at Hepburn Heights [in San Rafael]. Jerry lived down-stairs and Rock lived upstairs. The first time I went there and saw the place, I said, "Hey, this is nice!" It was modest. Jerry says, "This is Rock's place." Jerry's place was downstairs and was kind of like a college dorm room or something. It was covered with ashtrays and ash and not much of a view, because that was upstairs. And he had a closet with, I'm not kidding, twenty black t-shirts on hangers and five plaid shirts, jeans; and that was about it. Because he was solo then, no woman.

[On November 16, 1980] we were editing there and Rock inter-rupted us very politely—I always liked Rock, got along with him—and he said to Jerry, "I don't mean to interrupt, but Dylan's playing and they want to know if you want come down and sit in. I know you don't want to . . . he's doing the Christian thing . . ." And Jerry said, "Who's asking?" Rock says, "What do you mean?" Jerry says, "Who's asking—is it Bill [Graham] or Bob?" So Rock says, "I'll find out," and he comes back and says, "It's Bob." Jerry says, "Okay, get a limo at seven, get these guitars . . ." I thought, "Wow." Because everyone was shitting on Dylan at that time. But I took stock of Jerry and thought, "This guy is loyal and he's gonna help his buddy." That impressed me a lot.

JERRY GARCIA: I was surprised that the tunes were as difficult as they were. A lot of the tunes that he writes are deceptively simple-sounding, when in reality they're not. There was really only maybe two or three of the five or six that I played on that I wasn't doing anything besides trying to learn the tune.

It might be that he's been working with someone as far as the ar-rangements of the tunes are concerned, the compositions, or some-thing like that, but I was surprised. That was what was interesting about playing with him: the tunes were difficult, man. Some of them were like—"What?" The guys in the band were telling me that he changes them freely, and rehearsing is not necessarily security like in most situations. And then there's this additional double-whammy that happens. When you're playing with an artist who changes the material as you're playing, you develop this deep-seated insecurity, because you have to pay attention all the time. You never know what's happening; you don't know whether a bridge is going to come up, whether he's gonna use the same structure for whatever musical piece you're about to enter. And the guys in the band were talking about how it works both ways with Dylan. They develop that insecurity because he performs them differently, and then he throws them further by then being consistent. It's a very interesting space, something you can appreciate if you've had to work as a sideman.

BRENT MYDLAND (1981): I'm not playing enough synthesizer. I'm trying to work it in little by little. The problem is that you've got to have an idea of what you want and then find it. The way we go, by the time I figure out what I want, the music's changed and it's no good anymore.

If it doesn't keep growing and changing, usually you hear something about it. A few times I've set something up and let it go for a while, and hear "I thought it would never end!" Everybody's got their own expectations; that makes it a band. It's nice knowing that whatever you do, somebody can relate to it. The whole spectrum's there—country, jazz, classical. Everybody appreciates pretty much everything.

I only had two tunes on [*Go to Heaven*]. We'd do one one night, one the next night, back and forth. None of the other tunes were like that, and we did them so much I think the audience got burned out on them. They just got so little response compared to everything else that I felt embarrassed doing them.

BRENT MYDLAND: Last New Year's [December 1981], Joan Baez came and did a set in between our sets [at the Oakland Auditorium]. "You've to be me! We'll get warmed up, and then you guys are going to play a set with Joan Baez, then I'll come out in an hour and a half to two hours?" I went down to Jack London Square to a bar for a while, got back late, and missed a tune. I got some real positive stuff from not playing with [Baez]—more positive than negative. I made some fans there.

As far as rehearsing tunes that we play live, sometimes we'll just run through it at a soundcheck and that's it. I don't think we've ever run through a tune more than four or five times before we played it. Any other band I've been in, we've rehearsed over and over, grinding it into the ground. I can't say we do that, and I'm glad we don't. I like the looseness of this music, not feeling like I have to do the same thing every time. I like the Eagles, too, but this is a real release from that. I was used to that way before I started playing with [the Bob Weir Band]. Through Bob, I got an idea of where they were coming from. It's like, "Let's not rehearse it again, it might sound too good. Let's leave it a little rough, and that way we've got something to play with."

Sometimes Jerry just gets into playing and keeps going, and there's not the communication from one side of the stage to the other. It's too spread out—sometimes it seems like three completely different bands to me. There's Jerry and Bob, me and Phil, and there's the drummers. It's like we're all three playing the same tune at different times. A lot of that's our stage setup. Sometimes I don't think Jerry can hear me, or that Bob can hear anyone but Jerry. And I know a lot of times I can't hear what Jerry's playing, and sometimes I can't hear what Bob's playing.

MICKEY HART [1984]: Brent was fighting it for a while. He's not quite as crazy as we are. He's getting there. He didn't believe in the structureless form, that our form was valid. I think he just came to this as a job. He didn't have the passion at first. Then his attitude and his playing changed, and he relaxed.

BOB WEIR (1981): Being between Phil and Garcia, the most challenging thing is listening to them individually and in combination and intuiting where they are heading and what kind of chord is going to fit. I have to be there to supply that tonality, and maybe even lend some sort of leading harmonic development to it. Sometimes it works, and sometimes the magic just ain't there. But that's intuitive improvisational music at its most challenging for me. When we're playing more structured material, I just try to be an extension of what Phil's doing and fill in the spaces. Sometimes I think of myself as a brass section or a string section. When I'm onstage playing, I'm not really conscious of the guitar. I'm conscious of the notes and the sound and the demands of the music. And I'm trying to most aptly supply what the music needs in terms of sounds, textures, and harmonic development.

JON EZRINE (Musician): The Grateful Dead invented their own form of music, like jazz or blues or rock. It's a way to play music, an approach, and it's an ongoing evolutionary process. There is a core sound to the Dead that goes as far back as Magoo's Pizza Parlor, I'd imagine, that "it"—the sound of their DNA. It's a beautiful and unique noise, where what you are experiencing are exquisite musical sound effects that go beyond the restrictions of "songs" or "music."

The obsession begins with hearing something like the transition from "St. Stephen" into "The Eleven" on *Live Dead*. The combustion they created together when "it" was happening is the "musical crack," the addiction. Great songwriting—and they certainly had plenty of that—alone cannot foster that kind of devotion. I'm not knocking those aspects: as far as I am concerned there is no better songwriting. It's my bible. But people don't get addicted enough to be talking in chat rooms sixteen years after a band breaks up and throwing their lives to the wind when the band is touring at the expense of their futures for simply great songwriting. Or singing. Or virtuoso guitar playing. The drug is really those sounds and wavelengths that can alter brain chemistry. A lot of people, of course, got addicted to the lifestyle and the community, but I'm talking about the art of their music: how powerful it really is.

The approach evolved; they concentrated it, turned it more into a show rather than a bacchanal, between the late sixties and the late seventies. As they evolved they seemed to focus more on sleight-of-hand, musical parlor tricks, playing with time, the moment, playing with space, like musical [M. C.] Escher paintings: a different kind of psychedelia. I think this particular approach evolved as they mastered their instruments. By '81 it was like they were shining a spotlight on their obsession with the minutia of the moment, which was thrilling for me. Coming out of "Space," for instance, they'd give you these really outré, post-bop excursions that were as cutting-edge as anything coming out of the East Village at the time by "serious" jazz cats. Just jaw-dropping stuff, which I don't think the Dead get a lot of credit for. I really like that era: you're getting a musical maturity and cynicism they simply did not have in the seventies. They're right on the slender thread between youth and middle age.

Part of Weir's approach is akin to a pianist's. His sense of time is uncanny. His approach is as a jazz cat—not necessarily classic jazz, but more along the lines of Cecil Taylor or Sun Ra, open-ended— "What will work here, now? Where is this song going, what kind of new animal is it, what dimension is it in? What is it about now?" His love of folk and blues and rock is very deep, but his approach is jazz. I don't think he gets enough credit for his use of tones, how he creates moisture or dryness. Bobby is probably the most original player in the Grateful Dead. As wondrous as Jerry was, he was also much more rooted in a classic approach. Bobby loves to pull rabbits out of hats and let cats out of bags, and I think the "Ace" nickname suits him well in that light.

JERRY GARCIA: We feel Bob's the finest rhythm guitarist on wheels right now. He's like my left hand. We have a long, serious conversation going on musically, and the whole thing is of a complementary nature. We have fun and we've designed our playing to work against and with each other. His playing, in a way, really puts my playing in the only kind of meaningful context it could enjoy. Any serious analysis of the Dead's music would make it apparent that things are designed really appropriately. There are some passages, some kinds of ideas that would really throw me if I had to create a harmonic bridge between all the things going on rhythmically with two drums and Phil's innovative bass playing. Weir's ability to solve that problem is extraordinary. He also has a beautiful grasp of altering chords and adding color.

ALLAN ARKUSH: When I came up in '81, I went to a show or two and I told Jerry I was doing this science fiction movie [*Heartbeeps*]. He said, "Any way you want to get me involved in it, that's great." It was just talking, you know. Everyone always asked favors of Jerry.

I called him up with this idea of having the voice of one of the robots be like a guitar speaker, and that Jerry would do the guitar, because the robot was put together from spare parts, and one was an old Fender amp. The idea would be that he would talk like the sound of a Fender guitar, like an R2D2, but with a Fender.

He had a really interesting idea: He would just play lots of guitar, and he would use an electronic gate and speak the dialogue, and it would gate the guitar sounds like a vocoder. We kind of did a bunch of that stuff, but we never got it the way we wanted it. We came up with different methods, but Universal didn't want to spend the kind of money on sound effects that Jerry deserved to get. Jerry did it anyway.

And then Universal changed everything. I got taken off that picture after the preview, and they re-edited it and changed the sounds, made everything more conventional. It was one of the movies I've done in my life where I go, "Oh, well, that one didn't work." I have not watched it since the day it came out. Jerry's part was pretty much gone.

> In September 1982, at consecutive shows in Maryland and Maine, the Dead introduced two songs that would become keystones of the repertoire for the rest of their history: Hunter and Garcia's buoyant "Touch of Grey" became a latter-day anthem for the group, with its stirring "We will survive" refrain (even though the verses freely mixed cynicism with surrealism). And Weir and Barlow's "Throwing Stones" brought a surprising strain of blatant social consciousness into the Dead's already startlingly eclectic songbook. Hunter originally wrote "Touch of Grey" for a never-completed solo album; then, a few

years later, Garcia picked it up and rewrote the music, bringing out more of its optimism in the process.

ROBERT HUNTER: [I was in England, and] I had been up all night and I was looking blearily through the window the next morning wondering, "How do you survive?" And I thought, "You just do." And I sat down and wrote from the world-weary point of view I was experiencing right then. I started detailing the things that were happening to me.

[But] not precisely. In the song it talks about a seventeen-year-old kid who can't read, for instance, and I didn't have a seventeen-year-old kid. At the time I had two young step daughters and a five-year-old son. Maybe that was partly a comment on the punk movement from a parent's point of view. But I also wanted to get across the idea that I would survive.

JERRY GARCIA: Hunter sang "Touch of Grey" as a sort of dry, satirical piece with an intimate feel, but I heard something else coming through it. "We will get by" said something to me, so I set it to play big. My version still has the ironic bite of the lyrics, but what comes across is a more celebratory quality.

BOB WEIR: ["Throwing Stones"] is more or less just an anarchistic diatribe. It seems to me the people who are running the show aren't doing such a good job of it on either side. It's apolitical. It's anti-politics. I don't see politics as something that is doing much to serve humanity.

I was watching the news one night and I was struck by the absurd posturing that the big governments take over issues, and the fact that governments lie so readily and so blatantly and then stand by it. It occurred to me that governments are acting in the most inhumane and ludicrous manner. That got me pissed, and that rattled around in the back of my head for a while and a few lines emerged. I bounced those off of Barlow and a song eventually came out of it.

The world isn't all bad. But we wanted to paint a picture of the world as we both saw it that night. It took longer than a night, of course, but we had the form of it down in a night.

Sooner or later it's all going to collapse; the whole house of cards is going to collapse. I guess the thrust of the song is what we will or won't do in the face of that: "We will leave this place an empty stone / Or that shiny ball of blue we can call our home." Sooner or later we'll emerge triumphant as a race or we'll make our own graves.

BOB BARSOTTI (Bill Graham Presents): We had been dabbling with kids' rooms backstage [in the early eighties] at certain gigs. We hadn't really formalized it, but when they were there it was cool and went over well. But when you got to the next gig you didn't know if it was going to be there or not. The next time someone would come with all their kids, there'd be nothing; they had plans to get high and they'd have all their kids with them, and it was a bummer.

They were getting to the point where they had kids who were getting old enough where they were getting into trouble at the shows. It was the band members, and all those around the band. It was like a big family, anyway, with all the kids along. Now all of a sudden there were a lot of kids around that we needed to deal with. They would get in our way and into trouble.

One time [a band member's kid] and his friends ended up in a dressing room thinking they were snorting blow, but it was crystal LSD. They got really high. It was about that time I got a call from Rifkin saying, "We want a kids' room for every [Bay Area] show." That's when we formalized it and came up with a fee, a plan, and the particulars.

It started off small and grew, like everything else. By the time they were doing the multi-show Oakland Coliseum run, we had a big kids' room with a staff of fifteen or twenty. There'd be times at intermission where you'd have between fifty and a hundred kids in there.

Then there was the time at the Mardi Gras show that we decided the kids should be part of the balloon drop. We came up with a float that was Bill Walton's shoe. We asked if he would come to Mardi Gras

WAVY GRAVY: We would have sixty, seventy, eighty kids in there, not just the band members' children, but all of their friends' children. It was a very desired venue for short people. Little crawlers and toddlers had to have someone accompanying them besides us to keep their eye on them, because we didn't do that. When we did the bingo game, it was just such great fun. I would say the number B 10 and all the kids would go "B ten!" You could hear a pin drop. And it wasn't just bingo; I'd do video, double bingo, triple bingo for small prizes—but it was the big stuff they wanted to get to. And parents would come in asking if they wanted to go see some music; no, they're playing bingo.

and be in the float as a giant jester. We made him a seven-foot-tall jester outfit. We made a float that was a big high-top tennis shoe with spangles. There were benches in it, and we put the kids with Bill as part of the parade. It was fantastic!

WAVY GRAVY: We [the Hog Farm] were always operating on a fringe, but it was Bob Barsotti who reeled us in and realized that we would be good at [watching out for the kids]. In the beginning, we volunteered to do it, and did it for free for a long time. And then they said, no, we want to pay you. And not only that, but we were given a really nice budget to get stuff to intrigue short people. And I would go into toy stores and look for what actually lit up for me. And then as the kids came into the kids' room, all the cool stuff would be lined up. And they're like, "Whoa. How do I get my hands onto that?"

It helped us make our land payments in Layton-ville. That was extraordinary. And we worked very hard for it, too.

We got art projects going on, and we're teaching them juggling and that kind of thing. And we would take all of the kids out for New Year's, for the balloon drop. And that was always quite thrilling; they had a special place for us, and it was like a military operation to get them out for the balloon drop. Bill coming down dressed as a fruit fly or [whatever]. I don't think they ever became jaded to that.

It wasn't always a lot of fun. Every now and then, a kid would slip through our nets.

314

Garcia's health became an issue in the early eighties, as the effects of his drug use became more noticeable.

ALLAN ARKUSH: I had never seen anyone freebase before. [Jerry] became more distant the more that stuff dominated. I would bring him whatever I had directed, he'd look at the stuff, and then he would call me, and like it. Often, it was harder to get to talk to him before and after shows, because he was locked up during that period.

DENNIS McNALLY: There was always discussion about his condition. There was always worry. "We need to sit him down . . ." Once in a while there would be a sit-down, and he'd ignore it. And it just never stopped. And after a while, if you didn't want to get crazy, you kind of tuned it out. He was impervious to pressure.

[In early 1985, finally,] he had thrown in the towel and said, "Yes." I'm sure people offered to drive him [to rehab] and he said, "No thanks, man." My understanding, from what he said after, was that he was going to go someplace in the East Bay. He's driving from Marin, and he sort of talks himself into cutting through Golden Gate Park.

He had gotten this car he was driving from a drug dealer. There was something very shady about the car, and about the place [near the Polo Fields in the park]. I don't know whether the cop saw the plates and ran the plates first and went, "*Hmmm.* There's something wrong with this," or he saw what looked like a street person sitting inside the Beemer. At any rate, I assumed that Jerry did what I understand to be a fairly classic act of a drug addict prior to checking in: he did all the drugs he could. He was going through his empty [cocaine] bindles and doing his last bit.

Eventually, it was Chris Andrian, a Deadhead lawyer in Santa Rosa, who got him bailed out. Eventually, they got Jerry into a drug diversion program, which he did, getting up at the crack of dawn to go to a methadone clinic in San Francisco in the Tenderloin District.

JERRY GARCIA (1987): Drug use is kind of a cul-de-sac: It's one of those places you turn with your problems, and pretty soon all your problems have simply become that one problem. Then it's just you and the drugs.

There was something that I needed, or thought I needed, from drugs. Drugs are like a trade-off in a way—they can be, at any rate. There was something there for me. I don't know what it was, exactly. Maybe it was the thing of being able to distance myself a little from the world. But there was something there that I needed for a while, and it wasn't an entirely negative experience, but after a while, it was just the drugs running me, and that's an intolerable situation.

I was never an overdose kind of junkie. I've never enjoyed the extremes of getting high. I never liked to sit around and freebase until I was wired out of my mind, know what I mean? For me it was the thing of getting pleasantly comfortable and grooving at that level. But of course, that level doesn't stay the same. It requires larger and larger amounts of drugs. So after a few years of that, pretty soon you've taken a lot of fucking drugs and not experiencing much. It's a black hole. I went down that black hole, really. Luckily, my friends pulled me out. Without them I don't think I ever would have had the strength to do it myself.

> Also in early 1985, the Dead's friend Phil DeGuere hired Merl Saunders to serve as the music supervisor on his revival of *The Twilight Zone* for CBS-TV.

MERL SAUNDERS: I was thinking about going back up north. I really never did like L.A. Phil DeGuere came to me and said, "Merl, I'm leaving [the hit detective show] *Simon and Simon*. I have a project you can work on. You can't tell anybody what it is." I said, "Fine." He gave me all these tapes of old *Twilight Zone* episodes. This was before he went into production.

He said, "Do you think you could get the Dead involved in it?" I said, "sure," called up Jerry, and told him I was getting involved with *The Twilight Zone*. He said, "Fuck yeah, man!" I called up Mickey and went up to his ranch and started creating the theme. Mickey would show me different sounds we could mix with it.

Dealing with Grateful Dead time and Hollywood time are two

different things. I would have to deal with the Dead on Dead time. I would have 75 percent of the music already written so it'd get to Hollywood time. It was funny, but it worked. The fellas played just marvelously.

I brought in Huey Lewis on some things. I will never forget when Huey walked into Front Street. He was like a little kid, shaking. "I'm finally in here." Here he is, with a gold record, talking about being in "here."

BOB BRALOVE (Musician, tech): I was living in San Francisco, commuting to L.A. I met Merl Saunders on the Grammy stage when I was working with Stevie Wonder and Herbie Hancock and Howard Jones and Thomas Dolby for a Grammy presentation. It was a whole high-tech synthesizer thing, and Merl came up to me and said, "Do you operate all these machines?"

I said, "Yes."

He said, "Have you ever thought about doing a soundtrack?"

I said, "Yes, I'd love to do something like that!"

He said, "Oh, good. Here's my number. Call me when you're back in San Francisco."

I started with Merl on *The Twilight Zone*. I was writing some of the score, and I was producing stuff. I got involved with Mickey, who was doing sound design. I was the only principal in the scene who was working with both Merl and Mickey. I was the only one who knew what the entire soundtrack was sounding like. [The Grateful Dead, Merl, and Bralove did all the music] for at least one full season, and Mickey did some more.

The band did the theme song, and then members of the band were involved in the score, but Merl was going to deliver the score. We would compose the score; sometimes band members would come in and do things. I was also asked to sample the band; I would lock Bobby in a room and he'd come up with all these wild sounds off his guitar. We would drop them into, like, the opening of the box—the coffin opens and *wee-oww!*

JERRY GARCIA: They didn't give me any kind of guidelines. They might have given Merl some, but what we got to do was a collection of little music inserts called stings and bumpers—you know, little hunks of non-specific music of various lengths that have different moods. One might be a mood like "Don't open that door," or "Don't go into the attic." Or, "I'm going to work, honey. Are you sure you'll be okay alone?" They gave us a huge menu of those—forty that are like five seconds, twenty that are six and a half seconds, a bunch they can fade in and out. Then it's the music editor who actually fits them in the show.

In July of 1986, Garcia nearly died, throwing the Grateful Dead and Deadhead worlds into chaos.

DAVID NELSON: They were playing RFK stadium [July 6–7, 1986]—Tom Petty with Bob Dylan, and the Grateful Dead. It was a hot, hot summer night. RFK, Washington, D.C., you know how hot that can be: unbearable. Right after that, riding back in the van, Garcia says, "I'm so dry, my throat's gonna stick shut. You got any water, Nelson?" All I had, dammit, was a beer. Nobody had any liquid. He was dehydrated. When he got home, he collapsed of dehydration, and then the coma.

STEVEN MARCUS: When he was brought to the hospital, he was very agitated, so they gave him Valium, and they didn't realize he was allergic to it. He coded on the table, and that's what caused the coma for five or six days.

JERRY GARCIA: I had some very weird experiences. My main experience was one of furious activity and tremendous struggle in some sort of futuristic spaceship vehicle with insectoid presences. After I came out of my coma I had the image of myself as these little hunks of protoplasm that were stuck together kind of like stamps with perforations that you could snap off. They were run through with neoprene tubing, and there were these insects that looked like cockroaches, which were like message-units that were kind of like my bloodstream. That was my image of my physical self, and that particular feeling lasted a long time. It was really strange. It was DMT-like as far as the intensity was concerned, but it lasted a couple of days. It gave me a greater admiration for the baroque possibilities of mentation. The mind is so incredibly weird. The whole process of going into the coma was very interesting, too. It was a slow onset—it took about a week—and during this time I started feeling like the vegetable kingdom was speaking to me. It was communicating to me in comic dialect in iambic pentameter. So there were these Italian accents and German accents, and it got to be this vast gabbing. Potatoes and radishes and trees were all speaking to me. It finally reached hysteria, and that's when I passed out and woke up in the hospital.

DENNIS McNALLY: Did I see it coming for him? No. I was on the tour [before the collapse]. It was 100 degrees and 100 percent humidity, so disgusting [at the stadium shows]. But my comment afterwards always was, "He spent all but three hours in an air-conditioned trailer." He went home. On the flight home he was normal. There was nothing to notice. But then he went down, and I took him to the hospital.

People were very worried, but for some odd reason, I wasn't. I just had this weird faith. I was calm then. I just felt he was very strong, and it wasn't going to kill him. But I didn't go to the hospital. Mountain Girl and Hunter and Parish and band members went— you know, that was enough. He didn't need any more bodies there. Maybe I had to go once to talk to a doctor to prepare a press release or something.

Then, maybe a week after, I got laid off. I turned out to be the only person who got laid off at that time. Mickey and Phil were both noticeably freaking, trying to pretend that they were in charge and everything was going to be okay, so all they could think of was to grab one person and throw him off the boat. [A few months later] I said to Jerry, "I'd like my job back," and he looked at me and said, "Oh, yeah, you were the collateral damage to my meltdown. Yeah, no problem, we'll take care of it."

CAROLYN "MOUNTAIN GIRL" GARCIA: I was up in Oregon, out at the Country Fair helping my friend Camille set up her booth. We'd been out there all day and I didn't get home until about 11:30, and as soon as I walked in the phone rang. It was Jahanara [Wavy Gravy's wife] calling from Camp Winnarainbow [Wavy's summer camp] because Trixie [Jerry and Mountain Girl's daughter] was at camp. And she said, "Oh, I'm so glad you answered the phone. I've been calling you. Is Jerry going to be all right?" I said, "What?" I hadn't heard anything about it. She was the only person that called me. So I called the doctor and he said Jerry was going. I jumped on a plane at 6:30 the next morning and took the Airporter [bus] up to the hospital. I got there and the doctor was saying, "We're not sure he's going to live through the hour." They were saying, "We're readying him for a tracheotomy to help his breathing." I said, "A what? No, you're not!" I told them I thought that was a really bad idea. Obviously, if it was absolutely necessary as a last resort to save his life, that would be one thing, but . . .

LEN DELL'AMICO: You don't come out of a coma with your brain intact. And when I went to see him in the hospital with Merl it was like, "Wow, he's got a long way to go." I mean, when you go into the ICU of a hospital, you're prepared for that and you suck it up. But I was in the room when somebody handed him an acoustic guitar, and I remember thinking, "Really? He's only been conscious for about two days." He kind of looked at the guitar like "What is this?" and handed it back. It didn't look good, quite frankly. He was confused and weak and he would say things like "I don't know how to play. What makes you think I know how to play?"

God bless Merl. I don't know how he did it. It's got to be a musician thing that I can't understand. When it comes down to it, it's not the money or the fame—they love their music and they love each other, and they're just going to go through the scales on the piano. Merl's the guy who took it on himself. There wasn't anyone else. Merl had faith.

It was this massive infusion of faith, and Jerry talked about feeling the prayers that he was getting. It made him turn into a mystic.

MERL SAUNDERS: When he became sick, I was with him three months solid, every day. He was determined to play the guitar again. That's the type of person he was. The one thing he could do: when he picked up his guitar, regardless of his state of mind, he could play. That's the thing that I loved this guy for. Duke Ellington was in love with music. Music was his first love, and everything else followed. Jerry was the same way. His focus was good music.

STEVEN MARCUS: When Jerry got sick in '86 we had a lot of canceled shows, and the Grateful Dead had no money. They always lived check to check. Bill [Graham] loaned them money, but it was with the knowledge that he was not getting paid back. John Scher did, too.

ANNABELLE GARCIA [Jerry's daughter]: Dad wasn't really talking that much because he had a lot of things going on in his head. He spent a lot of time relearning how to play. He started with the banjo. He picked up the banjo and had to teach himself all these things. So he was awfully grumpy because he was mad—he had lost bits of him that he could rely on ever since he was a kid. He was frustrated. I remember seeing him banging the banjo hard, just pissed because he couldn't make his fingers do what was so easy just six months before. But he kept at it. He kept saying, "I've gotta try harder!" Instead of resting on his talent, he found himself in a situation where he had to actually work at it again, which I think was both rewarding and irritating at the same time. But I think the most positive thing it did was make him go off in some different directions and think about taking more control over his life.

KEN BABBS: While he was recovering, he came up here to Oregon to be with Mountain Girl, who was living at the time in Pleasant Hill [outside Eugene; it's also where the Kesey farm was]. The first thing we did together was, Mountain Girl's kids were in school and there was a school play. I had kids around the same age so we were there, and there's Jerry and Mountain Girl in the front row and he was just so happy to be there. So we chatted awhile, and the next day Mountain Girl calls me and says, "Babbs, how about taking Jerry out of the house and doing something with him?" I had this old [Lincoln] convertible, it was a nice day, so my wife, Eileen, and I went over there to pick him up and we decided to drive on up to Sisters, [a town] on the old road that goes up through the lava fields. So we spent the whole day driving up there and having lunch, driving back and shootin' the shit and talkin'—just a really, really good day. He was definitely still recovering and getting his strength back, but he was not weak; he was sharp. He was as normal with me as we'd ever been. We'd always been close and been able to talk to each other openly about anything. Considering what he'd been through, though, he was in good shape and in a really good mood.

LEN DELL'AMICO: [That fall], I was going to go see Los Lobos [at New George's in San Rafael] with Sue Stephens and Annette Flowers [both of the Dead office] and I said, "Jerry, you want to go see this band?" I thought it would be nice to get him out of the house and all, but I didn't think about the implications, because as far as I knew he hadn't been out socially in years, because the previous year he was being the working rock star. And before that he was just a heavy drug user, and you can't really be doing social things when you [need more drugs] every fifteen minutes. I hadn't thought about any of that.

So I went up to his house and it was basically his first time out in a long time. Mountain Girl said, "All right, but just the first show, and no drinking." "Okay, I'll have him back at eleven." So the four of us got a table there and people were remarkably respectful and polite. Actually, most people were completely shocked, because of the rumor mill. He was just a regular guy sitting there. And he had a drink. "I thought you weren't going to drink." Well, I guess he is. And that relaxed him a little. Then the show was on and after a while he was up dancing in front of the stage with some people. Then, after the set, we were backstage and [Carlos] Santana was there, too, and they had a very warm, heartfelt embrace and they talked for a while.

David Hidalgo [one of Los Lobos' two guitarists] and Jerry seemed to really hit it off. So then I'm thinking, "Well, it's time to go." But Jerry wasn't going anywhere. The second show comes; it's midnight, 1:00 a.m., Jerry has another drink, and then Los Lobos calls him up onstage, and they give him a guitar, and they played "La Bamba" and he ripped out this incredible solo. I was just overcome—it was all there; it was like nothing had changed. It sounded exactly like him.

The audience went nuts, of course; it was like a riot broke out, or something. This was the answer to everyone's question. It was going to be okay. And it was all there in that one moment.

The show goes on to its conclusion. It's 2:00 a.m., we're all thrown out and the house is emptying and Sue and Annette and I are looking around and we can't find Jerry. We look backstage and he's not there. I'm panicking, of course. "Oh, shit, I've lost him. Mountain Girl's going to kill me." So we walked outside and he was standing on the sidewalk, kind of loose and goofy with a big grin, talking to one fan after another. He was just sort of politely waiting for us.

CHAPTER 9
I'll Get a New Start

Jerry Garcia made his official return to performing with a Jerry Garcia Band show at the Stone nightclub in San Francisco on October 4, 1986.

FREDDIE HERRERA (Co-owner of the Stone): There was a red carpet. Broadway was blocked off. There were so many people there for Jerry. It's amazing how much everybody really loved that guy.

STEVE PARISH: He got knocked out pretty hard, and when he came back, he was almost babelike, in the sense that he had to relearn how to play the guitar. It was really scary to him, and it was a strange time. Merl Saunders would come over and get him started, and we'd all sit around there with him. I'd bring his guitar over to his house; at first he would just hold it and play it. He started off baby-stepping, and then he came back and he relearned it. It all came rushing back. But it took a while.

When we first came back, he was a clean gentleman. He was totally clear, okay? So when he played that [comeback] show, he was getting back to some of those early roots of guitar. The man loved guitar. You had to love guitar like he did to understand how deep his relationship went with that instrument.

JERRY GARCIA: The coma gave me that little midlife kick you need sometimes. It got me out of the doldrums, out of the becalmed somewhere in the early eighties when I said, "*Hmm.* Nothing much happening." It got my attention, let me put it that way.

I felt like, "Well, as long as I'm alive, I might as well try as hard as I possibly can to do all the things I want to do." And there's plenty left to do. So since then, I've been feeling pretty optimistic about things. It's a new beginning—and I've always been a fan of new beginnings.

The Grateful Dead returned with three emotionally charged performances at the Oakland Coliseum Arena, December 15–17, 1986. The first song, "Touch of Grey," was a perfect call. Throughout the run of shows, various lines from Jerry's songs took on great poignancy and drew responses from the crowd: "Hand me my ol' guitar," "I'll get a new start," etc. Two weeks later, a four-night run at the more intimate Henry J. Kaiser Convention Center (formerly the Oakland Auditorium) was capped by Bill Graham flying across the ceiling in an eagle suit at midnight on New Year's Eve.

PETER BARSOTTI (Bill Graham Presents): [New Year's Eve] was Bill's favorite thing of his life, period: that moment at midnight when everybody's looking at him, he gets everybody's energy and gets to be the person. He just loves it. It's not strictly just from an ego point of view. He would go to any end to please the audience.

Every year, we'd start with the wildest idea we could come up with and try to make it as fantastic as possible. Bill always had an idea, but the thing about him was, the best idea was the one we'd use. He wasn't stuck on it having to be his idea, but if you didn't want his idea you'd better have an even better one.

The very first one I worked on was in Winterland in 1977, when Bill came on an old Harley-Davidson motorcycle. We drilled a hole through the upstairs at Winterland and drew a cable all the way to the stage. Bill rode down suspended on this cable, dressed as a skeleton on this motorcycle. Harry [Popick], the Dead's sound guy, recorded a bunch of motorcycle noises down in the basement; [sound man Dan] Healy turned them up to 10. It looked like this motorcycle was driving over the top of the kids' heads.

One year, Bill was a butterfly. He was hidden in the back of this fake hippie bus, which drove through the audience. When he got to the mixer, Bill sprang out of the top of this bus clad as a butterfly and flew over the top of the cables, landing on the stage, where he was caught in a large butterfly net. The fun part of that was he had a helmet on with antennae. His hat fell down over his eyes as soon as he got out of the truck. He never saw a thing the whole time. When he landed, he was so mad that he couldn't see straight. He was upset that he missed it.

It was always a real seat-of-the-pants thing. We're always trying to pretend that it's together, but we're worried up until the last minute. There are always things going on. [One] year Bill was dressed as a shaman, coming down on an island with trees. The lights went out and we were just about to start, finding out we lost power to the motors that were running it. The band was already on stage, and we had to do it right then. One of the guys in the ceiling got his flashlight, found the plug, and plugged it in within one second. These things make our lives shorter.

One that Bill wanted to do that I talked him out of: when the Soviet Union disintegrated, Bill was contemplating taking a troupe of people over there to put on a big show to kind of commemorate their freedom. He said, "I've got the idea for New Year's: Russia. We'd build this big float that looks like Russia." I said, "Bill, what does Russia look like? What do you want me to do? Build a big blob and divide it up like a map?"

He goes, "I guess that won't work." So we went on to other ideas.

It's a big thing to worry about every year, for twelve months!

He's been on motorcycles, he's flown in on joints, he's been a butterfly, he was standing on top of a giant red mushroom, a glove, a lightning bolt. One year we had twenty-four people on top of a birthday cake thirty feet across. It was so monstrous that everybody said, "Do you really have to do that?" So the next year we switched to flying things.

One of my most favorite ones he ever did was an American eagle. It was like the Presidential seal, but it said "GRATEFUL DEAD." We had it up there [in the rafters of the arena] all four days, and everybody was saying, "What's the deal with the eagle? What's that got to do with the Grateful Dead?" So on New Year's Eve, we had a spotlight on the emblem; the spot switched to the back balcony, and there was a real live emblem, which was Bill Graham as the eagle. He jumped off the seal and flew to the stage. It was pretty spectacular. It was really hard to keep your arms flapping that long.

BILL GRAHAM: That moment is really my only relative understanding of what it's like to be a member of the Dead or of the Stones, but in the guise of Father Time. For a good thirty seconds—the rest of the time I'm throwing flowers, or trying to see where I am, or pushing some button that's going to do something—I get to see the absolute joy on the faces of the audience. I get to experience for just a few seconds what performers experience year round. It's pure joy. It's an awesome experience.

One year [1977–78], I was stuck—Santana [whom he managed] was playing at the Cow Palace and the Dead were playing Winterland. And Carlos asked me to do a [midnight] entrance at his show, so it became, "Well, I can do one or the other, so what should I do? Or, I can do both, but how can I explain to the Santana-Journey audience what my problem is?" And finally I decided I could explain it to the Dead audience and make a late entrance there. Only because I knew Deadheads would say, "Okay, why not?"

So when people came to Winterland that night, they got a little slip of paper with a Dead logo on it that said: "Due to circumstances within my control, New Year's will be at 12:30. Thank you. Cheers,

Bill." So I did my entrance at the Cow Palace, left there at two minutes after midnight, and while I was being driven to Winterland, I got into my Dead skeleton suit. I got to Winterland at 12:26, raced up the side, and went up in the balcony, got on the Harley-Davidson, and then at 12:29 went across the audience on a wire.

[No one] said, "Why did you do that?" And that has a lot to do with who the Deadheads are. As a large unit of people, they have literally said with life: "I'll try it. I don't know what you've got, but I'll try it."

Nineteen eighty-seven proved to be a gigantic year for the Grateful Dead: their studio album, *In the Dark*, and the first single, "Touch of Grey," both hit the Top Ten; they released a long-form video, *So Far*; rehearsed and toured with Bob Dylan; and, on the road, reached a level of popularity that created a whole new set of problems. In October, Bill Graham brought Jerry Garcia to Broadway: a series of shows at the Lunt-Fontanne Theater in which the Jerry Garcia Acoustic Band opened and the electric Jerry Garcia Band played two full sets.

ROBERT HUNTER: [To record *In the Dark*], the Grateful Dead for the first time did what they should have done all along: got themselves on a stage as though they were playing for an audience, and played live. Without an audience. The tape machine was the audience; it's a live record. Took it in the studio, processed it a bit, and neatened up the vocals, but the sound is live because it is live. You can't get this with people yowling and carrying on and pressures of performance. You're going to get a different thing. This is an ideal way to record, you know, with real cleanliness and separation. And yet live playing. We're not going to set out to make a hit record. We didn't set out to make one this time. It's just a coincidence—this tune seemed to click with some emergent factor in American consciousness. And *blammo*, there it was. The shoe fit this time.

I think "Touch of Grey" was a hell of a hot little tune. It was very, very well recorded, and released well, followed up with a hell of a video. I think we genuinely got ourselves a hit, and a hit does what a hit's supposed to do: propels a band to the top. I think it's as simple as that: we got a hit record.

JOHN CUTLER: The Dead is most successful as a live band. There's no reason why they can't be successful as a recording band, but I think it's apropos that they did their basic tracks in a live situation—as if they were playing live—because that's where their expertise lies. We had them set up onstage in the same places they would be for a concert, and I think that helped a lot. But it's definitely a studio recording.

BOB BRALOVE: Working on the record was the first time I really engaged Jerry. I was working on overdubs for both Mickey and Brent, and then some for Bobby, helping them get some new sounds, and Jerry and I ended up hanging out a lot, and I really got to see Jerry's audio playfulness as producer. When he mixed, he always used to talk about pairing people up. Depending on what the tune might be, he might view himself and Phil as a pair—they would occupy roughly the same space [in the mix] and have the same weight, and you would feel them as this pair through the song. Two other people might be another pair. It gave me a new fun way of looking at the band and listening to their music. It's always nice to have someone turn your head and say, "Hey, look at it this way." [*In the Dark*] gives you a good idea of how Jerry heard the Grateful Dead.

BRENT MYDLAND: The sessions seemed like they went a lot easier [than *Go to Heaven*]. This is only my second studio album with the band and I can tell a lot of difference between this and the last album. It feels a lot more natural and it feels more like us on stage.

JERRY GARCIA: Technically speaking, it's right on the top. It sounds as good as it could sound in this time. I think the band has never played better on an album, ever. I don't think we've ever had better singing, either.

MICKEY HART: I'm more than happy. This is one of the few Grateful

Dead records I can listen to. When we got it all mixed down, I took a cassette home and I listened on my little blaster. I sat there and turned into a Deadhead and I loved it. I think this record will go into the archives and sit well beside the rest of the Grateful Dead material.

BOB BRALOVE: They asked me to take the sounds that happened in those sessions on the road. "Horns" for Brent ["Tons of Steel"]; somebody described it as a calliope sound in the beginning of "Touch of Grey"—a little synth sound that kinda lifts the energy. Nobody else in their crew could take these sounds that I'd just created for the album and let them play them live. That's when they invited me to join.

I started out mixing the drum solos and designing the electronic drum stuff for the drum solos in the summer of '87 at Ventura—the train effect and the [electronically sampled] berimbau, that kind of stuff. I have a vivid memory of that drum solo. My impression of it was—electronically, anyway—that it was pure distortion from beginning to end, and pure havoc. It was one thing to work it out in the studio, but Mickey, in particular, live onstage, is a different animal than Mickey in the studio. So all of a sudden we went from this controlled scene in the studio to impassioned slamming of the drums and slamming the Beam [a large metal frame strung with piano strings, with pickups] and hitting the [electronic] triggers, and we went from fairly calculated routines to inspiration and changing ideas on the spur of the moment.

BRENT MYDLAND: I've been more or less playing acoustic instrument sounds instead of coming up with really out there stuff. I'm using sounds that are like real instruments—the violin, the sax, the piano (which is a synthesizer, actually)—and those blend real well. So if I want a little more attack on, say, the end of "Sugar Magnolia," I might drop in a horn part to help accent the piano part. Or on a ballad I might try to bring some strings in, but try to make it so you don't notice it too much. As opposed to just pushing a button and having an instrument there or not there, I'll blend it in with a pedal so I can listen to it, and if it seems to work I'll go with it, and if it doesn't I can back off of it and go on to something else. I have a lot of freedom with this new system.

> Cameron Sears joined the Grateful Dead management team in 1987.

CAMERON SEARS: I had been a river guide for about ten years, working to protect the Tuolumne River [which flows from Yosemite National Park down into California's Central Valley], and I was taking a lot of congressional people down the river—we were trying to introduce people to water politics in California. I was a Grateful Dead fan. I saw my first show in Boston in 1976 and probably saw 150 shows prior to working with them. I was also aware of their philanthropy [the Rex Foundation, started by the Dead to funnel the proceeds from their benefits to a variety of grassroots causes].

[Sometime in 1985] I wrote the band a letter and tried to get them on a river trip. I created a little letter and a brochure, and I had a friend who knew where their office was, so I walked it over there and handed it to Eileen [Law]. She was very friendly, as she always was, and a couple of weeks later I called her and said, "Any interest?" and I got the "Don't call us, we'll call you" response, which was fair enough. Then a couple of months later I got a call from Danny [Rifkin] saying, "I've got twenty-five people who want to go on a river trip with you; can we still do it?"

So I put together a trip. None of the band guys came; it was all office people. That time I took them on the American River, because it was a bunch of inexperienced people and the Tuolumne requires a little more experience. But Danny and I became great friends—he's still one of my dearest friends. We did another trip that fall and kept doing stuff together.

Then, in the spring of 1987, the Dead were getting ready to go out [on the road] with *In the Dark*. Jon McIntire and I had become friendly, and he called me up and said, "Why don't you come work for me? I need a capable assistant who can handle logistics and coordinate all this stuff for me. You'd be the perfect guy." So I said, "Okay."

He'd been on some river trips with me and saw me in action on multiple occasions and thought that skill set would translate, which it did. I had no preconception I was going to get involved in the music business. I thought I was going to be an environmental activist and go to law school, or something like that.

I was a probationary hire, which meant it was a temporary position —"Don't get your hopes up!"

The first gig that I did, we flew down to Ventura to play the County Fairgrounds there [June 12–14, 1987] and Jon got sick with the flu and was stricken to the point where as soon as we got to the gig, he went and laid down in a backstage trailer flat on his back. I went in to check on him and he said, "You're going to have to get the band onstage." I hadn't even really met these guys! I'd seen some of them in the office, and everybody knew I was going to be there helping Jon, but they hadn't seen me in this capacity. So I had to go around and basically introduce myself to everybody and say, "By the way, you're on in half an hour, I'll be back in twenty minutes, and we're gonna start the show . . ." And everybody was pretty decent, with the exception of Kreutzmann. Billy was up on stage, and I walked up to him and I gave him the same rap—"Hi, I'm Cameron, I'm helping Jon; he's sick so I'm trying to get everyone up here so we can start the show on time," etc. He [mumbles], "Yeah, yeah, yeah," and I start to walk away and Billy Grillo [of the road crew] comes up and taps me on the shoulder and says, "Hey, Billy wants to talk to you." So I turn back and Billy says to me, "Don't talk to me or any of my friends, ever again." I said, "Oh, okay, whatever."

The show happens, we get back to the hotel, and then, at about three in the morning, the phone rings and it's Billy. He's out of his mind: "So, you want to be the road manager for the Grateful Dead? You better get your ass down here right now, because your piano player is keeping me up and I want to go to bed!" So I go down there —Bill is completely trashed. Brent is completely trashed. The door to Brent's room is wide open and he's sprawled on the floor. There's broken shit everywhere. There's broken windows, a broken mirror. He's gone nuts, he's had a fight with his wife, and Lisa is gone. I had to get Brent cleaned up. Then Billy pokes his head out of his room and says, "So, you havin' fun yet?"

About a month later, we're on the road, and we're movin'—the album's out, we're doing stadium dates, it's a full-blown, full-tilt boogie. And one of Billy's bags is missing as we're distributing the bags at 2:30 or 3:00 in the morning, whenever we landed in Pittsburgh. He and Jon had had history in the past and he just went after Jon and destroyed him verbally. Jon called me up and said, "Cameron, I don't know how to tell you this, but I think I'm going to go home tomorrow, so you . . ." Then Billy called and said, "I've been thinking—you've been doing a really great job and I think you oughta take this on; you can handle it." Obviously Billy knew he'd crossed a line [with McIntire]. I said no to both of them. I said, "That's not gonna happen. I'm not gonna do that." Largely, I was saying to Jon, "Suck it up here. Don't let this become an issue. Let's do this. He's out of his mind. Calmer minds will prevail over the next twenty-four to forty-eight hours." Which they did, and it was fine. But in the space of thirty days, that's how far the pendulum had swung from "Don't ever talk to me again" to "So, you want the job?"

> Bob Dylan and the Grateful Dead announced a tour for the summer of 1987. Rehearsals took place at Club Front in May and early June.

DAVID NELSON: [Back in 1986, when the Dead played RFK Stadium on a bill with the Bob Dylan–Tom Petty tour], I'm standing in Healy's sound booth, watching. The Dead were gonna have Dylan sit in. He comes out and he plays one song, and I think the middle of the first song, he breaks a string. The Dead jam for a little bit. Parish goes to the guitar stash—they had these guitars that hadn't been used in years. Parish grabs a similar guitar to the one Dylan was using and hands it to him. Dylan grabs it, straps it on, plugs it in, steps up to the mic—and it was horribly out of tune. I know Garcia died a thousand deaths.

So [before the Dylan rehearsals began] Garcia calls me and says, "I hate to ask you to do this and not play, Nelson. I can't guarantee that you're gonna be able to play, but would you agree to come along and watch over all the guitars, keep 'em strung up and in tune?" I said, "Sure."

JERRY GARCIA (1987): I think that we'd all like to do something that none of us have done before. We're not that thrilled about just doing our stuff. We love Dylan's tunes but we know he's burned out on them to some extent. So the thing is really finding the material that we can all enjoy playing, and that the audience might dig.

[At the first rehearsals] there started to be a certain chemistry that was like something else. It wasn't us; it wasn't him. It was all of us together and it was starting to become something. If we all like it, then we'll probably do some shows. We're sort of keeping the doors open. We don't want to corner Dylan into doing anything, and I'm sure he has his own rate he wants to work at.

STEVE PARISH: Dylan walked into our studio with no entourage, just him, without a shirt, with just a leather vest on, and into our world. And we welcomed him with open arms. He was an amazing guy. He felt right at home there.

There's a lot of stuff about Bob that he said changed him at that time. He came there, and you could see that he had things to work out, and he did. He went on to play and play and play, and he realized that was what he loved. He's a really perceptive guy and a great guy to work with. He fit right in perfect, man. He liked all the things we liked. And he wasn't afraid to ask if it wasn't there. Some very strange things would come up but he could handle it all. He was [a] very game lad, a very game lad, and very perceptive.

STEVE PARISH: The first or second night that they were playing together, they were going through all of Dylan's old tunes. Dylan was so amazed that these guys knew some of his old stuff, 'cause he'd forgotten some of the words and all. Jerry started playing "It's All Right, Ma, I'm Only Bleeding," and Dylan started singing it. Jerry said, "Hey, Bob, how do you go home after writing a song like that and look your mom in the eye?"

Bob looked at him and said, "It wasn't easy."

335

LEN DELL'AMICO: I wanted to be there the day Dylan showed up at Front Street. My mother had given me his first record when it came out, so I was into Dylan when he was a folk singer. To me, he's the greatest recording artist of all time, period. There's no doubt in my mind. His output—what can you say? I'd never met him or worked with him. But I got the sense from Jerry that the two of them had a closer relationship than has been revealed by either one. Because once I got [Jerry] talking, it was clear they had talked on the phone a lot and they had spent time together in New York when [the Dead] played in New York. Bob had even given him a tour of New York City in his van. I think that was somewhere between '78 and the Christian tour in 1980.

So, Front Street, spring '87, Dylan's due any minute. Smoke. The door opens, there's Bob, he's got a man with him, and the crew is like, "Eh." You know the crew—their job is to cut down your hat size. They were incredibly effective at that. "Hey, come on in! This is everybody." "This is Bob." And Parish says, "We've already got a Bob. You're going to be Spike." To be treated like a shlub—Dylan loved it!

He was so slight, like a wisp of a man; the wispiest ghost-like presence you could imagine. The conversation in the room went to whatever it had been. It wasn't like, "Now we're going to talk about Bob, or Spike." I went to the bathroom and I came back in and, I swear to God, this literally happened: I'm sitting there and people were talking and I said to myself, "Wasn't there somebody famous here a second ago?" This is how weird Dylan is. I had to think for a second. "Yeah, Dylan was here when I left the room." And I looked around and he was still there. But his presence was as close to nil as I've ever experienced, at least in that setting. And then the next time I looked, he wasn't there and I didn't see him leave. I didn't notice. The total opposite of Garcia, who just dominated any room he was in and was so welcoming and outgoing.

BOB WEIR: When we were in rehearsal, Dylan didn't bring a guitar; there was some sort of mixup. We had to go get him one. We sent out to a couple of music stores and brought in a couple of Fender Strats, 'cause that was what he asked for. And on a whim, I also called up

Modulus, 'cause I was playin' Modulus guitars and they make a sort of a Strat knockoff. I said, "You got any Strat knockoffs that you can bring by?" And they did. And it was Pepto-Bismol pink.

At the end of a couple of days, we were wrapping up a rehearsal—it was just me and him left in the building at the time—and he was standing there scratching his head, lookin' at these three or four guitars that we had, and almost goin', "Eeny, meeny, miney, moe." I asked him, "Are you trying to figure out which one you're going to go with?"

He said "Yeah. This one sounds good; this one plays good." Then he looks at the Modulus and says, "This one's really the right color, isn't it?"

BRENT MYDLAND: I had a great time playing with Dylan. He let us play [his songs] pretty much the way we wanted. I liked that, but there were a couple of times when I thought, "God, someone please give me a clue of what to do here!" But it fell into shape. I think it sounded pretty good. There were some pretty loose moments. I had trouble hearing what Dylan was doing on guitar sometimes, and that made it a little tough to follow him.

The hardest thing was just learning all the material. It was a bombardment, and we didn't get to rehearse that much. And then he pulled out a couple we hadn't rehearsed at all! Down in Anaheim we did "Mr. Tambourine Man"—we'd never played it, and we did a pretty twisted version of it.

Jerry was sort of like the conductor. I listened to him as closely as I could because he's got a way of playing that I can tell which way the chords are going even if he's playing lead. He's real good at making sure you know what direction everything is going in.

LEN DELL'AMICO: I think Dylan rushed into the idea of working with the Dead without thinking about it. The previous year, it was Tom Petty [as Dylan's backup band] and it was Dylan in leather. Petty is a garage band and I thought it worked really well. Dylan is a garage band with whoever he has.

But the Dead is like an orchestra, and I think it was difficult for him to assert himself with six guys who had a very set way of doing things and counted measures. People think of the Dead as sloppy, but it's because they were improvisational; they were excellent musicians. So here's Dylan, being all loosey-goosey, and his tunes are being done by these guys. I can't picture him telling Phil what to do. So I think it was hard for Dylan emotionally and musically, and once he committed he realized, "Wow, this is not going to be my band, and I kind of have to adapt to what they're doing," which he wasn't used to. But I think it turned out pretty great, considering.

BOB WEIR (1987): [Dylan's material] is living and breathing. It's obvious when you first hear it that that's the way it is. The songs don't so much grow on me, like other songs do, as just introduce themselves and then keep unfolding. When I listen to his songs these days it's like listening to a new song because I just focus on the different aspects. They're so incredibly complex and varied, the little vision that he presents, it mutates over time. They're little alive pieces of something or other.

It takes a bit of footwork for us to remember the arrangements. A couple of the guys in our band, a few of the songs they've never heard. They know his hits. Being a real fan of his, I know most of his material, but even so, I haven't played it all. Keeping it all straight's a challenge for me—it must be quite a challenge for him to remember what is essentially a completely different repertoire than he was doing last year.

A lot of the *Blood on the Tracks*–era material was his suggestion—just stuff he hasn't gotten around to in a little while. Right after he wrote it, and performed that body of work for a while, he got tired of it, I think. And now, after distancing himself from it for a little while, absence makes the heart grow fonder—he wants to do it again. Different eras of his career—they pop up like that. The *Blonde on Blonde* era, for instance—he's doing that stuff. He didn't want to do it for a while, 'cause he was probably sick of it. Or just had enough.

The [song] endings are never gonna be right. Our endings are not famous for being neat as a pin to begin with. It's enough to rehearse forty or sixty songs, but to go over forty to sixty endings as well, you're askin' a lot. Besides, we don't know which ones we're gonna play until we get up on it. . . . He has a different way of working with bands than anybody else we've worked with.

I remember once we were in rehearsal and we were playing "Frankie Lee and Judas Priest." We weren't formally having a whack at it; it just sort of emerged. Jerry had been trying to get him to do it, because he loved that song. We were going through the tune and Bob didn't remember the lyrics, so it was Bob and Jerry and me going back and forth on the lines as they'd come up, and between the three of us we were getting most of them. As each line would arrive, it was as much a surprise to him as they were to us; we were just cracking up. Each new line was a shining new gem.

For that tour we rehearsed like a hundred songs and then proceeded to draw up a bunch of song lists consisting mostly of tunes we'd never played before.

LEN DELL'AMICO: Dylan was managed by Elliot Roberts, who was legendary, and still is. He's an amazing character; like out of central casting. He's obscene, he's funny. I got word from my team that we had to shoot some promo of Bob and the band to put on TV to sell tickets for the shows. "Here are the dates; Bob will be up rehearsing." I said, "What's my budget?" "Fifty grand, to come from the two artists and to be repaid by the promoters."

So I get there on that day, and the video truck arrives at Front Street. The band arrives; Dylan and Jerry are already in there. I'm working with my crew, and Elliot comes in and says, "Shoot's off." I said, "What are you talking about? We've already paid for this. Everybody's here. You think I can just send everyone home and say sorry?" He says, "Your guys don't want to do it anymore."

I don't think Elliot understood that I knew my guys, that it wasn't a typical who's-the-video-asshole thing. I said "Really?" So I go in and Weir is eating a potato chip and I said, "Did you say something about not wanting to do this?" He said, "No, I'm game." And I went to Phil. "No, what are you talking about?" Mickey, Bill, Brent . . . "No, we're fine." So I go to Elliot and he says, "Go in and talk to Jerry. He's in there with Spike."

So I have to suck it up and go in there, and each is sitting on a drum riser alone with acoustic guitars; they're working on an acoustic thing. So I say to Garcia very loudly, "Do you have any problem doing this promo shoot? Because Elliot says you do." And Jerry says, "No, it's not me, it's Dylan!" and he laughs. And I just looked at Dylan, and he didn't look up. And I said, "Okay." I lost my courage. I should have said, "Bob, you agreed to do this." I should have pressed the point. But it's fuckin Dylan, man. But Jerry was like, "Oh, we'll do it another day."

I'm thinking about the money, so I go to Elliot and I say, "Why are you here? You flew up from L.A. It's your job to tell your fucking client to do this." And he said, "What do you want me to do? He's crazy! I can't tell him what to do if he doesn't want to do it!" He was funny. I said, "Okay, but it's still fifty-fifty. Because they're my clients." And then Bobby says, "Nah, don't worry about it. We'll pay for it." So I had to go out and tell my crew to put it all away. And the shoot never happened.

DENNIS McNALLY: Jerry was healthy, happy to be alive, happy to be playing music again, and the rest of the band was, too. Eighty-seven was just a really sweet year in that way. It all fell together, with unintended consequences. They're healthy, they're focused, they have all this great material. They go [into the Marin Veterans' Memorial Auditorium] and they set it up exactly right. They play live but it sounds like studio. The basics [the main tracks for the album] are done in three weeks, a couple of more weeks of overdubs. On that level, it was the perfect situation for them to make a record. They're going to do the tour with Dylan, everyone was so stoked.

Then what happens: Dylan isn't in any great shape himself, and so the tour is frustrating and of minimal personal reward. And then we get a hit and everybody says, "This is charming!" Everybody is buying cars. Hunter buys a new house, and everybody thinks this is great. And then we have the unintended consequences: We have five thousand bonus people without tickets at every show. Something that we really never recovered from. [The sudden rise in popularity] only became flamingly noticeable after *In the Dark*.

This is my theory of Deadhead [evolution]: many of us became Deadheads because a friend or a sibling sat us down and said, "Listen to this. This is cool." We are sufficiently elderly now that it was not through tapes—because there weren't many tapes in 1972—it was records. So [the growth] was organic. And it has always been my argument, sociologically, that in addition to falling in love with this band, there was a certain set of ethics and protocols that were implicitly passed along that came along with it. Among other things, it was, "We're on to something good here; keep a low profile. You don't have to advertise us too much."

I will never forget the guy who took me to see the Dead, freaking at Ed McClanahan's article in *Playboy* ["Grateful Dead I Have Known"] in March of '72 and saying, "Oh, God, our cover's blown, we'll never . . ." Little did he know. To some extent, they were still in a paradigm of slow, organic growth until '87, when suddenly we're on pop-fucking-radio, and that song, that damn song. You've got literally thousands of people who hear the song on the radio, like that song, and think they'll go to the show. But they can't get tickets because it's already sold out; so they go down and check things out anyway, and see the biggest, best party that any nineteen-year-old could want—beer and girls, food, dope, acid—everything.

At Compton Terrace [in Arizona, August 18, 1987], even after all of this madness [stage manager Robbie] Taylor would hand me tickets to give away—and this is when we were begging people not to come without a ticket—and I went up to this kid in the parking lot at Compton Terrace and offered him a ticket. He said, "Oh, no, man, I just came for the party." I was like, "Oh, God!"

ROBERT HUNTER (1988): Once in a while I'll see kids who look like they just stepped out of 1968—their heads seem to be in the right place, and they're interchangeable with that era. Or perhaps those are some of the Heads who have been tripping back and forth between 1969 and 1988, for all I know. Maybe some of them have found a tunnel through. You never know. Maybe it isn't a new generation at all. First Deadheads were trying to get tickets to every city they could, now they're trying to get in every time. And they still can't get in—they're still standing outside saying, "I need a miracle!"

We've set ourselves up to weather all kinds of seas. The sea of fame and large, middle-of-the-road acceptance may be one of the roughest ones of all, and we could founder here. We could have foundered anywhere on the way to here. I have to believe we won't. I don't know where this goes, though, except down. It's impossible to think it's going to get bigger, because it seems like it would be impossible to get bigger. Where do you go from the stadium? To the point where you can no longer play gigs because it will be such a circus if we do? I hope not.

JERRY GARCIA (1987): What options [do we have]? There aren't any in existence that fill the bill in terms of the requirement of the band and the audience. The audience requires the band, the band requires the audience, you know what I mean? And anything short of live performances is short of live performances. So some sort of video isn't going to get it. Bigger venues isn't going to get it. When you're at the stadium, that's it, that's the top end, and that's already not that great . . .

As far as I can tell, we're at the cul-de-sac, the end of popular music success. It doesn't mean there's no place to go from here. But now we have to be creative on this level as well, and invent where we're going to go.

CAMERON SEARS: I think everybody was a little surprised by [the success], frankly. No one really saw it coming. I think they were able to enjoy it while it was enjoyable, and I think they were thrilled to have Jerry back. It was sort of validation that they were doing the right thing, in a sense. Jerry was in a really good place and they all enjoyed it until it became somewhat burdensome. It wasn't really until a year or two later that the largeness began to ripple through the whole situation. At the time, they had a great perspective on it, because it was never something they set out to do, necessarily. It was sort of like they were reluctant beneficiaries in a sense. I mean, they put an enormous amount of hard work into it, and it's always gratifying when the work pays off, but it wasn't their object to be on the cover of *Rolling Stone* or *People* magazine or be on MTV. Every time they intersected with that world it was sort of tongue-in-cheek—"We'll do it, but let's see how we can fuck with them at the same time."

STEVEN MARCUS (Greatful Dead Ticket Sales): I think the "Day of the Dead" on MTV is what fucked up everything. There was one solid day on MTV where like every third video was Grateful Dead–related, and then all day they did cut-ins from the Meadowlands parking lot [outside Giants Stadium] showing "what a great scene it is out here in the parking lots!" From that point on, the number of people in the parking lots tripled, and it was like—party time! Instead of going to Fort Lauderdale on spring break, you go on tour with the Dead, but you don't even go inside!

That day of TV got the Dead so much into the mainstream, particularly with young people; it's never been the same. When I first started working for the Dead in '83, the median age of our audience was about twenty-five to twenty-seven. In '87 and '88, the median age dropped to seventeen or eighteen.

It got to the point where the cities and buildings wouldn't allow us —'89 was the last time the Grateful Dead played Frost [at Stanford], or the Greek [in Berkeley]. The Stanford Police Department was out filming what was going on at Stanford, and they put together a half-hour video. And they sent instructions to the police departments of every city the Grateful Dead were playing, on what to do to control the Deadheads—and arrest as many as possible.

JAN SIMMONS (Grateful Dead Productions): [In the late eighties] there was a big influx of younger Deadheads that maybe didn't get it, and there were a lot more arrests going on outside of venues. So the older Deadheads were getting together to say, "We need to teach the younger ones how to do this." They were trying to put out information about being cool in the parking lots. "There are cops amongst us, and watch your activities"—just trying to educate people. I thought that was a really beautiful thing. But there was an element of people that came around the Dead in the later years that really weren't that interested in the music and were more interested in the party scene and drugs. And inevitably alcohol probably played a more negative part than the drugs that were being done. But there were people who came along figuring it was a great party, and they weren't part of the spiritual element of the theme, and I think that was a troublesome element.

In October 1987, Garcia went to Broadway with two bands, electric and acoustic.

BOB BARSOTTI: Bill [Graham] always wanted to do something on Broadway. We'd sit around in the dressing rooms talking with Jerry and the guys about different things. One of the things mentioned was doing a Broadway show. Jerry said, "Fuck you, Bill." But things progressed to the place where they thought about doing it. Jerry said, "Bill, are you serious about this?" and Bill said, "Now that there's some interest, I certainly will be." Within about a week we knew about the possible availability of all the Broadway theaters.

The Lunt-Fontanne had a space available in the time frame that Bill thought would work. It happened quickly, but it all worked out. It was the two bands: the Jerry Garcia Band and the Jerry Garcia Acoustic Band. It was an exciting thing. Ticket sales broke Yul Brynner's record with *The King and I* for first-day sales on Broadway in 1964. It was broken again later by Andrew Lloyd Webber with *The Phantom of the Opera,* but Jerry held the record for a while.

STEVE PARISH: I wanted Bill to do something special with us. He was on me all the time—me and him would hang out after shows in the Bay Area and have a smoke and a drink and talk. I said, "Bill, I can't take you to the East Coast unless you come up with something new." We came up with this idea of Broadway, which was a place we'd never been. I said, "That way I can take you into a market where I felt we wouldn't be offending [East Coast promoter] John Scher." But John got mad, of course, and then, to his credit, he forgave me and I was able to work with both of them.

That was a special run on Broadway. First of all, it was different from anything else. The rules and regulations of Broadway were in place. Bill was in his element in New York. He'd make us egg creams every night; he'd come backstage and hang out, and we had a rollicking time. There were a lot of celebrities come through. We had a Halloween bash where we had a great makeup team come in and do people.

Jerry told me one thing after that. "Never again," he says. "Never again something where we've got to do matinees on Wednesdays and Sundays." That really took it out of him to play those; it upset the "sched." But it was still memorable—the Lunt-Fontanne Theater and the beautiful Deadheads there. We took Broadway by storm.

LEN DELL'AMICO: New Year's '87. Al Franken has dropped out, Tom Davis is the solo host, Jerry's clean. Davis and I sit down [a few days before the show] and I say, "Tell me what you got." And Davis had this idea for a straight-arrow cooking show hosted by Chef Jerry in a white chef's hat and apron: "And Jerry will have this big bag of white sugar and he'll hold it up and look at it [longingly]."

I said, "I don't know, Tom. The ordeal he went through getting off drugs is not that far in the past. But let's you and me go to Front Street and pitch it. I'm behind you." So Jerry listens and he says, "Well, I don't think it's very funny." And Tom is like, "Trust me, Jerry. People are going to see this and think it's funny." And Garcia says, "You're kind of laughing at me, aren't you?" Tom says, "Yeah! But you want people to laugh, don't you?" So he said okay, we shot it at Front Street, and he killed on it! When they put it on the screen for the live audience that night, I could hear the roar of the crowd through the [video] truck walls.

TOM DAVIS: We were gonna do [a television broadcast] for New Year's Eve 1987. Len Dell'Amico, who was producing it, said, "Do what you want, Davis." So I started writing lots of stuff that needed to be produced.

A day before the show they had so much stuff to edit that there was no time to edit half the stuff I did.

I went, "You said to do anything I wanted to do."

Len said, "That was then, this is now." So I went up to Jerry, and he was having fun, talking to some girls at a table. I went, "Jerry, we need more money to get another edit room."

He said, "Goddammit, Davis, don't talk to me about money, or I'll send you over to Kreutzmann and that'll be the end of the whole thing!"

That's when I knew we were pals.

The best thing that came out of it: I did a [skit] with Jerry. He was clean now, no drugs, so, "What do you do, Jerry, with all this time before the show?"

"Well, I love to bake. Let me show you how you do it . . . I'm doing a layer cake now. Hand me the powdered sugar." It was this baggie with half an ounce of white powder. And Jerry looks at it and goes [*long sigh*]. It was hilarious. He could do comedy. He had great comic timing.

DENNIS McNALLY: Most of the Deadhead pieces [for newspapers and magazines] didn't need me [to set up interviews]—they just went to the parking lot and wrote about that. My favorite story in that regard was the classic example: it was at Frost [Amphitheater], late eighties, a young woman from the *New York Times* [Jane Gross] called me: "We'd like to do this story." I thought, "It's the *Times*, okay." So we talked, and I went on and on and on about the diversity of the Deadheads, about how "You're going to get in that parking lot, and you're going to see tie-dye, and it's going to be an almost sensorially overwhelming scene. You're going to assume that everybody's the same, and I'm telling you they're not. They're not all the same. We've got senators, we've got doctors, and also people who haven't taken off their tie-dye in the last ten years and live for this tour. We wouldn't be making the living we do if that was the majority, because they have to scuffle to get in." And sure enough, the opening sentence of her article was something like: "Wrapped in tie-dye, reeking of marijuana smoke . . ." So, for the Deadhead stuff [journalists] didn't need me, they just went ahead and did it, and it was superficial American journalism at its finest.

ROBERT HUNTER (1988): I think one reason that the Deadheads are growing and jumping aboard right now is we look like an alternative to a grave parentalism that is overtaking the nation. We're not parental. We say, "Do what you want to do." Like we don't take stands for or against drugs. There are individual stands—some people in this band have been through a few things like that, and they're sharing the wisdom of their information that this leads nowhere. Fine. But we're not taking a group stance.

And there's a group of Deadheads [the Wharf Rats] who have a [yellow balloon they meet under at the shows], and they're the drug-free Deadheads. They invite people to come gather around there. I like that. That's nice. I don't think that you need to be stoned out of your mind to enjoy the Grateful Dead experience. If you are stoned out of your mind, well, then you're experiencing that, too, in your own way. So long as you're not degenerating, ruining your body, ruining your brain, and bashing your head against the wall, I don't want to tell people what to do and not to do. I may personally view it with alarm, but it's not my province to tell other people what to do, except by example.

CAMERON SEARS: We all hated [stadiums] in a way. The experience lacks intimacy and it's complicated logistically in terms of, when you're playing a 60,000-seat stadium, you probably have a total of

ROBERT HUNTER: We're trying to be non-authoritarian. We find ourselves in stadium situations where suddenly we're responsible for any pandemonium that may ensue from things not being regulated properly. Therefore we are forced into that position, out of necessity. There's a bit of paradox: the size that we've become [and being] face to face with the responsibility we have for the safety and well-being of our audiences. It must be worked out in each individual situation, and the best that can be done is with the least

80,000 or 90,000 people around the venue in total—another 30,000 people could be out there on any given day, and they had no investment in the show, many of them, yet we were the ones being nailed to the cross over it. But it was more about the musical experience. Our production costs were enormous, in an effort to make it sound and look as good as it possibly could, to make what many would consider an inferior experience as positive as it could be. Everybody would have loved to see the band at the Fillmore, but those days were gone.

The security bills were enormous; all the bills were enormous. And yes, the grosses were big. Most of it was thought out in advance, but there would be times when there were surprises. You've got a security bill that might have 150 people on it, a police bill with a helicopter unit, police on horseback, a command center, a place to process people who get arrested. At a certain point I think we wondered, "Are we the cheese in the mouse trap?" There was an element of that, too. What are we doing, exactly? As caring people, that became a real conundrum for us.

We knew there were undercover units—DEA or local police—at every show. Part of our messaging to our fans was: there are going to be undercover agents, so consider yourselves informed. We did everything we could to make people aware of what was considered permissible and what wasn't.

We were conflicted, too, because we knew there was big business enterprise being undertaken [outside our shows] that was harmful to the fans. The whole nitrous oxide thing was pretty ridiculous. That was an organized crime thing in a lot of places —especially on the East Coast. There was one show where they confiscated something like seventy-five or eighty [nitrous] tanks, and there were actually hundreds of tanks there. At five bucks a balloon, somebody's making millions of dollars, when you think about it. So when that kind of money is being generated, you know that other elements are going to come into play.

> In 1989, recording commenced for a new studio album: *Built to Last.*

JERRY GARCIA: We started off this record like the last one: we thought, "We've hit on a good methodology—we'll go in and play the Marin Civic as though we were playing a regular show." But it really was not coughing up the kind of results we wanted to get. I think all of our consciousness about production and about excellence in the recording has gone up too much, where we can't accept things that aren't quite right anymore. Now we want to be able to pay attention to the music, not have to worry about avoiding the weak places. When you're dealing with a record that isn't quite perfect, every time that little place goes by where there's something a little funny, where there's a little glitch, you try to do things to disguise what it is that's wrong. We've never had the patience to really dig in very much, so the whole problem's always been, "How can we make this experience more enjoyable to us, in the sense that a live performance is enjoyable, and still maintain the microscopic attention to detail that a record requires?"

We started with the material, rather than the band as a performing unit. We went about it in a way that was a little more methodical, that at first seems kind of mechanical, but really it worked for us. Rather than have hundreds of takes of each tune to listen

control that's absolutely necessary to control a crowd. And the minimum authority.

This is our big, big problem now: what to do with the unruly factor now that's causing a large group situation to become aggravated and exhibit mob behavior. I don't know; I don't know that anybody's ever known, short of imposing absolute authoritarian control, and that is of course the opposite of what the Grateful Dead stand for. Will we be forced to become our own opposites? Interesting philosophical question.

through, and even do such things as picking out the best of each one and splicing them together, it would be interesting to do this as though there were only one take of each tune. And the way we would do it is to set it down in time on a piece of tape. We started off by setting a drum machine, which is like a metronome, essentially, and finding the rhythm that was closest to describing the general feeling of the song. We would start playing the tune, not thinking really in terms of the final rhythmic feeling, but in terms of the conversation between the instruments. We would start working out our parts together, using that as a context, the same piece of tape every time, the same tempo every time.

PHIL LESH: Whoever wrote the song played either the guitar or the piano, and a drum machine, just to start with, and each musician would add parts to that. It's kind of a layering procedure; we didn't do a lot of live playing on this record—which is 180 degrees from what we used to think would be the best methodology for us to use. In other words, we turned around; we actually made a studio record this time.

JERRY GARCIA: When we started to get our stuff shaped out, then we would have Bill come in. He'd put on the earphones and he'd hear the rest of the band playing. So his experience would be playing with the band, supporting the band the way he's used to playing live. Then his feeling would be on the tape—"Okay, here's how Bill's going to interpret this, he's adding this component. Now let's go change our parts," and so on—evolving the way it works, everybody at their own rate. 'Cause this is something you can come in and do when nobody else is here. So if Brent says, "I'd like to spend a couple of days just with this tune, and listen really carefully to what everybody else is doing and just fool around with my part until it falls into something," Brent would do that. And then Weir would come in and say, "Oh, Brent's got some neat stuff here; if I play this over here it'll work like that . . ." This is the normal evolutionary process that happens onstage, but it usually takes a couple of years with a piece of material.

PHIL LESH: There was no opportunity to interact with another musician and say, "Could you put that accent half a beat to the left?" So it was pretty much "work with what's there," which is a discipline unto itself. I found that fascinating, and I came up with some different kinds of playing than I would normally have done.

It was very easy to do the work because all the instruments were isolated, and you could mix them and set them up so you could have the perfect mix to play with. I'd come down [to the studio] alone and work the machines myself and do it till I was happy with my part.

That's one way to do it, but it certainly lacks the feeling of the other way. It's a real dilemma for us, because when we play live with two drummers [in the studio] we can't get the isolation on the instruments to make a good record. When we play separately in the studio, we don't have the right feeling, but it sounds good on a record. We do one or the other; hopefully one of these days we can figure out how to do both.

I do think *Built to Last* was one of the best-sounding records we've ever made. You can hear everything real clearly. But it didn't hang together that well.

I really believe if we hadn't had a deadline imposed on us by the record company [Arista] on *Built to Last,* we probably would've gone back and done the whole thing over again more in line with how we did *In the Dark.* [But] we took a big advance on that, which gave them the power.

JERRY GARCIA: ["Foolish Heart"] is one of those tunes where I had the melody written and the phrasing written before I talked to Hunter, so he wrote lots of different versions of lyrics before he settled into something. I've never been entirely satisfied with the subject matter of the tune in terms of what the lyrics mean, but the gesture of it—the unfolding of it—works real good for me, and that's what I really care about.

When Hunter and I were working on this tune, I said, "This is an advice song!" I mean the lyrics are "Never give your love, my friend / Unto a foolish heart." Is that really good advice? Is that what we want to say? Shouldn't we tell them, "Hey, brush your teeth twice a day!"?

BILL KREUTZMANN: "Foolish Heart" is a wonderful song. When Jerry first laid that song on us, everyone liked it so much they played everything they knew all at the same time! It was a mishmash, but we were excited. It was like, "Settle down, cowboys! Rein 'em in a little!" But after a few times, we got the feel for it better. It's evolved nicely. It's gotten to the point now where I can't wait to play it onstage. I get so excited; sometimes when I like a song I'll push it a little.

JERRY GARCIA: My original notion of it was much more "string-y." I had a kind of Pete Townshend kind of acoustic guitar thick rhythm notion, something between that and that kind of U2 uptempo roll, the fingerpicking roll. Something along those lines. But the evolution of the parts in the band made me completely rethink it. I eventually abandoned that idea totally.

The thing that's interesting about "Foolish Heart" is that nobody's playing chords in the song. Everybody's playing lines, and the lines hook up and tell you all you need to know about the harmonic content of the song. You don't wonder where it's going. It's so beautifully designed, it's like a clock. It's really lovely. It surprised me it came out so interesting and so perfect and so totally its own personality. That's the Grateful Dead in action, really.

BILL KREUTZMANN (1989): Sometimes I wake up at 4:30 in the morning and I can't drop back to sleep, so I'll get up and work on songs. Last night when I woke up I worked on "Victim or the Crime." I got up, put on earphones so I didn't wake up the family, and listened to a tape from yesterday and really thought about the parts I was hearing—Phil has some really great things on there that got me thinking in a certain direction. So from there I visualized myself playing a part in relation to him. Now today when I go in, it'll take me a couple of times through at the drums to get it, but the idea I have will probably be right because I worked it out in my mind first. It's like doing a storyboard for a movie instead of just being loose and shooting.

BOB WEIR: I had originally written ["Victim or the Crime"] for the

Grateful Dead in '83 or '84. I wrote a snatch of chorus and then I showed that to my friend Gerrit Graham and we talked about it a little bit, and then he fleshed it out lyrically, and I fleshed out the music as well. When I originally brought it around to the band, the way I wrote it and the way it came together, it's a very complicated piece and it didn't get a whole lot of attention because there was other material we were working on at the time. So I did it a little bit with [Bobby and] the Midnites, then did it solo, and then brought it around again to a warmer response. So at that point we started putting it together as a Grateful Dead song.

We started trying to soften up some of the stuff that we knew we were going to encounter resistance with, like the J-word. [The first line is "Patience runs out on the junkie."] We tried to come up with stuff like "Patience runs out on the monkey," or then we tried to take it all the way in that direction—"Patience runs out on the bunny." But none of that worked. Then the whole rest of the song just wouldn't stand up, because it has an integrity about it. You can't dick with it.

I'll be the first to admit that it's not "Sugar Magnolia." But I can't do that exclusively for the rest of my life. There are little corners of my soul that I'm going to want to explore and investigate, and people are paying me to do this. It's my charge to do this, to investigate myself—stuff in general—and every now and again I'm going to peek into a dark corner. If I see something there that I've got to write about, then I'm going to write about it. And if people tell me I can't do that, that's just going to fuel the fire.

It's tension, and you keep expecting release. Release does occur, but there's a lot of tension. There's a lot of "ponderosity" to it that a lot of people consider pompous, and perhaps it is pompous. There's that part of all of us. The questions posed in this song are not unique to this boy.

PHIL LESH: I didn't particularly care for the attitude of the song, but I have to admit it's grown on me. I've found things to play in it, whereas first it was a just question of going *boom-boom-boom-boom.* I'm beginning to hear the music in it now. I don't quite understand why Bob feels he has to sing this song, but I'll defend to the death his right to sing it. And to have us play it, too—if he can make it stick.

JERRY GARCIA: "Victim or the Crime" is fascinating because it defies, almost, any effort to play freely through it. You have to know it. It has changes in it, and they're very strict, and they have lots of real dissonant moments. The angularity of it was fascinating to me, the tonality was, because it's one of those things where you really have to stretch to figure out something appropriate to play to add to the tonal mood of the tune.

I don't believe I've ever actually listened to all the words to it. Ever. I have the gist of it; by now I probably could recite it if I really had to, but the text of it is more of the same, in a way: it doesn't have a whole lot of light in it. It's very dense, and it's angst-ridden to boot. So it seemed to me when we were starting to record it, in order to save it from an effort to make it more attractive, I thought that what would work with the song would be to just go with it, to go with the sort of asymmetrical way it's structured, and play to expose that.

An early possibility that occurred to me was that this would be an interesting song to do something really strange with. This is where Mickey comes into the picture, 'cause he's one of the guys that holds down the strangeness corner; he's always a willing accomplice in these ideas. So I thought about the Beam, which is an instrument that people feel about the way they feel about "Victim or the Crime" —I thought, "Let's take two of the things that really have a huge potential for really upsetting people and combine them in a happy marriage. Something that will be a real horror show." And it's turned out to be strangely beautiful. I really enjoy it now. When me and Mickey started working on it, I'd be sitting there listening and say, "You know, I may be going crazy, but I'm starting to like this."

It's one of Weir's stunningly odd compositions, but it's also very adventurous. It's uncompromising; it's what it is, and the challenge of coming up with stuff to play that sounds intelligent in the context has been incredible, but also appropriately gnarly. I really wanted that part of it to work. I think we did a nice job on the record with it. It works. Whatever it is, it works. I'm real happy with it because it was one of those things that was like, "What are we going to do with this?" It's like having a monster brother that you lock in the attic. It's like a relative that you—"God, I hope nobody comes over when he's eating."

BOB WEIR: "Picasso Moon" is a piece of music that I wrote for another lyric that Barlow had written called "It Doesn't Matter." I had it pretty much finished when I learned that Barlow had given it to Brent to work on, because he assumed that I was ignoring it or something. We're not entirely sure why. So I figured, well, I'll just get started on something else here.

We were sitting around in the front room here during a rehearsal and everything got sort of quiet for a moment, and Phil said, "Picasso Moon. I don't know why I said that, but there it is. You can see that, can't you?" We weren't talking about anything at all, anything specific; he just popped. And it took a couple days to settle in on me, but I was riding my bicycle one day, and in my head I was listening over the chorus, wondering what that was all about, and "Picasso Moon" just sort of floated in and hung there. And I could see that little Picasso moon hanging up there in the sky, and things got real weird for a minute and I almost fell off my bike, and then I knew what the song was about.

And then I started working with Barlow on it, and it took me a while to get across to him what it was that I was seeing. Finally we got it together, and I think the song hangs together pretty well.

JERRY GARCIA: Characteristically, Bob doesn't finish the song until about a week before delivery time. So just about then, he's still working on the thing. And a lot of times he'll pick a melody which is virtually unsingable. Either it's out of his range, or it's got notes that don't appear anywhere in music, or things like that. I've been through this process with him enough times to know that at the end something's going to come out of this that's probably going to be pretty neat. So you have to just go along with that, even though I had no idea how that song was going to sound until the week we mixed it. The vocal didn't go on, and the vocal background parts didn't go on, and no sense of the shape of the song.

You have to develop a faith in the process and assume that what's going to come out is going to be a song. But you're disadvantaged because unless you get him to sing it right away, or something like it, you don't know where the vocal's going to go, so you don't know where the melody goes, and you don't know whether you're stepping on it or not when you start to construct a part to go along with the song. Weir's songs sometimes evolve from the bottom up in kind of a strange way—the melody is the last thing that's written, so you have to approach it differently. "Picasso Moon" is typical in the sense that he writes them back to front, so to speak.

BOB WEIR: Often, when I'm writing a song, I'll engineer it for it to be a stretch for me—something I either can't sing or play to some degree—and then work on it. I usually won't bring it around to the band until I can more or less handle it, but I like there to be room for growth. I like to give myself a challenge, and when you challenge yourself you make yourself more capable in the long run. You expand yourself. I view every song that's presented to this band—by myself or by anyone—kind of that way: that this is a song I can't play, but if I work at it, I can. To varying degrees, others in the band view it that way, too, so we all have to stretch and learn the new material. And in so doing, a lot of what new capabilities we have to achieve to be able to play new material splashes over into the other tunes we play.

JERRY GARCIA: "Standing on the Moon," for me, is one of those perfect songs. Hunter wrote a lyric that was so absolutely perfect, I just wanted to do nothing to interfere with what it says. I wanted to keep it just as close to the bone as possible, I didn't want to hear any solo voices in it, I didn't want to hear any suspended chords, I only wanted to hear pure triads; I wanted to hear the emotion just as pure as it could be. And it came out really nicely. It works—for me, that's the only test: does the thing work emotionally? For me, it works emotionally.

PHIL LESH: "Foolish Heart" and "Blow Away" are my two favorites on this album. [With] "Blow Away," what knocks me out about it is the horn-imitation parts that Brent put on with the synthesizer. It reminds me of a great big-band sound. It's a thrill to hear that kind of thing in one of our records, especially done as well as it is.

BOB WEIR: Brent tends to be a bit more prosaic than either Garcia or I do in our writing, and that's probably real good for the Grateful Dead in general, as sort of a grounding influence, I would think. And also at the same time I feel like I'm just cut loose. 'Cause I hear Brent's writing, and I can do stuff like "Picasso Moon" and "Victim or the Crime" and not have to worry about keeping it down to earth.

JERRY GARCIA (1989): After ten years, you can hardly call [Brent] "the new kid." He's not the new kid anymore, he's Brent, and this record gives us a chance to let him be what he is. He's always been an incredible singer and an incredible player, and a guy with wonderful ideas. And he's been so conservative in terms of letting himself out into the band. He's been a model of conservative bandsmanship all this time, and now he's starting to come out a little. The songs speak for themselves, and every one of them is good. They're all good, and the performances on them are excellent. It's really fun to work with him.

On "Just a Little Light," I thought it would be a good chance to imitate the guy [guitarist Kenny Withrow] in [Edie Brickell and] the New Bohemians who imitates me [on the 1988 Top Ten single "What I Am"]. All I heard in this last year was, "Have you heard that guy that sounds like you?"

JERRY GARCIA (1988): It used to be that a lot of what we were doing was going from one song into a wholly different kind of song, where the transition itself would be a piece of music. Lately it's much less that. It's more that we're able to come up with transitions that are very graceful in a real short amount of time, because we've tried almost everything by now, in terms of going from one kind of thing into another. It's not that transitional music doesn't exist anymore. It's just that we've worn out the pathways.

Eventually you know all the music you have. So even though we have a hundred and fifty tunes, or a hundred and forty, or ninety, or whatever it is, we know those songs well enough to know the places between them—all the hypothetical places between them—because if we haven't gone from one song to another specifically, we've gone from one like it to a song like it. In that sense, there aren't many surprises left. So that's why you have to create new material—to create new spaces out of which to build things.

We need the stuff that lets us play at that edge of chaos, but doesn't require rehearsal, dig? 'Cause we don't have the energy to rehearse like [we did back in 1968]. Then, we used to rehearse seven, eight hours a day—when we were youngsters. We needed to have our chops up because we were still all learning our instruments.

When I choose to go from one song to another, I like the doorways. Bob doesn't seem to care about them one way or another. A lot of times we'll discuss an idea before the second set, like Weir will say, "Let's do 'Playing in the Band' into 'Uncle John's Band' into something, something." "Okay, sounds good." And more often than not they tend to chop off, they tend to splice into each other. If it's a Bob segue—if it's his design—he tends to like them like that. We've never really discussed it, but generally speaking I prefer the doorways and he prefers the splices. It just seems to work out that way.

The more you play together, the better you get at playing together. There's no question about that. So the more time you can spend with the same group of musicians, the better the music's going to be, the more personality it's going to have. The thrust of everybody's musical ambition is to keep getting better at it. My perception of it is that the Grateful Dead is still improving. It may be that age will run us off before we get to where we really could go, because of the energy involved.

Every time we do a tour now, the first two nights it's like just getting back to being able to finish a show. Goddamn! Even the guys who are really physically conscious, like Weir and Mickey, are exhausted. The nature of what we do is that it's difficult physically. So time itself is our greatest enemy.

BOB BRALOVE: Jerry wanted the simplest, easiest way to make music. He just wanted to play the guitar. It was really fun to give Jerry a new [MIDI] sound and then watch him check it out. My first experience with Mickey in the drum solo and giving him sounds is he'd go through zillions of sounds—he'd go crazy going through all the different sounds. But Jerry would want to play one new sound during a whole night. He'd want a sound that he could play with for an entire "space" section or whatever he was going to investigate. That's why you'd hear the double reeds come back or the trumpet come back. He wanted to master that sound.

When he would do the trumpet sound, he'd do the slides and all these little trumpet things, but with his fingers. He tried to play a trumpet line like a trumpet player might do it—where the trails are, where the vibrato is, even the embouchure.

Sometimes he was a horn section. There was one time he played "Midnight Hour" and I swear you could practically see the horn section he was doing standing up, sliding back and forth. He had this huge grin on his face. He could get totally out there, too, playing helicopters or thunderstorms.

JERRY GARCIA (1989): This is the first time I've had a guitar that I can use both the guitar sound and the MIDI sounds interchangeably, so it's like a whole new language. It means that you have a whole new vocabulary to play with. And if you produce a sound that's convincingly like, say, a French horn, you start to think French horn ideas. They just tumble into your head. I don't have the discipline to sit down and learn how to play French horn, but if I can make sounds like a French horn, I'll find 'em.

[Horn sounds] are the ones that are most playable for me right now. I go on how much my touch can be transferred to the MIDI realm. What's interesting is that if I play harder on the horn things, I can actually overblow it, just like you can with a horn. So what I'm

359

looking for is some of the expression you get from a horn, except on guitar. I look for things that are most interactive and that I can affect by my touch. But I'm still on the ground floor of this.

I tend not to think of specific players, but I do think of a color. So while I might not think of Coltrane specifically, I might think of "Ascension"—not a part of it, but the whole way it unfolds. Or, more to the point, I found myself thinking at one point of "My Favorite Things," but more Eric Dolphy than Coltrane, because one of the [MIDI] saxophones has a very good soprano sax register. That's the thing about the guitar; it crosses the registers. Sometimes you find yourself in a place—like with the flute—you're playing in a register that doesn't exist for the instrument, but you still recognize its characteristics. There's a soprano saxophone–like thing I can get to that has this very pure Steve Lacy sound—very open and enunciatory, and different than a jazz tone. To me, that's very appealing.

CAMERON SEARS: [By 1989] there were a couple of things going on. The fan base was expanding, and there were two components to that—there was the parking lot scene and then there was the camping thing. The two were intertwined, but they were also distinct, because one went on 24/7 and the other one went on when the lots opened and kind of ended when the lots closed. So there were two different constituencies being served. There were the local kids who came down during the day and maybe went to the show and after the show was over, maybe hung out for an hour or two and then split. But then there were other people who essentially lived there. It had evolved out of a sort of self-policing community—take care of your neighbor, look out for one another. "Oh, great, you made it to the next show!" That sort of thing. Then, the people who exploited that scene started taking advantage of it—like the nitrous oxide vendors. After a point, there was a lot of enterprise going on that became detrimental to us being able to do what we were there to do.

A place like Alpine Valley [in rural Wisconsin] was particularly difficult because the locality wasn't very favorable at all from the get-go, even though it's a large space. The authorities were very aggressive on the roads coming in there. It was not something they wanted to endorse. At the same time, they didn't want Deadheads floating through and winding up in Farmer Joe's fields. So the best thing was to try to get it contained.

In the cities, a place like Hartford was tough because the lawn of city hall is adjacent to the arena, so—bonfires in front of the state house? I don't think so. It was problematic. And we had problems in all the big stadiums as everything got bigger and bigger. Then, when we went to the smaller places [arenas] in the spring and the fall, all of that kind of got condensed. There weren't the same numbers of people, but there was still that element of people who were there to take advantage of it that didn't shrink. It was probably the same number of people feeding off a smaller group of fans.

BOB WEIR: I ran away with the circus when I was sixteen, and it turned out to be this band. I've hung with it ever since. Our approach has got a fair bit of adventure to it, and there are going to be kids in any generation who are going to share that appreciation of the adventures that life can hold for you. And some of those people are going to identify with us, our approach as expressed through our music and our way of doing things. And they're going to want to get in on it as best they can, so maybe that means packing up and following the band around for a summer or whatever.

JERRY GARCIA (1989): Success in the concert world is getting to the point where there's a whole new set of kinds of problems. I guess really it has to do with local municipalities who are upset by the large numbers of Deadheads camping out when we play a three-day stretch in a small town. We've got lots of noise about that kind of stuff, and I think it's probably not so much the specific behavior of the audience or Deadheads—I think they're generally pretty well-behaved and not a terribly disruptive influence. I think it's just part of the large numbers of new strange people in these places. America is essentially a xenophobic kind of place, and anybody who's different, I think there's a certain scare there.

At any rate, it's difficult now for us to play three days someplace, and a lot of places don't want us to play there and we can't come back because we represent too large of a problem in terms of logistics, traffic, and so forth. In that case, success is no success at all.

The whole structure of America is, you can rise to a certain level of success, and then you have to start defining what success means on your own. There's no further definition provided by the world at large. The end of that story is stadiums, and you can't really get any more people than that into a concert. And it also means a certain dilution of the concert experience. I mean, when you're in the back row of one of those stadiums, you're not getting a really rich experience. I don't know where this is leading us, but it certainly represents whole new worlds of problems. The main ones from my point of view are the production problems, trying to still project a good show to every seat in the house. The exterior social problems that arise, I think, are probably the things that affect our audience most. But in that area, success is problematical.

My instincts are to leave everything alone. If people want to vend stuff, fine. I have no control over them, and I don't want to have control over them. But it's at the point now where I guess we're asking Deadheads to govern themselves. This is hard to do, because we don't know who it is they're offending. Those people don't speak to us. The people that do speak to us are the people who they complain to, see? So we get it from the police and the mayor and the city council and that sort of stuff and those kinds of semi-official bodies, and our only recourse is to speak to the Deadheads, and it's a blind-alley situation. We're saying, "Well, people are very offended for some reason, and it seems to have something to do with all of us being there at the same time. If you can do something about it by cleaning up your act or these various alternate possibilities of ways to behave when you're at a Grateful Dead show, then that may be what's going to be required."

I feel that there's a certain railroading going on, that there's kind of a bias against our audience. Professional sports still draw more people than rock 'n' roll does, and you don't hear this kind of hysteria about those crowds.

DENNIS McNALLY: The band's response [to the crowds outside shows] was to shrug and accept it until we got the letter from Giants Stadium in the Spring of '89. It basically said, "We love you, we want you. However, if you do three shows, that means we need to provide essential city services to ten thousand people [outside the stadium] for five days—sewage, porta-potties, security, food. We'll have that so-called overnight parking; de facto camping. There will be at least that many people. We can't do that. We can't afford it."

Jerry had no desire to be the mayor of a traveling city. Giants Stadium [in East Rutherford, New Jersey] wasn't going to deal with that, and why should they? It was far beyond their obligation as the venue. So we declared two things: One was no camping or overnight parking. And the other was no merchandising.

Now, the overnight parking worked fine. People were told that if you're not out of here in an hour, we're going to tow you. I never heard of that ever being a problem. The no-merchandising caused endless problems. We all may have noticed that Deadheads have an inclination to be somewhat entitled at times, so first there was this incredible reaction of "You can't mean me, because I'm good vibes." And there was a lot of "Oh, the band is just getting greedy. They want the money."

Why ban merchandising? Because it created, as they say in urban planning circles, an attractive nuisance: a focus for people to hang out in. And if there wasn't a Shakedown Street [the scene outside], maybe there would be fewer people hanging out.

Most of [the bootleg shirts], in any other time, would have been fine. Make fifty, sell fifteen, and do your tour: no problem. Now, the guys that were transparently counterfeiting our t-shirts—organized crime, basically—we were not thrilled by that, and we tried to chase them around with our two security guys in a parking lot. There was no way it was going to make a dent in it most of the time, and we never really did. But there was a lot of criticism, especially on me, because I was the messenger. To this day, I still live with a particular insult that one of the early Deadheads said, that I sounded like a shill for the tobacco companies because I was defending these policies. And I was like, "Gee, I wasn't really aware that the Grateful Dead were selling merchandise that caused death," but whatever. I had a lot of Deadheads tell me they couldn't stop vending. But our ability to tour was at risk in '89.

CAMERON SEARS: Every night I would get the band onstage and then I would walk the lots. If I got there early enough before the show, I'd go out there, look around and make sure the ingress was good, and get a general sense of what the vibe was—how the kids were being treated, what was going on. Because you can tell, based on just a few interactions, what's really taking place. But every night, after we turned out the lights and the band hit the stage, I'd go back out and see what's going on.

We were also having problems with people running up to the doors. When you start having assaults on the building and the staff, it creates a confrontation you never want to see. That happened in multiple places. And it's not something at the end of the day the fans are going to win. So you're trying to prevent it from occurring in the first place. It puts the security people in a bad place, too, because if they're bracing for an "assault"—they're ready to go; their adrenaline is up. It's a bad situation. And you'd hear kids saying, "Oh, man, Jerry wants me in there," and this and that.

Ultimately, we wrote up our own manual of how to handle a show, from the outside to the inside. I would go out and advance dates with the authorities—"Okay, this is what we expect, this is how we'd like to do it." We would go through the specifics of who was going to be deployed where. How is the event going to run? Where are people going to go when it's over? What's going to be the city's response when this happens or that happens? We really rolled our sleeves up, for a couple of reasons: one, out of concern for the well-being of our fans; but secondly, out of a sense of trying to preserve our business. We were dependent on our ability to go to these places to be able to play. And if the municipalities were getting burned out on it, we were running out of the places to play, so that would affect the economics of our organization.

JERRY GARCIA: We have been on the road enough and been doing this enough that we're like an institution. If we come to town, we're not people that blow in once and rob everybody blind and then are gone forever. They know we're going come back next year, or we're going to come back within six months, so we've become something more than that, in a way. We're no longer a one-shot. We're now part of the environment. We may only be part of the environment once every six months, but we are a part of it. And if there are a lot of Deadheads in town, we represent a sizable amount of influence there. Some towns, we bring in enough money to keep the town from falling over. You know, we provide enough economic strength for that weekend or whatever it is that just pushes that community over what it needs because there are a lot of people contributing to the local economy.

Anti-authoritarianism has found its way into every nook and cranny of American life. It no longer has its original face or demeanor, but it's everywhere now. That's essentially what the Grateful Dead audience is acting out: their version of how much freedom is there to go for a wild ride. What's left is, you can follow the Grateful Dead on the road. It's part of what it means to find yourself in America. It's hard to join the circus anymore, and you can't hop a freight; what do you do? You have your adventures, your car breaks down in Des Moines and you need to hitchhike someplace and a guy picks you up and he's a Deadhead. These are your war stories, your adventure stories.

BOB WEIR: The ones that catch your eye are the ones that are basically people who live on the road and follow us around. They're a small percentage of the audience, but they're quite visible. The ones who aren't visible are the stockbrokers, lawyers, doctors, housewives. You know, the stockbrokers, their hair isn't long and full of leaves and stuff like that, so they don't catch your eye. They're wearing the tie-dye, so they don't stick out, but you don't see them. The ones you see are the ones with the leaves in their hair, the matted hair and all that kind of stuff. But that's only a few of them. Those are just the highly visible ones. In that audience, the bulk of people don't look like that every day.

Built to Last was released on Halloween 1989, and though it was successful by old Grateful Dead standards—it sold around 800,000 copies—it didn't have nearly as much impact as *In the Dark* two years before. This time there was no hit single (though "Foolish Heart" did get a lot of radio play). Still, the Dead juggernaut continued to roll and the scene outside of shows kept growing. Many Deadheads believed that musically, 1988 through the spring of 1990 was a new golden age for the band.

"Drums and Space" had been a permanent fixture since the spring of 1978. When mythologist Joseph Campbell saw the Dead in the late eighties he gave a sort of imprimatur to the band's show structure, moving from order to chaos and back again.

JERRY GARCIA: We want to maintain some area [of the performance] that is absolutely and totally unstructured. It finds structure. It finds expression, if we're lucky. This is one of those totally subjective kinds of experiences: there are times when you are really clicking into something—but you definitely have to be alert in a certain way. You have to be ready, and also you have to discard notions that are fondly held by a lot of musicians—about sequences and notes and about scales and musical systems as a whole. If you think of music as a language, the "space" part is where you throw out all the syntax.

PHIL LESH (1990): "Dark Star" has always had the potential to go absolutely anywhere. We designed it that way in the first place. And it turned out to be a very appropriate vehicle for trying a whole lot of different things through the years. That was the one we sort of tacitly agreed upon where anything was okay. I guess maybe in some way, we felt for a long time that if we couldn't do justice to it, we didn't want to do it at all. Or, for whatever reasons, the impulse to do it just wasn't there. Maybe it didn't feel right. I don't know.

Beyond that, all I can say about what it's like now is that it evolves because we evolve. It's grown or shrunk or disappeared because we have our ups and downs. Anyone's work will do that—it grows and shrinks with them. It rises and falls with them.

BOB WEIR: There is a continuum that I feel when we're playing "Dark Star" that I've felt all along. There's a sort of deep, dark-planets-and-space feel to it that I've always felt about that song.

You know, in '69 we stayed in basically a blues mode in "Dark Star" all the way through it. We would push it to maybe a couple of new tonalities, but these days [early nineties] that blues mode sometimes lasts only about 16 bars and then we go elsewhere. The wheels come off, the antennae go up. It's a fun tune to play. Obviously it's totally different every time we do it, which is part of what keeps it interesting. Each version, particularly the way we've been playing it, has its own character.

MICKEY HART: The band as a whole moves as an organic unit, and the people dancing to our music are finding their own way to dance to it and lock into a rhythm that they feel comfortable with. We're not trying to make the beat fall right on the two or right on the one or wherever, and that gives everybody the freedom to find what they want in it. It allows for personal nuance. It's not assault music where we're dictating how to respond to it by laying down some fixed thing; it's participant music. And when everyone's really into it, that's when you get this giant animal breathing as one, and that's what's so thrilling about the Grateful Dead. You can have all these guys playing polyphonic parts, but we're playing as one; it's just different pieces of the pie. And the same is true of the audience. Everyone's dancing differently, but they're part of the same thing. That's magic.

Entrainment is [one] of the major laws at work in the Grateful Dead. Billy and I are entraining when we're up there—beating efficiently together. There's a lot of power in that, and a surprising amount of subtlety, too—a lot the band can play off of; little nuances we can add because we're playing together and off of each other, and don't have to be totally concerned with just keeping time. We can drift off a little bit, maybe even go into trance states, and then pull each other back. If I go a little too far out, the band won't fall apart; same with Billy. It's not like losing consciousness, really; it's changing consciousness. We're actually courting that space. When we can relax and things flow seamlessly—with no effort, with no thinking, just feeling it—you're there, man. But you can't force it, either, and you have to be ready for change every second. It's the razor's edge. It's dangerous. But when the music is right and the feeling is right, it's heavenly. It's as good as making love.

> Although *Built to Last* had been something of a showcase for Brent's songwriting (he had four tunes on the album) and he was featured more than ever before on the spectacular spring 1990 tour, personally he was going through a very rough time.

LEN DELL'AMICO: Toward the end, Brent really got it down. That was a good fucking band, and he was the perfect colorist. He accepted the role and made it into its highest art form. I think Jerry loved him. Brent was such a sweet guy, but so self-destructive. I mean, when Garcia sang "Stella Blue," you'd literally cry, it was so beautiful and so sad. And then you'd see him backstage fifteen minutes later, and he's having a drink and laughing. He'd been performing. But when Brent sang "Blow Away," you were afraid he'd get up and kill himself right there. It was right from his heart. There was no separation between the man and the work, and that always scared me.

CAMERON SEARS: Brent had OD'd [on heroin] at the end of '89. His wife found him and he was able to be resuscitated. But when you're in possession, they can arrest you, so he was in the clink and I needed to bail him out. That call came into the office; Dennis [McNally] was there, too. So we got together the bail and then we had to go get him and take him home, and we ended up spending the night with him because he was livid that his wife had called the ambulance and he'd been busted. We didn't want to leave him in that agitated state, back in the scene of the crime, so to speak.

We talked to everyone about the situation, and he was put on notice by the band. He recognized he'd crossed a line, but I don't think [the OD] in and of itself had cured him of anything. It just made him aware that people were on to him. Because up until that point, nobody realized that's what he was up to. He did have an alcohol problem and people were aware of that. And he had a volatile personality when he was under the influence. Brent was a really sweet guy, but it was like a Jekyll and Hyde thing—when he was drunk he wasn't such a sweet guy. It was sad. So his rock's been turned over a little bit, he's on notice, and he's trying to keep it together.

He was a lonely guy in a lot of ways, and I don't think he had the best people around him, necessarily, and eventually he got back into it. I don't know that he ever wasn't into it, to be honest; he just got better at hiding it.

The interesting thing about heroin is that during the day, when you have to function, as long as you got that itch off your back by taking a little chip or whatever, you can be somewhat functional. But then when you get home and clock out and have your way with it, nobody's the wiser. I honestly don't know how long he'd been at it before that incident [in '89], but suffice it to say, it was the last straw for his wife, and they started living apart. He was on his own more, and the people around him who he thought he wanted to have around him weren't the greatest friends to him in the end.

At any point—and this was an issue that people now have a better perspective on—what kind of steps do people take to help somebody who's in a situation like that? How do you confront it to ultimately have a positive outcome? It's an issue that continuously confronts us in rock 'n' roll bands, but also in families and society at large, and we are ill-equipped to deal with it effectively. The treatment modalities aren't there. These guys [the Grateful Dead], especially coming from the place that they came from, had a difficult time separating individual choice and decision-making, with effects that are life-threatening. Because they all had their moments with something like that. It is hard to tell other people how to live their lives, and often times when you do confront it, people will say, "Oh, I hear you, brother. Tomorrow it will be different." And you want to believe it for two reasons: one, you want to believe they do think that; and two, you're relieved that you don't have to go deeper into it.

When Brent died [of an overdose on July 26, 1990], I think Jerry was the most affected by it. It was like, "Shit, this again . . ." But everybody was heartbroken. Brent was a great musical component to the band. He was a presence. And so soulful. He was at a creative place, too. He was writing a lot, and the other guys weren't writing as much.

LEN DELL'AMICO: Everyone knew Brent had issues. I remember at the *So Far* news conference [in 1987] somebody mentioned Brent and someone in the band said, "Brent's going to jail." [A reporter] said, "Do you care to elaborate?" and Garcia said, "No, I won't!" Very fast, and everybody laughed. So he had a date with rehab. [He did not go to jail.]

It was clear to me that Garcia was hit harder than the others, or was showing it worse. As a department head, I was in on the first meeting after Brent died. They were scheduled to go to Europe. Would there be video in Europe? Would there be recording at all? Because they were planning to record the whole thing and have a huge product release the following year. But it was clear that we were now not going to be recording, because they wouldn't be ready [as a band]. I remember thinking, "Is this meeting too soon? Should I even be here?" I didn't even know if the band had had a meeting on their own. This was in August, before they'd even hired a replacement, because that was an agenda item.

The meeting is grim. Nobody wants to look at anybody. And Garcia "down" is scary. It just emanates. Because Garcia "up" would fill the room endlessly. I guess McIntire or somebody breaks the ice and says, "First thing we ought to decide is whether we're going to do this European tour or cancel." Long pause. Waiting for Jerry to say something—because it truly was a democracy where everyone had the same voice, but at this point you've got this extremely wise person, and everybody knew that, so why wouldn't you want to see what he thinks? So Jerry says, "Let's figure out if we have a band first." At that point I said, "I don't think I should be here for this," and I left.

Obviously, they decided to do the tour and to find a keyboard player in four weeks and rehearse him. I thought that was a huge mistake. They should have canceled the tour and taken as much time as they needed. I think ultimately it was the family pressure. You've got at least fifty people who were dependent on this, and I gather they did not have a rainy day fund big enough. I don't think the fifty-person extended family overtly applied pressure, but I think they remembered what happened in the mid-seventies [when there were serious financial difficulties] and that was their biggest fear.

CAMERON SEARS: I think Jerry knew immediately how difficult it was going to be to replace Brent and the challenge that presented. It was a lot of work amongst all the other things that were resting on everyone's shoulders—the parking lots, the size of the venues; all these things were an omnipresent force in our decision-making, so this was the last thing anyone wanted to deal with. But they decided to soldier on.

STEVEN MARCUS: We used to have a Jerry's birthday party at the ticket office; we would have a barbecue and stuff. If Jerry was in town, I never bothered him or anything, but after Brent died [five days before Garcia's forty-eighth birthday], I called him up and I said, "We're having a birthday party for you. We have it every year, but we never invite you. We've got burgers and hot dogs and it's just the employees of the ticket office—nobody from the main office, no road crew, nobody else, no friends, just us. And there's a burger with your name on it." He said, "I'll be there in ten minutes."

I told everybody, "Please don't bring up Brent. If he wants to talk about Brent, he'll do it." And he did, and one of the first things he said was, "I dread going up on stage and not having Brent there." And he asked, "What should we do?" And I said, "There's a lot of shit that's been going down. I think you guys should take six months off and reevaluate the situation." Everybody in the ticket office was aghast, because basically I was saying we're giving up our jobs. Everybody else came up with ideas: you don't really need a keyboard player; you should just go and do the shows without one.

Or maybe you can bring in so-and-so, or whatever.

Eventually, he did what the band said, and the band said they had to tour. So they canceled Shoreline [Amphitheater in Mountain View, California], and did everything else. It was just really sad.

CHAPTER 10

Vince and the Early Nineties

Bruce Hornsby was approached about replacing Brent Mydland in the Grateful Dead. He was unwilling to give up his thriving solo career, but did agree to tour with the band for a while as they brought a new player up to speed: Vince Welnick, former keyboardist for the theatrical rock group the Tubes and for Todd Rundgren.

DENNIS McNALLY: My theory was that Jerry to some extent took some responsibility for Brent's death. He recognized that the internal dynamics of the Grateful Dead—the way they treated each other as human beings—was a fraud, was non-supportive, non-any-thing that any human being would want to be a part of. Look how these guys managed to pick the same personality four times. Pigpen was the starter: all three of his successors had the same emotion-ally vulnerable personality. They had four guys [audition for the keyboard chair] —Vince, the guy from Dixie Dregs [T Lavitz], Tim Gorman, and Pete Sears—and Jerry was distraught just from the process of valuing and judging. "We want to play music."

If he had been able to sing, it would have been Pete [Sears], I think. The point I argued—not that anyone was going to listen to me—was, knowing that [Bruce] Hornsby was going to be there after ten shows, I said, "Go out as a five-piece. It'll be different. It'll be a challenge. The audience is not going to complain because they don't hear a keyboard there." But they were so devastated, and being "manly men," they wouldn't talk about it, they wouldn't confront it, they just tried to put themselves in total denial, get another keyboard player, and keep going. It was almost archetypal, the way they failed to deal with what had just happened to them. I think Jerry knew this, whether he wanted to admit it out loud or not, and it put him in a bad place, and you can hear it in his guitar playing for the rest of his life. How many great shows are there in the nineties that you know of [from] him?

CAMERON SEARS: They wanted somebody local so they could rehearse and work things up, and beyond that, somebody who could play well and sing the high parts. When Vince came in, I think they liked his free spirit and easy-going nature, and he could definitely play and sing the high parts.

You make all these decisions in a vacuum, in a sense, because you don't really know people's psychological makeup. You're starting to live with them essentially; you don't really know everything you might want to know about them in an intimate relationship like that.

Vince really loved it. He was really down and out when he got the call, so he recognized the gift that it was, in that respect. So he didn't take it for granted, not for a second, and he really worked hard at maintaining his playing at the highest level possible.

VINCE WELNICK: I had met Jerry before, in the early seventies, when the Tubes played a three-night run with Jerry and Merl Saunders at the Lion's Share in San Anselmo. We did a three-day run and Jerry was real cool about it. He said, "We'll switch billing every other day." Whoever got the headline billing was the unfortunate one. They wouldn't go on until 1:00 a.m. and a lot of people would've gone home. But we didn't know each other that much.

Later, he told Lori [Vince's wife] that when I walked into the room he was impressed by my dress and the fact that I looked squeaky clean. I was pretty comfortable with the songs I went in with. [Once I'd been chosen], they gave me copies of some of the recent tours they'd recorded, and then Bob Bralove would assign me ten songs from a tape, and I'd work on them at home and then come in and play them the next day. I listened to the CDs, too, and there are even a couple of songs where I basically learned Donna's harmony part, because I liked the blend she got with them sometimes.

I knew most of their songs from the sixties [having played in a psychedelic band in Phoenix] and a few from the seventies. But I was surprised how much great newer material they had. I loved learning the songs. There are so many beautiful arrangements, like the bridge part of "Wharf Rat"—I feel like crying every time I sing that. It's amazing. "Terrapin"—another incredible tune.

At some point, Jerry said he was thankful we were going over some of these songs because there were some they hadn't hashed over in ten to twenty years and some of them had transmogrified or gone in a bad direction and they'd forgotten their singing parts. Phil hadn't sung the high parts for years and Bobby decided to change some of his parts. He would jump on certain people's parts and it became apparent he had learned it a certain way and wasn't going to learn it another way, so I sometimes had to change my position. So we went over that sort of thing. And if it got to be where the problem part was Bobby, then I would have to rewrite my singing part to work with Bobby's.

Jerry would give me a history of a song sometimes or say, "This is cousin to this song," meaning it was closely related structurally. He was like ol' granddad sitting sonny boy down, telling you how the feel of it should go. But mostly he said, "Play anything; have fun with it."

At first, I thought [the music] would tighten up considerably after rehearsal, but then at some point I realized I had to trade in my feelings about the strictness and consistency of the songs in favor of playing freely, which was something that I didn't get to do with the Tubes or Todd Rundgren. Very seldom would Jerry or Bobby tell me not to play something, unless it was dead wrong or it wasn't the right dynamic. They had the ability to go down to a whisper way more dynamically on the quiet end, the tender side, than Todd or the Tubes. So that became something I focused on, as well as the freeness and spontaneity. And then I'd try to nail my harmony part the best I could.

I'd run home [after a show] and, if not that night, the next day, put the tape on and check it out. I'd put on headphones and sometimes I'd be so elated there would be tears pouring down my cheeks and I'd rant and rave about how good this tune or this jam was, and I was making copious notes: "'Bird Song' turned into 'Flight of the Bumble-bee' here," and analyzing the shit out of it, but in a good way. I knew they connected with that, but they weren't as impressed with it as I was. The phenomenal part about it had sunk into them a long time ago, and they were more blasé about it.

BRUCE HORNSBY: In '86, '87, we were traveling around touring the world on our first record [Bruce Hornsby and the Range, *The Way It Is*], which went a long way in a semi-hurry. We had to learn how to become headliners on nine songs. We needed to flesh out our set, so we played some covers. We played "When I Paint My Masterpiece" the way the Band played it—that was my favorite version, with all that Garth Hudson accordion. Made me want to play accordion. We would segue from "Red Plains" into "I Know You Rider," and that was a popular moment in our show.

Out of the blue, we got a call from the Dead asking us to open for them at the Laguna Seca Raceway in Monterey [May of '87, with Ry Cooder also on the bill]. We met them before we played. They were so nice. They were fans of our record. Phil and Jerry seemed to be the two biggest fans; the most effusive, anyway. They were very warm to us all, and made us feel welcome. It was a great time. And then we opened for them a couple of times a year for the next three years after that. The second year, they asked me to sit in with them at Buckeye Lake. Then I asked Garcia to play on our third record [*A Night on the Town*], on "Barren Ground" and "Across the River"; he played so great on both of them.

I would show up and sit in with them when I wasn't opening

for them. I first just sat in on accordion, 'cause that seemed easier, logistically, and Brent was already playing the piano. It was a little limiting, frankly, because I'm a pretty shitty accordion player. But I was very comfortable, because I knew the music. And it was simple music. "Sugaree" and "Stuck Inside of Mobile with the Memphis Blues Again" were the first two songs I did at at Buckeye Lake [June 25, 1988].

Obviously, these are crystal-clear memories for me, because it was quite a time. The music of your youth—from age ten to twenty-two, say—is very powerful for the rest of your life. For most people, they never go past that. They listen to that music for the rest of their lives. I'm not that guy, but still, the music of my youth is still very powerful for me, and Grateful Dead was a big part of that from, say, eighteen to twenty-two, and of course onward. Standing next to Garcia, trying to trade licks with him—what could have been better? Fantastic.

It was just this growing relationship that culminated, sadly, with the death of Brent and them asking me to help them out.

Garcia and Phil came out to the Concord Pavilion in August of 1990 and asked me to join the band.

I said, "I'll certainly help you out through this time, 'cause I know this is rough, but I've got this thing of my own going pretty well. I've spent a lot of time trying to get this thing off the ground, and it's off the ground now. If this had happened in 1984, then I'd have lived happily ever after as your piano player." That would have been great. Had they found me in '84, I would probably have been totally satis-fied being their piano player and just doing what everyone else did, which was have their own side projects. In 1990, I had four or five years of nice success in my own group, so I did that. I told them they needed to look for somebody permanent.

I think my twenty months with them served as a bridge between Brent's death and the time that Vince got comfortable. Vince came in not really being aware of the music. He didn't know very many of the songs; I knew a lot of them. I knew about forty to fifty Grateful Dead songs, and that meant that I didn't know about a hundred and forty. It was a steep learning curve for me, too, but I had a pretty good head start. I wasn't fearful at all about it, because I had played with them;

I knew them personally. It didn't feel daunting to me, because of my background and my fairly solid knowledge of their music and their approach to their music. But also the fact that the guys seemed to be so interested in having me play with them. They just were really warm and welcoming.

Frankly, I thought that with two keyboard players, people would always wonder why there were so many times when I played with the Dead where I would sit there and not play, 'cause there were lots of times when I would do that. I felt that there was so much going on that anything I would add would make an already thick soup impenetrable. So I would sit there and wait for the dynamic level to subside a bit. Or play in an arrangemental fashion—wait for the chorus, lay out in the verse, things like that; things to add some focus to it. But mostly it was, "Man, there's a lot of people playing! Anything I do is gonna be wrong, completely unnecessary."

BOB BRALOVE: There was a big shift when Vinnie joined the band after Brent's death, because Vinnie was more of a piano player than a synthesist.

After Brent, Jerry asked me to lose the [Hammond B-3 organ] from the rig. I don't know why; he never really articulated it. He wanted to move somewhere else with it. It may have been an emotional connection with Brent. I think Vinnie would have preferred to play the B-3, and he did play a lot of piano sounds.

With Brent, I was pretty much organizing his access to the things that he liked and my enhancement of whatever sonic worlds I could introduce to him. But it was about his access to those worlds. Vince was so busy getting on top of the tunes that he gave me more freedom and leeway to orchestrate his sounds.

VINCE WELNICK: At first I was somewhat taken aback by having to take solos, because here I am just getting used to the scene and I'm pretty profoundly impressed by what band I'm playing with, and to have Jerry give me the nod and the encouragement to insert my deal into their scene was gratifying and scary at the same time. In the Tubes, there were two really loud guitars going on, and synthesizer, and if I was the keeper of the piano part, there were few times it would come down to a level where soloing would make a bit of difference. And Todd Rundgren was the keeper of the piano parts in his band. The Dead were saying, "Play anything you want," but Bruce being there made it even more complicated because now I had to think, "Okay, do anything you want but don't be a piano player."

One thing the band didn't realize is, [when I joined] I had no equipment. I learned every song in the book on a piano, so now all of a sudden I show up sitting on Brent's old gear and I haven't practiced on it more than five hours in those ten days [of rehearsal before the first tour], and then I'm out on the road with those guys, and I'm on Brent's stuff, but not a real organ, a fake organ, and playing the synthesizer stuff. And the big rule of thumb is "Don't think like a piano player," even though I learned every song on the piano at home. So that fucked me up more than helped me out, having Bruce there on a lot of the songs. Although at the time he was definitely the most authoritative player, if you were to hear me on the piano and hear him on the piano. Also, I never owned a grand piano in my life, up until '92, so I didn't really have the hands to play a big nine-footer and beat the shit out of it.

There were certain songs where Bruce would let me take it, because he didn't know it as well or I had the piano part down. When it finally got to where it was just me [in mid-1992], it became easier because I played piano at least half the time after that.

BRUCE HORNSBY: When I first started playing with the Dead, I got the feeling that there were some people in the crowd going, "What is this fucking Top Forty guy up here doing playing with these guys?" They would send me DeadBase ["The Complete Guide to Grateful Dead Set Lists"], and they'd have people reviewing the concerts. I remember some guy in particular saying—it was a nice article, actually—"I learned a lesson in prejudice today, concerning Bruce Hornsby." Because I'd had a bunch of hits, this guy thought that I was going to inflict some dreaded Top Forty disease on the Dead. But he realized that that was bullshit.

CAMERON SEARS: The European tour [October 13–November 1, 1990] was an attempt to break out of the regular touring mode for a bit, break the cycle of what was going on in the States, and try to find some other markets we might be able to develop, and that was successful to a point. When you take tour support from a record company, you're just borrowing from yourself, so unless you really need it, you probably don't want to do it, because they're recouping it out of your royalty stream.

BILL BELMONT: Arista didn't provide any money. The tour was done in spite of Arista. They wanted a record; they got a record [the live album *Without a Net*]. They got a tour that was tailored around the record—the artwork and everything. But it was seventy-five band people on the road including the road crew plus production folks.

DENNIS McNALLY: The Europe tour was a total triumph, except for Sweden; except for the first show [October 13]. Even then, it's amazing what people will swallow if they don't know what they're supposed to be getting. I had any number of Swedish friends telling me it was a wonderful show.

VINCE WELNICK: Stockholm was sincerely bad. They thawed out some old Bill Graham pot cookies and gave Jerry a whole one and I remember between that and jet lag and being over there, he had to sit down; he could barely stand up for the first set. There wasn't any one person who could save the night. It sounded fuckin' horrible to me, and then at the end of the night I felt like, "God, bands break up over less shit than this," but Ram Rod said, "That's what jet lag sounds like," and not a single one of them had any regrets about it or any kind of judgment about it one way or another. Just another gig. You win some and lose some.

DENNIS McNALLY: I heard it was a chunk of hash. Jerry was a zombie. Vince came off the stage at "Drums" almost in tears, convinced that he was causing all of this. And I just said, "No, Vince, there are times when the Grateful Dead play really, really badly, and tonight's the night. Don't blame yourself. Relax."

BILL BELMONT: I've heard stories that Jerry was using [on the tour], but I took him to bookstores, we went to a museum together and did a bunch of stuff, and he just seemed like Jerry. So if it was happening, it wasn't really visible to me. He was really sick at Wembley [at the end of the tour], but that was an illness.

VINCE WELNICK: I was unaware of any drug use [by Jerry]. When I got into the band, nobody came out and said it, but I was under the impression that the whole band was clean, and they knew I was clean, too—I don't count herb as being a drug. Part of the reason I got hired is I'd been clean since I was playing with Todd.

I assumed no one was on drugs. I just thought Jerry was fragile, healthwise. He could really hold up his end when he was up on stage, and he also could really run through a lobby faster than anybody. I'd heard stories that he'd gone through health problems and the heroin thing, and I thought it was pretty much behind everybody, especially after having Brent die the way he did. I'm sure the last thing they wanted was another drug scene to go down.

The Europe tour, to me, was very unremarkable. But it was fun. We had a really good time. That's when I was meeting all the Grateful Dead's friends and the followers and going up to the Bobby suite and having pizza. Bobby always had a suite which was like the designated party room if you were up after the gig and you had nowhere to go or nothing to do. You were always welcome at Bobby's. He'd usually be at the bar [in the hotel] until closing time, and if there were people down there he'd been talking to, he'd invite the whole bar up to his room. So there'd be lots of folks there and we'd order up room service and make unusual demands of the staff in the middle of the night. Jerry wasn't a big drinker, so he didn't attend any of these things; you'd never see him over at Bobby's room.

I remember in Germany, I ran this guy down in a phone booth—he had a "The Pope Smokes Dope" t-shirt—and I said, "I want what the Pope's on." Nobody brought any drugs over with them, so you had to cop there. So I got some hash and I invited everyone over to the room because I figured anyone who wanted to smoke hadn't had any for some time. So I mostly wound up with the crew, and we ended up emptying each other's minibars and telling stories.

ROB KORITZ (Drummer, Dark Star Orchestra): In Berlin, they played "Let it Grow" near the end of the first set. It went on and on and on, and everybody in the band got quieter but kept playing, and Hornsby took off on that theme and extrapolated it, varying that theme. Before you knew it, almost nobody else in the band was playing. Bobby actually sat down on the drum riser and put his chin in his hand and was just staring at Hornsby, mesmerized by what was going on. That was a kind of a light bulb moment for me: it was just cool to see guys getting turned on by what someone else in their group was playing.

BILL BELMONT: Individually they all had a great time; collectively they complained that it lost money. But I can tell you places where they threw more money out the window than the tour cost them. And they spent the money. One band member insisted on the Maharajah Suite at a certain hotel; and this other guy insisted on this and this guy insisted on that. But that was fine—they hadn't been to Europe in years.

DENNIS McNALLY: We brought everybody to Europe—wives, family, you name it. And everybody was renting Porsches so they could do 180 on the Autobahn, and just laying it on thick, and we ended up losing a smidgen by their standards. I think it was $100,000. It was a promo tour.

VINCE WELNICK: It was all expenses paid, bring your family, your money's no good, it's all on the house. I'd never seen anything like it in my entire life. They came back and they had spent every dime they earned and $175,000 of their own. I thought to myself, "Well, this is far out—I just got in the band, and on our first tour we lost money!" But it was meant to be that way. They wanted to go to Europe, so it wasn't about money for them.

CAMERON SEARS: It was a luxurious tour in some respects, even though we were traveling by bus. We had been traveling on private planes [in the U.S.] and when we got there we were on buses, because that's the more efficient way to travel in Europe. They stayed in great hotels and everybody had a pretty good time at it. They were playing six- to twelve-thousand-seat venues across the board.

I think if we had kept at it, we could've grown that business a little bit. But at that point, they weren't feeling particularly entrepreneurial or adventurous. It was like, "We can do a tour in Europe where we can break even or make a little, or we can do a tour for three weeks in the States and make a lot. What do you think we want to do, Cameron?" But in terms of building an audience, you can't go to Europe one year and then not go back for five. You have to chip away at it, and I think if anybody had a chance to break those markets open, it would've been the Grateful Dead.

BRUCE HORNSBY: For a while, there was a new spark. They were interested in doing new things—like, you may remember that sometimes at the end of ["Drums"] there would be these little [trios] that happened. "Let's go out and play Phil and Bruce and Bob . . . Vince and Jerry and Billy"; whatever they decided. It was different from what was going on, but it didn't last very long at all. It lasted for a little while. Europe had a little bit of that spark, but it seemed like the [six] nights [at Madison Square Garden in New York, preceding the European tour]—this is just my sense of it from where I sat on the piano bench—had all that vibrancy and sense of adventure; in Europe it was waning a little bit, but it still existed. For instance, Garcia said, "Hey, why don't you go out and play some variations on a theme of 'Dark Star'?" "Sure, okay, fine." I did that. That's what became, I think, "Silver Apples of the Moon" [on the 1991 live "Drums and Space" album *Infrared Roses*, produced by Bob Bralove]. It's just me playing at Wembley Arena, by myself. I think they gave a writing credit to Vince, and that's fine, I don't care, but it was just me playing with a MIDI hooked up to my piano.

So that was still happening, but then gradually it receded and became more straight. I don't know why. These guys have been playing for a long time. Maybe they just didn't have the energy to try new things. Through my tenure with them, I would always say, "Why don't we start the night with 'Drums and Space?'" "Why don't we start the night with just two of y'all goin' out there and playing some old folk tune?" The Deadheads, I think, would have loved anything that was different. They were the most forgiving audience in all of music, to me, and they were so ready to receive. I think they were fine with everything being sort of codified, the same most nights, but I think they would have loved all this. I would mention this [to the band] and they'd say, "Hey, sounds great," but it would never happen. I didn't feel it was my place to push that, so I would throw out these ideas, and let them inevitably sink.

JEFF MATTSON: I really hated the fact that "Drums" and "Space" were always in the same place [in the second set]. Instead of the old days—when we got into "Space" it was because the music took you there. Now, it's prescribed; whether it makes musical sense or not at that time, "We will now play 'out.'" I'm still glad they did do that, because nothing gave me more glee than to be in a stadium of 80,000 people and watch them play just completely dissonant music for twenty minutes.

I remember seeing a Giants Stadium show [June 17, 1991] where they opened the first set with "Eyes of the World," and it was like, "Oh, okay! This is Bruce's influence. He's kickin' their ass to get them out of their routines." But then "Eyes of the World" went into "Walkin' Blues," or something, and it was like, "Okay, enough with that!" But he just kept fucking with them, going into "Dark Star" in between every song.

LEN DELL'AMICO: In the spring of 1991 I got a call from ABC. Phil DeGuere [who most recently worked with the Dead on the revived *Twilight Zone* TV series in the mid-1980s] had an *In Concert* [TV] show at eleven o'clock Friday nights for two hours, and he wanted to put the Grateful Dead on. It was a handsome venue, as they say, for video product. It was going to come from a couple of shows at Giants Stadium [June 16–17, 1991]. He put me in touch with ABC: "This is what we want to do. This is how much you're going to be paid." It was a lot of money for work we were already going to do [because the Dead always shot multi-camera video of their stadium shows in this era], so it was like found money.

By this time, Phil [Lesh] had taken over [responsibility of the video side of the Grateful Dead], so I call him up and tell him about it. As Jerry said, Phil's "high German," an intense guy, knows what he wants at all times, very strong opinions, sometimes gruff, but he's earned it. A no-nonsense guy, didn't suffer fools, unlike Bob and Jerry, who would suffer fools, quite frankly. He listens and he goes, "What does Jerry say?" I said, "You're the guy now, remember? I call you now." "Oh, yeah." And he said, "Fuck 'em!" "Really?!" "Yeah." Oh, okay, I guess he doesn't want to do the video.

So I called ABC and said, "The band considered your proposal very carefully and decided to pass at this time." Literally. But then quickly it came back. In 1988, we'd done this rainforest benefit at Madison Square Garden [a star-studded affair in which the Dead played with the likes of Mick Taylor, Suzanne Vega, and Hall and Oates]—that was a huge video product that has never come out. And since that, we'd done work with the Rainforest Action Network and Greenpeace, and someone came up with a plan that we could hook that up with ABC and benefit these groups. I thought it was a great idea, but I said, "Tell the band to tell me, because they already told me no." Somebody changed the band's mind, so we went ahead. I went into full production mode.

Then, the night of the first show, we had a run-in with the ABC censors. I'm at the show getting ready and someone comes in and says, "ABC wants to talk to you." So I get on the phone and the voice at the other end says, "You're in a lot of trouble. You can't say stuff about the destruction of the rainforest, because we have commercial breaks, and, well, you can't do that." Their position was we couldn't criticize American corporations without letting an American corporate representative give the other side. Imagine that. I said, "So you don't want our show? It's in *TV Guide*. It's on in three nights." And he was like, "Oh . . ." We already had their money. What were they going to do, run a movie instead and disappoint everybody? So they backed down. And it ended up being the largest audience that ever saw [parts of a Dead concert] at once—four million people. It started out with a helicopter shot looking down at the stadium, and talking about the rainforest.

JERRY GARCIA (1991): What we're doing is, by its very nature, non-formulaic. There's no way that you can make it happen by intention alone. It's something that you have to sort of allow   to happen, and you have to allow for it to happen. It's not something you can force into existence. And the kind of music we're doing is largely experimental; we don't know how it's going to turn out. We don't know what it's going to be like. We don't know anything about it, except that we recognize it when it's the way it ought to be, and we recognize it when it's not the way it ought to be. Apart from that, it's an intuitive walk. It's something you have to feel your way through. You can't say, "Well, the last time we played, I did this and this and this and this, and everything worked out." It doesn't work that way. You can't repeat things, because each time is different. The universe has changed. Everything has changed. And so each time you go out with this idea, you have to learn it all over again from the ground up because it's a new time, it's a new experience, and consequently, everything you know about it, you have to disallow. It's new. So some things may work, but they definitely won't work every time. Some things may work at various times.

BOB WEIR: Sometimes the magic works and sometimes it doesn't. Yet another of our family values—that you don't know when it's going to work.

JERRY GARCIA: Yeah, and you can't make it work. It's not a matter of will. You allow for the possibility that something miraculous could happen.

BOB WEIR: That's the whole faith in the process.

JERRY GARCIA: You need a certain amount of will there. Will alone is not enough to make it happen, but it's definitely a requirement. It needs to be there. Sometimes it takes innocence, sometimes it takes guile, sometimes you have to be clever. The audience participates in this process with us, so they know it the way we know it. They know that it's exploratory and you coax and you squirm and you wheedle and you fool around and do all this, and you try all these different things, and things start coming together, and you can feel it coming and stuff like that, and then the closer you get, you go, "Yeah, yeah, yeah!" Sometimes it never does quite focus down.

BOB WEIR: Sometimes it's a huge amble, where you're just on top, on the lid, and it's not going anywhere, and sometimes you walk on the stage and from the first note, the afterburner kicks in and you can't stop it.

JERRY GARCIA: Right. Either way, it's not about control. So then you can infer from that, that since it's not about control, then the whole way of doing things validates itself.

STEVEN MARCUS: Sharing the wealth was the Grateful Dead philosophy. I remember when Vince got hired. He was at a meeting, and he said, "I don't mean to be rude, but how much am I getting paid?" And they said, "You're getting a thousand dollars a day," and he said, "How many shows do we do a year?" Eighty. "So, eighty thousand." And they said, "No, a thousand a day: you get three hundred and sixty-five thousand a year, plus you get a bonus at the end of each tour, and a Christmas bonus. And you get paid exactly the same as everybody else in the band."

Garcia's attitude was there was more than enough money to share the wealth. So the road crew was the highest paid road crew. The managers didn't work a percentage; they got a salary. What other band had a manager that was not getting 10 percent or 15 percent? We were all employees, and when it came to Christmas bonuses, they were pretty equal. People did very well. I think in thirteen years [in the ticket office], I had a turnover of eight people who left. When you have a staff of thirty-five, that's not much. Two of them died, the rest were college students.

BOB WEIR (1991): We have all the dynamics of a family. If you took a bunch of people and adopted them and raised them, you'd have nothing different than what we have and what we are. We're not related through blood, but we're related through shared experience that has depth far beyond what most families have because we live a life that has a depth of experience that goes a lot deeper than most people ever get to. We've also been together much longer than most families stay together.

JERRY GARCIA (1991): We've had people born and people die, all the things that blood families have, and probably more intense in a way. Our family has the same thing that blood families have, in that you don't really choose who your family is. It's like you get them, and that's what you get.

I know that my relationship with the Grateful Dead family is way closer than anything I've got with any of my blood relatives, such as they are. I barely see them. In fact, my brother is a member of my family because he works in the Grateful Dead community more than the fact that he's my blood brother. He's part of that world. Otherwise, I'd never see him.

It's a family that works. I don't know how hard other people work at it, but we work at it. We do work at it.

LEN DELL'AMICO: Vince was a peculiar character in my very limited interactions. He didn't do the eye contact onstage I was used to [from Brent]. He tended to look down. He was on a little riser behind Jerry, so it's conceivable he could see Jerry without looking up. But he was in his own little world and he was put up there by [Bruce's] grand piano. I thought there might be a little bit of tension there. I thought it must have been a little hard for Vince. I didn't like the optics of it [directing the show video], and musically it seemed to me to be a difficult thing to try to do, and I sort of wondered why they let it develop like that. I think Jerry really liked Bruce personally and liked his playing—Bruce had a big range; he could play jazz and everything. He did killer eye contact with everybody, and Jerry loved that.

BRUCE HORNSBY (1993): Brent was a more retiring, shy cat. I'm not that way at all. When I show up on anybody's gig, I'm going to try to kick their ass. That's my nature—I'm a real jock at heart. Garcia always responded to that, and I think that's why he likes playing with me.

CAMERON SEARS: There were hints of insecurity [from Vince], but when you jump on a bus like that, that's moving at 180 miles an hour, who wouldn't feel that? And for the first two years he was probably hanging on for dear life. But they were very supportive of him as a person. It was a different band, obviously, and there were other dynamics in the band that influenced things.

Vince had the unenviable problem of being compared to Bruce, because they were two totally different types of players. Bruce was more like Keith, because he played the grand piano. [After Bruce left in 1992], Vince would hear, "I wish Bruce was still there," or, "It was great when you and Bruce were doing it together." But that wasn't going to last because Bruce had his own career, and also Bruce had his own frustrations with the band and the music and what was happening and how it was happening. Looking back on it, it looks crystal clear, but at the time it was a little murky.

MICKEY HART (1991): From where I sit, I think we have a better feeling in the band than we've ever had. Personally, the grooves feel real warm to me. They're solid and they're warm, and it just feels good. Everybody's having a good time. It seems happy. Personally, everyone is getting along very well, as we normally do, actually. We don't ever really get along poorly, but it's sometimes better or worse, and it's just one of those upswings.

Bruce and Vince—it's a fresh wave. It's fresh air and everybody has to be on their toes, because it's different than it was. So we're trying to reinvent ourselves again, and when you reinvent yourself, it's always exciting. So there's always a bit of excitement in the air, wondering if the new guys can make the changes or where are we gonna take them now, or where are they gonna take us now or how are we gonna get there together. All these things crop up 'cause we're intuitive. We know each other so well, the five of us, that Bruce and Vince are now plugging into the stream of consciousness, and it's becoming intuitive to them, as well. You just got to keep playing over and over together, and then it becomes easier and easier. So that's the process that's going down now. They're trying to entrain with the Grateful Dead and doing a wonderful job at it. There's a power on the left side of the stage that makes me feel good. So, that's how we're doing as far as I can see. I give the Grateful Dead—the doctor gives it a good report. Its heart is beating, there's life inside, there's still life left in the beast.

BRUCE HORNSBY: "Space" to me was a situation where sometimes it was really amazing, and lots of times it was not. It was a real hit-or-miss proposition. I think the Dead would say the same thing. Sometimes "Space" would get into some great things, other times I'd be sitting there, "I don't really see where this is going . . ." I'm all for the "Space" concept, but totally improvised music is a hard thing to make work. I know a lot of players in the jazz world who play freely, and a lot of them tell me, "More times than not we're up there scuffling to find something to play together." This was no different. If there's no structure, it makes it much harder for the music to be coherent and have meaning.

I'm all for playing freely, but I've been in too many instances where

I've thought that the level of listening was not up to the demands that are required for this sort of playing to really be meaningful. Sometimes I felt that there were real conversations going on between people, and other times I didn't.

VINCE WELNICK: I wanted to tour a whole lot more. They'd play for three weeks and be all cranky and want to go home, and I'm thinking, "Jesus Christ, I used to play two hundred nights a year with the Tubes, sometimes two shows a night. Look at these great crowds of people, and people can't get in, and they'd obviously love to see us play some more. Let's get it goin'!" But they were very strict about "We can't go beyond eighty gigs this year." They believed that if you went above and beyond this time frame, band members would start falling apart, relationships would be strained, wives would soon be wreaking havoc with their husbands.

On October 25, 1991, the music world was stunned to learn that Bill Graham had been killed in a helicopter crash while flying home to Marin County from a show at the Concord Pavilion featuring Huey Lewis and the News. Bill Graham Presents had been intimately involved with putting on hundreds of Grateful Dead shows from 1966 on, and had been especially active during the eighties and early nineties, always striving to make their productions somehow special, and also working with the Dead to try to control the problems that were cropping up outside so many of the venues they played.

BOB BARSOTTI: Before Bill died, I went to him and said, "Listen, I don't feel so comfortable being a front for this thing." At the beginning it was great, because we were doing something that was really cool. We were creating community, business, and a profitable and safe scene. A lot of people were having fun while we were revitalizing old buildings and going to places that didn't have much going on. I was proud of that. Eventually it became difficult to stand up in front of a city council and say, "These [Deadheads] are good people. Let them stay in your park for three days." It wasn't so easy to say that anymore because of the weird shit going on—the syringes and thefts.

I went to Bill and said, "I think I want out." There was a point in my career when I used to do all the shows. The Dead's business in the eighties got to the point where it was so big they needed one person to focus just on them. Bill asked me to do it. I said, "You've got to understand, if I do this, I'm shut off from the rest of the company that I've been part of for a long time. It means I'm shut off from the music. I'm doing this one band over and over, which is kind of limiting. I'm not so sure I want to do this." He said, "Look, I really need you. You are the person who knows how to do this. I'll take care of you." Then it gets to the point where I'm not having fun anymore.

The Dead had fired [Bob's brother] Peter. He was Bill's representative in their midst. It bugged them that he would have something to say about everything. I'm not sure that the production managers on the East Coast were the same. They had a hands-off thing with those guys, but we were energetically connected to the center, and working with them.

I told Bill I wasn't so proud of what was going on anymore and they should take a break to regroup and figure out what they were doing. This was just before Bill died. He said, "Look it's a huge thing for me to replace you. What are we going to do?"

I said, "Well, they just fired my brother, and I don't feel this thing is morally supportable. I always felt good about it before, Bill, but I don't feel good anymore." He could not disagree with me.

It seemed to me there was an awful lot of moving forward with blinders on, and having this one thing dangling in front of them: the top-grossing band in America every year. That led them down this path. They didn't want to examine things carefully. I kept saying to Bill that we should do something about it. He said, "What can we do?" I said, "Why don't you find someone else? I'll help you find someone you can hand this off to." Months later, he died. The whole company asked me, "So you can keep the Dead now, right?" I said, "Of course." I was stuck there and was the one doing it.

LEN DELL'AMICO: Nineteen eighty-six to 1990 was our second chance. We got a four-year spurt there, and after that Brent died and then a year later Bill [Graham] died, and I don't think Jerry could shoulder it. It was staggering. It was like a fighter getting hit.

JERRY GARCIA: [In a press conference two days after Graham's death, the night of the first of four Grateful Dead shows in Oakland]: I couldn't believe it. I thought about Bill as indestructible, if I ever thought about it at all. It never occurred to me, really. I expected Bill to get old with the rest of us. It was a huge shock and I'm not over it yet. I don't know if I ever will be.

The thing about Bill is, his relationship with us was, on a lot of levels, like our relationship to each other. It was intimate. There's a certain level of friendship that you have when there's somebody who understands you, and Bill was there from day one just about. . . . We miss the personal thing—the guy who understands us. That's what hurts.

[He] was the guy who was respectable enough to talk to the rest of the world while we were out on the fringe. Bill could talk to the community and the mayor and stuff like that, and we never did pick that stuff up, so now we're going to have to start learning how to do that kind of stuff.

MICKEY HART: We'll maintain and go on. You know, they say you're not dead when people can still remember your deeds and what you've done. And as far as we're concerned he isn't dead, because he'll live on in all of us and in the things that he's done and the people he's helped.

JERRY GARCIA: He's a large part of us. And on a lot of different levels. We're carrying along some piece of him into the world and the future as we go along.

> The Dead headlined a free memorial concert at the Polo Fields in Golden Gate Park on November 3, 1991. Other acts included Jackson Browne; Santana; John Fogerty (backed by the Dead);

Journey; Crosby, Stills, Nash, and Young; and more.

BOB BARSOTTI: We always tried to get the Dead to play Golden Gate Park. Sometime in the eighties, Bill approached the Dead and said, "I want to come to one of your meetings." He gave a heartfelt plea for playing for free in Golden Gate Park once again. They said, "Bill, you're crazy. We'll never be able to get the permits." He said, "If I can get the permits, will you let me do this?" They said, "Sure, we'll do it." We asked the mayor how to get permits without having a public hearing. We went around and around and couldn't get him to do it. We said, "If you have public hearings it won't be possible. If you don't have public hearings it will be a fun, legendary San Francisco thing. It'll be good for tourism."

CAMERON SEARS: We talked about it, but it was complicated. "We can't play out on a flatbed truck anymore!" And once you decide you need a stage, that takes a few days to build, and how do you keep that secret if you're trying to be discreet about it?

BOB BARSOTTI: The city couldn't deal with it. If you announced it too far in advance, there would be too many people there. We felt we could pull this off. We got turned down; it was the one gig we could never do until Bill died. I called Cameron and said, "Now will you play Golden Gate Park for free? We're doing it next Sunday." He called me back a half hour later and said, "Yup, we're on." Bill got his wish, but he wasn't there to see it.

Bruce Hornsby continued to play with the Dead through the spring of 1992 as his solo touring schedule allowed. His final show with the band (except for scattered guest appearances) was at the Palace in Auburn Hills, Michigan, March 23, 1992.

BOB WEIR (1992): We're in the post-Brent era, I guess. Things are starting to step solidly forward for me. There was a "directionless-ness" that I think we experienced for a while, while we were regroup-ing and coming up with a new identity for the band. I think that period of the new era is over. I think now the band has something of a new identity, and now the challenge is what to do with it. Part of finding our new identity is learning to live with that situation; to live with the two faces—with Bruce and without Bruce. Therein we've had to look for our own strengths, and having found some of them, we've also looked at everything we do as a little newer and a little fresher. That's good for us.

Bruce is spectacularly colorful, and real playful. And Vince is finally becoming real solid. He's starting to become a real fixture. His influ-ence on the music is subtler right now, but as pervasive as Bruce's. Vince is a little more integrated into what we're doing now than I see Bruce becoming. Bruce more or less imposes his personality on the band—which is not a bad thing at all. Vince has been endeavoring to become one of us, whereas Bruce is just playing with us. But also, in learning to play with the two of them, we've opened up to the point where we can play with other players now. It's taught us to be a little more responsive to sit-in guests.

BRUCE HORNSBY: In the end, I said it was time for Vince to be the guy, time for me to go. They understood; they said "fine."

BOB WEIR: Maybe [singing] is the last aspect of Vince's integration that we need to polish. His playing is starting to fit real well, to my way of thinking. His singing—he can cover the same parts as Brent. Every now and again we start hinting at the new blend with Vince. But it took a long time to establish a blend with Brent, too. I guess the voice is the most personal instrument, and when you get in to trio singing or quartet singing, then us actually singing well is the cherry on the sundae for this group. It needs to be hammered and polished more, but it'll come in time. We just need to sing together a lot more and learn each other's moves, and not just do it in rehearsal, but live, because that's what counts. We sing together live and it just doesn't feel to me to be quite knit like it should be yet.

MICKEY HART (1993): The band is getting better and it's becoming a new band. Another skin is being shed. Vinnie is adding his piece to it. Remember, it always goes from chaos to order, then back to chaos, and so forth. This is the duality of the band.

> In the summer of 1992, Garcia's health issues once again came to the fore. Shortly after his fiftieth birthday (August 1), he had another systemic meltdown, though this time there was nothing so acute that he had to be hospitalized. Instead, over the next several months, he remained mostly at his house, and various physicians, holistic healers, and physical therapists came by to get him back into shape. The fall '92 Grateful Dead tour was canceled, and the band didn't play again until that December, when a leaner and happier Garcia made his second triumphant return from the brink. There were rampant rumors that the Dead's touring schedule would be curtailed, and Garcia even fueled those rumors in a couple of interviews, but in the end the status quo prevailed, including the summer cycle of humongous stadium shows, which Garcia said he did not particularly enjoy.

JERRY GARCIA: [On the summer 1992 tour] I was getting to the place where I had a hard time playing a show. I was in terrible fucking shape. I mean, I was just exhausted. I could barely walk up a flight of stairs without panting and wheezing. I just let my physical self go as far as I possibly could.

LEN DELL'AMICO: I remember as early as the spring of 1991, Garcia was making noises about not playing stadiums at one of the meetings. Talking about the summer, he started out by saying, "Is it only me that doesn't ever want to play a stadium again?" It was one of those come-to-Jesus moments. *"Whaaat?"* They were like the highest grossing band of 1987 and they were still really huge. He's saying, "They sound like shit." But they decided to do it, of course, and he went along with it.

JOHN SCHER: Jerry never said anything to me about not playing stadiums. I think the band in general, and Jerry in particular, were always very conscious of giving the kids their money's worth. That's why they put huge opening acts on the bill with them—Bob Dylan; Tom Petty; Crosby, Stills, and Nash; Sting; Traffic; Steve Miller. Because they wanted to give kids more than their money's worth, and quite frankly, to make being in a stadium a better experience for everyone. They didn't like stadiums, and they were trying to hold ticket prices very low. If the average stadium show was thirty dollars, they wanted theirs to be twenty-five dollars because they knew that the experience musically of being in a stadium couldn't possibly be as rewarding to the audience as it was in an arena. And they knew it wasn't as rewarding in an arena as it was in a theater, but they'd long since abandoned any hope of being able to play theaters. So we added a strong second act, and did that every year. I think Jerry was content with going that way. And the truth is, the Grateful Dead played some great shows in stadiums in the nineties.

BOB BRALOVE: I was in constant awe of the fact that in a performance situation in front of 70,000 people the band would still go out there and play these quiet ballads and, even more remarkable, "Space." The band's attitude was, "We're going to go out there and not have anything planned. Nobody knows exactly where it's going to go and what it's going to be, and it can be abstract or concrete or obtuse." That kind of risk in front of that-sized crowd is phenomenal.

MICKEY HART (1993): I like stadiums, myself. I like to get the big groove going, and I like to see all the people enjoying themselves at one time. I know it's not a peak musical experience necessarily for me, but I've had great times in stadiums, just like I've had great times in the little theaters. It's a different kind of communication, it's a head space, and we're getting better at it. Moving large audiences is different than playing in small places.

I always thought that if the Grateful Dead lasted long enough, it would be a powerful force. I never thought that it wouldn't be, but seeing it is certainly gratifying. No one ever thought this far in advance and said, "Hey, man, some day the Grateful Dead will assume this position and will be visiting the White House." We never really thought about that, but it's not odd to me because it was always a special thing. If you can maintain and keep it special forever, then it just builds steam, like a snowball going downhill. If it don't crack up, it's enormous by the time it gets to the bottom of the hill. That's what we've got here—a snowball. Then history took over. And the books were written, and the records were made, and the mystique and the mythology has grown.

> The last burst of songwriting to come from the Hunter-Garcia partnership was three songs introduced in February 1993: "Lazy River Road," "Liberty," and most powerful of all, the ballad "Days Between."

VINCE WELNICK: Jerry went on a writing spree with Robert Hunter. They got together in Hawaii and wrote some songs, and they came back and they were pretty much done. He was excited because he'd written these songs and they were somewhat effortless in the way they were constructed. They didn't take a lot of time and they kind of came gushing forth.

The only one I thought I had much of a hand in shaping was "Days Between": the piano part. For the beginning he had a sort of broken fingering pattern and I started playing this piano thing. I really connected with that song the most of the later ones—that and "So Many Roads." I like those poignant tunes. I thought "Days Between" was very majestic. He was thinking out loud and he'd say, "We're going to come out just with the piano on the first verses, and then the band will come in," and then he'd change his mind and not want to build until later. It was one he didn't have as much a handle on as far as the feel of it goes. But I felt very definite about the feel of that song. It was one of those tender songs, reflecting on the past.

STEVE SILBERMAN: Towards the end, Garcia's weathered quality became part of the plot. A young man would not have been able to sing "Days Between" or "So Many Roads." I get the chills when I listen to "Days Between." There was this autumnal quality. The great thing about the Dead in those later years is, if you'd been with them your whole adult life, as many of us were, it attained the magnitude of a great novel or something—this long, wonderful American story, inexhaustibly rich, and one that included the possibility of revelation. We need a story like that.

PHIL LESH (1994): I enjoy playing a tune like "Days Between" because it's a song that really stretches your capability to play in time, because it's so slow. It makes the whole feeling of the presentation of it more legato, if you will; it's less chopped up. You can think in larger units, as it were. On the other hand, playing something like "Corrina," it's really nice to get into that pulse and work off the different subdivisions you can agree on. I think "Corrina" has gotten pretty interesting. It's been a long time coming, but the feeling, the groove, is starting to happen.

BOB BRALOVE: "Corrina" was one of the things that I had developed for a drum groove. We were performing it in the "Drums" section, and while we were performing it, Bobby came up to me and said, "Remember this." I came up to him after and I asked, "What was it that you wanted me to remember?" He said, "I want to use that for the intro to 'Corrina.'"

That musical groove was [played off a tape at] the beginning of the song. I faded it out on Bobby's cue to me. Sometimes Bobby wanted to take it somewhere else, so he could call it to leave at any point. Once we had the [intercom] system, they could communicate in my in-ear and tell me something. They could get whatever they wanted, y'know? They could order off the menu. It didn't have to just be "cut" or "go." He could have me kill that track at any point. If he felt like he wanted to take it faster that night, he could kill the track early. If he wanted to hang out and play with the track, and explore it in a more spacy thing, it would hang out longer. I had huge amounts of it, just to be on the safe side.

ROB EATON: When they went to in-ear monitors [in 1993, allowing for even more individualized mixes for each player], I'd sometimes go through their mixes [at the side-stage monitor console], and Vinnie was not in their mixes. I think Mickey was the only person who listened to Vinnie. That's part of the reason why everything was so disjointed in '93, '94, '95. Once they went to in-ears, they stopped playing as a band. They stopped listening to each other. Phil listened to Kreutzmann's kick drum, some vocals, a little bit of himself, a little bit of Jerry. Hardly anybody listened to Mickey. It was very bizarre. I'd go through these mixes and my jaw was on the floor. Mickey's mix was the best of anybody's, but it was eight decibels louder on his left side than the other 'cause he was deaf. Weir's mix was stereo—he had the vocals panned, but he was still not listening to Vinnie. Phil's and Kreutzmann's were pretty much mono. Garcia didn't listen to Vinnie, either.

DENNIS McNALLY: What Don Pearson [of the sound crew] told me about that was that nobody listened to anybody but themselves. That was what it really boiled down to.

[Basically] they were going on auto-pilot. The justifications for [using the in-ear monitors] were they'd be able to save their hearing, which didn't work. Mickey's severely hearing-impaired. Bobby is severely hearing-impaired.

> On the spring 1994 tour, there was a major offstage change to the Dead's sound. Dan Healy was dismissed from his position as front-of-house mixer and replaced by John Cutler, who had held that position for many years with the Jerry Garcia Band, and also had co-produced several albums and mixed the Dead's various radio and TV simulcasts for a long time.

BOB WEIR: The last couple of years before that, we had been working a lot more closely with Cutler, and we had more of a simpatico going with him. I don't want to talk out of school, but we were all having problems with Dan in the live situation, and at one point enough became enough. No one had issues with Cutler, so we said,

"Let's see what he can do out front." And that's what happened. I'm sure it wasn't that easy for Cutler—not technically, of course; that was no problem. But just the thing of replacing someone who'd done it so long.

PHIL LESH (1994): There was a new transparency to everything for me, partly because of the sound, and partly because four of the guys in the band [Phil, Mickey, Bill, and Bob] are now doing yoga. Billy and I agreed it made a big change in our perceptions.

It's a question of your perspective, of where you're coming from. It's hard to describe. But there were points where I had a very centered feeling, which is rare—usually I'm more scattered because I'm not just myself onstage; I'm also those five other guys, and I'm concentrating so hard on what everyone is doing. This was a new experience. I was able to balance that perception with a new feeling of centeredness. Whatever caused it, it allowed Billy and me, in particular, to lock in better.

Anyway, I think both the yoga and the new sound space had a real effect on the music this tour. On the very first night [in Chicago, March 16, 1994], the beginning of the second set, on "Scarlet Begonias" and "Fire on the Mountain," everyone was playing different stuff—placing their notes differently.

Lesh's enthusiasm notwithstanding, by mid-1994 there was tremendous concern within the band and among Deadheads about the obvious recurrence of Garcia's drug issues, manifested by an alarming listlessness and lack of focus onstage. But even more disturbing, perhaps, was that he was clearly having some sort of physical problems that were affecting his dexterity as a guitarist for the first time. Suddenly he was unable to execute certain lead lines that had never been a problem for him before. In 1993, he had revealed that he was dealing with carpal tunnel syndrome, but worsening hand issues in

1994–95 might well have been associated with his ongoing
battle with diabetes (which first appeared during the 1986
health crisis)—it's not uncommon for diabetics to lose feeling
in their extremities.

JERRY GARCIA (1993): There are problems associated with playing
an instrument over a long term. But there are also a couple of different schools of physical motion that are kind of a holistic philosophy
of movement. They train you about your physical relationship with
your instrument, mostly posture things. They're mostly aimed at
classical string players, because they're the ones that suffer from this
stuff where it matters most. If you're a symphony violin player, you
can't get away with sloppiness. If there's anything funny about your
fingers, you're fucked. There's something called Alexander Technique
that has to do with everything—stress, relaxation, and that sort of
stuff. It's designed to overcome those kinds of problems if you're a
musician.

There probably are [exercises to treat it], but I'm not aware of
them. I have things that my chiropractor has given me that are designed to open up the pathways, because you have sheaves of muscles
and your nerves are in between them. When you play a lot, your
muscles develop in that certain restricted way. They get flat and hard
and they squash the nerve, which changes the signal. That's the thing
of it slowly getting dead, where you slowly lose sensation.

VINCE WELNICK: Jerry talked about his drug thing very little, and
the only time he tried to explain it to me, he was trying to describe
his relationship with [heroin] and how he was what he called a "main-
tenance user." He said he didn't do it to get high. It was becoming
apparent in the mid-nineties—about halfway through my tenure—
when it was pretty much out of the closet and it was pretty obvious
that he was going to do what he was going to do. Better blatant than
latent, though he never did the shit in front of you. He didn't do it to
party, and he just did enough to make himself feel "normal."

He could be playing and nod out and then he'd wake up and find
himself still playing it. It's a sick fucking drug, but I wouldn't want to

play on that angle too much, because Jerry wasn't about that drug. That was incidental to what Jerry was.

And it was also obvious he had a lot of blood sugar and heart problems that could have affected his performance. He had nerve issues, the onset of diabetes.

BRUCE HORNSBY: [By 1994] it was a much larger, and way less discerning audience. If you're playing for 50,000 people, you just can't expect to have 50,000 knowledgeable, discerning fans. I would guess that 15,000 of that 50,000 were that, and that's a hell of a lot of people who are completely involved and interested and knowledgeable and intelligent about what's going on, and can tell when you're sucking or not, or can tell when this is a special moment. It's pretty amazing that they were able to have, every night, probably 15,000 people that were knowledgeable, but most of the people were not; some of them were just there for the party. That's fine, too, but [it meant] they could get away with a lot. That was alarming for me at that time.

I sat in with them a couple of times [in stadiums]. In '94, I remember playing with them at Giants Stadium, and it was just horrifically bad. They all knew it, the [band members] were all bummed and embarrassed. I'm looking out at the audience, I'm playing accordion, and I'm standing there in the midst of a sea of mediocrity on the bandstand. Everyone knew it—it wasn't just me—and you're looking out and seeing these people going completely crazy, and you're going, "This is surreal and strange." It was hard. It was tough for everybody, because no one seemed to be able to reach Garcia. That was tough.

CHAPTER 11
Summer Flies
and August Dies

CAMERON SEARS: Once the manifestation of Jerry's choices were becoming more and more apparent, it was forcing a conversation to happen that got a lot more attention. We did confront him. We did have a lot of meetings internally. People were genuinely concerned from a personal perspective for him and the music was not what people felt it should be, so there were a lot of things being discussed. But the X-factor in the whole thing was really Jerry's reaction to it and what he wanted to do. Because at the end of the day it was his life to live how he chose.

Initially, he was [dismissive]. Most people in that situation are. It's the rare person who says, "You're right. Thank you." It doesn't happen that way very often, in my experience.

There were other physical problems. I had taken him to doctors, so we were aware. I took him to a hand specialist in the city and they were doing some treatments with him, to some success. His heart condition was also apparent. His approach to that, of course, was, "I'll adjust my diet," and he attempted to do that to some extent.

He wasn't a fool. He knew he needed to do things, but it's very hard for anyone—no matter who it is—to stop what you're accustomed to doing because you have to. Nobody wants to be told they can't do something ever again. And he had multiple sets of things where he was being told that. "You need to lose forty pounds. You can't smoke. You can't eat this. You have to exercise." At a certain point you're kind of like: "Fuck this," which you can picture Jerry saying internally. But because he was an intelligent and thoughtful and considerate person, he did want to take those steps, but they're huge steps. Anybody who, in the best situation, has to lose twenty pounds, it's an enormous undertaking. We all wish we worked out more and ate better. It's not a simple thing. And in his case it was very complicated.

JAN SIMMONS: It was heartbreaking sometimes, watching Jerry being in such poor health that it was hard for him to walk up and down the stage stairs. And it was very painful to see somebody just loved that much, and respected that much, being in so much trouble. He had his good times and his bad times during the years I was with them. And it was not easy sometimes.

STEVE SILBERMAN: I went on tour in the fall of '94 and I said to myself at the end of the tour, "Something is wrong, because I just saw fifteen shows or whatever and I can only think of three or four really transcendent moments." Whereas in the past, up through '91, if I saw three shows, I'd be able to think of two purely transcendent moments in one set that [were] incredible, that defined what their new shape was going to be.

I would talk to kids who were fully as much of a Deadhead as I ever hoped to be, and they would tell me that fall tour '94 was the high point of their life. Am I to say: "But dude, if you were around in '72 you'd change your tune"? Where's that at? There's so much beauty there, that even if you got on the bus in '94 there was enough.

I think every Deadhead relates very positively to the way the band sounded when they first got on tour. It's like the geese bonding with the first object they see. People were still getting off, and having the experience, and being psychedelic, and the collective process was undiminished even if the music was not what it had been.

ROB KORITZ (Musician): The musical quality declined over time, and I think part of that was having two drummers. There were a lot of other factors. I hate to say it, but we can't deny what drug use did. Not just drug use, but alcohol as well, because I know some drinking also took place.

I remember one time when I was talking with Billy. He was talking about the nineties in particular, when Jerry was out on the smack again. He said, "Most of that stuff was terrible, but no matter what, even if Jerry was out of his mind, every night there was at least one song—or sometimes it was just three minutes—when the magic would happen. And even when it was bad in the nineties, those three minutes of magic every night were worth it for me to stay there."

PHIL LESH: [Dylan's] "Visions of Jonhanna" is such a great song, and [Jerry] had such an identity with it. It's a mystery to me why we didn't start playing it earlier. Even without the teleprompter, he could usually remember most of it. And his guitar playing is just so moving. I just love the song, and I love his rendition of it. It's him. It's really him. "The ghost of electricity howls in the bones of her face." Whew, yeah.

> In 1994 there was a very tentative attempt to make a
> studio record.

BOB BRALOVE: Jerry was not in good form, but the band was play-ing really great, so they were putting down some really good tracks. Things were sounding pretty good, but nothing really gelled, so there weren't any finished performances with vocals. The energy around it was kind of confusing, because there was this really positive energy coming from the band, but it was missing a key ingredient. He'd come late; he might be pissed off.

DENNIS McNALLY: In 1994 we played a gig at this airstrip in High-gate, Vermont [Franklin County Field, July 13, 1994]. It was almost a guerrilla thing. We went in, it was comfortable, we got out. The venue had been pristine, because nobody knew about it. This time [June 15, 1995, with Bob Dylan opening] every piece of land in the immediate vicinity of the venue was rented out—you can't tell a bunch of Yankee farmers that they can't make a buck off the passing circus, so they didn't—and there were nitrous tanks and camping. So all of the people that had to stay moderately sober the previous year because they had to drive back to Burlington didn't have to stay sober.

There wasn't a riot there; there would have been if we hadn't opened the gates, but they made the rational decision that you're not going to ask security guards making five dollars an hour to de-fend that gate with their last breath. Thousands of people [without tickets] were massed in front of the gates. They were going to come through the gates no matter what. So they opened the gates and then 10,000 more people were inside than should have been.

So, right away, that's a bad sign [at the beginning of the tour].

Jerry was in alarming health. [Earlier] that year, Vince and Gloria [DiBiase, who were longtime assistants to Garcia] told me that his blood sugar reading, which is supposed to be in the mid to high 90s if you're healthy, was at 200. I actually do remember saying to people in January, "If we get to Boston this fall . . ." I knew. His physical health was crumbling.

So he's out of it in Albany [June 21–22, 1995], kids get hit by lightning at RFK [Stadium in Washington, D.C., June 24, 1995]—that's where the "tour of doom" thing started.

When we first got to Deer Creek [for shows on July 2–3, 1995—the venue is a lovely amphitheater in Noblesville, Indiana; the band had played every year since 1989], Kenny Viola [tour director of security] takes the band into a back room, then comes out and tells me what he did: he played them tapes of threatening phone calls that the venue had received against Jerry. Threatening to kill him—if I remember correctly, because Jerry had stolen his girlfriend, metaphorically, or literally, or otherwise. Look, we're talking about a disturbed person. And Jerry's going, "And?" So Ken asked if they wanted to play the show, and they said, "Of course we're going to play the show. Don't be ridiculous."

CAMERON SEARS: It was Jerry's choice to play. He was pissed. He was not happy about the whole situation.

DENNIS McNALLY: They ended up playing the show with the lights up. We also had brought in metal detectors that the audience came in through. And we had several Secret Service–trained audience spotters. That is to say, cops who were looking for anything wrong in the audience.

Nothing happened—except, of course, the 10,000 people who came over the back fence [in the middle of the first set]. And the band, for the first time ever, witnessed not only the people coming over the fence, but the people on the inside—people who they thought were their fans—kicking it out to make holes so people could come in through the fence. It was apocalyptic. I was in the pit along with the cops looking for shooters, and going, "Oh, shit!" These people they loved were acting like lunatics, like louts, which is why, throughout this period, during every tour we had, we did phone messages, taped messages, for the promoter or whatever saying, "If you don't have a ticket, don't come." Jerry would never do it because he thought it was being authoritarian, and he couldn't bring himself to do it. Phil and Bobby did, and Billy; I probably used them all.

CAMERON SEARS: Once the fences started coming down, I had to go out and see what was happening. Deer Creek had a big hill you had to climb and a big fence all the way around it, and once they started rushing the fence, security said, "You know what, we're out!" What could they do?

The most troubling aspect of it was the people inside cheering them on. It was a very twisted sense of entitlement. These were kids that really just didn't give a shit what anybody said to them. You could say, "I work with Jerry, and no, Jerry doesn't want you to tear down the fence," and they'd say, "Fuck you!" They were anarchists, in a sense, and once people are in that place, there's no reasoning with them. You don't have a whole lot of alternatives in terms of how do you corral this. It's crazy. It's like an altered state. Some of them were these young skate punk hippie kids. A lot of them were Phish kids, too. They would go back and forth. Phish was having all the same problems as we were.

DENNIS McNALLY: It was also really creepy leaving that night. We have this insane scene; people start panicking. We had one bus there, the production bus, [but most of us] had come in vans. So we get another van to take the sound crew home. We put the women and children, whoever were their guests, in a van, and they left in the middle of the second set. [After the show] we put the band in the bus and leave. This is twenty minutes after the show, and you had to go through the parking lot a long way at Deer Creek. There's no back-door entrance or exit.

Then there were these people pounding on the side of the bus and there were people deliberately walking in front of the bus; it was basically a "fuck you." It was really freaky and disconcerting. Then going on these back roads, which are really narrow, with sharp turns, the bus got stuck in a ditch, which actually broke the tension. We got out, and looking at it, all of it was so horrific, it was like it had descended into farce. And everybody sort of relaxed, and this local farmer lent us a miniature tractor. They're trying to drag a bus out of a ditch, Ram Rod and [fellow roadie Billy] Grillo were digging at the tire, and trying to do this and that. Eventually a tow truck came and pulled us out and we went back to the hotel.

The next day, on the way in, Cameron says to me, "Draft a press release." The cops had said, "We'll direct traffic for you outside the venue, but we will not work inside. We're not going to risk our lives to defend your property."

So the band decided, "Well, we can't do a show without the police. That's it." So I wrote a very strong press release [from the band to the fans] saying: "If you guys quit on us in terms of ethics, don't forget we can quit on you," and Jerry signed it. He was truly shaken. It was appalling.

I did think, "You know, the Grateful Dead's karma about touring for thirty years was remarkably lucky." There were some famous moments where their [equipment] truck almost didn't get through. But I don't know how many, if any, shows the Grateful Dead ever had to cancel, but surely not many, and certainly not any because of the audience.

JAN SIMMONS: It was the tour from hell, as far as we were concerned. The relationship between the entourage and the Deadheads, as far as I could tell, it was pretty good up until that time. Ticket sales were 100 percent and I really, until that last tour, maybe the last two tours, I wasn't aware that there was that much bad activity going on.

CAMERON SEARS: I don't think anyone saw it coming to the extent that it manifested itself. We all were aware of the fragility of the situation. Every gig was kind of like a pressure cooker. But who would predict that someone would phone in a death threat to a show? Who would predict that at a campground a porch would collapse and people would get killed? Who could have predicted a lightning strike [at RFK Stadium]? We were all kind of looking at each other and saying, "Really? Is this all happening now?" It was a culmination of a lot of little things, and in each case it had nothing to do with us.

RICHARD LOREN: That last tour was the metaphor for the end. It really showed the collapse of the thing they tried to keep up for so long. The fact that [the Grateful Dead] weren't savvy enough to not play that last year they played—they didn't need the money and they could have served their fans another way. They could have created something, done a show somewhere, telecast it, whatever. They could have taken that collective spirit—that socio-musical spirit—and shared it with the rest of the world.

STEVEN MARCUS: When I started working for the Dead in '83, Jerry was not doing well. I asked Eileen, who was in charge of the Deadheads, "Do you go to the shows?" And she said, "Very rarely, and when I do, I stand where I can't see Jerry." And this was '83, '84. And then by '85, he was in really horrible shape. Eighty-six was horrible. And in '92, he collapsed again. People didn't realize how bad it really was.

When he was clean, he was so wonderful to be around. And he would be backstage in the hospitality area, where Joe Schmo could come in with a sticker [backstage pass], and he was open to everybody. When he started using again, he would go back.

By '95, he would actually go into his dressing room backstage, shut the door and lock it, and take a nap. I remember one show where Parish and Cameron and a bunch of other people were pounding on the door trying to wake him up. They couldn't find anybody with a key. Eventually, he did wake up.

I remember seeing him on the last tour at Three Rivers Stadium [in Pittsburgh, Pennsylvania], and he was pale, like a ghost, in horrible, horrible shape. He always walked around with his briefcase; it was practically handcuffed to him. He would just get out of the van, go to his dressing room, disappear, and then twenty minutes before the show would start, he would go up to his cubicle on stage and nobody would see him, you know? It was so hard and so sad. It was just impending doom.

ALLAN ARKUSH: I remember the last time I saw them play, and it's emblematic of my relationship with him. They were in Giants Stadium, and I came before the show; I rode out with Candace. Sitting backstage, with the sun, the people coming in, [Jerry] asked me what I was up to. I said, "I'm in New York, producing and directing this show for CBS called *Central Park*

ALLAN ARKUSH: You would say things to Garcia, like: "So, Jerry, you have a record in the Top Ten." And he goes, "It's not my fault." He'd crack you up. You knew what he meant. He said, "Whatever we do, we seem to be stumbling uphill." The conversations were like that.

West. It'll be on Tuesday nights at nine on CBS. It's a big glossy night-time soap. It's not your kind of thing, but really, I'm enjoying it."

"Good for you, man." We're looking out at Giants Stadium filling up, and I said, "It's funny. You're filling Giants Stadium here for two nights. I remember seeing you guys at the Cafe au Go Go in June of '67." He looks at me and he says: "It's amazing, isn't it?" And he says: "Hey! CBS at nine on Tuesday nights is playing Giants Stadium." It was that kind of deflection, you know.

We had another conversation like that, around the time Brent died. He was saying that Brent had no life other than the Dead. He had no things he looked up to, aspired to, beyond it. And once you had what you wanted, you didn't aspire anymore; you lost your direction.

In a way, that was kind of what happened to Jerry. He didn't take his own advice that way. He lost that spark—I mean he had it, but his life became a burden.

WAVY GRAVY: My last memories of Jerry are sitting with him backstage going through the sculpture books of Andy Goldsworthy, page by page. Jerry and I always used to communicate about good art. If ever I saw good art, I would always bounce it to Jerry, because he loved it.

STEVEN MARCUS: The last time I saw him was at the last Soldier Field show [July 9, 1995]. Jan [Simmons] put me and my then-partner in Jerry and Vince's van going back to the hotel. We were in the very back; Vince was shotgun, and Jerry and Deborah [Koons Garcia, his wife] were in the first row. There was somebody else in the second row. We stayed until the fireworks were over, and we had the police escort back to the hotel. Jerry looked horrible, but he was very excited about the show and couldn't stop talking about the fireworks. He loved the fireworks. There were heart-shaped fireworks, stuff like that. We had this police escort through Chicago and ended up at the Four Seasons. He got out, and there were a bunch of people asking for autographs; he signed a couple of autographs and disappeared with Deborah up in the elevator. That was the last time I saw him alive.

413

CAMERON SEARS: We knew Jerry was going into rehab [at the Betty Ford Clinic] after the tour, and we were thrilled that was happening. The fact that he was being proactive about it—we were all completely supportive of it. I was telling everybody, "We need to give him as much time as he needs. We have a tour booked, but that tour will wait. This is the first time something of this magnitude has happened with him. This is a very positive development." And everybody agreed. So we were very hopeful he would stay the course and do what he needed to do.

Then he left early [just a couple of weeks into the program]; that took my breath away. That was a horrible idea. I knew that he was now probably in the most dangerous place he could be in, which is to say, he comes out feeling much, much better, and then somebody taps on his shoulder and he goes back to his old thing. So I was very concerned. Everyone was. It was premature; we all knew that.

> Garcia left the Betty Ford Clinic prematurely and returned to the Bay Area, but shortly thereafter checked himself into the Serenity Knolls drug treatment center in Marin County. In the early morning hours of August 9, 1995, he suffered a fatal heart attack.

CAMERON SEARS: The last time I saw Jerry, Cassidy and I were out running an errand and he was in his car pulling out of the Wendy's drive-thru where he was getting, presumably, a chocolate shake, French fries, and a cheeseburger, as he was wont to do. He waved at us. This is the day he died. [Later] he drove out to Serenity Knolls. Again, that was a great concept in his mind of doing something. He recognized that he had dabbled and wanted to stop, but he didn't choose a place that was able to deal with the extent of his medical conditions. The reason Betty Ford was a good place is it was attached to a hospital.

He had been to a cardiac specialist in Marin [back in 1992] and was offered surgical options that he didn't want to consider. After the [1986] coma, he never wanted to go back to a hospital. I think that might have played a role in why he wanted to leave Betty Ford. I also think people were recognizing who he was [there] and that was uncomfortable for him. What appealed to him about Serenity Knolls was it was local, down home, and out in the woods—more his style, maybe. But he needed to be in a medically supervised place. Hindsight is twenty-twenty, but there are a lot of treatment programs that are attached to hospitals for just that reason. That's not to say they could have brought him back when he had the heart attack. You need to be hooked up to the machines. If you flatline, you need to be hooked up for anyone to notice. If you're asleep, as he was, and he also had sleep apnea. People with sleep apnea sometimes die.

When the phone rang at 4:30 or 5:00 in the morning, I was like, "C'mon, I just saw him yesterday." I didn't believe it. I got the call from John Scher, because it was already on the radio on the East Coast. Nobody out here had turned on their radio yet.

So then I was the guy who had to make the phone calls to convey that news to the band. It was awful.

STEVEN MARCUS: I got the call and immediately turned on the radio. I went into the office. There were already a bunch of flowers at the ticket office, but not at the main office. For some reason, they were bringing everything to the ticket office. TV crews were in front of the ticket office. I think Calico was already there, and there was a candle burning in the window. Eventually, Dennis [McNally] showed up. Everybody showed up at the main office, and Dennis read a statement.

I said to Cameron, "We need to stop filling orders." He said he thought we should keep going. I said, "Cameron, the tour is not going to happen. We are going to stop filling orders. This is ridiculous." I think he really was frazzled; he had already lost Brent, and now he had lost Jerry.

The next day, we were told to let go of most of the staff. And everybody—band members, crew members—everybody's salary was cut in half immediately. And then the next week, cut in half again. At the ticket office, I had held a slush fund because in '86 we had no money to pay our employees to send refunds and stuff; they came and did it anyway on a volunteer basis. So I always kept $150,000 in case of an emergency. I used it to handle the refunds, and shut down.

We put the house that we rented back exactly the way it had been. There was still $60,000 to $70,000 left, and we turned it over to Grateful Dead Productions. And that was it. It was horrible.

I have to say, I went into a depression for a good fifteen years.

PETER McQUAID (Former CEO, Grateful Dead Merchandising): I think there's an important legacy here. The Grateful Dead were amazingly determined, and kind of unwavering, in their commitment to their community and a way of life, which really did not change fundamentally in thirty years. They maintained that better than anyone ever did and probably more than anyone ever will. Even the groups today that are known for their independence and their commitment to social values—nobody comes close to what the Grateful Dead achieved in that regard; I don't think there's any comparison. You can talk about the amazing legacy of these 2,400 concerts and all that, and it's true—I don't think anyone will ever do that again in the same way. But it was more how they inspired so many people to adopt this lifestyle and the belief system. It was pretty remarkable. It's still fantastic. This commitment to community was never compromised.

CAMERON SEARS: I feel so fortunate to have experienced through them what I experienced. I hold all of them in very high regard. There are things that have occurred that don't always go down as sweet as you had hoped, but that's life. I still maintain that my perception of the ethos of what it represented is a set of ideals: Be kind, be fair, give more than you take, take care of the environment, be creative, follow a path that's true to yourself. Don't compromise on things you believe in, even though the odds may be stacked against you. Those are great life lessons I think the Dead fully embodied.

KEN KESEY: They weren't just playing what was on the music sheets; they were playing what was in the air. When the Dead are at their best, the vibrations that are stirred up by the audience is the music that they play. Consequently, when we'd go to L.A. you'd get one kind of thing, and when we'd go to Portland, Oregon, you'd get a completely other kind of music. That means that the band has to be supple enough to really read the notes written on the wall, and [to know] that they're changing all the time. I don't know of any other rock band that could have done it. It sort of started when we went to see the Beatles. They went up to see the Beatles with us in the bus. I saw power like I'd never seen it, never imagined it before. When one of the Beatles—when George—would turn his head you'd hear this screaming wave. What the Beatles were saying was, "Come closer, come closer. Love me do." And the people were pressing closer and closer. But they didn't know how to sing that moment, and the moment needed to say, "Don't come closer. Stay back, stay back."

[Deadheads are] looking for magic. When I did my writing class, I started the writing class by showing people [a magic trick]. The reason I like to do that is because there's a moment when you see something like that, there's a crack in your mind. You know it's a trick, but you can't figure it out. That crack lets in all the light; it opens up all the possibilities. When that little split-second thing happens when the Dead are playing and everybody in the audience goes, "Wow! Did you see that?" That's the moment. And kids will watch five hours of mediocre music to have that one click happen, because that puts them in touch with the invisible.

OWSLEY STANLEY: There has never been and never again will be a band like the Grateful Dead. Of all the strange and wonderful things I have done in my life, the years I worked with the Dead are the very pinnacle. After some consideration, I also believe those particular years constitute the real golden age of the band. We were a madcap bunch of very close friends out having an absolute ball together. When I returned from jail, I kept looking for that, but it had gone and was never to return. Not that the band did not grow ever more skilled and continue to expand their musical world. But a certain special spirit and larrikin sense of camaraderie had been lost. As if the Pranksters had forgotten to prank—or how much fun it was to do so. Kesey's Pranksters liked to remind us: "nothing lasts."

Courtenay Pollock, Tie-Dye Man

> Courtenay Pollock's Grateful Dead journey was a unique and magical happenstance. Beginning in 1970, he worked with the Dead for more than a decade; he created magnificent tie-dyed backdrops for shows at the Greek Theater in Berkeley three years running in the early eighties.

COURTENAY POLLOCK: I had a head shop in Greenwich Village, New York, on MacDougal Street, and then I opened a boutique on Bleecker Street. Some guy came in selling some tie-dye scarves which were just random colors swirled together. I loved the look of them—it reminded me of something from my childhood, and the bright swirling colors that I used to paint in my art compositions. I decided that I was going to try my hand at it.

Around the same time, this beautiful exotic woman came into my boutique wearing a bed sheet. It was a tie-dye, a sunburst; she had put a hole in the center and pulled it over her head, and it was very fetching. I started figuring out how a sunburst was made, musing on a method to achieve that. At some point later, I had occasion to be in upstate New York. I got to sample some dyes and got some cloth together, and put into practice this method that I theorized, and it worked like a charm. And I had seen no other people's methods, or read any books on tie-dyeing, or had no idea how other people created this. It's not like I had to think outside of the box, because I was never in any box.

From the get-go, it was geometric, psychedelic designs, and I realized I had come up with something extraordinary and that it was just a gift from the cosmos. I had long since understood that my mission in life was to bring joy and light. I just wanted to turn on the world.

At the end of the summer of 1970, our lease was up [on our commune in Vermont]. I threw the I Ching. In the first paragraph, it said "Fortune in the West." So I got on a Greyhound bus headed west.

When I ended up in San Francisco, I went to this little hole in the wall off Haight called the Switchboard. I'm saying, "I'm looking for a place to rent—rolling green hills," kind of like the place I had left in Vermont, which was a five-hundred-acre farm on the river.

The guy says, "You want to live in Marin County where all the rich rock 'n' rollers live."

I said, "Yeah, that sounds perfect." Mr. Naïve.

He said, "Well, that ain't going to happen."

And then this fellow says, "Somebody is calling from Marin County; wants to share his house." They gave me the phone, and this guy says, "I'll meet you at the Greyhound station in San Rafael at five o'clock, and we'll go out to the place."

Five after five, this blue Volkswagen pulls up and a guy in a polyester suit and glasses gets out. He looks so painfully straight. I'm in patched jeans, tie-dyes, long hair, and a little wispy beard.

He started driving out to west Marin. He explained that he wasn't happy with the straight world, and he was listing on the Switchboard in order to meet someone from the counterculture.

We drive to Nicasio Valley, and there on one side of the road are rolling green hills, and on the other side are old-growth redwoods. We pull into this driveway and through these beautiful stately trees to this little cottage built around two giant redwood trees. They grew right through the house. It was a 150-acre private estate that he had lucked into. His friend was running the ranch across the street, which was also part of the estate, and had tipped him off about the cottage. It was two bedrooms, all the mod cons, stone fireplace, lovely little patio, under this wonderful stand of great old-growth redwood trees.

He said, "The rent is eighty dollars a month."

"No way I've got eighty dollars."

He said, "No, no—your half is forty dollars. The owners got a good break in their younger years and had good fortune, and they want to pass that good fortune on to younger people." It was just an idyllic situation.

I got up in the morning, put a bag of tie-dyes on my back, and walked down Nicasio Valley Road looking for a freak ranch. I was looking up the driveways, and about a mile down the road I looked up this driveway and I got the feeling that yeah, there's definitely freaks living here.

I go bang on this farmhouse door and this beautiful little elfin gal with a ring in her nose opens the door. "Hello, I'm new into the neighborhood; would you like to see some of my tie-dye work?"

"Sure, come on in. I'll get some coffee going." She comes out with the coffee, and I've got tie-dye pieces hanging around the living area, and she goes, "Oh, these are absolutely beautiful. The guys will love these. They should be back up the road any minute. And here they are now!" These trucks pull in and these rowdies tumble out and rumble through the house; they stop in the middle of the room and look around, and they go, "Far out, man. You can do our speaker fronts." And another says, "Yeah, I'll make it happen tomorrow morning."

"Who are you guys?"

They said, "We work for the Grateful Dead." This was [crew members] Rex Jackson, Sonny Heard, and Joe Winslow.

It was Rex who put the wheels in motion, and Frankie—who was Weir's partner at the time—was the little elfin lady with the ring in her nose. She said, "Weir should be back in a day or two, and we'll make it official."

The next day, I'm walking up from my house up towards the

Rucka Rucka Stud Ranch, which is what they called their little ranch because they had horses in the field. Of course, the name was really based around *them* as the stallions, rather than the horses. This car pulls over and someone says, "You want a ride?"

I say, "Yeah, sure."

He says, "Where are you headed?"

"I'm going down to meet up with some friends. It's only a mile down the road at the Rucka Rucka."

He said, "Oh, that's my place."

I said, "You must be Bob Weir." We got down to the ranch and he looked at some of my work, and he said, "Oh, yeah, these are great. I'll make sure it's all in motion for you. You can come down and start measuring cabinets and getting the contract together. What are you doing for work right now?"

I said, "I'm just looking for opportunities," and he said, "Well, until we get your commission going, if you want to just do some stuff around the ranch, you're welcome to stay here."

I already had a place, but I did help out—stacking wood, feeding the horses, whatever. I started meeting the rest of the fellows, and probably three days later I was down on Front Street measuring cabinets for a gig that was coming up in a couple weeks.

The Deaducation of Gary Lambert

New York-born Gary Lambert was the driving creative force behind the *Grateful Dead Almanac* beginning in the nineties, and is the cohost (with David Gans) of *Tales from the Golden Road,* a weekly call-in show on SiriusXM Radio's Grateful Dead channel.

GARY LAMBERT: [In 1966], the Dead weren't really on my radar. I think the name, probably, was off-putting, and one of the first images of them I ever saw was that incredibly weird Bob Seidemann picture [sold as a poster in head shops in 1966–67] of them in Daly City looking like an alien biker gang. I was this Beatlemaniac—"All You Need Is Love"—and my favorite American band was the Lovin' Spoonful. I was into that very happy kind of hippie rock 'n' roll thing. I had nothing bad to say about the Dead's music, because I wasn't familiar with it, but I thought, "These guys seem really odd!"

I literally stumbled upon them in Central Park [in New York] on May 5, 1968. My brother, who had seen the Jefferson Airplane the night before at the Fillmore East, called me on Sunday morning and said, "Hey, you should get into the city—the Jefferson Airplane is playing a free concert at the band shell."

I just knew that I was getting up and going to see the Airplane in Central Park. I get to Central Park and catch the last few tunes of the set by the Paul Butterfield Blues Band and the Airplane set. I get up to leave, and Marty Balin says, "Stick around, the Grateful Dead are coming up next." And I decided to stick around.

The Dead were terrific. They were the best band of the three that day, but it wasn't like I resolved to follow them to the ends of the earth.

Seeing the two drummers was a revelation. There may have been other bands doing [it], but not the way the Dead played the polyrhythmic stuff. They played some of the material that would turn up on *Anthem of the Sun:* "The Other One," "New Potato Caboose," though I didn't know those songs by name. I recognized "Morning Dew" from the first album. They finished with "Turn On Your Love Light," which I loved. It just struck me as amazingly creative, unlike most of the rock music I was hearing in that period. The collective aspect of the playing appealed to me—the fact that there was so much simultaneity of creation going on.

I understood it, because I was a jazz fan and I was into some pretty weird music already. I've always thought that the thing that best prepared me for the Grateful Dead was that through sheer coincidence and wonderful timing, I got turned on to the Beatles and Charles Ives at about the same time. Ives totally appealed to me. I don't know what it was about my upbringing that made that so easy for me to love, but I did.

I was also way into jug band music—the jug revivalists, especially the Jim Kweskin Jug Band. I think the Lovin' Spoonful were my favorite American rock band for a while because they brought jug band into the pop realm.

So everything the Grateful Dead were playing seemed somehow connected to music that I already loved. That made them very attractive to me right away.

I didn't hear them again until early 1969. They were opening for Janis Joplin and her new band at the Fillmore East [February 11–12, 1969], so they were restricted to playing exactly an hour. I just marveled at how they compressed so much into that hour. It had all the elements of what I would come to love about Grateful Dead music, but played with incredible concision and focus. It was like condensed cream of Grateful Dead soup. Notably, given the force of nature that she was, the Dead kind of blew Janis off the stage, 'cause she didn't really have that new band roadworthy yet. And she said that herself.

It was a few months later, in the summer of 1969, that I really had my Road-to-Damascus moment with them, where I could not imagine the idea of not going to see them if they were playing anywhere near me. I went to the shows at the Fillmore East in June and the New York State Pavilion shows the next month. This repeated exposure to the Dead revealed more and more about them, the depth and variety of the music, and you would learn how each show was different from the one that preceded it and the one that followed it, and the more I saw that the more knocked out I was.

Once I got to see them a few times, I realized that there was great joy in the music and there also was wit in the music. One thing that I immediately admired about them was they had no compunction about dragging you—in the middle of your happy hippie reverie—to the edge of the abyss and making you stare into it. You'd be in the middle of these cartoony songs like "Dupree's Diamond Blues" or "Doin' That Rag," harking back to the jug band feel, but then suddenly they're playing "Death Don't Have No Mercy" and "Morning Dew," which in Bonnie Dobson's original telling is a very touching, very pretty kind of English madrigal. The Dead really brought out much more of the depth of sorrow in that song, with that line "I guess it doesn't matter anyway"—that terrible feeling of resignation. The more I got to hear them play, the more I was impressed with how they could balance seriousness with sheer goofiness, as well as the joy and exhilaration they could create.

What I immediately found attractive about the music, and what has continued to keep me somewhat at odds with the more Garcia-centric of the Deadheads, was the sense of music being made collectively. They made music that was conversational, rather than a soloist being supported by sidemen. There was some improvisation going on in rock that I found less than satisfying because there was a "Yo, check this out!" aspect; an exhibitionism to it that the Dead generally didn't succumb to. Anyone at any time could be leading the music in a satisfying direction. Garcia was certainly the primary soloist in the band, but even his solos were more about serving the context than they were about calling attention to the awesome guitar playing. I was very keyed in to those soloists in jazz, like Lester Young, who said, "Just tell me a story" to his sidemen. And the Dead were always about telling the story. Even when the music was extremely abstract—when there was no discernible story to be told—they managed to present this kind of narrative, this conversational context, that was really what I was looking for in music.

CODA NO. 3

Ned Lagin: Electronic Whiz Kid

> Ned Lagin was a student at Massachusetts Institute of Technology (MIT), playing jazz and experimenting with electronic music, and hosting a show on the campus radio station.

NED LAGIN: My friend said, you gotta listen to the Grateful Dead. He took me to two shows on December 29 and December 30 [1969] at the Ark [a short-lived venue in Boston]. The first night, they didn't start for an hour or two after they were supposed to, and they all were sort of like sitting on their amplifiers or languishing around. I wasn't sure who the musicians were. Then they got up and started playing. I was there in a jacket with leather patches, looking professorial, except that I had sort of an Afro and a goatee and a turtleneck sweater on. I was a jazz musician.

The Grateful Dead were just remarkable. I wasn't sure how that related to my jazz improvisational–avant-garde music, but they were remarkable.

My friend urged me next to write them a letter telling them what I was doing. He had wanted to get me interested in them, and now I guess he decided that they should get interested in me. So I wrote them a letter. I think at that time a lot of people perceived the Grateful Dead as, in a sense, an open entity. There was a view of Mount Olympus on the West Coast of all these musicians—the Grateful Dead, the Jefferson Airplane, Quicksilver Messenger

Service, Country Joe and the Fish, the Youngbloods. We heard they played together and hung out together, and they did all these things in Golden Gate Park together. The view of the Grateful Dead at that point was that they had all these different musical experiences, and they all got on a bus and toured around; it was the Tom Wolfe *Electric Kool-Aid Acid Test* view of the Grateful Dead. So it didn't seem unreasonable that other musicians would enter that sphere of influence in one way or another.

I wrote Jerry Garcia a letter, and I talked about how I was doing all this music that was attuned to particular spaces and things. I ended up getting a double degree in humanities and science: biology and music. I was learning to transcribe Renaissance music, music written in the 1450s to 1460s, and found that this religious music—mostly Catholic Mass music written for specific cathedrals—was written with tunings and rhythmic-harmonic-contrapuntal relationships that were in tune with the acoustic spaces of the particular cathedrals or chapels that they were performed in. They were all performed on a basic pulse called the tactus, the heartbeat. So if you looked at these little illuminated manuscripts you'd see these choruses of singers doing these performances and each would have his hand on the next guy's shoulder, actually feeling the pulse of the person next to him.

I never heard anything back.

Then my friends and I got the idea to invite the Grateful Dead to do a concert at MIT. I helped organize that. They arrived on May 4, 1970, having just come from Yale. Kent State [where four people protesting the war in Vietnam were killed by National Guardsmen] had just occurred. They all drove their own vehicles at this point—they didn't fly from gig to gig—and Garcia was driving a rented station wagon with his amplifiers in the back. I met him in the motel parking lot and introduced myself. He got out of the station wagon and ran away down the parking lot, yelling, "Phil! I found the guy! I found the guy!"

It turned out that the letter had had a tremendous effect on him. This started an association that then went on for several years.

I invited them to a concert of the 8-track, 4-tape-recorder piece I had scheduled to perform at the MIT chapel, which is this circular, cylindrical building. I set up eight speakers around that circle, and we sat in that circle—a bunch of MIT people and friends, and Mickey and Jerry and Phil—and they listened to my electronic music composition, and then Jerry, sort of rubbing his beard, said, "This guy would really like to play with a 16-track recorder, I'm sure," and Phil said, "I'm sure he would." That's how I got invited to California.

The next couple of days, they played an outdoor gig at the student center, the same place that I practiced piano in every night, under very cold and tough circumstances. And the next night they played with the New Riders inside the auditorium next door. Between that time, Phil and I and Jerry and I—alternately, 'cause I could only take one at a time—would go down into the basement and play the first computer game, Space Wars. We played Space Wars through the night.

During the day, they would come and get me at my dorm room in East Campus, so you'd see Pigpen and Jerry and Mickey and Phil come into my dorm room and close the door. I had had an old, not very well-tuned upright piano in my dorm room. There was one occasion when Pigpen and I played piano, one guy playing the bass line and one guy playing melody, and then vice-versa, while Jerry and Phil sat on my bed and listened.

I thought that Pigpen would probably be on the opposite side of the planet from me, but he turned out to be a very sweet person. To him, I was like one of those whiz-kid-rocket-scientist-genius kids that he always wanted to have access to, but he was on a different school bus going to a different place. But we could sit together and play together and hang out together, and later on he was responsible for me covertly sitting in on some of the gigs where I'd be standing by his organ when they would go from "Truckin'" or something into "The Other One" and he would just pull me in.

CODA NO. 4
Editing *The Grateful Dead Movie*

In 1975 and 1976, when he wasn't on the road with his bands or Keith and Donna's group, or working on any number of Grateful Dead and Round Records projects, Garcia was devoting much of his time to working on the Grateful Dead film that had been shot at Winterland at the final pre-hiatus shows in October 1974. Like so many projects in Grateful Dead world, it was open-ended, improvised, and under-funded. Work on the film would stretch from the end of 1974 until the film's release in the summer of 1977.

SUSAN CRUTCHER (Film editor): I had heard about this movie. It was about a band I'd heard of but never heard. I liked jazz and had a big world music collection, and my sister is an ethnomusicologist, so I was real interested in music, so I thought, "That sounds like fun, a concert film." I managed to track down Eddie Washington [the film's producer] and I met him down at the Sweetwater [club in Mill Valley]. We talked, and he hired me as an assistant editor. They had shot the concerts already and they had about 100,000 feet of film to sync up. They had used a very experimental, at that time, system for synching the seven cameras using a SMPTE time code system. At that point it had never been used with 16-millimeter cameras or Nagra [recorders] as far as I know. Still it took nearly five months to get everything in sync.

I had a hidden agenda, which is I wanted to cut the film [be the main editor], so as it went along I learned about the Dead's music and their following. Jerry was around quite a bit during all this, and I got to know him a bit. And I also got to know Ron Rakow, who was working with Jerry in this endeavor called Round Records. Ron was pretty much the producer of the film. Leon Gast [who had supervised the shoot] disappeared, and then there was a long period when they were trying to hire every famous editor in the universe, and nobody really wanted to do it. I don't think there was any money to hire anybody, anyway. I sort of waited around for the smoke to clear and then finally stepped forth and said to Jerry and Rakow, "Well, how about me?" I went out to Rakow's house in Stinson Beach and showed them some of the work I'd done, including a film about the Haight-Ashbury Free Medical Clinic. They seemed to like it, and at one point Rakow said, "Well, I think we have everyone we need to make the movie right here." That was the three of us and Rakow's wife, Emily, part of the deal as an assistant, which was fine. As it turned out, she was a crack assistant editor and we ended up working together for fifteen years after that.

So we just started working. We rented this equipment so I could screen six cameras at the same time. It was fascinating to see what six camera people were doing at the same moment in the same song. We had great camera people, so it was almost all really high-quality work. A few of them had never seen a Dead show, so that was quite an experience for them.

Jerry's view was that even if something was very strong visually, if he wasn't completely happy with it musically, he didn't want to use it. It also took him a while to get used to looking at himself on camera. But actually, he was good about that, better than a lot of people I've worked with. He was more concerned with his playing.

I did a lot of the editing myself, because Jerry went out on the road a lot, both with his band and with the Dead. I tried to be true to the instruments. If Phil was doing something wonderful, I tried to be on him, or if Bob was doing something wonderful, I tried to be on him. But I was working with Jerry, and the other band members didn't come around very much, and I can honestly say I felt Jerry was the focus of the band. It wasn't something I knew intellectually, because I didn't know much about them before I started. But it's something I felt in the music. So if there's an error in the point of view, if it sometimes feels like it's too much on Jerry, that's my error, not Jerry's.

We built in the complexity of the music. We get into the jazzier, more free-form music towards the end, and it's also a reflection of a certain pseudo-highness. We've got the little nitrous oxide scene. It gets weirder and weirder and weirder and it gets out to a place where it's just weird enough, and then it comes back around to some good-time tunes, just like at a real Dead show.

There were a lot of serendipitous things like that that contributed to the quality of the footage and how to convey the experience. That was one thing I drew on as I was trying to learn about it. Then the other thing I drew from was Jerry, who was so good at articulating what he was thinking, and of course has such a tremendous musical knowledge. Cutting the film with him ended up being quite an education in music for me.

At one point I had some Hells Angels in the editing room visiting. I was cutting some footage with Jerry and talking about one song we had a couple of performances of, and we were analyzing which one we liked better and why. We were having a standard day-at-the-office conversation; we're very candid with each other. The only difference was we had four Hells Angels sitting behind us watching. At one point I said something to Jerry criticizing the music in a gentle but honest way, and this Angel says to Jerry, "Who is that bitch?" Jerry just calmly turned around and said, "She's my editor. She's working with me." I figured after that, no producer could ever intimidate me. I've had Hells Angels in my editing room!

Terrapin Trailways

Norm, Sandy, Jasmine, Justin, and Tasha Ruth live in Albuquerque; they followed the Grateful Dead around the West in a bus for several years. Over that period a couple of hundred people joined the tribe and rode the bus at various times.

NORM: I ended up in New Mexico via a circuitous route from Michigan to Long Beach to Santa Cruz to Sante Fe. I'd always had a vision of going on the road as a jewelry merchant, traveling in a step van. In 1981, I ended up trading some furniture and a little bit of cash for a bus.

My brother took me to [see the Dead at] Duke University in 1982. The next night, we went to the Scope in Virginia.

I took the bus to see Bobby and the Midnites in Santa Fe in 1982. From that point on, the bus took on the life of going to see the Grateful Dead. It was a such a cool-looking bus—1948 White Motor Company. When we first started cleaning it, we rubbed off some of the paint that had been sprayed over some markings and discovered the words "Atomic Energy Commission" under that paint. So we spent our time exorcising the bad energy out of it and putting the good energy into it.

SANDY: In Michigan, they painted the turtles and came up with the name.

NORM: My mom [did] the lettering, and we painted "TERRAPIN TRAILWAYS" on the front of the bus. It evolved from there.

The most people we had on the bus was summer 1982. The band played Veneta [Oregon] and then Seattle. We ended up with thirty-two people, I think, leaving Seattle. We stopped in Portland, hippies got off . . . we ended up going to L.A., and at that point we had less than ten. That was just before the Us Festival [Labor Day weekend of 1982]. We found a couple of odd jobs in L.A., cleaning floors and warehouses. We discovered that a lot of change falls at drive-through restaurants and people don't pick it up, so we worked that. We'd scoop it up. We gave plasma.

After the Us Festival, we put on the UCLA ride board, "Bus going to Albuquerque." We got five Europeans who got on the bus in L.A., and we went via the Grand Canyon. It gave them a view of the country. Some of the people were okay with it; some were really scared. I think the more adventurous ones comforted the ones who were scared, to keep them on board. They helped pay for gas. We all made it back to Albuquerque.

After that trip, I came down from the blacksmith shop to the big city to meet a woman, and Sandy was that woman.

SANDY: His roommate worked with me, and that's how we met. They parked the bus in the parking lot right behind the college bar I worked at, and they were painting it.

NORM: We did the experiment of "Let's get a bunch of paint and a bunch of people and see what happens." It was kind of a mess. After that, we decided, "Let's do it right." We met Leo Romero, a sign painter and mural artist and general all-around awesome dude. He did the first real paint job, and I made his wedding rings in trade.

We drove it up to the Oakland Auditorium for five nights of the Grateful Dead. We got to park the bus right along the side of the Oakland Auditorium. Rock Scully saw the bus, and he saw the jewelry I had made. He said, "I can get you New Year's tickets. Wanna trade?" And then on New Year's Eve, no Rock Scully, no tickets, no nothin'. Sandy goes up to the front of the building and sees Nicki

Scully. "Nicki, Rock was supposed to get us into the show . . ." She comes back to the bus with Sandy: "Get your stuff! Come on in!" And she walks us all in.

SANDY: Not just the five of us: everybody who was on the bus!

Talk about your first Dead shows. It was amazing. I was hooked. Great guy, best bus, great band, great people. You instantly connect.

When we got back [to Albuquerque], the place I worked at had closed down. We moved into the bus. Summer tour [1983] was Jasmine's first experience: two and a half years old, and she saw the whole summer tour.

Back then, the parking lot scene was barely existent. We noticed that there was no food, especially for the hippie crowd. We started cooking stir-fry. We were one of the first food vendors. There was another person who used to walk around selling avocado sandwiches, and that was it. It was us and them.

NORM: Hot stir-fry was a big deal in the bus in '83–'84, and pancakes in the morning.

SANDY: We'd have lines of people waiting. We would leave right when the encore started, and we would cook for two hours.

We also gave away a lot of food. We knew how much gas we needed, and we knew how much ticket money we needed. And then we'd go, "All right, we've made what we need." We had our little advertiser [Jasmine] right there. She would scream out the window, "STIR FRY!" And she was so damn cute, I think that's why we got such a great following.

People would fly into Albuquerque just to take the trip with us. We had the two benches, and we used to put wood planks between [them]. We had people underneath, everywhere, wherever you could fit 'em. Norm would pull over and everybody was sleeping—

NORM: The only place I had to sleep was the driver's seat, so we decided to build a loft.

The adventure of driving the bus in a heightened psychedelic state was more fun than driving it straight. Our crew knew that if I was driving, it was very likely that I was tripping.

SANDY: We didn't do that when we had the kids in the bus.

NORM: Whenever I would do Grateful Dead Ticket Sales mail order, Calico would always send a nice note: "Best bus in the lot!"

JUSTIN: I remember when you bought the ship's wheel in San Francisco.

SANDY: Once we added the loft, that's when the whole thing got gutted and we redid it, with redwood ceilings and the benches. Diane Barone—a really good friend, another Terrapin Family member—did the tie-dyed curtains and the material for the cushions.

We would go to shows and people would say, "Whose bus is this?" A lot of people would say, "Norm," but Norm and I would say, "It's everybody's." It was built by the love of a lot of family members. So many people put things into it. The walls are covered with pictures, different things people over the years contributed.

We had a little "bus fare" box for donations.

NORM: It's pretty extended. Friends of friends have made marks. Little connections. You know how it gets.

TASHA: I remember being in Japan, and we went to this Grateful Dead store. The owner had a picture of the bus on the wall of the store. I didn't speak much Japanese at the time. I was trying to communicate with the owner, telling him, "My dad has this bus that's painted with the Grateful Dead," and he goes and gets this book. It's all in English, and he flips to the page with this biography of Terrapin Trailways. I said, "Yeah, that's our bus!"

NORM: We've had a few famous people visit the bus. Calico [from the Hog Farm and Grateful Dead Ticket Sales]; Allen Woody and Warren

Haynes [of Gov't Mule] brought us some mushroom stickers for the bus. Neil Young. David Byrne. Billy and Mickey came by for fajitas in Telluride, and Phil visited the bus in Vegas.

JUSTIN: I feel like the family on the bus were my family. My parents' friends that were always on the bus felt more like aunts and uncles than they did my parents' friends.

JASMINE: I think the biggest thing is just seeing the family my parents made over the years. I don't think I realized how unique it is until I got older. They have a family that they've kept in touch with for years and years, shared stories with, through all the good times and bad times. I think that's pretty neat, and something that they cherish.

NORM: When Jerry died, the local news came to us. The whole family was together, and they interviewed us.

SANDY: "The biggest Deadheads in New Mexico," they called us.

CODA NO. 6

Confessions of a Teenage Deadhead, Early Eighties

DAVE LEOPOLD: I grew up in Harrisburg, Pennsylvania, and in the tenth grade I got turned on to Dead tapes: the acoustic set of Harpur College [May 2, 1970]; Fillmore East, September 20, 1970; Red Rocks '78—that "Estimated" > "Other One" and "Wharf Rat" > "Franklin's"—great stuff that I still like to listen to. Around the same time [my identical twin brother] John and I got into a lot of the surrounding literature—*The Electric Kool-Aid-Acid Test,* Kesey, Vonnegut. It seemed like a whole world was being revealed, and the Grateful Dead ended up being the magic carpet through that world.

I had only been to a handful of concerts before my first Dead show at the Spectrum in Philadelphia on May 4, 1981. My mom was taking my older sister to see a road company of *Annie* in Philadelphia, and we were going to the show with a guy who lived outside of Philadelphia that we'd met through our synagogue youth group. For some reason my mother agreed to drive us down the Pennsylvania Turnpike and leave us off someplace, where we jumped over a fence and our friend's mother was waiting in a car to take us back to their house. So it was an adventure from the word go.

We were living in this totally gray world where nothing ever happened, and then all of a sudden there was the Grateful Dead. Right away we sort of "got it." We'd had some sense of what it could be, and

441

then we were there and we *loved* it. So then we started wondering, "How are we going to get to the next one?"

Our second show was in Buffalo, September 26, 1981, and that was a really good show. The logical show for us to go to on that tour would have been at the Stabler Arena [at Lehigh University in Bethlehem, Pennsylvania], because it was only two hours away, but there was a family event so we couldn't go. But we had convinced a guy who worked at the B. Dalton bookstore at the downtown mall [in Harrisburg] where John and I worked to drive us if we paid for his ticket and all his gas. We had a place for us to stay, with a friend of a friend.

We weren't even driving yet. When John and I took driver's ed, the driving teacher would always say, "Where do you want to go?" And we'd always say we wanted to go to this travel agency that had a Ticketron. We'd go in there and ask, "Any Dead tickets on sale?" because we didn't know how else to find out about shows. And the answer was usually "no." One day we went in there and they said, "Tickets go on sale tomorrow for these shows." So we get up early and go down there, and there are two guys at the front of the line from Penn State who had gotten money, it seemed, from everybody at Penn State; they were buying something like eighty tickets. We thought we'd never get good seats. But when the Ticketron people came in, they recognized us, and when they saw the Penn State guys were buying all these tickets, they said, "Oh, let these boys get their tickets first." And they let us. We got tickets in the second row.

By the time we went to see them at the Spectrum again, in April of '82, it was obvious we were really getting in to it, and my dad says to us during this tour, "Hey, I'd love to check out what you guys are into; I'd love to go to a show. What's the next show?" They were playing at the Baltimore Civic Center [April 19, 1982]. John had dated a girl in Rockville, Maryland, so we called her up to get tickets. She said, "Oh, at my local liquor store, if you buy thirty dollars of liquor they'll give you two tickets to see the Dead." We were all under age, and my father, God love him, never asked where or how we got the tickets. The tickets turned out to be seventh row center, and it was a great show. I ended up seeing about three hundred shows, but this was one of the strangest nights I spent with the Grateful Dead. During "Drums," they wheeled out two giant nitrous oxide tanks out onstage. I'm at the show with my dad! Billy and Mickey are laughing uncontrollably and they start coming out with bird calls. Then Phil recites "The Raven" [Edgar Allan Poe lived and died in Baltimore]. It was totally weird.

Soon after that, we went to a high school party. We heard that the older brother of the girl who was throwing the party was a Deadhead; we spend the party hanging out with him and talking about the Dead, and as we leave, he says, "Hey, we're going to go out to Red Rocks this summer. Do you guys want to come along?" And we're like, "Yeah!" If you ask [my dad] Sandy Leopold today, "What's the biggest mistake you ever made as a parent?" he'll say, "Letting the boys go to Red Rocks"—because as foaming at the mouth as we were before that, after Red Rocks, well, we had *done* it. We traveled across the country in a pickup truck. It really opened our world to us. I'd never been farther west than Chicago. We were with a bunch of college or just-out-of-college folks. We were sixteen. We went to the three Red Rocks shows, and at the same time at the Naropa Institute [in Boulder, Colorado] they had a conference on the Beats. We had read Kesey and Ginsberg and all these people, and suddenly we're at a Grateful Dead concert with them. It was surreal. The last night we had to sneak in over these mountains and then we had to get tickets, and we ended up in the front row. Classic Grateful Dead war story, and in our case it was totally true.

When we went to college in the fall of '83, my dad sat us down and said, "Boys, you're going to college for an education, not to go to more shows." We were like, "Of course!" And we totally meant it. Within the first week at school, we were walking down the street, I was wearing my Red Rocks '82 shirt, which is such a classic, and another Head sees it and we start talking, and we end up going to a bunch of shows on the fall tour, separately and together. John goes to [Madison Square] Garden and sees the [revival of] "St. Stephen." I go to Hartford and see the second "Stephen." I felt like every show had some remarkable thing happening. I know this is a period with the Grateful Dead when they were personally going through some turmoil, and Jerry was sinking into it, but for us it was this incredible open door. I had such a great time at those shows and I still listen to them.

By the spring of '84, we did the entire tour except for two nights when we had to go home for Passover. We missed a killer "Other One" at Niagara Falls. Summer of '84, we did some of the East Coast shows together, but John had a job, and I went into the Midwest with some other friends and we did all those shows. At Cuyahoga Falls in Ohio they did "Scarlet" > "Touch of Grey" > "Dear Mr. Fantasy." They were doing "Why Don't We Do It in the Road." At Alpine Valley, they brought back "Lovelight." It was great! We would stay in cheap hotels, or maybe we'd start driving to the next show, because we were up. We'd drive as far as we could, maybe sleep on the side of the road. It was that great time when we had zero responsibilities. We had the set lists we sold with a collage of band photos on one side and all of the set lists from the previous year on the back—those cost us twenty-five cents to make and we sold them for a dollar, and if other people sold them for us we gave them fifty cents for each. Our goal wasn't to make money. Our goal was to not lose money, and to keep us in gas, tickets, and food; so we were happy. At the same time, if we got into town early enough, I'd go to the art museum, or go to something interesting in whatever area we were in. That totally opened up my world.

What I took away from it all was the sense of possibility. Because as much as we liked the scene outside of shows and the adventure of getting there, we were always so excited about what was happening onstage—the idea that nobody knew what was going to happen until it happened. I thought that was the paradigm you'd want to aspire to. It was very liberating.

Jim and Doug Oade: A Tale of Two Tapers

JIM OADE: I first started taping the Grateful Dead in 1980. In Birmingham, Alabama [April 28, 1980], I talked to a kid who was taping the show and found out that the Dead were totally cool with it. I thought, "I want to take some of this home with me."

Doug, the technical wizard, helped me pick out a pair of microphones, and I believe he gave me his old JVC portable tape deck. I went to Boulder, Colorado, Folsom Field [June 7–8, 1980], snuck myself down in a good spot, and taped the show. Crappy recording by today's standards, but it was a wonderful feeling to be able to share it with folks who couldn't make it to the venue.

Doug started getting interested in recording. He redefined good recording by making equipment that was better than anything that was currently available. That gave us a feeling of satisfaction, capturing in as accurate a format as possible the incredible experiences I had had.

DOUG OADE: It took me a while to believe you could squeeze that onto a piece of tape, hand it to somebody, they could extract the experience, and derive as much pleasure from it as if they were there. Once I got that idea, there was no stopping us.

JIM OADE: Some of the recordings would very easily transport you back to the venue where the magic was occurring, as opposed to getting a soundboard [recording] that sounds really clear but it doesn't put you in that space and time. I remember one kid telling me that one of the recordings I made had completely changed his life.

Maybe that was an easy way to justify blowing all our cash on going to shows, but we saw that nobody else was making a recording that totally satisfied us.

> The Oade Brothers also ran a retail audio shop in Thomasville, Georgia.

DOUG OADE: What we wanted was a way of generating income with things that we enjoyed. Nobody was going to pay us to smoke pot and go see a Grateful Dead show, so what was left was to help people get the music experience in their lives. We wanted to be able to take off three to six months out of the year to experience such a potent thing.

JIM OADE: Once we got enough good gear in the right hands, we felt more laid back, didn't have to go to as many shows, knowing that somebody else was there recording it with the same caliber of gear and the same level of passion that we were.

DOUG OADE: We did it because we were following our hearts, following our passion, wanting to share a beautiful experience. It's an old Christian notion: it's more blessed to give than to receive. We got more than we gave; that's a fact.

JIM OADE: We had a great place to stay in every town we traveled to, probably as a result of being so generous with the music.

DOUG OADE: [Before taping was formally "legalized" by the Dead in 1984] you had to sneak your gear in and hide it before the show. As soon as the lights went down, the mic stands went up and the gear came out. You got good at dropping the thing quickly at the end of the set, before the lights came up, because we'd be hassled by venue security.

JIM OADE: Hiding the gear under women's dresses was one common way to get it in there—probably the funnest way to get it in there.

DOUG OADE: It was often a group effort with eighty to ninety pounds worth of PCM gear—two pretty large boxes that comprise the recorders, the [videocassette] tapes, the microphones, cables. It was very rare that an individual could do it by himself, although I did it a number of times with just two people.

JIM OADE: I'd carry in a backpack, and oftentimes just look at the crew that was taking tickets, etc., look at the person that seemed to be the happiest, and—the Jedi Mind Trick, just kinda walk right in.
    At one show, a couple of friends had to create a diversion as they went in, acting like they were fighting while I cruised in with a backpack full of PCM gear. There were a lot of different ways you could get it in.

DOUG OADE: The "bringing a birthday present to a friend at the show" trick. There was a whole host of 'em.

JIM OADE: I've seen people get it in with a twenty-dollar bill, too, for that matter.

DOUG OADE: And then there were those who you could tell by the look on their face, clearly knew what you were doing and approved. Those were the best.

JIM OADE: As [the band] gained in popularity, there were a number of notoriously bad rooms.

DOUG OADE: The "Distortatorium" in Miami [Hollywood Sportatorium]. In those bad-sounding buildings, we always left with a recording that was substantially better than what you experienced at the show, because we were able to select microphone patterns, position the microphones, and set up the correct angle between the microphones to make the best compromise between rejecting building acoustics while still getting an impressive image that would transport you back through time to the venue.

The Frost [Amphitheater, at Stanford University] was my favorite place to record, because of the sound. It's just absolutely stunning. I don't know whether it was the grass around it, the trees surrounding it, the gentle slope of the field that you set up in, but it had a level of detail, clarity, and warmth that produced the most luscious recordings.

JIM OADE: At Red Rocks, when they hit the right frequency the rocks around you would resonate—an experience that's beyond description.

The Greek Theater also had its pluses. Not only did it sound wonderful, but the shape of the bowl was such that Phil could fill it up and then play around with it. You had the entire earth around you resonating, as well as Phil dropping the bombs.

DOUG OADE: It was such an intimate experience at the Greek. Even if you were separated by distance from your friends, who traveled from all over to see the show, you could see them. It was so small, and the depth of the bowl was such that it was easy to see friends' faces smiling throughout that. It had an intimacy that was a beautiful thing to experience. That's probably my second favorite, the third being the Starlight Amphitheater in Kansas City, September 3, 1985. Absolutely gorgeous recording.

JIM OADE: The Dead made the venues sound as good as possible, and as the years went by, every venue, as they figured more stuff about it, they made it sound better and better. So the big gnarly sounding halls, after going in there several times, you knew how to get a better recording. But part of the art form of this is that you're always changing. What works in one venue won't work in another venue.

DOUG OADE: You have to use your ears. If you walk around and listen, you can actually find the spots where the PA sounds cohesive, and rather than hearing two separate speakers, what you hear is where the sound locks in, takes on a character of a cohesive wall of sound, and the distance between you and the PA disappears. I call that "image center," the spot where you're just bathing in the sound.

JIM OADE: That was part of the drive—to fine-tune the recordings, making them better and better: to allow somebody else to have that experience. It gave you a great feeling of satisfaction, without a doubt.

DOUG OADE: Yeah! To be massaged by the sound of Jerry's guitar—it doesn't get much better.

Hanging Loose with Al and Tipper

CAMERON SEARS: The day the band went to the White House [in 1993], Bobby and I were having a meeting with Interior Secretary Babbitt in his office, so we didn't get to go. But we did have a great dinner up at the Vice President's house one night. Al and Tipper Gore were friends of Mickey, principally, Tipper being a drummer. I think it was '94 and we were in D.C. playing RFK Stadium [July 16–17, 1994]. There was a comet that was racing across the sky, and we had an off night. The Vice President's residence is at the Naval Observatory, which has a telescope on it, so Phil said, "I'd like to see if I can go up and use the telescope with my boys and see the comet." Calls were made, approval given; that's great. Then, on one of the van rides to the gig, somebody overheard somebody saying, "Phil's going up to the Vice President's house to look at the comet." A couple of other people said, "Well, I'd like to go . . ." and, "If you're going I want to go. . . ." So all of a sudden, a party of four that was going to go up for milk and cookies and to look through the telescope was now a party of thirty and we're having dinner at the Vice President's house. The Gores had been in California, but we were told to show up at 5:30 that evening and we'd have dinner. We were at the gate with the security detail checking us in when their chopper lands on the front lawn; they're just arriving.

We go in and they have the Naval staff and there's wine and beer and hors d'oeuvres. I think all the band members were there. Al and Tipper were upstairs taking a shower while we were down there hanging out in their house. They come down and it's all great. Cassidy and I were the last people seated and we got to sit with Al and Tipper. We had dinner with them, and it was a lot of fun. [Actor] Woody Harrelson had come with us, and he and Jerry had gone into the powder room and enjoyed a puff or two. There's a Secret Service guy standing outside the door. They open the door and it's like a Cheech and Chong movie. Finally, the party is winding down and it's time to go, and Phil's saying, "I still want to go up in the observatory." But it was like, "We're out!" and in the end I don't think he got to see the comet, and he was pretty upset about that.

Sources

CHAPTER 1

More Than Human

"I was with": Sidon '14; "It goes back to": DG '14; "I was offered": Van Matre '88; "I got to be": BJ '96; "I remember in": DG '92; "He was so mean-lookin'": DG '92; "Weir and Jerry were": BJ '96 ; "I think there are": Wanger, KZSU '64; "The jug band was fantastic": BJ '96; "I saw Jerry": Eisen '14; "I think it was": DG '12; "In those days": BJ '96; "Anyway, so": DG '12; "I couldn't believe": DG '97; "Our earliest": BJ, GR27; "It was always": BJ, GR27; "We used to": Eisen '14; "The first gig": DG '14; "We did": Wenner, Signpost '72; "Jerry used to": BJ GR27; "I met Jerry": DG '81; "Good God": Childs '74; "[Phil] decided": Bakshe '80; "[I learned in]": Childs '74: "We played in": Harris '66; "In '65": BJDG '14; "I remember watching": DG '97; "We played": BJ GR21; "We'd do songs": Watrous '89; "Phil was my": BJ GR21; "I first had": Unknown Radisson '81; "We were trying": KFRC '66; "It was time": DG '14; "It's a genre ballad": Helix '67; "Jerry takes me": DG '12; "Everybody's mom": DG '92; "The Pranksters usually": Hepperman '08; "It was kind of": Ibid.; "They were really": Ibid.; "We were colorful": Ibid.; "I remember going": DG '12; "There was no barrier": Hepperman '08; "[It was] like": BJ GR22; "For most people": Greenfield '07; "A lot of people": Alderson '89; "[Playing on acid]": BJ GR21; "There's a thing": Sievert '78; "By putting the tape": BJ GR22; "This short lag": BJ '96; "Even when the Dead": BJ GR22; "I was amazed": DG '14; "[After an Acid Test]": BJ '96; "The Acid Test was like": BJ '96; "[When] we started": Talbot '86; "It wasn't one": Alderson '89; "All I can say": Haas, '79; "I think the Acid Tests": Hepperman '08; "When I fell in": Watrous '89; "We all saw": Rheingold '91; "If there was": Ibid.; "Yeah. So he filled": Ibid.; "It's still working": Ibid.; "I came to love": BJ '96; "We were roaring": Harrison '70; "The Fillmore Acid Test": BJDG '14; Fillmore Acid Test '66; "I thought, 'These guys'": DG '91; "The Trips Festival": DG '12; "Everybody there was":

Press conference '91; "[After being in the]: DG '12; "There was [Bill Graham]": BJ '96; "At the very end": DG '12; "That was the only": Harris, '66; "For me, it was": BJ '95; "It was just": Fong-Torres '76; "We didn't invent": BJ '96; "We moved into": Harrison '70; "From the very beginning": DG '12; "We'd met Owsley": Greenfield '07; "I never set out": Ibid.; "Of course, the biggest": DG '14; "I think my knowledge": BJ '96; "I remember one" : BJ '96; "We didn't have": BJ-DG '14; "We were going": BJ '96; "The devolvement of": BJ '96; "If the Acid Test": Fong-Torres '76; "We were never": BJ '96; "I miss the looseness": Watrous '89; "When we left": BJ '96; "We came back": Wenner '72; "[The main house]": BJ '96; "Novato was": Wenner '72; "When the Dead were": BJ '82: "[That summer] had": BJ '96

CHAPTER 2

San Francisco

"The Dead and": DG '84; "What was": DG '86; "Graham used to": Itkowitz '70; "Graham would call": BJ-DG '14; "[Chet Helms]": Harris '66; "If you walked": BJ-DG '14; "I think [psychedelics]": Garbarini '81; "We were": Watrous '89; "Back in the": Sievert '91; "It taught me": Trachtenberg '76; "The thing that happens": Helix '67; "A song like 'Viola'": BJ-DG '14; "We had been to": DG '14; "I could carry": BJ '06; "We did the first": Harris '66; "It's better than": Ibid.;"The [Vancouver] Trips": Ibid.; "Back then,": BJ-DG '14; "One of the things": BJ-DG '14; "Everybody always": BJ '96; "Everything Owsley did": BJ '05; "We called it: BJ '05; "When it was working": Garry '70; "The thing was": unknown '67; "I think Bear's idea": BJ '05; "With Tim and Bear": BJ '05; "When the band": BJ '05; "There is a small": Groenke '67; "[The first]": BJ GR3 '84; "We said, 'That's got'": BJ '14; "[The skeleton]": Rowland '91; "[The San Francisco]": BJ GR3 '84; "People really would": BJ GR4 '84; "When [Phil and I]": DG '14; "You come in": BJ '96; "At the very beginning": BJ '12; "I had a firehouse": BJ '14; "At 710, they": DG '14; "I did not know": DG '14; "We're legendarily": DG '84; "Many first-person": McGee '14; "When there was the Be-in": Wenner '72; "In early 1967,": Troy '91; "The record company": McGee '14; "At that time": Wenner '72; "Garcia played": BJ GR6 '85; "RCA Studio A": BJ '05; "[The songs on the album]": Wenner '72; "I wish I could have": BJ GR6 '85; "The Golden Road": DG '92; "[The artwork]": BJ GR3 '84; "We waited for Mouse": DG '92; "I think our album": Groenke, GR7 '85; "I think it's": KMPX '67; "The album came": BJ '96; "I had heard of them": Silberman '95; "We're getting into": Gleason/KPIX '67; "I think Garcia didn't really": BJ '14; "There was a lot": BJ-DG '14; "That was the lamest": BJ GR25 '91; "It was the first rock": Artisan '07; "I

was thankful": Peerless '11; "I helped": Troy '91; "Just for a while": DG '86;
"I'm not sure there was a": BJ '12; "What was happening": BJ-DG '14; "We're
moving": Helix '67; "I had the drum": DG '11; "I was there": BJ-DG '14; "I
worked out": JB GR21 '89; "[The Potrero]": BJ '96; "[Phil and I]": DG '12; "In
1967, Bob": BJ '11; "Mickey joining": BJ '14; "The thing that made": DG '07;
"I was not living": BJ '96; "I can't say": Childs '74; "The arrests were": Rifkin
'67; "That was the first song": Tamarkin '86; "I was arrested": DG '84; "We
went on our": DG '14; "Pigpen was the musician": DG '84; "Dave Hassinger":
DG '84; [Anthem of the Sun]": BJ '05; "It was an album": BJ-DG '14; "[Phil
and I]": DG '89; "There was one": DG '89; "We went to L.A.": BJ '05; "That
was my": BJ '95; "I was pretty sure": BJ-DG '14; "I was very straight": BJ
GR6; "Phil is a perfectionist": BJ '96; "I remember": BJ GR6 '85; "There was
a great deal": DG '84; "I just looked": BJ GR6 '85; "We started out": Wenner
'72.

CHAPTER 3

All Graceful Instruments Are Known

"I met the Grateful Dead": BJ GR5 '85; "There was always": BJ '06; "I got
the Northwest": DG '14; "We had some": BJ GR5 '85; "Tall Tales"; "We had
some": Ibid.; "That Oregon energy": BJ '96; "Most of those guys": BJ '14;
"On January 17, 1968": BJ '96; "We were young": BJ '09; "What was clear":
BJ '96; "The Carousel was": Platt '81; "We ran into": BJ '96; "We couldn't":
BJ '96; "[After the Carousel]:" BJ GR17 '88; "Garcia always": BJ '96; "If you
listen": BJ '14; "When the band": BJ GR27 '93; "He was our": Ibid.; "We'd
go back": DG '84; "In the early": BJ '14; "'Dark Star' is": BJ GR3 '84; "It was
'Dark Star'": BJ '96; "We walked into": Platt '81; "Using feedback": Childs
'74; "[In 'The Eleven'": BJ GR18 '88; "It was really": BJ GR23 '90; "The second
trip": BJ '96; "I was a junior": Bernstein '08; "I remember how": Ibid.; "We
thought it": Robinson '70; "The Haight-Ashbury": Selvin '92; "We were happy": BJ '96; "As time went on": BJ '12; "Whether you marry": DG '14; "I was
out": BJ '96; "I had a bedroom": BJ-DG '14; "People were in": BJ '84; "The
Carousel closed": DG '91; "When we were": DG '84; "From the early days":
DG '84; "Next thing": DG '84; "We were the": BJ GR27 '93; "Bobby was": DG
'14; "[If the firing]": BJ GR27 '93; "I thought they": DG '11; "It wasn't": BJ
GR26 '92; "My memory": BJ GR27 '93; "Because of the": BJ-DG '14; "[The
'firing']": DG '12; "We were practicing": BJ GR26 '92; "In the winter": DG
'13; "All I remember": Ibid.; "It was a charming": BJ '96; "It was the basic":
GR25 '91; "I was sleepin'": Ibid.: "That's right": Ibid.; "Everything was": Ibid.;
"I wanted": Ibid.; "Simply wouldn't": Ibid.; "He'd be playing": Ibid.; "It was ac-

tually": BJ '14; "Babbs was on": BJ '96; "Sometime in there": BJ '14; "Shortly after": DG '91; "In March": DG '14; "That big lab": Ibid.; "Bear was": Ibid.; "Owsley's an": BJ '96; "I was hired": DG '14; "Oh, yeah, his": Ibid.; "Aoxomoxoa was": BJ '05; "We did all": DG '10; "The 16-track": BJ '05; "The way most": BJ GR21 '89; "A lot of that": Lake '74; "Everything was": BJ GR3 '84; "I was doing": Paul '14; "We were finishing": DG '14; "It's good": Wenner '72.

CHAPTER 4
Psychedelic Americana

"In 1969": DG '11; "I knew": DG '11; "[The Western motifs": BJ '04; "I remember": BJ '10; "I remember Phil": BJ '04; "Jerry wanted": Platt '81; "[Woodstock producer]": BJ GR20 '89; "Once I got there": Rolling Stone, "Woodstock" '89; "We were supposed": BJ GR20 '89; "The rotating": BJ '06; "So there we": BJ GR20 '89; "There was": BJ '06; "After I don't": BJ GR20 '89; "We could hear": Ibid.; "All day": Ibid.; "Hello, people": Woodstock tape; "It was raining": Rolling Stone, "Woodstock" '89; "What I": BJ '96; "Rock Scully": DG '14; "It was going": Wenner '72; "Finally, we got": DG '14; "It was certainly": BJ-DG '14; "We were in": BJ '96; "There's no question": Goodwin '70; "Jerry never": DG '14; "You never would": DG '86; "I think the Angels": Itkowitz '70; "Altamont made": BJ '96; "There was this": DG '14; "What the Grateful": DG '14; "Jerry said": DG '14; "It's been insinuated": BJ-DG '14; "There were these": DG '01; "I wanted Bill": BJ '96; "Lenny seemed": "The day I": BJ '96; "Lenny and Gail": BJ '14; "What Lenny was": DG '14; "I met him": DG '14; "I compare this": DG '14; "Mickey was": BJ-DG '14; "Around the same": BJ '96; "When Lenny was": DG '14; "Lenny Hart disappointed": DG '14; "[After that]" DG '14; "I had already": DG '01; "In the year": DG '04; "There were a couple": DG '89; "He's more": Grueber '71; "His being a": BJ-DG '14; "Keyboard technology": DG '12; "They got into": DG '10; "They had listened": Silberman '95; "After the experience": BJ '05; "Bob would": DG '10; "When I delivered": DG '14; "That was a different": BJ-DG '14; "It's what Garcia": Selvin '92; "We didn't mean": Goodwin '70; "You try to": Scoppa '71; "With a Miles": DG '84; "[Playing with]": Davis '89; "We had to": DG '86; "Sam Cutler was": BJ GR6 '85; "When we played": Robinson, '70; "I think the": Ibid.; "Mickey had a": DG '14; "On that train": Ibid.; "There were two": BJ GR6 '85; "I guess it": DG '14; "I think someone": BJ GR6 '85; "The Festival Express": BJ-DG '14; "Rock Scully says": DG '14; "You can go": Scoppa '70; "After all this": Itkowitz '70; "In 1969": DG '10; "The first four": Robinson '70; "I think that's": BJ-DG '14; "John Dawson had": DG '07; "'Truckin' is": DG '87; "['Sugar Magnolia']": McNamara '78; "It's a good-time": Fermento '88; "The first time": McNamara '78; "They called me": BJ GR3 '84; "A long time": Goodwin '70; "Mike Bloomfield": DG '90; "Everybody knew": BJ '14; "At the [February 18, 1971]": DG '11; "It was okay": BJ GR 21 '89; "I remember being": DG '11; "In those days": BJ '96; "It looked like": Stuckey '71; "I kept trying": BJ '11; "The second time": DG '95; "With the best": DG '95; "'Deal' and": BJ '04; "We did a lot": BJ GR21 '89; "Garcia took": DG '92; "I believe they": BJ '04.

CHAPTER 5

Let It Grow

"Warner Bros. had": DG '10; "The Dead always": BJ GR6; "Oh, we wanted": Hunt '84; "I grew up": DG '11; "In this scene": Perry '73; "I loved his playing": BJ GR21; "When he rehearsed": BJ GR6; "It happened pretty quick": BJ-DG '14; "He was a fine player": BJ '94; "Keith was a real": DG '11; "Texas was great": White '71; "Rock Scully was really": DG '14; "The Grateful Dead has become": Fedele '71; "Sam Cutler did": DG '11; "I was brought": DG '14; "I could've been": BJ '12; "I adored Keith": BJ '11; "When the Dead came": DG '13; "This big, boomy": BJ '11; "Magically, one by one": McKaie '72; "It's a boon": BJ '12; "Jahrhunderthalle": DG '11; "We would take": DG '11; "We were so delighted": BJ '93; "He couldn't drink": BJ '93; "Pigpen was very": DG '11; "The equipment guys": BJ '11; "On that tour": DG '03; "I was so stoned": BJ '12; "While we were in": DG '95 ; "The audiences in Paris": DG '11; "It started in Paris": DG '95; "We canceled the gig": BJ '11; "When everyone": BJ GR6 '85; "There was a report": Ibid.; "If Garcia sings": British radio '72; "The Lyceum Ballroom": Giles 2011; "On that tour": DG '95; "Billy was so there": DG '11; "Europe '72 [the]": Crowe '73; "They came back": DG '14; "It was divine": BJ '96; "I really didn't want": BJ-DG '14; "There are a lot": Crowe '73; "The songs that came": BJ '14; "The songs that came" through "I don't remember": BJ GR25 '91; "I can sort of see": BJ '04; "The Grateful Dead has": BJ GR5, '85; "They wanted to develop": BJ '96; "It's dumb": Crowe '74; "If it were up": BJ '96; "The record company": Wasserman '73; "Why should we": Ibid.; "This company represents": Johnson '74; "I had been in radio": BJ-DG '14; "Pigpen had been": BJ GR27 '93; "God knows": Ibid.; "During that period": Ibid.; "I don't think it was": Ibid.; "I was at home": Ibid.; "For Pigpen to die": Ibid.; "I chose the booze": Ibid; "[At the funeral]": Ibid.; "I just remember": Ibid.: "We'd been getting": Ibid.; "We played without": Ibid.; "It was heavy": BJ '14; "He was genuinely": BJ GR18 '88.

CHAPTER 6

Independence

"["Dark Star"]: Fricke '80; "Sometimes in shows": BJ '96; "When I was a student": BJ '14; "[Playing with the Allmans]": Crowe '73; "After I saw them": BJ '14; "We were talking": Liberatore '73; "By Thursday night": Siegel '73. "I thought the Dead's": BJ '14; "There were numerous": Liberatore '73; "Sam Cutler was": BJ '95; "His worldview": BJ '11; "We're recording": Crowe '73; "We made this record": "'Stella Blue' is": Sievert '93; "The first production": BJ GR6 '85; "Looking back on": BJ GR16 '88; "Frankie Weir": DG '14; "I would go": DG '14; "We couldn't support": DG '14; "When the Dead said": DG '91; "It's easy to": BJ '05; "On a normal": Epand '74; "Bear would walk": BJ '05; "[The Wall of]": Wasserman '74; "We did the Wall": BJ-DG '14; "It was really": BJ '05; "We'd start at 8:00": Sievert '88; "Another thing that": DG '14; "Imagine walking": DG '11; "['Scarlet Begonias' is]": BJ '04; "[Musically], it": BJ GR25 '91; "The sessions started": BJ-DG '14; "I always got": BJ '96; "The first step": Childs '74; "I loved making": BJ '14; "It was a congenial": BJ-DG '14; "We're not the band": Lake '74; "Before we were into": Childs '74; "Ned Lagin, Mickey": Ibid.; "After about a": DG '08; "I was told frankly": DG '01; "They had this tour planned": BJ-DG '14; "By the time we got": DG '01; "I do [acid]": Childs '74; "The whole band": DG '01; "A few more miles": BJ-DG '14; "That was the last": DG '77; "That night when": BJ '14; "At the end": Ibid.; "We haven't broken": Herbst '74; "I don't remember there": DG '11; "I never understood": BJ '84; "Rakow was": DG '14; "No one ever said": BJ-DG '14; "We've been in a group": James '75; "I would rather fail": Sekuler '75; "Branching off": Lazar '76; "The hiatus allowed": BJ '14; "The Grateful Dead is": Bream '75; "[Blues for Allah]": Lazar '76; "We had a formula": White '90; "They started recording": BJ-DG '14; "We're trying to": James '75; "Bob wanted me": DG '11; "Workingman's Dead": Rowland '80; "We made this": DG '84; "When Phil Garris": BJ GR6 '85; "It's the first of our": Grissim '75; "It was an extremely": DG '98; "Jerry, Keith": BJ '14; "That really slow": BJ '03.

CHAPTER 7

On the Road Again

"I thought the": BJ '95; "When we went": BJ GR5 '85; "We went through": BJ '06; "When they came": DG '13; "They were playing": DG '13; "In smaller places": BJ '14; "Jerry once": BJ '14; "We have been": Hafferkamp '76; "I remember taking": DG '13; "Music has a": Bream '75; "Kreutzmann was": BJ '14; "We've had to": DG '77; "I wouldn't": DG '13; "It limits you": DG '12; "I don't know whose": DG '04; "We got stretched": BJ '96; "The movie was": BJ-DG '14; "Rakow was": BJ '95; "I got splattered": BJ '96; "When Lenny": BJ '14; "Rakow was bright": BJ '14; "The movie was": BJ-DG '14; "I thought Clive": BJ '95; "The independence": Adamson '76; "We proved": Fricke '80; "There was something": DG '88; "In November": BJ '96; "Of the guys": WBRU '78; "They played a couple": BJ '96; "I think [Keith Olsen] has": Hall '77; "The band had to": Selvin '77; "Everybody told me": BJ GR21 '89; "We learned a lot": DG '77; "Everybody, at": DG '04; "Keith Olsen was": DG '84; "We had nothing": BJ '10; "On 'Terrapin'": Bell '78; "There was something": DG '84; "It's a shame": DG '04; "For me, the movie": Adamson '76; "The reason Keith": BJ GR6 '85; "Whenever [Jerry]": DG '13; "We chose to mix": BJ '96; "The movie works: Block '77; "Mickey and Rhonda": BJ '14; "I do wonder": BJ-DG '14; "I had just": Mulvey '88; "We had outgrown": BJ '96; "We had worked": Alson '78; "I think a really": BJ '14; "I saw 1974": DG '13; "After the jamming": DG '12; "We chose Lowell": Bell '78; "George produces": Ibid.; "Lowell George was different": BJ '95; "Lowell George was mad": DG '84; "It's really a pity": White '90; "I was Jerry's": DG '14; "Phil and I": DG '84; "In the late sixties": DG '08; "There was talk": BJ GR8 '85; "Then, of course": DG '08; "That had always": Campbell '79; "This is kind of": SF Chronicle '78; "We went over": BJ '14; "You know a desert": BJ GR7 '85; "Those Egyptians": BJ '14; "It was a blast": Turkel '79; "When we were in": Adamson '79; "Billy [Kreutzmann] fell": BJ '14; "In 1978": DG '08; "They found out": BJ GR7 '85; "I never even": DG '08; "One of the highlights": BJ GR7 '85; "Most of the": Ibid.; "After the concerts": DG '08; "We called it": BJ '14; "I was drafted": DG '08; "Hamza was like": BJ '14; "In Hamza's village": DG '08; "I also went": BJ '11; "In Cairo": DG '08; "We stepped out": Sutherland '81; "It was a wonderful": Ibid.; "We were hoping": BJ '95; "Obviously we": DG '08; "If we had nine": BJ GR8 '85; "[The Egypt trip]": Adamson '79; "My thing with": BJ '95; "Lorne Michaels": DG '09; "The whole band's": Ibid.; "We started to": BJ GR6 '85; "Arista is": Adamson '79; "I don't know [why]": Turkel '79; "When I started": Haas '79; "There's a certain": Adamson '79; "In the early": Turkel '79; "Englishtown '77": DG '12; "[Keith] got wedged": DG '81; "We were really wasted": DG '98; "First we decided": Witmore '80.

CHAPTER 8
Hungry for Color

"What we always": BJ-DG '81; "I was born": DG '81; "Bobby gave me": BJ GR15 '87; "He had the chance": DG '84; "The Grateful Dead is": BJ GR15 '87; "Keith had": Sutherland '81; "Our textures": Joseph 80; "I think Brent": Bashe '80; "There were a lot": DG '12; "When it came": DG '10; "I was think-ing": BJ GR15 '87; "The idea [for]": DG '84; "We can get that": Garbarini '81; "We wanted to play": Fricke '80; "My major reservation": BJ GR9 '86; "No-body was very": Sutherland '81; "We'll start out" through "It's his need" (Bill and Mickey): Hurwitz '79; "In the Grateful Dead": Fewel '79; "Since we've been": Rowland '80; "Getting in shape": Hurwitz '80; "It doesn't feel": Fricke '80; "As hard as we": Bream '80; "We cling": Fricke '80; "In 1990": Peck '80; "I think there's": Haas '79; "We thought that": Unknown Radisson '81; "I had shot the band": BJ '14; "Long before I met": DG '09; "We'd shoot these": BJ '14; "[The fall 1980]": Unknown Radisson '81; "We edited the videos": BJ '14; "I was surprised that": BJ-DG '81; "Last New Year's": DG '81; "I'm not playing enough": Ibid.; "Brent was fighting": DG '84; "Being between Phil": Sievert '81; "The Grateful Dead invented": DG '11; "We feel Bob's": Sievert '81; "When I came up in '81": DG '13; "[I was in England": Van Matre '88; "Hunter sang": Peters '99; "['Throwing Stones']": BJ GR9 '86; "We had been dabbling": DG '14; "We were always operating": DG '14; "I had never seen anyone": DG '13; "There was always discussion": BJ-DG '14; "Drug use is kind of": Gilmore '87; "I was thinking about": DG '90; "I was living in": DG '12; "They didn't give me": BJ GR6 '85; "They were playing RFK": DG '07; "When he was brought": DG '14; "I had some very weird": Brown '93; "Did I see it coming?": BJ-DG '14; "I was up in Oregon": BJ '96; "You don't come out": BJ '14; "When he became sick": DG '90; "When Jerry got sick": DG '14; "Dad wasn't really": BJ '96; "While he was recovering": BJ '14; "[That fall,] I was": BJ '96.

CHAPTER 9
I'll Get a New Start

"There was a red": DG '14; "He got knocked": DG '03; "The coma gave": Morse '90; "[New Year's Eve]": DG '14; "That moment is": BJ GR8 '85; "To record": DG '88; "The Dead is most": BJ GR14 '87; "Working on the": Ibid.; "The sessions seemed": Ibid.; "Technically speaking": Ibid.; "I'm more than happy": Ibid.; "They asked me": BJ GR26 '92; "I've been more": BJ GR15 '87; "I had been a": BJ '14; "I'm standing": DG '07; "[On July 7, 1986]": DG '07 ;

"I think that we'd": Rense '87; "The first or second": DG '03; "Dylan walked": Ibid.; "I wanted to be": BJ '14; "When we were in": BJ '05; "I had a great": BJ GR15 '87; "I think Dylan": BJ '14; "[Dylan's material]": DG '87; "Dylan was managed": BJ '14; "Jerry was healthy": BJ-DG '14; "Once in a while": BJ GR16 '88; "What options": BJ GR14 '87; "I think everybody": BJ '14; "I think that the 'Day'": BJ GR27 '93; "[In the late eighties]": DG '14; "Bill [Graham]": DG '14; "I wanted Bill": DG '03; "New Year's '87": BJ '14; "We were gonna do": DG '13; "Most of the Deadhead": BJ-DG '14; "I think one reason": DG '88; "We all hated": BJ '14; "We're trying to be": DG '88; "We started off": Simmons '89; "Whoever wrote": DG-BS '89; "When we started": Simmons '89; "There was no": DG-BS '89; "['Foolish Heart'] is": BJ GR21 '89 JG; "Foolish Heart is": BJ GR21 '89 BK; "My original notion": Simmons '89; "Sometimes I wake up": BJ GR21 '89; "I had originally": DG-BS '89; "I didn't particularly care": DG-BS '89; "'Victim or the Crime' is": Simmons '89; "'Picasso Moon' is": DG-BS '89; "Characteristically, Bob": Simmons '89; "Often, when I'm": BJ GR20 '89; "'Standing on the Moon'": Simmons '89; " 'Foolish Heart' and": DG-BS '89; "Brent tends to": DG-BS '89; "After ten years": Simmons '89; "It used to be": BJ GR18 '88; "Jerry wanted the": BJ '96; "This is the first": BJ GR21 '89; "[By 1989]": BJ '14; "I ran away": DG-BS '89; "Success in the": Simmons '89; "The band's response": BJ-DG '14; "Every night": BJ '14; "We have been on": Rheingold '91; "The ones that catch": Ibid.; "Antiauthoritarianism": Watrous '89; "We want to maintain": Rheingold '91; "'Dark Star' has": BJ GR23 '90; "There is a continuum": BJ GR26 '92; "The band as a": BJ GR24 '90; "Toward the end": BJ '96; "Brent had OD'd": BJ '14; "Everyone knew Brent": BJ '14; "I think Jerry": BJ '14; "We used to have": DG '14.

CHAPTER 10
Vince and the Early Nineties

"My theory was": BJ-DG '14; "They wanted somebody": BJ '14; "I had met Jerry": BJ '91,'97; "In '86, '87": DG '13; "At first I was": BJ '91; "There was a big": DG '12; "When I first": Silberman '93; "The European tour": BJ '14; "Arista didn't provide": BJ '96; "The Europe tour was": BJ-DG '14; "Stockholm was": BJ '97; "I heard it was": BJ-DG '14; "I've heard stories": BJ '96; "I was unaware": BJ '97; "In Berlin": DG '11; "Individually they": BJ '96; "We brought everybody": BJ-DG '14; "It was all expenses": BJ '97; "It was a luxurious": BJ '14; "For a while": DG '13; "I really hated": DG '13; "In the spring": BJ '14; "What we're doing" through "Right. Either way" (Jerry and Bob): Rheingold '91; "Sharing the wealth": DG '14; "We have all": Rheingold

'91; "We've had people": Ibid.; "Vince was a peculiar": BJ '14; "Brent was a": DG '93; "There were hints": BJ '14; "From where I sit": Ruhlmann '91; "'Space,' to me": Silberman '93; "I wanted to tour": BJ '91; "Before Bill died": DG '14; "Nineteen eighty-six": BJ '96; "We always tried": DG '14; "We talked about it": BJ '14; "The city couldn't": DG '14; "We're in the post-Brent": BJ GR26 '92; "In the end": DG '13; "Maybe [singing]": BJ GR26 '92; "The band is": Mulvey '93; "[On the summer]": DeCurtis '93; "I remember as early": BJ '14; "Jerry never said": BJ '96; "I was in constant": BJ '96; "I like stadiums": Mulvey '93; "Jerry went on": BJ '97; "Towards the end": BJ '96; "I enjoy playing": BJ Dupree's '94; "'Corrina' was": DG '12; "When they went to": DG '12; "What Don Pearson": BJ-DG '14; "The last couple of": BJ '10; "There was a new": BJ Dupree's '94; "There are problems": Sievert '93; "Jerry talked about": BJ '91; "[By 1994,]: DG '13.

CHAPTER 11

Summer Flies and August Dies

"Once the manifestation": BJ '14; "It was heartbreaking": DG '14; "I went on tour": BJ '96; "The musical quality": DG '11; "['Visions of Johanna']": DG '97; "Jerry was not": BJ '96; "In 1994": BJ-DG '14; "It was Jerry's": BJ '14; "They ended up": BJ-DG '14; "Once the fences": BJ '14; "It was also": BJ-DG '14; "It was the tour": DG '14; "I don't think anyone": BJ '14; "That last tour": BJ '95; "When I started working": DG '14; "You would say": DG '13; "My last memories": DG '14; "The last time I saw": DG '14; "We knew Jerry": BJ '14; "The last time I saw Jerry": Ibid.; "I got the call": DG '14; "I think there's": BJ '14; "I feel so fortunate": BJ '14; "Seeing the Dead": Shapiro '93; "There has never": BJ '06.

CODAS

No. 1, Courtenay: DG '14; No. 2, Lambert: DG '11; No. 3, Lagin: DG '01; No. 4, Grateful Dead Movie/Crutcher: BJ '96; No. 5, Terrapin/Norm Ruth: DG '14; No. 6, Confessions/Leopold: BJ '14; No. 7, Oade Bros.: DG '07; No. 8, Al and Tipper: BJ '14.

Bibliography

PERIODICALS AND BOOKS

Adamson, Dale. "Jerry Garcia Says Grateful Dead Aren't Dead—They Are Just De-controlled." *Houston Chronicle,* March 28, 1976.

———. "Grateful Dead: Still Treading the Path of Uncertainty." *Houston Chronicle,* January 7, 1979.

Alson, Bob. "Bob Weir Lets It Grow." *Relix,* May–June 1978.

Artisan News Service. Interview with Bob Weir on fortieth anniversary of Monterey Pop. August 19, 2007.

Bashe, Philip. "What a Long Strange Trip It's Been: A Conversation with Jerry Garcia." *Good Times,* April 22, 1980.

Bell, Max. "The Grateful Dead's First Annual Pyramid Prank." *New Musical Express,* September 30, 1978.

Bernstein, Barbara. Interviews with Bob Merlis and Alan Senauke (commis sioned by DG), 2008.

Block, Adam. "Garcia on Garcia '77." *BAM,* December 1977.

Bream, Jon. "The Dead: Grateful Fans Follow Band Through Fifteen Years of Changes." *Minneapolis Star,* May 30, 1980.

———. "The Grateful Dead May Be Coasting to New Undertakings, Its Leader Says." *Minneapolis Star,* November 24, 1975.

Brown, Jay and Rebecca Novick. "An Interview with Jerry Garcia." *Magical Blend,* Fall 1993.

Campbell, Mary. "Success Surprises Grateful Dead." Weekend Vistas/AP, June 29, 1979.

Childs, Andy. "Conversation with Phil Lesh." *Zig-Zag,* no. 46, October 1974.

Crowe, Cameron. "Ghost Stories from the Dead: Semi-Startling Conversa tions with Bob Weir." *Rock,* June 30, 1973.

———. "The Grateful Dead Flee Big Business." *Circus,* October 1973.

———. "Grateful Dead Show Off New Bodies; Their Heads Are Something Else Again." *Creem,* January 1974.

Davis, Miles with Quincy Troupe. *Miles: The Autobiography.* New York: Simon and Schuster, 1989.

DeCurtis, Anthony. "The Music Never Stops: Rolling Stone Interview with Jerry Garcia." *Rolling Stone,* September 2, 1993.

Epand, Len. "State of the Artful Dead." *Zoo World,* August 15, 1974.

Fedele, Frank. "'Fuck No, We're Just Musicians: An Interview with Jerry Garcia" *Long Beach Sunset Press,* December 1971.

Fewel, Clifford. "Grateful Dead: You've Got to Hear Them." *Sacramento Union,* June 30, 1979.

Fong-Torres, Ben. "The Grateful Dead Lives On, Thanks to a Free Spirit." Detroit Free Press, via *Rolling Stone,* January 10, 1976.

Fricke, David. "The Grateful Dead Celebrate Fifteen Long Strange Years with White Suits and a Cosmic Giggle." *Circus,* July 1980.

Garbarini, Vic. "In Search of the Grateful Dead." *Musician,* September–October 1981.

Garry, Mac. "The Grateful Dead." *Zigzag,* June/July 1970.

Gilmore, Mikal. "The New Dawn of the Grateful Dead." *Rolling Stone,* June 16, 1987.

Greenfield, Robert. "The King of Acid," *Rolling Stone,* July 12, 2007.

Greuber, Mike and Charles Beichman, Rex Browning, and Hank Baig. "The Dead Just Keep on Truckin'." *Harvard Independent,* March 4, 1971.

Grissim, John. "The Dead After a Decade: 'Allah' Means Business." *Rolling Stone,* November 6, 1975.

Groenke, Randy and Mike Cramer. "One Afternoon Long Ago: A Previously Unpublished Interview with Jerry Garcia, 1967." *Golden Road,* no. 7, summer 1985.

Haas, Charlie. "New Life for the Grateful Dead." *New West,* December 17, 1979.

Hafferkamp, Jack. "The Grateful Dead Return From Limbo." *Chicago Daily News,* June 26, 1976.

Harris, David. "The Grateful Dead." *Mojo Navigator* R&R News, August 30, 1966.

Herbst, Peter. "A Message from Garcia: Nothing Exceeds Like Success." *Bos ton After Dark*, November 19, 1974.

Hurwitz, Miles. "A World of Drums: A Candid Interview with Grateful Dead Drummers Bill Kreutzmann and Mickey Hart." *BAM*, August 17, 1979.

————. "Mickey Hart: Up the River and Other Tales." *BAM*, August 29, 1980

"Interview with Jerry Garcia." Unknown author. *Helix* magazine, vol. 1, no. 8, July 1967.

Itkowitz, Jay. "Rapping with the Dead's Jerry Garcia." *Action World*, November 1970).

Jackson, Blair. "In Phil, We Trust: A Conversation with Blair Jackson." *Dupree's Diamond News*, no. 28, spring 1994.

————. "The Album: In the Dark." *The Golden Road*, No. no. 4, summer 1987.

————. "Alton Kelley: Art for Fun's Sake." *The Golden Road*, no. 3, summer 1984.

————. "Brent Mydland: Steppin' Out." *The Golden Road*, no. 15, fall 1987.

————. "Bill Kreutzmann: Long Distance Drummer." *The Golden Road*, no. 21, fall 1989.

————. "Bob Bralove: Growing, Pruning and Feeding Infrared Roses. " Co-interview by Steve Silberman. *The Golden Road*, no. 26, 1992 annual.

————. "Dave Hassinger on Producing the Dead." *The Golden Road*, no. Six, spring 1985.

————. "Dead Ducats: An Interview with GD Ticket Czar Steve Marcus." *The Golden Road*, no. 27, 1993 annual.

————. "Donna: The Greatest Story Never Told." *The Golden Road*, no. 6, spring 1985.

————. "Dupree Come Out With a Losing Hand: A Closer Look at 'Dupree's Diamond Blues.'" *The Golden Road*, no. 21, fall 1989.

————. "Garcia on Film, Video, and 'The Twilight Zone.'" *The Golden Road*, no. 6, spring 1985

————. "Garcia/Hunter: Words/Music." *The Golden Road*, no. 25, spring 1991.

————. "Garcia: Listen to the Music Play . . . " *The Golden Road*, no. 18, fall 1988.

————. "Mickey Hart: Drums and Dreaming." *The Golden Road*, no. 24, fall 1990.

————. "On the Bus With Ken Kesey." *The Golden Road*, no. 2, spring 1990.

————. "The Once and Future Bob: An Interview with Bob Weir, 1/3/92." *The Golden Road*, no. 26, 1992 annual.

————. "Out in the Wild Blue Yonder with Tom Constanten." *The Golden Road*, no. 3, summer 1984.

————. "Pigpen Forever: The Life and Times of Ron McKernan." *The Golden Road*, no. 27, 1993 annual.

————. "Recording 'Built to Last': An Interview with Garcia." *The Golden Road*, no. 21, fall 1989.

————. "Robert Hunter: The Song Goes On." *The Golden Road*, no. 16, spring 1988.

————. "A Short Break with Bob Weir." *The Golden Road*, no. 9, winter 1986.

————. "The Sound Ideas of Dan Healy." *The Golden Road*, no. 5, winter 1985.

————. "Tall Tales, Part One," *The Golden Road*, no. 5, winter 1985.

————. "Tall Tales, Egypt '78," *The Golden Road*, no. 7, summer 1985.

————. "Tall Tales, Part Two." *The Golden Road*, no. 6, spring 1985.

————. "There's a Band Out on the Highway: An Interview with Grateful Dead Manager Jon McIntire." *The Golden Road*, no. 17, summer 1988.

————. "Time Out with Bill Graham." *The Golden Road*, no. 8, fall 1985.

————. "We Want Phil: An Interview 4-18-90." *The Golden Road*, no. 23, spring 1990.

————. "WEIRd Notions: Catching up with Bob Weir." *The Golden Road*, no. 20, summer 1989.

————. "Will Success Spoil the Grateful Dead." *The Golden Road*, no. 14, summer 1987.

James, Viola. "Garcia Takes Legion on Funk Crusade." *Circus*, July 1975.

Johnson, Nels. "Grateful Dead Records: An Idea Worth Many Millions." *Marin Independent Journal*, August 16, 1974.

Jospeh, Ted. Unknown title. *Illinois Entertainer*, January 1980.

Lake, Steve. "Rock 'n' Roll Misfit." *Melody Maker*, September 14, 1974.

Lake, Steve. "Weir: Rock Has Ceased to Progress." *Melody Maker*, September 21, 1974.

Lazar, Randi and Jim Maxwell. "Weir on the Dead and Kingfish." *Newsbeat*, March 22, 1976.

Liberatore, Paul. "Grateful Dead: Group Plays Famous Eastern Gig." *Marin I Independent Journal*, August 17, 1973.

McKaie, Andy. "Bob 'Ace' Weir: Inside Straight on the Dead's Full House." w*Crawdaddy*, August 1972.

Morse, Steve. "The Grateful Dead: Celebrating 25 Years, Jerry Garcia and Bandmates Still Relish 'New Beginnings.'" *Kansas City Star* via the *Boston Globe*, June 29, 1990.

Mulvey, Sally and Michael Mulvey. "Conversations at the Edge: An Interview with Mickey Hart." *Dupree's Diamond News*, no. 25, August 1993.

Paul, Alan. "Lyricist Robert Hunter on Finding Words for the Grateful Dead," *Wall Street Journal* online, July 18, 2014.

Peck, Chris. "Dead Dares for New Grateful Fans." *Spokane Spokesman Review*, June 13, 1980.

Peerless, Beth. "Back from the Dead: Bob Weir and Phil Lesh Come Full Circle as Furthur Pulls in to Monterey County Fairgrounds." *Monterey Herald*, unknown date.

Peters, Stephen. *What a Long Strange Trip—The Stories Behind Every Grateful Dead Song*. Thunder's Mouth Press, 1999.

Platt, John, "Rhythm Devil. An Interview with Mickey Hart." *Comstock Lode*, no. 9, autumn 1981.

Rense, Rip. "Back from the Dead." *Los Angeles Times*, April 19, 1987.

Robinson, Lisa. "Creem Interview with Grateful Dead." *Creem*, December 1970.

———. "Elvis Costello and Jerry Garcia: Strange Bedfellows." *Musician*, March 1991.

Rowland, Mark. "Bring Me the Head of Jerry Garcia." *St. Louis Post-Dispatch*, 1980

Ruhlmann, William, "Mickey Hart Interview." *Relix*, October 1991.

Sekuler, Eliot. "Grateful Dead and Round: Innovative Independence." *Record World*, April 12, 1975.

Selvin, Joel. "The Grateful Dead Decides to Try a Guiding Hand." *San Francisco Chronicle*, July 28, 1977.

San Francisco Chronicle. "The Grateful Dead Play the Pyramids." *Washington Post* news service, September 15, 1978.

Sidon, Rob. "The Common Ground Interview: Bob Weir, Gratefully." *Common Ground*, November 2014.

Siegel, Joel. "Watkins Glen Jam Tops Woodstock; 600,000 Fans," *Rolling Stone*, August 30, 1973.

Sievert, Jon. "Bob Weir: More Than Rhythm Guitarist for the Grateful Dead." *Guitar Player,* August 1981.

————. "Jerry Garcia, Bob Weir: Lately It Occurs to Me . . .". *Guitar Player,* fall 1993, special issue.

————. "Jerry Garcia: For More Than a Decade the Patriarch of the San Francisco Sound." *Guitar Player,* October 1978.

————. "Jerry Garcia: New Life with the Dead." *Guitar Player,* July 1988.

Silberman, Steve. "An Egg Thief in Cyberspace: An Interview with David Crosby, 1995." *Goldmine,* July 7, 1995.

Stuckey, Fred. "Jerry Garcia: It's All Music." *Guitar Player,* April 1971.

Sutherland, Steve. "Tripping in the Timeless Zone." *Melody Maker,* March 28, 1981.

Tamarkin, Jeff. "The Greatest Stories Never Told: Robert Hunter Talks About the Dead's Greatest Hits." *Relix,* April 1986.

Troy, Sandy. *One More Saturday Night.* New York: St. Martin's Press, 1991.

Turkel, Chris. Unknown title, *New York Daily News,* January 12, 1979.

Unknown interview with Jerry Garcia, 1967.

Van Matre, Lynn. "Voice of the Dead: The Mystery Man Who Writes Grateful Dead Lyrics." *Chicago Tribune,* April 10, 1988.

Wasserman, John L. "The Expansion of the Grateful Dead." *San Francisco Chronicle,* October 12, 1973.

————. "The Dead: Committed to Sound Perfection." *San Francisco Chronicle,* March 22, 1974.

Watrous, Peter. "Touch of Gray Matter: The Grateful Dead are Different from You and Me." *Musician,* December 1989.

Wenner, Jann and Charles Reich. *A Signpost for a New Space.* DaCapo Press, 2003. From an article originally published in *Rolling Stone,* January 20, 1972.

White, Timothy. "From the Beatles to Bartok: Jerry Garcia and Bob Weir Trace the Roots of the Dead." *Goldmine,* November 1990.

Witmore, Sam. "The Dead Go to Heaven (And Come Back to Life)." *Sweet Potato,* June 1980.

"Woodstock Remembered: The Artists." *Rolling Stone,* August 24, 1989.

AUTHOR INTERVIEWS

Allan Arkush (DG 12/13); Ken Babbs (BJ 6/96, 11/14); Stephen Barncard (DG 4/10); Bob Barsotti (DG 10/14), Bill Belmont (BJ 4/96); Jerilyn Brandelius

(BJ 5/14); Bob Bralove (BJ 2/96, DG 3/12); Steve Brown (BJ-DG 6/14); Betty Cantor-Jackson (BJ 6/05, DG 3/10); Tom Constanten (DG 12/89, 1/12); John Cooke (DG 10/14); Susan Crutcher (BJ 3/96); John Cutler (DG, 8/08); Sam Cutler (DG 7/14); Tom Davis (DG 3/09); Len Dell'Amico (BJ 8/96, 10/14); Rob Eaton (DG 1/12); Jon Ezrine (DG 11/11); David Gans (BJ 11/14); Annabelle Garcia (BJ 7/96); Carolyn "Mountain Girl" Garcia (BJ 5/96); Jerry Garcia (BJ-DG 4/81); Tiff Garcia (BJ 2/96); Donna Jean Godchaux (DG 3/98, 4/04, 12/11; BJ 11/03, 8/14); Bill Graham (DG 10/84); Mickey Hart (DG 11/84, DG 9/07, BJ 10/11); Dan Healy (BJ 5/06); Gail Hellund (DG 6/14); Freddy Herrera (DG 8/14); Bruce Hornsby (DG 1/13); Robert Hunter (DG 2/88), BJ 6/04); Paul Kantner (DG 6/86); Jim Koplik (BJ 10/14); Rob Koritz (DG 11/11); Bill Kreutzmann (BJ 5/05); Ned Lagin (DG 2/01); Gary Lambert (DG 12/11); Eileen Law (BJ 1984); Phil Lesh (DG 7/81, 10/89 with Bonnie Simmons, 9/95 with Marty Martinez, 5/97); Richard Loren (BJ 12/95; DG 8/08); Bob Matthews (DG 7/92, 4/14 , BJ 5/05); Jeff Mattson (DG 1/13); Rosie McGee (BJ 3/96; 9/12; DG 1/12); Jon McIntire (BJ 4/96, 2/11; DG 3/11); Dennis McNally (BJ-DG, 9/14); Peter McQuaid (BJ 12/14); Jerry Moore (DG 1/08); Connie Bonner Mosley (DG 7/92); Brent Mydland (DG 4/81); Michael Nash (DG 12/13); David Nelson (BJ 12/95, 4/10; DG 7/07, 1/12); Keith Olsen (DG 8/77; BJ 4/96); Steve Parish (DG 9/03); Dave Parker (2/96); Ron Rakow (BJ 11/96); Jonathan Reister (BJ 4/96); Brian Rohan (DG 8/14); Sara Ruppenthal (BJ 4/96); Norm and Sandy Ruth (DG 3/14); Roy Siegel (BJ 1996); Merl Saunders (DG 6/90); John Scher (BJ, 10/96); Rock Scully (BJ-DG 6/14); Tim Scully (BJ 5/96); Cameron Sears (BJ 11/14); Steve Silberman: (BJ 5/96, 12/14); Jan Simmons (DG 7/14); Owsley Stanley (DG 1/91; BJ 10/96, 6/06); Rhoney Stanley (DG 11/14); Sue Swanson (DG 7/92, BJ 2/93); Rick Turner (BJ 5/05); Ron Tutt (DG 3/14); Wavy Gravy (DG 9/14); Bob Weir (DG 8/77, 11/81, 7/87, 10/89 with Bonnie Simmons, 9/95 with Dennis Martinez, BJ 4/09, 8/10); Vince Welnick (BJ 2/91, 5/97); Ron and Susan Wickersham (BJ 7/05, DG 11/14); John Zias (DG 11/11).

OTHER INTERVIEW SOURCES

Alderson, Jeremy. Interview with Jerry Garcia, July 3, 1989, hotel room in Buffalo, NY, from jerrygarciasbrokendownpalaces.blogspot.com.

Bernstein, Barbara. Interviews with Bob Merlis and Alan Senauke, commissioned by DG, 2008.

British radio interview with Bob Weir, May 27, 1972.

Eisen, Benjy. Onstage interview with Bill Kreutzmann, "So Many Roads" conference, San Jose State University, November 6, 2014.

Fermento, Dan. Rock Stars radio interview with Jerry Garcia, May, 7, 1988.

Fillmore Acid Test Craziness, January 8, 1966; thanks to Key-Z Productions.

Giles, Bill. Email to David Gans, 2011.

Gleason, Ralph J. *The Maze.* KPIX-TV (San Francisco), April 8, 1967.

Goodwin, Michael. Jerry Garcia interview, October 1970, from deadsources. blogspot.ca/2013/12/october-1970-jerry-garcia-interview.html.

Hall, John. "True Confessions in Hartford." Relix, November-December 1977.

Hepperman, Ann and Kara Oehler. Hearing Voices no. 113 (public radio docu mentary), 2008.

Harrison, Hank. Interview with Ron "Pigpen" McKernan, May 1970.

KFRC (San Francisco) radio interview with Jerry Garcia, Bob Weir, Pigpen, and Bill Kreutzmann, 1966.

KOFM (Oklahoma City) radio interview with Bob Weir, October 18, 1973; Mike Flanagan, interviewer.

McGee, Rosie. Letter to the authors, 2014.

McNamara, Denis. Interview with Robert Hunter for WLIR-FM (Garden City, NY), March 1978.

Press conference with Jerry Garcia, Bob Weir, and Mickey Hart after Bill Graham's death, Oakland Coliseum, October 27, 1991.

Rheingold, Howard. Interview with Jerry Garcia and Bob Weir, April 1991.

Selvin, Joel. Interviews with Jerry Garcia and Robert Hunter, April 1992.

Silberman, Steve. Interview with Steve Silberman, October 14, 1993.

Simmons, Bonnie. Interview with Jerry Garcia, September 28, 1989.

Talbot, Stephen. Interview with Carolyn "Mountain Girl" Garcia, 1986.

Wainger, Pete. KSZU (Stanford, CA) radio interview July 1964, "Live from Top of the Tangent," from Mother McCree's Uptown Jug Champions CD, 1964.

WBRU (Providence, RI) interview with Jerry Garcia, March 11, 1978.

Unknown interviewer, Jerry Garcia at the Radisson Hotel, St. Paul, MN, July 1981.

Photo Credits

Page 3: Ron "Pigpen" McKernan, 1967. (Photo by Herb Greene)

Page 47: Grateful Dead, 1966: Jerry Garcia, Ron "Pigpen" McKernan, Phil Lesh, Bob Weir, Bill Kreutzmann. (Photo by JimMarshall)

Page 95: Grateful Dead at Columbia University, New York City, May 3, 1968; Sunshine Kesey at Jerry's knee. (Photo byRosie McGee)

Page 127: Grateful Dead at the Fillmore East, January 2, 1970. (Photo by Amalie R. Rothschild)

Page 177: Grateful Dead, 1972: Jerry Garcia, Bob Weir, Donna Jean Godchaux. (Photo by Barrie Wentzell)

Page 209: Grateful Dead and the Wall of Sound, May 12, 1974: Bob Weir and Phil Lesh. (Photo by Bruce Polonsky)

Page 245: Grateful Dead, 1976: Keith Godchaux, Bill Kreutzmann, Jerry Garcia, Mickey Hart, Donna Jean Godchaux, Bob Weir, Phil Lesh. (Photo by Jim Marshall)

Page 291: Brent Mydland, July 1984. (Photo by David Gans)

Page 325: Grateful Dead,1987: Mickey Hart, Jerry Garcia, Phil Lesh, Bill Kreutzmann, Brent Mydland, Bob Weir. (Photo by Herb Greene)

Page 373: Jerry Garcia, Bruce Hornsby, Vince Welnick, August 17, 1991. (Photo by Bob Minkin)

Page 405: Jerry Garcia, photographed for magazine ads for Alvarez Guitars, November 8, 1994. (Photo by Jay Blakesberg)

Index of Speakers

Arkush, Allan, 118–19, 187, 247, 261,
    311, 315, 412–13
Arthur, Brooks, 91–92

Babbs, Ken, 41, 43, 100, 120–21, 321–22
Barncard, Stephen, 163–65
Barsotti, Bob, 313–14, 344, 391–92, 394
Barsotti, Peter, 326–28
Belmont, Bill, 142, 380, 381, 382
Bildman, Bernie, 278
Bogert, Dick, 68–69
Bralove, Bob, 317, 330, 331, 359, 378,
    397, 399, 407
Brandelius, Jerilyn, 235–36, 263–65, 274,
    275, 276, 280
Brown, Steve, 16–17, 48–50, 51, 54, 77,
    203–4, 216–17, 223, 225–26, 227,
    230–31, 234, 238–39, 240–243,
    251–52, 253

Cantor-Jackson, Betty, 124, 151–52,
    153, 177, 295–96
Cipollina, John, 97–99
Constanten, Tom, 89–90, 104–5, 117,
    124, 125, 132, 150, 151
Cooke, John, 160, 161
Crosby, David, 71, 152
Crutcher, Susan, 261–62, 431–433
Cutler, John, 276–77, 278, 280–81,
    282, 330
Cutler, Sam, 138–140, 184–85

Davis, Miles, 156
Davis, Tom, 284–86, 304, 346
Dawson, John "Marmaduke," 195
Dell'Amico, Len, 302–4, 305, 306,
320–321, 322–23, 336, 337–38,
    339–40, 345–46, 368, 370–71, 384–86,
    389, 393, 396–97
Dryden, Spencer, 178

Eaton, Rob, 250, 288–89, 295, 400
Ezrine, Jon, 309–10

Freiberg, David, 44–46

Gans, David, 72, 81, 103–4, 200
Garcia, Annabelle, 321
Garcia, Carolyn "Mountain Girl," 8,
    21–23, 24, 26, 27–28, 36, 37, 42–43,
    60–61, 67–68, 71, 80, 99–100,
    107, 110, 119, 121, 135, 137, 143–44,
    274–75, 279, 320
Garcia, Clifford "Tiff," 6–7
Garcia, Jerry, 7–8, 11–12, 13, 16, 18–21,
    25, 26, 28, 29–30, 34–35, 37, 39, 43,
    44, 48, 50, 51, 52, 53, 56–57, 58–59,
    67, 68, 69, 71, 72, 73, 77, 94, 104,
    106–7, 109–110, 116, 119–120, 126,
    134, 135–36, 137, 153–54, 158,
    162, 163, 165, 167, 168–69, 172,
    179, 184, 185, 189, 199, 200, 202,
    203, 206–7, 209, 211, 215, 216, 222,
    225, 227, 236–37, 239, 240, 241,
    249, 254, 256, 260–61, 262–63, 274,
    276, 281, 283, 287, 288, 291, 294,
    295, 297, 299, 300, 301, 302, 305,
    306–7, 310, 312, 315–16, 317–19,
    326, 330, 335, 342, 349–50, 351, 352,
    354–6, 356, 357–60, 361–63, 365,
    366, 386, 387, 388, 393, 396, 402–3
Giles, Bill, 196–97

Godchaux, Donna Jean, 179–183, 186, 187–88, 189, 190, 197, 207, 224, 226, 237, 239–240, 242, 243, 244, 246, 249, 250, 253, 259, 260, 261, 268–69, 279, 286, 289–90
Graham, Bill, 47–48, 112–14, 155, 212, 273, 282–83, 328–29
Grant, Laird, 205

Harris, Dave, 52
Hart, Mickey, 77–79, 81–83, 86, 89, 90–91, 96–97, 102, 104, 106, 112, 114, 130, 242, 259, 260, 265, 269, 270–71, 281, 293–94, 298, 299–300, 301, 308, 330–31, 367–68, 389–90, 393, 396, 397–98
Hassinger, Dave, 68, 69, 92, 93, 94
Healy, Dan, 95–96, 201, 246
Hellund, Gail, 144–47, 148–49, 158–59, 237–38
Herrera, Freddie, 325
Hornsby, Bruce, 376–78, 379, 383–84, 390–91, 395, 398, 403
Hunter, Robert, 6, 86, 120, 125, 129, 153, 167, 173, 174–75, 200, 218, 225, 312, 329-30, 341–42, 347, 348–49

Jarnow, Jesse, 268

Kantner, Paul, 48, 75–76, 136–37
Kelley, Alton, 59, 70, 167–68
Kesey, Ken, 24–25, 26, 27, 32, 33, 417
Koplik, Jim, 210–213
Koritz, Rob, 382, 407
Kreutzmann, Bill, 8, 13, 17–18, 26, 52, 80, 171, 174, 182, 212, 223, 257, 296, 298, 352–53

Lagin, Ned, 141, 229–230, 231–32, 232–34, 427–29
Lambert, Gary, 15–16, 28, 53, 71, 74, 75, 85, 106, 107, 156, 173, 183, 191, 192, 193, 197, 423–26
Law, Eileen, 237
Leopold, Dave, 441–444
Lesh, Phil, 223, 226, 227–29, 232, 236, 243, 266, 287–88, 350, 351, 353–54, 356–57, 366–67, 399, 401, 407
Loren, Richard, 214, 246, 252, 254, 269, 271–73, 279–80, 281–82, 283, 411

Marcus, Steven, 318, 321, 343, 371–72, 387–88, 411–12, 413, 415–16, 343, 371–72, 387–88, 411–12, 413, 415–16
Matthews, Bob, 5–7, 13, 17, 20, 51, 55–56, 69, 70, 71, 87, 91, 114–15, 123–24, 125–26, 152–53, 174, 220–221, 270–71
Mattson, Jeff, 246, 248, 249–50, 384
McDonald, Country Joe, 132–33
McGee, Rosie, 38–39, 44, 46, 60, 61, 62, 65–67, 76–77, 80–81, 84–85, 92–93, 110–11, 138, 186, 218–219
McIntire, Jon, 101, 102–3, 172, 182, 186–87, 188, 189–90, 191, 206, 214–15
McKernan, Ron "Pigpen," 31, 32, 33, 38, 56
McNally, Dennis, 253, 265, 315, 319–320, 340–41, 346–47, 363–64, 373–74, 380, 381, 382, 400, 408–9, 410–11
McQuaid, Peter, 416
Merlis, Bob, 168-69
Moore, Jerry, 229
Mosley, Connie Bonner, 6, 70
Mouse, Stanley, 59, 61–62
Mydland, Brent, 291–93, 294, 296, 307–8, 330, 331–32, 337

Nash, Michael, 267–68
Nelson, David, 9–11, 21, 23–24, 34, 35, 36–37, 38, 129–30, 157, 159–60, 166, 195, 318, 334–35

Oade, Doug, 445–449
Oade, Jim, 445–449
Olsen, Keith, 255, 256, 257–58

Parish, Steve, 223, 325–26, 335, 344–45
Parker, Dave, 10, 148, 171–72, 201–2, 252–53
Pollock, Courtenay, 419–422

Rakow, Ron, 102, 103, 142–43, 198–99, 202, 203, 239, 251
Riester, Jonathan, 100, 102, 111, 122, 133, 142
Rifkin, Danny, 85
Rohan, Brian, 63–64, 97
Ruppenthal, Sara, 30
Ruth, Jasmine, 439
Ruth, Justin, 438, 439
Ruth, Norm, 435, 436-9

Ruth, Sandy, 435, 436, 437, 438, 439
Ruth, Tasha, 438

Saunders, Merl, 169–70, 316–17, 321
Scher, John, 265–66, 397
Scully, Rock, 31–32, 41, 48, 53–54, 73,
     74, 75, 79–80, 89, 92, 104, 112–13,
     116–17, 130–32, 135, 140–42, 147,
     151, 153, 160–61, 165, 183, 189,
     199, 205, 206
Scully, Tim, 41, 57–58
Sears, Cameron, 332–34, 342–43,
     347–49, 360–61, 364–65, 368–70,
     371, 374, 380, 383, 389, 394,
     405–6, 409–10, 411, 414–15, 416,
     451–52
Segal, Roy, 226
Senauke, Alan, 109
Silberman, Steve, 105–6, 209–10, 246–
     48, 266–67
Simmons, Jan, 343–44, 406, 411
Stanley, Owsley "Bear," 25, 27, 33–34,
     39, 40–41, 43–44, 54–55, 112,
     121–22, 131, 132, 136, 149, 221,
     417–18
Stanley, Rhoney, 134–35, 140, 143, 149
Swanson, Sue, 13–14, 21, 70, 71, 205–6

Tork, Peter, 74, 75

Trist, Alan, 205
Turner, Rick, 221
Tutt, Ron, 243

Walker, George, 22
Wavy Gravy, 39–40, 314
Weir, Bob, 4–5, 28–29, 30, 32, 50, 52, 56,
     57, 64–65, 73–74, 86–87, 88–89, 93–94,
     100, 109, 114, 116, 117, 124–25, 131,
     133, 150, 154–55, 157–58, 161–62, 167,
     173, 187, 188, 192–93, 196, 197, 205,
     206, 216, 234–35, 236, 239, 240, 249,
     259–60, 266, 269, 273, 275–76, 281,
     287, 288, 289, 290, 294–95, 296–97,
     300, 308–9, 312–13, 336–37, 338–39,
     355, 356, 357, 361, 365, 367, 386, 387,
     388, 394–95, 395, 400–401
Welnick, Vince, 374–76, 378–79, 380,
     381–83, 391, 398
Wickersham, Ron, 221, 222, 223
Wickersham, Susan, 122

Zias, John, 127

Index of Names

Abbey Road, 27
ABC–TV, 384, 385
Abrams, Jerry, 99
Academy of Music (New York), 185
"Accidentally Like a Martyr," 270–271
Ace, 183
Acid Test at "Big Nig's" House, 23
Acid Tests, 22–34, 37, 39–43, 56, 120.
    See also individual acid tests
"Across the River," 376
Adler, Lou, 73
Africa/Brass, 162
Afterthought (Vancouver), 52, 53
"Ahab the Arab," 179
Alembic studios, xxi, xxiii, 194,197–98, 218,
    219,
Alexander Technique, 231, 232
Alioto, Joe, 110
"All By Myself," 243
All Good Things, 271
"All You Need Is Love," 423
"Alligator," 81, 86, 104
Allison, Luther, 47
Allman, Duane, 210
Allman Brothers, 210, 212, 213
Altamont Festival, 135–38
"Althea," 297
American Beauty, xix, 119, 128, 148, 162,
    164, 165, 167, 171, 198, 229, 242, 269
American Recording, 91, 93
Ampex, 121, 123
Andersen, Eric, 158
Andrian, Chris, 315
Annie (road company), 441
Anthem of the Sun, 89, 90, 103, 116, 124, 128,
    152, 154
Aoxomoxoa, 112, 118, 119, 123, 124, 125,
    128, 152, 154

Apocalypse Now, 297
*Apocalypse Now Sessions: The Rhythm Devils
    Play River Music,* 297–98
Arista Records, 253–54, 268, 287, 351, 380
Ascension, 360
"At a Siding," 259
Atee, Abdul, 271, 272, 279
Atlantic Records, 199
"Attics of My Life," 164
Autumn Records, 123
Avalon Ballroom (San Francisco), 30, 45, 47,
    48–49, 51, 58, 59, 100, 122, 125
Aykroyd, Dan, 121–22, 134, 144, 145, 286

Babbitt, Bruce, 451
Babbs, Eileen, 322
Babbs, Ken, 9, 31, 42, 120, 121
Baez, Joan, 4, 15, 307
Baker, Ginger, 106
Balin, Marty, 68, 271, 424
Baltimore Civic Center, 442
BAM magazine, xiii
Band, The, 129, 157, 158, 210, 212, 213, 376
Barlow, John, 255, 296, 311, 312
Barncard, Stephen, 241
Barone, Diane, 438
"Barren Ground," 376
Barsotti, Bob, 273, 392
Barsotti, Peter, 273, 392
Basie, Count, 77, 301
Batdorf and Rodney, 292
Bear. See Stanley, Owsley "Bear"
Bear's Lair (UC Berkeley), 129
Beatles, xiv, xv, 11, 12, 33, 59, 63, 74, 75,
    417, 424
Beau Brummels, 72, 81
Bee Gees, 276
Bell, Richard, 161

Belli, Melvin, 134
Belushi, John, 284, 286
Bennet, Joe, 77
Berio, Luciano, 14
Berry, Chuck, 3, 11, 47
"Bertha," 177
Betts, Dickey, 211, 212
Betty Ford Clinic, 414
Beverly Hillbillies, The, 5
Bickershaw Festival, 194, 195
Big Beat Acid Test, 22, 30
Big Brother and the Holding Company, 53,
    62, 65, 76
Big Pink. See Music from Big Pink
Bill Graham Presents, xix, 273, 313, 326, 391.
    See also Graham, Bill
"Bird Song," 376
Bishop, Elvin, 118
Bitches Brew, 156
Black Mountain Boys, 4
"Black Peter," 153
Blonde on Blonde, 338
Blood on the Tracks, 338
Bloomfield, Mike, 47, 169
"Blow Away," 356, 357, 368
Blues Brothers, 287
Blues for Allah, 238, 240–41, 242–43, 245,
    247, 257
Bob Weir Band, 292, 293, 308
Bobby and the Midnites, 353, 435
Booker, James, 244
"Born Cross-Eyed," 86, 93, 103
Boston Music Hall, 220
Boulez, Pierre, 89
Bourne, Christie, 119
"Box of Rain," 224
Bralove, Bob, 317, 375, 383
Bramlett, Bonnie, 159
Brand, Stewart, 31, 36
Brandelius, Jerilyn, 145, 280
Brightman, Candace, 284
"Bristol Girls," 225
Bromberg, David, 204
Brown, Steve, 233
Browne, Jackson, 292, 393
Brubeck, Dave, 63
Bruce Hornsby and the Range, 376. *See also*
    Hornsby, Bruce
Brynner, Yul, 344
Buckeye Lake (OH) show, 376, 377
Buckmaster, Paul, 260
Buena Vista Hill, 51
Built to Last, 349, 351, 366, 368

Burdon, Eric, 75
Burke, Solomon, 179
Butterfield, Paul, 47, 48, 118
Byrds, xx, 15
Byrne, David, 439

Cabale (Berkeley, CA), 5
Cafe Au Go Go (New York), 72, 413
Cage, Buddy, 183
Cage, John, 89, 105
Cal Expo (Sacramento, CA), xiii
Calico, 415, 438
California Hall (San Francisco), 51
Camp David, 274, 275
Camp Winnarainbow, 320
Campbell, Joseph, 366
Cannon, Gus, 5
Cannon's Jug Stompers, 5
Cantor-Jackson, Betty, 123, 124, 173, 174,
    219
Capitol Theatre (Passaic, NJ), xiii, 302
Capitol Theatre (Port Chester, NY), 173
"Cardboard Cowboy," 81
"Cards, Trains, and Crows," 129
Cargill, Melissa, 21
Carousel Ballroom (San Francisco), 100,
    101–102, 112, 142
Casady, Jack, 118, 163
"Casey Jones," 285
Cassady, Neal, 9, 28, 29–30, 31, 36, 42, 43,
    60, 207
"Cassidy," 222
"Caution," 81, 104
CBS (corporation), 75
CBS Studios, 224, 226
CBS-TV, 316, 413
Central Park West, 412–13
Chad and Jeremy, 12
Charlatans, 19
Charles, Ray, 268
Chateau D'Herouville (France) show, 172, 173
Chess Records, 11
Chiarito, Gert, 15
"China Cat Sunflower," 125, 245, 267, 268
"China Doll," 200, 224
Christgau, Robert, 183
Cipollina, John, 45, 46, 95, 241
Clapton, Eric, 106
"Cleo's Back," 12
Closing of Winterland, The, 287
Coast Recorders, 69
Cohen, Brett, 280
"Cold Rain and Snow," 153

Coleman, Ornette, 18
College of San Mateo, 14
Collier, Greg, 292
Coltrane, John, 80, 154, 162, 360
Columbia Records, 123, 141, 255
Columbia University, xxii, xxiii, 108, 109
"Comes a Time," 183
Compton Terrace (AZ) show, 341
Concord Pavilion (Concord, CA), 377, 391
Constanten, Tom, 14, 89, 90, 92, 117, 149, 150
Cooder, Ry, 376
Cooke, John, 160, 161
Cooke, Sam, 179
Coppola, Francis Ford, 297
Corea, Chick, 183
Corman, Roger, 261
Coronation Park (Toronto), 157
"Corrina," 399
"Cosmic Charlie," 245
Country Joe and the Fish, xxi, 428
County Fairgrounds show (Ventura, CA), 333
Cow Palace (Daily City, CA), 221, 223, 328–29
Cowell, Henry, 89
Cramer, Floyd, 183
"Crazy Fingers," 240
Cream, 106
Creedence Clearwater Revival, 163.
Crosby, David, 144, 152, 153, 163, 165, 241
Crosby, Stills, and Nash, xx, 128, 152, 397
Crosby, Stills, Nash, and Young, 163, 394
"Cryptical Envelopment," 86, 115
Crystal Ballroom (Portland, OR), 97
Curcio, Paul, 123
Curl, John, 221
Cutler, John, 400–401
Cutler, Sam, 134, 136, 137, 138, 148–49, 157, 186, 194, 214, 237, 238, 252
Cuyahoga Falls (OH) show, 444

Daily Flash, 53
D'Amato, Maria. See Muldaur, Maria
Dana Morgan Music (store), 4, 5, 11, 13
"Dancing in the Street," 245, 250
Dancing with the Dead (McGee), xxi
"Dark Star," 81, 86, 103–105, 119, 126, 209, 230, 247, 278, 366–67, 383, 384
Dark Star Orchestra, xx, xxi, 246, 250, 382
Dave Clark Five, 5, 12
Davis, Clive, 141, 253–54, 255, 287, 296
Davis, Miles, 155
Davis, Tom, 285, 302, 303, 304, 305, 345
Dawson, John "Marmaduke," 129, 130, 166

"Day of the Dead" (MTV), 343
"Days Between," 398–99
Dead Ahead, 306
Dead Heads. See Deadheads
DeadBase, 379
Deadheads, xiii, 4, 217, 218, 245, 266, 273, 274, 282, 305, 315, 323, 328, 329, 330, 341–42, 343, 346–347, 361–65, 366, 384, 391, 406, 411, 412, 417, 425, 439, 443
"Deal," 173
"Dear Mr. Fantasy," 444
"Death Don't Have No Mercy," 150, 425
Debussy, Claude, 230
Deer Creek (Noblesville, IN) show, 408, 410
DeGuere, Phil, 316, 318
Delaney and Bonnie and Friends, 157, 158
Dell'Amico, Len, 346
"Desert, The," 242
Desmond, Paul, 63
Dharma Bums, The (Kerouac), 9
Diamond, Neil, 91
DiBiase, Gloria, 408
Diddley, Bo, 197
Diga, 247, 251, 252
Diga Rhythm Band, 251
Diggers, 49, 62 65, 77, 102, 134–35
Dilbert. See St. Dilbert
Dillon Stadium (Hartford, CT), 210
Dixie Dregs, 373
Dobson, Bonnie, 425
"Doin' That Rag," 128, 425
Dolby, Thomas, 317
Dolphy, Eric, 317
"Don't Ease Me In," 13, 51
Doors, 271
Doors of Perception, The (Huxley), 50
Downbeat magazine, 88
"Drums," 381, 383, 384, 399, 443
"Drums and Space," 298, 366, 383, 384
Duke University, 435
"Dupree's Diamond Blues," 119, 124, 128, 154, 425
Dylan, Bob, xiv, 11, 63, 129, 306, 307, 318, 329, 334, 335, 336–40, 397, 407, 408

Eagles, 308
Eastman, Linda, 64–65
"Easy to Love You," 296
Ed Sullivan Show, The, 7
Edie Brickell and New Bohemians, 357
"Edward (the Mad Shirt Grinder)," 244
8 ½ (film), 261
Eisenberg, Cookie, 264

"El Paso," 209
El Rey Theater (Los Angeles), 204
Electric Kool-Aid Acid Test, The (Wolfe), 9, 428, 444
"Eleven, The," 80, 106–107, 112, 119, 309
Ellington, Duke, 301, 321
Emergency Crew, 19
Eric Burdon and the Animals, 12
Ertegun, Ahmet, 199
Escher, M. C., 309
"Estimated Prophet," 255, 257, 441
Estribou, Gene, 51, 52
Europe '72, 197, 198
"Eyes of the World," 200, 209, 215, 384

Fairfax Street Choir, 235
Family Dog, xix
Family Dog on the Great Highway (San Francisco), 19, 47, 49, 59, 100, 143, 145
"Far From Me," 296
"Faster We Go the Rounder We Get, The," 86
Faulkner, William, 175
Fellini, Federico, 261
Fender Company, 75
Festival Express, 157–161
Festival Express (film), 157, 160
Fierro, Martin, 243
Fillmore Acid Test, 31, 32-33
Fillmore Auditorium (San Francisco), 30, 45, 47, 48–49, 51, 58, 65, 77, 83, 95, 96, 100
Fillmore East (New York), xix, 118, 129, 169, 191, 423, 424–25, 441
Fillmore East 2-11-69 (film), 119
Fillmore West, 102, 113, 125, 155, 156
Finkel, Shelly, 210, 211, 213
"Fire on the Mountain," 247, 266, 267, 278, 401
Fireside (San Mateo, CA), 16
Flatt and Scruggs, 5
Fleetwood Mac, 255
"Flight of the Bumblebee," 376
Flo and Eddie, 158
Flowers, Annette, 322, 323
Fly By Night (travel agency), 218, 219, 237
Fogerty, John, 393
Folsom Field (Boulder, CO) show, 455
"Foolish Heart," 351-52, 356, 366
Fox Theater (St. Louis, MO), 220
Franken, Al, 302, 303, 304, 345
"Frankie Lee and Judas Priest," 339
Franklin County Field (Highgate, VT), 408
"Franklin's Tower," 243, 441
Free City Convention, 102

Free Jazz, 18
Free News, 102
Freiberg, David, 278
"Friend of the Devil," 165
Front Street Studio. See Le Club Front
Frost Amphitheater (Stanford, CA), xiii, 343, 346, 448
Full Tilt Boogie Band, 158
Further (bus), 9

Gale, Eric, 169
Gans, David, xiii, xiv
Garcia (album), 174
Garcia: An American Life (Jackson), xiii, xvii
Garcia, Carolyn "Mountain Girl," xx, 45, 46, 119, 120, 135, 137–38, 145-46, 173, 191, 206, 240, 275, 277, 279, 319, 320, 321-22, 323
Garcia, Deborah Koons, 413
Garcia, Heather, 4
Garcia, Jerry, xx, xi, xii, xxii, xiii, 3, 4, 5–7, 8, 9, 10, 11, 12, 14, 15, 20, 21, 23, 34, 35, 53, 54, 55, 60, 61, 62, 68, 69, 71, 72, 75, 77, 78, 79, 80, 82, 83, 85, 86, 90, 92, 95–96, 97, 102, 103, 104, 105, 106, 114, 115, 117–18, 119, 120, 122, 125, 129, 130, 135, 136, 137, 138, 139, 140, 141, 142, 145, 146, 147, 148, 151, 153, 157, 159, 160, 161, 162, 163, 164, 166, 169, 170, 171, 173, 174, 181, 182, 183, 196, 198, 199, 202, 203–4, 206, 213, 215, 218, 224, 225, 226, 227, 229, 230, 238, 239, 240, 241, 242, 243, 244, 247, 250, 251, 252–53, 254, 255, 256, 257, 260, 261, 262, 266, 267, 268, 269, 270, 271, 277, 278, 279, 280, 281, 285, 289, 290, 294, 295, 302, 304, 306, 308, 310, 311, 312, 315, 318–23, 325, 326, 329, 330, 334, 335, 336, 337, 339, 340, 342, 344, 345, 346, 352, 359, 363, 368, 370, 371, 373, 374, 375, 376, 377, 378, 380, 381, 383, 385, 388, 389, 393, 397, 399, 400, 401–403, 405–7, 408, 409, 410, 411–12, 413–15, 425, 426, 428–29, 431, 432, 433, 439, 444, 449, 452
Garcia, Sara, 4, 5, 6, 10, 21
Garcia, Trixie, 320
Garris, Phil, 242, 243
Gast, Leon, 234, 432
Gathering of Tribes. *See* Human Be-In
Gazer, Tosca, 159
George, Lowell, 268, 269
Giants Stadium (East Rutherford, NJ), 282, 343, 363, 385, 412, 413

Gilmore, Mikal, xvi
Ginsberg, Allen, 443
"Gloria," 17
Go to Heaven, 295, 196, 297, 307, 330
Godchaux, Donna Jean, 179, 182, 186–87, 244, 257, 263, 264, 278, 279, 284, 286, 289, 290, 293, 294, 375, 431
Godchaux, Keith, 179, 180–83, 186–87, 189, 190, 197, 215, 244, 253, 259, 261, 279, 286, 289, 290, 293, 294, 295, 389, 431
Godchaux, Zion, 226
Golden Gate Park (San Francisco) shows, 49, 65, 134, 238, 315, 393, 428
Golden Gate Studios, 19
Golden Road, The, xiii
"Golden Road (to Unlimited Devotion), The," 69
Goldsmith, Jerry, 68
Goldsworthy, Andy, 413
"Good Morning Little Schoolgirl," 83
Good Old Boys, 238
Gore, Al, 451–52
Gore, Tipper, 451–52
Gorman, Tim, 373
Gov't Mule, 439
Graham, Bill, xxiii, 30, 34, 35, 36, 47, 48, 49–50, 64, 82, 100, 102, 113, 114, 133, 142, 210, 211, 212, 241, 264, 270, 271, 273, 279, 284, 306, 321, 326-28, 344, 380, 391–94
Graham, Gerrit, 353
Grant, Laird "Barney," 12, 35, 56–57, 61
Grass Roots, 97
Grateful Dead, The (album), xix, xxi, 177
Grateful Dead Almanac, The, xxi, 423
Grateful Dead from the Mars Hotel, xxiii, 224, 226, 230, 237, 241
Grateful Dead Gear (Jackson), xiii
Grateful Dead Hour, The, xii
"Grateful Dead I Have Known" (McClanahan), 341
Grateful Dead Merchandising, 416
Grateful Dead Movie, The, xx, 251, 253, 260, 261, 264, 271
Grateful Dead Productions, 343, 416
Grateful Dead Ranch, 111
Grateful Dead Records, xix, xxi, 198, 215, 217, 237, 247, 250, 254
Grateful Dead Ticket Sales, xxi, 343, 438, 439
Gravenites, Nick, 169
Great American Music Hall (San Francisco), 238
Great Society, 19

Greek Theater (Berkeley, CA), xiii, 343, 419, 448
Greene, Herb, 70
Greenpeace, 385
Gretchin' Fetchin', 120
Grey, Zane, 130
Griffin, Rick, 216
Grillo, Billy, 333, 410
Grisman, David, 269
Grogan, Emmett, 134
Gross, Jane, 346
Guaraldi, Vince, 170
Gurley, James, 78
Gutierrez, Gary, 262
Guy, Buddy, 157, 158

Hagen, John, 87, 100, 134, 145
Haight-Ashbury Free Medical Clinic, 432
Haight-Ashbury Legal Organization (HALO), xxii, 60
Hall and Oates, 385
Hamza el-Din, 280
Hancock, Herbie, 317
"Happiness Is Drumming," 247
Hard Day's Night, A, xv, 11, 128
Harpur College show (Binghamton, NY), 441
Harrelson, Woody, 452
Harrison, George, 257, 417
Hart, Lenny, 122, 140–49, 170, 252–253
Hart, Mickey, xix, 77, 80–81, 85, 87, 111, 113, 119, 122, 129, 140, 141, 142, 143, 146, 147, 158, 159, 170, 171, 177, 228, 235, 256, 242, 245, 249, 250, 251, 257, 259, 263–65, 266, 269, 274, 279, 280, 281, 297, 298, 316, 317, 319, 330, 331, 339, 354, 359, 400, 401, 429, 439, 443, 451
Hart Valley Drifters, 4
Hassinger, Dave, 164, 254
Haynes, Warren, 438–39
Healy, Dan, 87, 91, 93, 94, 96, 97, 98, 112, 113, 219, 220, 231, 233, 305, 327, 334, 400
Heard, Sonny, 134, 190, 192, 421
Heartbeeps, 311
Heaven Help the Fool, 292
Heider, Wally. *See* Wally Heider Studios
Hells Angels, 102, 104, 135–36, 137, 302, 433
Hellund, Gail, 138, 143, 144
Hellzapoppin', 261
Helms, Chet, 30, 100, 134, 143, 145
Hendrix, Jimi, 73, 74, 75
Henry J. Kaiser Convention Center (Oakland, CA), 307, 326

Hepburn Heights, 306
"Here Comes Sunshine," 200, 215
Herman, Woody, 155
Hidalgo, David, 322
Hog Farm, xx, 120, 130, 438
Hollywood Bowl (Los Angeles), 204, 228
Hollywood Sportatorium (Los Angeles,), 447
Hopkins, Lightnin', 4, 22
Hopkins, Nicky, 243, 244
"Horns," 331
Hornsby, Bruce, 373, 374, 379, 382, 383, 384, 389, 390, 394, 395
How to Keep Your Volkswagen Alive (Muir), 120
Howlin' Wolf, 11
Hudson, Garth, 376
Huey Lewis and the News, 391
Human Be-In, 65–67, 76, 94
Hunter, Robert, xv, 3, 9, 10, 85-86, 112, 119–120, 130, 145, 151, 153, 157, 158–59, 166, 173, 174, 207, 215, 216, 255, 260, 311, 312, 319, 340, 351, 356, 398
Huxley, Aldous, 50
"Hypnocracy," 218

"I Know You Rider," 197, 376
Ian and Sylvia, 159
Ice Nine Publishing, xxiii
If I Could Only Remember My Name, 165
"Iko Iko," 248
"I'm a Woman," 5
In Concert, 384
In Room (Belmont, CA), 16, 17
In the Dark, 329, 330, 332, 341, 351
Indian Valley College, xx, 263
Infrared Roses, xix, 383
"It Doesn't Matter," 355
"It Must Have Been the Roses," 174–75
"It's All Right, Ma, I'm Only Bleeding," 335
Ives, Charles, 18, 424

"Jack Straw," 183, 267
"Jackaroe," 248
Jackson, Blair, xiii, xvii, 134, 145
Jackson, Rex, 100, 102, 192, 235, 236, 421
Jagger, Mick, 134, 136
Jahrhunderthalle (Frankfurt), 188
Jarvis, Felton, 179
Jefferson Airplane, xx, xxi, 4, 45, 19, 44, 47, 48, 54, 60, 63, 65, 68, 69, 71, 72, 73, 100, 118, 141, 157, 163, 178, 180 271, 423–24, 427,
Jefferson Starship, xx, 238
Jensen, Rhonda, 263–64

Jerry Garcia Acoustic Band, xxii, 329, 344
Jerry Garcia Band, xxii, xxiii, 243-44, 325, 329, 344, 400
Jim Kweskin Jug Band, 5, 6, 424
Joe and the Sparkletones, 77
Joe's Lights, xix, 187
John Wesley Harding, 129
"Johnny B. Goode," 13, 177, 230
Jones, Casey, 154
Jones, Elvin, 18
Jones, Howard, 317
Joplin, Janis, xx, 78, 118–19, 158, 159, 160, 161, 424
Journey, 394
Junior Walker and the All-Stars, 12
"Just a Little Light," 357

Kahn, John, 169, 243, 244, 279
Kanegson, Bert, 103
Kant, Hal, 147
Kantner, Paul, 71, 141
Kaukonen, Jorma, 4
"Kaw-Liga Was a Wooden Indian," 45, 46
Keith and Donna (album), 182, 240
Kelley, Alton, 58, 62, 70
Kennedy, Robert, 102
Kent State University, 428
Kerouac, Jack, 9, 50
Kesey, Ken, xv, 8–9, 21, 22, 25, 28, 31, 36, 37, 41, 130, 164, 120, 206, 237, 271, 279, 282, 321, 418
Kesey, Sunshine, 80, 119
Keystone Korner (San Francisco), xxi, 181, 244
Kezar Stadium (San Francisco), 238
KFOG Deadhead Hour, The, xii
King, Albert, 48
King, B. B., 48
King, Freddie, 47–48
King, Martin Luther, 102
"King Bee," 13
Kingfish (group), 247
Kinks, 13
KPFA radio, 15
Kreutzmann, Bill, 11, 17, 23, 48, 53, 60, 69, 72, 77, 78, 79, 80–81, 82, 106, 161-62, 163, 164, 170, 173, 174, 182, 197, 198, 236, 248, 250, 257, 258, 276, 278, 279, 285, 297, 298, 304, 333, 334, 339, 345, 346, 350, 367–68, 383, 385, 400, 401, 407, 409, 429, 443
Kreutzmann, Brenda, 110, 115
Kreutzmann, Shelly, 276

KSFO radio, 16
Kweskin, Jim, 5. *See also* Jim Kweskin Jug
    Band

"La Bamba," 323
Lacy, Steve, 360
Lagin, Ned, 226, 228, 229, 231, 427
Laguna Seca Raceway, 376
Lambert, Gary, 423
Lang, Michael, 130
Lavitz, T, 373
Law, Don, 210
Law, Eileen, 237, 332, 412
"Lazy Lightning," 247
"Lazy River Road," 398
Le Club Front (San Rafael, CA), 268. 293,
    295, 297, 317, 334, 336, 339, 442
Leary, Timothy, 25, 65, 66, 76
Leopold, Dave, 442
Lesh, Phil, 14, 16, 18, 20, 23, 33, 38, 53, 60,
    62, 72, 75, 78, 79, 80, 81, 82, 84, 86, 87,
    89, 92–93, 95–96, 97, 110, 114, 115, 117,
    122, 127, 128, 132, 135, 136, 141, 147,
    162, 163, 164, 171, 188, 190, 196, 199,
    204, 225–26, 228, 229, 231, 233, 243, 257,
    258, 270, 271, 272, 286, 308, 309, 310,
    319, 330, 338, 339, 352, 355, 375, 376,
    377, 383, 385, 400, 401, 409, 428, 429,
    432, 439, 443, 448, 451, 452
"Let It Grow," 382
"Let Me Sing Your Blues Away," 215
Lewis, Huey, 317, 391
"Liberty," 398
Life magazine, 42, 70
Light and Sound Dimension, 173
Lindley, David, 292
Lion's Share (San Anselmo, CA), 374
Little Feat, 268
Little Richard, 183
Live Dead, xiii, 125, 154
Living with the Dead (Scully), 161
Long Strange Trip, A (McNally), xviii
Longshoreman's Hall (San Francisco), 30
Look magazine, 70
"Loose Lucy," 200
Loren, Richard "Zippy," 270
Los Lobos, 322–23
"Loser," 173
Love (group), 155, 444
Lovin' Spoonful, 423, 424
Lunt-Fontanne Theater (New York), 329, 344,
    345
Lyceum Ballroom (London), 196

Lydia, 142
Lyons, Gary, 295, 297

McClanahan, Ed, 334
McDonald, Country Joe, 133
McGee, Rosie, 38
McIntire, Jon, 138, 144, 145, 147, 148, 158,
    198, 205, 215, 332, 333, 334, 370
McKenzie, Scott, 73
McKernan, Ron. *See* Pigpen
McMahon, Regan, xiii
McNally, Dennis, xvii, 368, 415
McPherson, Jim, 235
Madison Square Garden (New York), 383,
    385, 443
Magoo's Pizza (Menlo Park, CA), 13, 17, 18,
    309
Mann, Michel, 173
Manson, Charles, 75, 241
Maples Pavilion (Stanford University), 200,
    201
Marin Veterans Memorial Hospital, 340
Marin Civic Auditorium, 349
Maroney's (liquor store), 6
Marshall Tucker Band, 265
Martyn Ford Orchestra, 259
Masakela, Hugh, 73
Massachusetts Institute of Technology (MIT),
    427, 428
Matrix (San Francisco), 19, 78, 118, 128,
    169–70
Matthews, Bob, 12, 13–14, 60, 129, 130, 167,
    173, 219
Mattson, Jeff,
Mauceri, John, 292
Mayer, Mary Ann, 168
"Me and Julio Down by the Schoolyard," 225
Meadowlands (East Rutherford, NJ), 343
Medicine Ball Caravan, 162
Memorial Auditorium (Eureka, WA), 97
Mercury Records, 123
Merry Pranksters, xv, xix, xx, xxi, xxiii, 9, 21,
    24, 28, 29, 30, 34, 35, 37, 41, 42, 120, 130,
    418
Meters (group), 302
"Mexicali Blues," 183
Meyer, John, 221
Michaels, Lorne, 284
Mickey and the Heartbeats, 118
"Midnight Hour," 359
Midnight Special, The, 15
"Might As Well," 157
Mighty Fine Distributing, 203

Miller, Steve, 219, 397
Mills College, 14
Mills Memorial Hospital, 264
"Mission in the Rain," 243
"Mississippi Half-Step Uptown Toodeloo," 215
Mitchell's Christian Singers, 244
Mittig, Paul, 36
Mojo Navigator magazine, 52
Monck, Chip, 134
Monkees, 74
Monterey College, 75
Monterey Peninsula Artists, 144
Monterey Pop Festival, xxiii, 73–74
More Than Human (Sturgeon), 41
Morgan, Dana, 13, 14. *See also* Dana Morgan Music
"Morning Dew," 425
Morrison, Van, 91, 241
Mosley, Connie Bonner, 12
Mother McCree's Uptown Jug Champions, 6, 8, 11
Mountain (group), 158
"Mountains of the Moon," 119
Mouse, Stanley, 58–59, 60, 70
"Mr. Tambourine Man," 337
MTV, 343
Muir, John, 120
Muir Beach Acid Test, 27
Muldaur, Geoff, 5
Muldaur, Maria, 5
Murphy, Ann, 31
Murray, Jim, 45–46
Music from Big Pink, 129
Music Never Stopped, The (Jackson), xiii, 242
Music of Upper and Lower Egypt, 280
"My Drum Is a Woman," 269
My Favorite Things, 360
Mydland, Brent, 290, 293, 295, 304, 308, 329, 331, 339, 350, 355, 357, 368–72, 373, 377, 378, 379, 381, 389, 393, 394, 395, 413
Mydland, Lisa, 333

Naropa Institute, 443
Nash, Michael, 153
Nathan, Florence. *See* McGee, Rosie
Navarro Hotel, 284
NBC-TV, 285
Nelson, David, 9. 10, 129, 130, 164, 239
Neville Brothers, 302
New George's (San Rafael, CA), 322
New Musical Express, 195

"New Potato Caboose," 86, 90, 424
New Riders of the Purple Sage, xx, xxii, 130, 157, 165, 166, 178, 180, 183, 195, 196, 204–7, 214, 219, 237, 265, 287, 429
New World Pictures, 261
"New Year's Day Wail," 65
New York State Pavilion, 425
New York Times, 346–47
Newcastle-Upon-Tyne (England) festival, 172
Newman, Laraine, 284
Nichols, Chet, 163
Nicki, 113
Night Beat: A Shadow History of Rock and Roll (Gilmore), xvi
Night on the Town, A, 376
Norman, Jeffrey, 282
Norton Buffalo, 263
"Not Fade Away," 177, 197

Oade, Doug, 445–449
Oade, Jim, 445–49
Oakland Auditorium. *See* Henry J. Kaiser Convention Center
Oakland Coliseum Arena, 313, 326, 436
Oakley, Berry, 211
Odom, Bunky, 210
Official Book of the Dead Heads, The, xiv
Ohio State University, 210
Old and in the Way, 271
Olmstead Studios, 87
Olompali. *See* Rancho Olompali
Olsen, Keith, 255, 256, 259, 260
Olympia Theater (Paris), 188, 191
Olympic Hall (Munich), 231
On the Road (Kerouac), 9
One Flew Over the Cuckoo's Nest (Kesey), 9
101 Strings, 259
"One More Saturday Night," 183, 230
Oracle, The, 65
Original Joe's, 225
Ostin, Mo, 63–64
"Other One, The," 81, 86, 90, 104–105, 161, 162, 177, 424, 429, 441, 444
Out of Town Tours, 237
Owens, Buck, 214

Pacific High Recording, 394
Pacific Recording Studios, 118, 123, 125
Palace (Auburn Hills, MI), 394
Palo Alto High School, 6
Parish, Steve, 184, 258, 270, 302, 319, 334, 336, 412
Parker, Bonnie, 10, 147, 199

Parker, Dave, 10, 147, 199
Paul Butterfield Blues Band, 424
Paul Revere and the Raiders, 71
Pauley Pavilion (Los Angeles), 42, 220
Payne, Sonny, 77, 78
Pearson, Don, 400
Pendleton Roundup, 100
Peninsula School, 4
People magazine, 343
Peraza, Armando, 170
Peterson, Bobby, 12, 86, 224
Petty, Tom, 318, 334, 337. 397
Phantom of the Opera, 344
Phillips, John, 73
Piaf, Edith, 191
"Picasso Moon," 355, 356, 357
Pico Acid Test, 41
Pierson, Clark, 161
Pigpen, xvii, 4, 6–7, 11, 12, 13-14, 18, 32, 36,
    53, 54–55, 60, 72, 80, 83, 88, 97, 98, 103,
    104, 114, 115, 116–18, 140, 147, 149–50
    179, 189, 196, 373, 429
"Pig's Boogie," 243, 244
Pine Valley Boys, 9
Pistol-Packin' Mama, 239
Playboy, 334
"Playing in the Band," 177, 183, 247, 266,
    267, 358
Pollock, Courtenay, 237, 419
Polo Fields (San Francisco), 65, 66, 315, 393
Popick, Harry, 327
Portland Acid Test, 52
Potrero Theater (San Francisco), 80
Pranksters. *See* Merry Pranksters
Presidio Theater (San Francisco), 103
"Pride of Cucamonga," 224, 225
Professor Longhair, 294
"Promised Land," 13
Public Television, 287

Quicksilver Messenger Service, xix, xx, 44,
    45, 47, 60, 65, 76, 95, 97, 99, 112, 180,
    427–28

Raceway Park (Englishtown, NJ), 265–66
Radio City Music Hall (New York), 302, 304–6
Radner, Gilda, 284
Rainbow (London), 187
Rainforest Action Network, 385
Raizene, Sparky, 276
Rakha, Alla, 102
Rakow, Emily, 432
Rakow, Ron, 100, 101, 133, 142, 143, 145,

198, 202, 203–4, 218, 237, 241, 251,
    252–3
Ram Rod, 87, 100, 113, 131, 134, 146, 158,
    173, 194, 235, 277, 278, 279, 304, 380,
    410
"Ramble On Rose," 183
Rancho Olompali, 44, 52
RCA Records, 63
RCA Studios, 67, 68, 69
Record Factory, 203
Record Plant, 215, 240
Red Dog Saloon (Virginia City, NV), 19
"Red Plains," 376
Red Rocks Amphitheatre (Morrison, CO),
    441, 443
Redding, Otis, 47, 48, 179
Reed, Jimmy, 11
Relix, 229
Rex Foundation, xix, 332
RFK Stadium (Washington, D.C.), 210, 318,
    334, 408, 411, 451
Rich, Buddy, 79, 155
Richards, Keith, 12
Riders of the Purple Sage, 130
Riester, Jonathan, 103, 135
Rifkin, Danny, 44, 48, 61, 62, 70, 75, 98, 140,
    141, 205, 214, 332
Roberts, Elliot, 339, 340
Rocking the Cradle, Egypt, 1978, 282
Rohan, Brian, 63, 123
Rolling Stone magazine, xvi, 84, 164, 343
Rolling Stones, xiv, 3, 11, 13, 15, 18, 68, 134,
    136, 137, 139, 276, 305, 328
Rolling Thunder, 263, 264
Romney, Hugh. *See* Wavy Gravy
Roosevelt Stadium (Jersey City, NJ), 265
"Rose for Miss Emily, A" (Faulkner), 175
Round Records, 218, 228, 237, 238, 240, 250,
    253, 431, 432
"Row Jimmy," 200
Rubaiyat of Omar Khayyam, The, 59
Rucka Rucka Stud Ranch, 422
Rundgren, Todd, 373, 375, 376, 379, 381
Rush, Goldie, 271
Rush, Tom, 160
Russell, Leon, 213
Ruth, Norm, 435–439
Ruth, Jasmine, 435–439
Ruth, Justin, 435–439
Ruth, Sandy, 435–439
Ruth, Tasha, 435–439

Sadat, Anwar, 272, 274

Sadat, Jehan, 274, 275
"Samson and Delilah," 245
"San Francisco (Be Sure to Wear Flowers in Your Hair)," 73
San Francisco Chronicle, 83, 181
San Francisco Mime Troupe, 17, 89
Santana (group), 170,
Santana, Carlos, 123, 170, 322, 328
Saturday Night Fever, 250
Saturday Night Live, xx, 284–85, 299, 302
Saunders, Merl, 169, 241, 243, 316, 317, 318, 320, 325, 374
Scaggs, Boz, 219
"Scarlet Begonias," 222, 224, 225, 227, 401, 444
Scher, John, 302, 321, 345
Scope Arena (Norfolk, VA), 435
Scorpio Records, 51
Scott, Tom, 257
Scully, Rock, 61, 62, 70, 98, 111, 134, 136, 140, 142, 161, 184, 214, 306, 436–37
Scully, Tim, 37–38, 39, 52, 56–57,
"Search for the Secret Pyramid, The" (Kesey), 271
Searching for the Sound (Lesh), 271
Sears, Cameron, xxiii, 332, 394, 410, 412, 415
Sears, Pete, 373–374
Sears Point Raceway (Sonoma, CA), 135
Seastones, xxi, 228
Segal, Roy, 224, 225
Seidemann, Bob, 423
Serenity Knolls, 414–15
Sgt. Pepper's Lonely Hearts Club Band, 152
Shady Management, 70
Shakedown Street, 268, 269, 270, 271, 283
Shankar, Ravi, 18, 73
Sheffield High School, 179
"Ship of Fools," 224
Shoreline Amphitheater (Mountain View, CA), 372
Showtime, 302
Shrine Auditorium (Los Angeles), 247
Shubb, Rick, 9, 10
Shurtliff, Lawrence. *See* Ram Rod
Sierra Club, 76
Silver (group), 292
"Silver Apples of the Moon," 383
Simmons, Jan, 413
Simon, Paul, 73, 74, 225
Simon and Simon, 316
Sinatra, Frank, 70
SiriusXM Radio, 423

Skaggs, Boz, 219
Skeletons from the Closet, xi
Sketches of Spain, 156
Skull and Roses, 177–79, 198, 217
Skullfuck. See Skull and Roses
Sledge, Percy, 179
Slick, Grace, 19, 78
"Slipknot," 243
Smith, G. E., 284
Smith, Joe, 62–64, 123, 153
SNACK benefit, 241
Snyder, Gary, 66
"So Far," 329, 370
"So Many Roads," 398–99
Soldier Field (Chicago, IL) show, 413
Sonny and Cher, 12
Sound City Studios (Van Nuys, CA), 258
Southern Comfort (group), 179
"Space," 310, 384, 390
Spectrum (Philadelphia, PA), 185, 441, 442
Sphinx Theater (Egypt), 277
Springsteen, Bruce, xiv
St. Dilbert, 218
"St. Stephen," 119, 245, 309, 443
Stabler Arena (Bethlehem, PA), 442
Stallings, Ron, 169
"Standing on the Moon," 356
Stanford University (Stanford, CA), 4, 8
Stanley, Owsley "Bear," 21, 33, 37, 39, 44, 51, 52, 55–56, 57, 62, 66, 96, 97, 122, 125, 134, 143, 144, 149, 201, 219, 220, 221, 222
Stanley, Rhoney, 144
Staples, Mavis, 155
Staples Singers, 155
"Stayin' Alive," 276
Steal Your Face, 251–52
"Stealin'," 13, 51
Stegner, Wallace, 8
Stephens, Sue, 280, 322, 323
"Stella Blue," 215, 216, 368
Stevens, Cat, 225
Stevens, Ray, 179
Stills, Stephen, 112, 153, 154
Sting, 397
Stockhausen, Karlheinz, 89
Stone club (San Francisco), 325
Stoneman, Scotty, 18
Straight Theater (San Francisco), 78, 79
Strand Lyceum (London), 195
"Stuck Inside of Mobile with the Memphis Blues Again," 377

Studio Instrument Rentals (SIR), 93, 225
"Study Number Three," 90
Sturgeon, Theodore, 42
"Subterranean Homesick Blues," 11
"Sugar Magnolia," 167, 331, 353
"Sugaree," 243, 267, 377
Sullivan, E. J., 59
Summer of Love, 76–77
Sun Ra, 310
Sunset Sound, 91
"Sunshine Daydream," 167
"Supplication," 247
Surrealistic Pillow, 68
Swanson, Sue, 36, 60, 84
Sweetwater Music Hall (Mill Valley, CA), 431

Tales from the Golden Road, 423
Tangent (Palo Alto, CA), 8
Tarot, 150
Taylor, Cecil, 310
Taylor, Mick, 385
Taylor, Robbie, 341
Teller, Al, 251
Ten Years After, 155, 157
"Tennessee Jed," 183
"Terrapin Flyer," 259
Terrapin Station (album), xxii, 258, 260
"Terrapin Station" (song), 255, 256, 259, 260, 266, 375
Terrapin Trailways, xxii, 435–39
Tex, Joe, 179
"That's It for the Other One," 86
"They Love Each Other," 200
Thomas, Bob, 144
Thompson, Bill, 73
Thompson, Eric, 10, 23
Three Rivers Stadium (Pittsburgh, PA), 412
"Throwing Stones," 311, 312
Thunder Mountain Tub Thumpers, 4
"Throwing Stones," 312
Tibetan Book of the Dead, The, 20
Ticketron, 442
Tiger Rose, 175
"Till the Morning Comes," 163
Tiny Tim, 42
Tivoli (Copenhagen), 187
"To Lay Me Down," 159
"Tons of Steel," 331
Tork, Peter, 74
"Touch of Grey," 311–12, 326, 329, 331, 444
Townshend, Pete, 269, 352
Traffic, 157, 397

Transcontinental Pop Festival, 157
Trips Festival, 11, 31, 34, 36, 37, 52–53,
Trist, Alan, 218, 272, 276, 279
Troupers Hall (Los Angeles), 39
"Truckin'," 167, 429
Tubes (group), 373, 375–76, 378, 391
"Turn On Your Love Light," 424
Turner, Rick, 121, 221
Tutt, Ron, 243
TV Guide, 386
Twilight Zone, The, 316, 317, 384
Tyson, Sylvia, 159

U2, 352
Uncalled Four, 4
"Uncle John's Band," 358
United Artists, 250, 251, 252
Universal Records, 311
University of Nevada, 223
University of New Mexico, 184
"U.S. Blues," 200, 224
Us Festival, 436

Varese, Edgard, 89, 151
Vancouver Trips Festival, 52–53
Vega, Suzanne, 385
Ventura County Fairgrounds (Ventura, CA), xiii
"Victim or the Crime," 352, 354, 357
Vietnam War, 37, 65, 77, 108
Village Theater, 87
Viola, Kenny, 408–9
"Viola Lee Blues," 51, 69, 74, 153
"Visions of Johanna," 407
Vitt, Bill, 169
Vonnegut, Kurt, 441

Wake of the Flood, 215, 216, 217, 226, 237, 242
Wakefield, Frank, 239
Wales, Howard, 164, 181
Walker, T-Bone, 4
"Walkin' Blues," 384
"Walkin' the Dog," 13
Wally Heider Studios, 153, 163, 173
Walmart, 178
Walton, Bill, 282, 313
Warfield Theatre (San Francisco), 302, 303, 304
Warlocks, 8, 11, 12, 14, 15, 16, 19, 22, 71, 77,
Warner Bros. Records, 63, 67, 68, 70, 87, 103, 123, 124, 141, 145, 146, 147–48, 153, 172,

177, 178, 186, 198, 199, 203
Warner Music Group (WEA), 199
Washington, Eddie, 261, 431
"Washington at Valley Forge," 7
Waters, Muddy, 11, 12, 47
Watkins Glen, xxi, 210, 211–14, 215, 238, 265
Watts Acid Test, 39
"Wave That Flag," 200
Wavy Gravy, 42, 130, 132
"Way It Is, The," 376
"Weather Report Suite," 200, 215
Webber, Andrew Lloyd, 344
Weidenheimer, Troy, 4
Weir, Bob, 4, 5, 6, 7, 11, 13, 23, 36, 51, 60, 70, 72, 79, 80, 82, 83, 86, 90–91, 104, 114, 115–16, 118, 120, 152, 163, 164–65, 167, 183, 196, 204, 205, 215, 218, 224, 226, 231–32, 240, 241, 242, 243, 247, 255, 256, 257, 258, 267, 268, 277, 279, 286, 290, 292, 293, 295, 296, 303, 304, 308, 310, 311, 317, 329, 350, 354, 355, 358–59, 399, 400, 401, 409
Weir, Frankie, 218, 219, 237, 421
Welnick, Lori, 375
Welnick, Vince, 117, 373, 374, 375, 377, 378, 381, 383, 384, 387, 389, 390, 395, 396, 400, 408
Wembley Arena (London), 187, 381, 383
"Werewolves of London," 270
Wexler, Jerry, 199
"Wham Bam," 292
"Wharf Rat," 177, 347, 375, 441
"What I Am," 357
"Wheel, The," 174, 245
"When a Man Loves a Woman," 179
"When I Paint My Masterpiece," 376
White House, 398
Who, The, 73, 74, 75, 155, 273. 303

"Who Was John," 244
Whole Earth Catalog (Brand), 30
"Why Don't We Do It in the Road," 444
Wickersham, Ron, 121, 123, 144, 220, 221
Wickersham, Susan, 144
Wildwood Boys, 4
Williams, Hank, 45
Wilson, Davey, 285
Wilson, Wes, 58, 168
Winslow, Joe, 194–5, 276, 421
Winterland, 106, 124, 180, 234, 235–36, 238, 261, 267, 287, 304, 327, 328-29, 431
Without a Net, 380
Withrow, Kenny, 357
Wolf, Billy, 235
Wolfe, Tom, 9, 428
Wonder, Stevie, 317
Woodstock (film), 133
Woodstock Music and Arts Festival, 130–133, 134, 210, 211, 214, 265
Woody, Allen, 438
Woolworth's, 179
Workingman's Dead, 119, 123, 128, 129, 148, 151, 152, 153, 154, 165, 171, 198

"Yellow Moon," 174
You Can't Always Get What You Want (Cutler), 137
"You Don't Have to Ask," 83
Young, Jesse Colin, 219
Young, Lester, 426
Young, Neil, 439
Youngbloods, 428

Zabriskie Point, 145
Zeigfeld Theater (New York), 264
Zevon, Warren, 270
Zodiacs, 4